STRATEGIC SOCIAL MARKETING

STRATEGIC SOCIAL MARKETING

JEFF FRENCH & ROSS GORDON

 SAGE

Los Angeles | London | New Delhi
Singapore | Washington DC

Los Angeles | London | New Delhi
Singapore | Washington DC

SAGE Publications Ltd
1 Oliver's Yard
55 City Road
London EC1Y 1SP

SAGE Publications Inc.
2455 Teller Road
Thousand Oaks, California 91320

SAGE Publications India Pvt Ltd
B 1/I 1 Mohan Cooperative Industrial Area
Mathura Road
New Delhi 110 044

SAGE Publications Asia-Pacific Pte Ltd
3 Church Street
#10-04 Samsung Hub
Singapore 049483

Commissioning editor: Matthew Waters
Editorial assistant: Molly Farrell
Production editor: Nicola Marshall
Copyeditor: Gemma Marren
Proofreader: Audrey Scriven
Marketing manager: Alison Borg
Cover design: Francis Kenney
Typeset by: C&M Digitals (P) Ltd, Chennai, India
Printed and bound by CPI Group (UK) Ltd,
Croydon, CR0 4YY

Library of Congress Control Number: 2014951096

British Library Cataloguing in Publication data

A catalogue record for this book is available from the British Library

ISBN 978-1-44624-861-4
ISBN 978-1-44624-862-1 (pbk)

At SAGE we take sustainability seriously. Most of our products are printed in the UK using FSC papers and boards. When we print overseas we ensure sustainable papers are used as measured by the Egmont grading system. We undertake an annual audit to monitor our sustainability.

From Jeff
To Alice French (1925–2014)
Inspiration, rock and friend

From Ross
I would like to dedicate this book to Nadia (ZNB), and my friends
and family – particularly Mum, Dad, Gavin and Calum for your love
and support; and to the people of Scotland and especially my
hometown Glasgow for the inspiration and motivation to become
involved in working for social good. Finally, G'day and thanks to my
adopted home of Australia.

CONTENTS

ABOUT THE AUTHORS

Jeff French (Professor Jeff French PhD, MBA, MSc, DipHE, BA, Cert.Ed. CEO Strategic Social Marketing) is a global thought leader in social marketing, social programme planning, evaluation and health communication. Jeff has published over 90 papers and three books. Jeff is a visiting Professor at Brighton University and a Fellow at King's College London University. Previously Director of Policy and Communication at the UK Health Development Agency and a senior civil servant in the UK Department of Health. In 2005 Jeff developed the UK government review of social marketing and set up the National Social Marketing Centre in 2006. In 2009 Jeff became the CEO of Strategic Social Marketing Ltd.

Strategic Social Marketing works internationally with private companies, NGOs and governments on the development and evaluation of social programmes that aim to influence behaviour.

Jeff is a member of several national and international policy committees and is a member of the editorial board of four professional journals. Jeff is the organiser of the European and World Social Marketing Conference and a member of the International Social Marketing Association Executive and the European Social Marketing Association Board.

Jeff has worked on behaviour change, health communication and social policy programmes in over 29 countries and has just completed a technical guide on social marketing for the European Centre for Disease Control. Jeff leads the social component of the EU funded ECom Programme and has worked on many occasions for WHO and ECDC on health promotion and communication issues. Jeff is a keen kendoka, dancer and painter.

Ross Gordon is a Senior Lecturer in Marketing at Macquarie University in Sydney. He previously worked at and remains a member of the Centre for Health Initiatives at the University of Wollongong, and also worked at the Institute for Social Marketing at The Open University (ISM-Open) and prior to that the ISM at the University of Stirling.

Ross is also President of the Australian Association of Social Marketing (AASM). His expertise lies in social marketing, consumer cultures, and critical marketing teaching and research. He has been a principal or named investigator on projects attracting over $6.5m in research funds in Australia, UK, Europe and India.

He has extensive experience managing and conducting research using mixed methodologies including longitudinal quantitative surveys, systematic reviews and meta-analyses, focus groups, depth interviews, observation research, ethnography, content analysis, and experimental studies.

His current research interests include, social marketing theory and practice, strategic and systems level social marketing, consumer cultures, critical social marketing, energy efficiency sustainability, marketing ethics, and critical marketing. Ross is also a specialist on the topic of alcohol marketing, and more recently gambling consumption. He has acted as expert advisor to the Scottish Government, the European Commission, Cancer Institute, and a range of other NGOs on various social marketing topics.

He has published 60 academic journals, book chapters and conference papers including in outlets such as *European Journal of Marketing, Journal of Business Research, Marketing Theory, Journal of Macromarketing,* and *Journal of Social Marketing;* and has delivered numerous client reports and invited speaking engagements. Ross is a keen player and follower of sports including football, tennis and cycling, loves travelling, enjoys current affairs, and is a big music fan and occasional techno DJ.

FOREWORD

We live in an age of multiple, persistent and complex problems. There are few simplistic answers to these problems but the good news is that we now know a lot about how to develop, deliver and evaluate interventions to tackle these problems. If we apply this understanding in a systemic way we can make a significant contribution to further improving the human condition. This book is dedicated to the proposition that the application of social marketing principles to social policy selection, programme strategy development and operational delivery is one of the key ways to bring about more efficient, effective, ethical and equitable societies.

The new age of citizen centric social policy

We have seen significant changes in the human condition over the last twenty years. There are at least seven billion people in the world now but also in every region with the exception of Africa populations are starting to age (United Nations, 2001). We continue to experience human accelerated global warming (Peters et al., 2013). The world suffers massive health and social inequality (Wilkinson and Marmot, 2003; Marmot, 2008). Obesity is a rapidly growing global problem (WHO, 2002). We also continue to experience the major global threats from nuclear, chemical and biological weapons and radical groups who seek to use violence to achieve their objectives. However, we have also experienced an unprecedented period of economic growth over the last two hundred years with corresponding health and wealth creation (Ridley, 2012). We have witnessed a massive absolute general positive improvement in global health (UNICEF, 2011) and literacy (UNESCO, 2012). We have also seen significant positive shifts in the developed world with regard to smoking, drug and alcohol abuse (WHO, 2014). We are also experiencing an ongoing technological communications revolution leading to 'always on, always connected' citizens.

These and other factors are resulting in the rise of more citizen empowerment leading to the development of what Sandel (2009) describes as new forms of government but also new kinds of citizenship. The relationship between the governed and governments is changing rapidly to one characterised by more dialogue and more joint responsibility and co-production of solutions to social challenges. Clarke et al. (2007) argue this new relationship is informed by the increasing expectation on the part of more literate and wealthy citizens to be treated with respect. People want government and their agencies to emulate many of the customer centric approaches in the commercial sector. Citizens' expectations about levels of quality of service from public institutions are increasing. People, especially those living in advanced democracies, want governments to inform them, consult them, incentivise good behaviour and do less dis-incentivising and banning when it comes to social policy interventions (Duffy et al., 2010).

However, the desire to engage, trade and seek collaborative interactions is not a new phenomenon. Ever since groups of humans have existed, they have tried to influence each other. Evolutionary psychologist Buss (2004) and historian Jenkins (1997) might agree that one key reason for the development of the species has been a focus on mutuality and cooperation, both of which involve exchange and seeking to influence the behaviour of others for their good and the good of the group. The essentially collaborative trading nature of humans together with the application and power of collective intelligence (Leadbeater, 2008) is a powerful cocktail. These ingredients have combined to advance the human condition and promote social good, from the inception of the earliest human societies in Catalhoyuk, Uruk, and Mesopotamia to the civilisations of Egypt, Greece, Rome, the Aztec empire, and the Xia dynasty to the present day. The desire not only to trade but also to generally act in a socially reciprocal manner may well be hardwired into the human condition (Ridley, 2012). If this is the case, it could obviously be argued that humans are natural marketers and social marketers – *Homo sociomarketus*!

However, it is also clear that small groups of powerful elites have also always sought to define 'social good'. These elites have used all manner of influencing strategies including oratory, law, rituals, religion, communication, entertainment and force to persuade people to behave in ways that they believed to be beneficial for the wider group and for the elite itself (Marr, 2012). As these elites are challenged by general economic development, literacy and mass connectivity the need for new forms of social discourse and development such as social marketing are beginning to emerge to reflect these new forms of power relationship.

A central tenant of social marketing is that governments, non-governmental organisations (NGOs) and businesses need to look beyond the development and provision of expert selected and designed policy, services, and products to solve social problems. This is because we live in a world where more and more people in both the developed and developing world are better educated, healthier, more empowered and have more choice. In this environment governments, NGOs and business all need to develop sustained reflexive strategies that are based not only on evidence and data but also on a deep understanding about what citizens value, believe, know, feel, need and will support.

Governments also need to harness the power and energy of citizens to understand and solve the big social challenges they face. Citizens often want to be part of the process of creating solutions to social challenges. The increasing development of citizen involvement processes by governments is a manifestation of this phenomenon, as is a growing emphasis on co-production, co-design, co-delivery and the blurring of consumption and production in the form of prosumers in both the public and private sectors. Citizens also bring to the process of co-production insights about what will and will not work, and how best to design and deliver interventions.

Why the world needs another social marketing book

We decided to write this book because despite the growing number of social marketing books that exist, they all tend to focus on the nature and mechanics of what we call 'operational social marketing'. By 'operational social marketing' we mean the application of marketing theory and techniques to improve the performance of social intervention projects. Framed in this way these books reinforce a form of myopia that confines the contribution that social marketing can make. The application of social marketing to operational delivery is obviously worthwhile as it has the potential, and a growing track record, to increase the effectiveness and efficient delivery of social programmes. However, it is our contention that marketing principles can also add considerable value to policy making and strategy development, and that these contributions have the potential to make a far more significant impact than those made at an operational level. In this book we set out why and how social marketing can add value to social policy, strategy development and delivery.

We also argue that the principle objectives of 'strategic' social marketing are to create social good by developing social value that results in more equitable, sustainable, healthy, happy and productive societies and individuals.

To deliver this set of objectives we also believe that it is time to move away from a singular focus on 'voluntary' behaviour change as the core focus of social marketing, and to renounce similar simplistic and formulaic interpretations of social marketing. It should be recognised we believe that an interdisciplinary, and wider spectrum of influence is required and that it is most often necessary to use a broader toolbox of theory and interventions to influence behaviour, environments and other determinants of behaviour, as well as the policy making process itself. The example of banning smoking in public places and the impact that it has made on public health in many countries is a good example of the need for a broad approach to intervention selection. The development, introduction and maintenance of such non-voluntary behavioural interventions can also massively benefit from being informed by social marketing.

Social marketing can and has informed decision makers about which forms of interventions would work. It has also helped in engaging citizens in co-creation and support for interventions as well as informing and shifting social opinion and norms and encouraging compliance. Therefore, it is also important to acknowledge that social marketing is about more than changing individual behaviour. We believe it should also be applied to shifting attitudes, perceptions, values and social norms as well as influencing environments, systems policies, products and services, and even in informing how markets are managed and regulated. This broader conception of both the nature and focus of social marketing sits at the heart of this book. What we hope that the book demonstrates is that rather than a simplistic and formulaic process the practitioners need to learn and apply in unaltered fashion, a more interdisciplinary, reflexive, critical and strategic mindset is required. It is through the application of this kind of critical and reflexive approach that we believe that social marketing will make its biggest contribution to preventing and solving social problems. Our favourite analogy is one based on cooking. Rather than following a set of prescribed recipes that require exact preparation and cooking times, and a fixed set of measured ingredients – what we need is a more creative approach that is characterised by using different, fresh and creative blends, prepared in novel ways. The essence of this book can be set out in five underpinning conclusions that we explore and expand in the chapters that follow. We believe that there is a need for:

1. A more interdisciplinary, systemic, reflexive, creative and critical approach to the application of social marketing that more accurately reflects the complexity and reality of dealing with complex issues in dynamic environments; and less application of simplistic analysis and limited formulaic responses.
2. A greater emphasis on the contribution of social marketing to the midstream and upstream environment, to policy and strategy development, and to social programme selection and delivery.
3. More focus on social value creation as a means to achieving greater social good. Social value creation should be seen as a central principle of social marketing within the context of the reality of multiple complex webs of exchange and relationships that underpin the creation or destruction of social good.
4. The need for a broader focus on objectives that go beyond a predominant focus on individual or group behaviour to include influencing attitudes, beliefs, practices, social norms, environments, systems, processes, services, experiences, products, policies, and markets.
5. The need for increased power sharing, co-creation and engagement in the selection, development, delivery and evaluation of social programmes as a process for the development of greater citizen, stakeholder and societal value.

Book structure and content

This book is conceptually divided into three sections focused on why social marketing is important in the social, cultural, policy and strategy arenas, what the nature and process of social marketing and strategic social marketing is, and finally how social marketing can be applied both strategically and operationally and be embedded into all social programmes.

In Chapter 1 we consider the potential contribution of social marketing to the social policy and strategy development process and some of the reasons and drivers of why it is being taken up around the world as a central component of social policy design and delivery.

In Chapter 2 we set out to examine and develop what we believe to be a contemporary conception of social marketing that is supported by modern marketing theory and evidenced based practice. In this chapter we also review the history of social marketing and some of the common criticisms and misunderstandings about its nature and focus.

In Chapter 3 we explore the scope of how marketing can be used to promote social value and ultimately social good. We also explore why influencing and engaging citizens now needs to sit at the centre of social programme design thinking.

Chapter 4 expands the issues raised in Chapter 3 by examining the nature of how social marketing is operationalised through the social marketing intervention mix. 'Types' and 'Forms' of potential intervention are reviewed as are the interdisciplinary contributions from marketing and other techniques such as public relations, lobbying, advocacy, branding and media promotions. Chapter 4 is the first of three chapters that explore in some detail the nature and focus of social marketing practice.

Chapter 5 describes and defines the nature of strategic social marketing and its contribution to the design of social policy selection and implementation. The concept and definition of 'strategic social marketing' are introduced and contextualised.

Chapter 6, which sits at the centre of the book, also represents one of the central propositions of this book: that societal value creation is the defining feature of social marketing. The nature of value creation from a marketing perspective is reviewed and the implications that derive from this for social marketing practice are set out, alongside how value creation contributes to the selection, design and delivery of social interventions that bring about net social good.

From Chapter 7 onwards the book focuses on how the application of a strategic and reflexive approach to social marketing can be put into practice. Chapter 7 explores the significance of systems thinking, theory and systemic analysis in the development and delivery of effective social marketing programmes. It also makes the case for a more holistic and comprehensive approach to problem analysis, strategic planning and the delivery of social marketing as part of social programme design and delivery.

Chapter 8 reviews the importance of theory when analysing and developing interventions that seek to influence individuals, groups and society and why a bespoke and open approach to the application of theory to guide strategy development and programme implementation is often needed.

Chapter 9 explores the relevance and application of different research paradigms that inform social marketing research, and situational analysis and how these data can be used for evaluation.

Chapter 10 considers the basics of research method selection design and research ethics, with particular relevance to the social marketing paradigm.

Chapter 11 takes a practical look at the scope and nature of strategy development and how social marketing can enhance this process. The chapter reviews some of the common strategic tools and forms of strategic analysis and strategic prioritisation.

Chapter 12 sets out a practical guide to applying social marketing principles to the development of a specific social intervention. It describes a comprehensive step-by-step approach to planning social marketing interventions and also introduces readers to a variety of the more commonly used social marketing planning tools that exist.

Chapter 13 is devoted to an exploration of why social marketing should be embedded in all social programmes and how to bring this about. The chapter sets out a number of diagnostic and influencing tools and tactics to encourage and sustain the use of social marketing within organisations.

Finally, Chapter 14 introduces the concept of 'critical social marketing' and sets out a rationale for why it is a key element in any strategic approach to the application of social marketing. The nature and application of critical social marketing are reviewed together with its implications for wider social policy.

To assist readers we have used a common format for each chapter in this book. Each of these begins with a set of key learning objectives for that chapter. At intervals in each we have inserted a number of discussion questions that readers – whether they are students, teachers or practitioners – can use to explore theoretical, technical and ethical issues posed in the chapter content. We also illustrate key concepts or approaches introduced in the book with cases studies in each chapter to help readers relate the theory that is presented to real life interventions. Each chapter ends with a set of self-review questions designed to test readers' understanding of the learning objectives of the chapter. Further reading and suggested web based resources are also provided to encourage more self-study.

Final thoughts and thanks

Through an exploration of how social marketing can add value to the policy and strategy development process we hope that this book makes a contribution to the development of a broader conceptualisation of social marketing theory and practice. Additionally we hope it promotes a greater recognition of the added value of applying marketing to policy and strategy development in the governmental, NGO and not-for-profit sectors.

We believe that this book marks a milestone in the development of a more contemporary and sophisticated conceptualisation of social marketing, incorporating a greater emphasis on its contribution to strategic analysis and planning and consequent system-wide effects. We hope it makes a contribution to the momentum that is building to move beyond a conception of social marketing that is focused only on improving the operational delivery of social programmes, using simplistic theoretical models with an over-concentration on individual behavioural factors. We argue that this kind of approach reinforces a dominant neo-liberal paradigm that is complicit in creating inequalities and social problems in contemporary societies. We also argue that it is time for a more socially progressive model of social marketing to emerge.

We hope that the arguments, examples and evidence we set out will encourage readers to apply and test some of the concepts, techniques and tools that we recommend. It is also our hope that in so doing readers will help build understanding about the contribution social marketing can bring to social programme design. We finally hope that this book stimulates others to further test and develop these ideas and their application.

We would like to thank the many people who have helped us to develop this book. We also want to acknowledge those people who worked with us to develop the case studies used in the book and generously gave their permission to use the material. This book would not have been possible without the work of many of our colleagues, and the advisors and reviewers who have helped us refine our thinking. We would especially like to thank the publishing team at SAGE for all their advice, support, patience and encouragement in bringing this book to fruition.

References

Buss, D. (2004) *Evolutionary Psychology: The New Science of the Mind*. Boston, MA: Pearson.

Clarke, J., Newman, J. and Smith, N., Vidler, E. and Westmarland, L. (2007) *Creating Citizen Consumers: Changing Publics & Changing Public Services*. London: SAGE.

Duffy, B., Quigley, A. and Duxbury, K. (2010) *National Health? Citizens' views of health services around the world*. Available at: www.ipsos-mori.com/researchpublications/publications/1395/National-Health-Citizens-views-of-health-services-around-the-world.aspx (last accessed 17 November 2014).

Jenkins, K. (ed.) (1997) *The Postmodern History Reader*. London: Routledge.

Leadbeater, C. (2008) *We-think: Mass Innovation, Not Mass Production*. London: Profile Books.

Marmot, R. (2008) *Closing the Gap in a Generation: Health Equity through Action on the Social Determinants of Health*. Geneva: WHO.

Marr, A. (2012) *A History of the World*. London: Macmillan.

Peters, G., Andrew, R., Boden, T., Canadell, J., Ciais, P., Le Quéré, C., Marland, G., Raupach, M. and Wilson, C. (2013) 'The challenge to keep global warming below 2 °C', *Nature Climate Change*, 3: 4–6. Available at: www.nature.com/nclimate/journal/vaop/ncurrent/full/nclimate1783.html (last accessed 17 November 2014)

Ridley, M. (2012) *The Rational Optimist*. London: Harper Collins.

Sandel, M. (2009) 'A new politics of the common good', BBC Radio 4, 4 July. Available at: www.bbc.co.uk/programmes/b00lb6bt (last accessed 17 November 2014).

UNESCO (2012) 'Adult and youth literacy', UNESCO Institute of Statistics, Fact Sheet No. 20, September. Available at: www.uis.unesco.org/FactSheets/Documents/fs20-literacy-day-2012-en-v3.pdf (last accessed 17 November 2014).

UNICEF (2011) *UNICEF Annual Report 2010*. New York: UNICEF.

United Nations (2001) *World Population Aging 1950–2050*. New York: UN. Available at: www.un.org/esa/population/publications/worldageing19502050/ (last accessed 17 November 2014).

WHO (2002) *Diet, Nutrition and the Prevention of Chronic Diseases: Report of a Joint WHO/FAO Expert Consultation*, 28 January–1 February. WHO Technical Report Series 916. Geneva, Switzerland.

WHO (2014) European databases for alcohol and tobacco. Available at: http://data.euro.who.int/tobacco/ and http://apps.who.int/gho/data/?showonly=GISAH&theme=main-euro (last accessed 17 November 2014).

Wilkinson, R. and Marmot, M. (2003) *Social Determinants of Health: The Solid Facts* (2nd edn). London: World Health Organization.

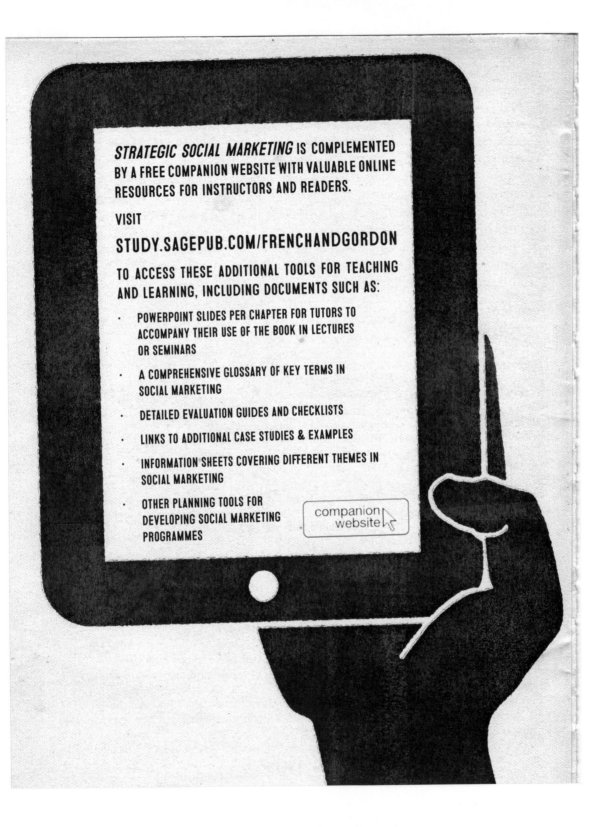

PART I
WHY?

1 THE IMPORTANCE OF SOCIAL MARKETING FOR SOCIAL POLICY

Learning objectives

By the end of this chapter, readers should be able to:

- understand why social marketing is increasingly being incorporated into strategy development as well as the operational delivery of social programmes
- articulate some of the key weaknesses associated with many current approaches to social policy and strategy aimed at influencing behaviour
- describe the key added value associated with the adoption of a strategic marketing approach to social programme and policy development.

Introduction

In Chapter 2 we explore and define the nature of social marketing and strategic social marketing but it is worth beginning this book with two key definitions of what social marketing is.

Social marketing was defined by Lazer and Kelley (1973: ix) as follows:

> Concerned with the application of marketing knowledge, concepts, and techniques to enhance social as well as economic ends. It is also concerned with the analysis of the social consequences of marketing policies, decisions and activities.

In 2013 the first consensus definition of social marketing was developed by the International Social Marketing Association in collaboration with the European Social Marketing Association and the Australian Association of Social Marketing. These organisations defined social marketing as follows (iSMA, ESMA, AASM, 2013):

> Social marketing seeks to develop and integrate marketing concepts with other approaches to influence behaviours that benefit individuals and communities for the greater social good.

> Social marketing practice is guided by ethical principles. It seeks to integrate research, best practice, theory, audience and partnership insight, to inform the delivery of competition sensitive and segmented social change programmes that are effective, efficient, equitable and sustainable.

As can be seen from these two definitions despite the intervening forty years the key focus of social marketing has remained constant, centred on the application and use of marketing principles, concepts and techniques to bring about social good.

Those forty years have seen social marketing become increasingly prominent in both marketing academe and in the social policy arena driven by increasing evidence that suggests it can be an effective social change approach in its own right (Gordon et al., 2006; Stead et al., 2007) and also because it can make positive contributions to social policy (French, 2011). Building on existing developments, the field is now proffering new ideas relating to management of the social marketing mix (Tapp and Spotswood, 2013), upstream marketing and policy (Gordon, 2013), interdisciplinarity, and strategic orientation (this textbook), applying service logic (Russell-Bennett et al., 2013), critical thinking (Gordon, 2011), value creation (Zainuddin et al., 2011), sustainability (Smith and O'Sullivan, 2012), and transformative thinking (Lefebvre, 2012). Calls are also being made for a broader, 'systemic' view of social marketing to be adopted (Hastings and Domegan, 2014).

Given its orientation towards practical social policy intervention design and delivery, social marketing also attracts significant research and development funds often not available in commercial marketing academe. The consequence is that social marketing is proving to be a testing ground for the conceptualisation, application and evaluation of new generic as well as social marketing concepts and theories. As Andreasen (2012) and others explain (Polonsky in Dibb and Carrigan, 2013) the opportunities are considerable for social marketing to inform marketing, and indeed social policy and change management, as its acceptance as a legitimate discipline increases. However, to realise this potential social marketing needs to break out of the confines of being a field of study and application focused on just the operational delivery of social programmes and campaigns, and seek to influence the development and selection of social policy and strategy.

Out with the old, in with the new

This book aims to signal the need for a move away from an operationally focused conception of social marketing, a position that could be called *social marketing myopia*, towards a broader concept of social marketing, that we term *strategic social marketing*. Strategic social marketing is focused on the potential for social marketing to add value not only at an operational level of programme delivery that seeks to influence groups and individuals, but also at the structural, environmental, political and social level (Goldberg, 1995; Andreasen, 2002; Gordon, 2013).

The authors argue that a narrow conceptualisation and a myopic focus on operational implementation have led to unnecessary and erroneous criticisms of how social marketing has developed and limited its contribution to solving social challenges around the world. The authors seek to remind both advocates and critics of social marketing that even as it was first emerging, select scholars proposed a broader remit (Lazer and Kelley, 1973) than just the systematic planning and delivery of marketing-based social interventions.

Specifically, the strategic, holistic, and interdisciplinary approach to conceptualising and operationalising social marketing presented here seeks to describe how it can facilitate a more comprehensive and multi-faceted approach to social change, by applying marketing principles, concepts and techniques that can be utilised at individual, microsystem, mesosystem, exosystem, macrosystem and chronosystems levels, and also be employed as a tool for engaging in wider critical systems analysis and thinking to address systems, marketing and organisational factors that cause social harm or promote social good.

Marketing focused social programme design

The processes associated with developing effective social programmes designed to influence behaviour and bring about social progress are a challenge faced by all governments as well as a challenge faced by all public, private and NGO organisations. Social marketing, if it is to deliver its full potential to assist with the development, selection and delivery of such social programmes, needs to be an integral component of all social policy formulation and strategy development rather than, as it is often currently conceived, as a second order operational function that is applied after policy and strategy have been agreed.

To date the vast majority of the social marketing books that have been published, with the exception of sections within Andreasen's (2006) book *Social Marketing in the 21st Century* and Hastings and Domegan (2014), have promulgated a view that social marketing is a positivist, individual psychology of behaviour and persuasion approach that is applied to social change, largely ignoring wider socio-cultural factors and forces that influence social outcomes.

This framing of social marketing and its contribution to social programmes we believe has been useful, but ultimately diminishes the impact that social marketing can have on social policy and programmes, and ultimately the effectiveness and efficiency of those programmes and consequently their impact on specific social problems.

A central contention of this book is that marketing and indeed social change theory principles and practice have expanded over the last forty years beyond programme and promotions management but most social marketing texts do not reflect this fundamental shift in theory and practice.

As a counterweight to this situation, in the ensuing chapters we have focused on how social marketing can be applied to influence policy, strategy and operational planning as well as the tactical delivery of social programmes designed to influence behaviour. Through this more comprehensive framing of social marketing we have sought to show that the application of current marketing principles can enhance policy formulation and strategy development as well as the operational delivery of social programmes. In essence this book seeks to reflect the need for social marketing to extend the exploration of how it can be and is being applied 'upstream' (Goldberg, 1995; Gordon, 2013) to frame social policy and strategy as well at operational and tactical delivery in a coordinated way. We focus on exploring the challenges and benefits of applying social marketing at the policy and strategy level and in so doing hope that social marketing will increasingly be seen, just as marketing is in much of the for-profit sector, as an integral strategic component of all social policy and strategy development activity.

Social marketing informed social programme design

It is vitally important that social marketing is incorporated into social policy and programme design as we believe that it can, alongside other approaches to social improvement, make a significant contribution to social good. This contention is supported by a growing body of evidence and experience about the limitations, drawbacks and unintended consequences of implementing social policy that does not take into consideration citizen needs and wants; and we explore these issues in Chapter 3. This evidence is also supported by emerging new understanding about how people take decisions, and how they can be influenced to act in socially and personally rewarding ways.

This understanding and its consequences for social policy and programmes are covered in Chapter 8. New understanding about how to design, implement and track social interventions has also been emerging as evidence informed policy making has gained momentum over recent years (Bullock et al., 2001). Learning from this evidence is reviewed in Chapters 11 and 12. Yet further evidence and insights are emerging from the management science, communications industries, webscience, the datafication of society, community engagement and empowerment methodologies and social design; we explore these issues in Chapters 4, 6, 7 and 10.

Books like *Nudge* (Thaler and Sunstein, 2008) and *Thinking, Fast and Slow* (Kahneman, 2011) and many others that seek to popularise some of our new understanding have hit the bestseller lists. Their contents are scrutinised by politicians and public policy makers and the recommendations that they make find their way into social policy solutions, from encouraging people to build up a pension, encouraging organ donations, the introduction of mandatory costs for disposable plastic bags, and minimum pricing for units of alcohol. However, rather than such a piecemeal or cherry picking uptake of ideas such as 'framing' or the application of behavioural 'defaults' it is necessary that we develop and apply a more systematic and cohesive approach to designing interventions that aim to influence people's behaviour. This is one of the key strengths of social marketing, just like other integrating methodologies such as lean production (Womack and Jones, 2007). Social marketing is not dependent on situation specific factors such as brilliant innovation, creativity, strong organisational culture leadership or even on governmental support. Rather it is its focus on core processes and the application of core principles and concepts that deliver its added value.

The fantastic consequence is that while specific situational brilliance and leadership can't be copied, superior development delivery and evaluation processes can. This means that social marketing informed social programme design is a globally applicable process.

CASE STUDY

EPODE: *'Ensemble, Prévenons l'Obésité des Enfants'* (Together, let's prevent childhood obesity)

EPODE is an acronym in French for *'Ensemble, Prévenons l'Obésité des Enfants'* [Together, let's prevent childhood obesity]. EPODE began in Fleurbaix and Laventie in 1992, which, at the time, had a population of 6,600 people between them. Everyone, from the mayor to shop owners, school teachers, doctors, pharmacists, caterers, restaurant owners, sports associations, the media, scientists and various branches of town government joined in an effort

(Continued)

(Continued)

to encourage children to eat better and move around more. The towns built sporting facilities and playgrounds, mapped out walking itineraries, and hired sports instructors. Families were offered cooking workshops, and those at risk were offered counselling. EPODE is a systemic coordinated, capacity-building approach aimed at reducing childhood obesity through a societal process in which local environments, childhood settings and family norms are directed and encouraged to facilitate the adoption of healthy lifestyles in children (i.e. the enjoyment of healthy eating, active play and recreation). In 2014 there were 25 EPODE programmes operating in 15 countries serving over 150 million people: this represents the world's largest coordinated obesity intervention network.

The primary EPODE target groups are children from birth to twelve years old and also their families. The other target groups of the EPODE methodology are the local stakeholders, decision makers and people who influence the social and economic life of the community in relation to healthy lifestyles. The EPODE approach involves the development of a town, area or city based strategy and action plan. The EPODE philosophy is based on:

- a positive approach with no stigmatisation of any culture, socio-economic status (SES) or individual
- a concrete and step-by-step learning and sharing experience of healthy life-style habits
- the tailoring of messages and actions to the targeted population (e.g. according to age, SES)
- a sustainable implementation of the programme to enable communities to plan actions and environmental changes in the long term.

Social marketing is one of the four pillars of the EPODE approach:

1. A strong political will, thanks to the involvement of political representatives.
2. A coordinated organisation and approach based on social marketing methods.
3. A multi-level, multi-stakeholder approach, involving public and private partners.
4. A sound scientific background, evaluation and dissemination of the programme.

EPODE is a long-term programme and methodology embedded into the daily life of the family and its constraints. It is a positive, concrete and step-by-step learning process, in line with the related national recommendations. A wide range of local stakeholders is involved to build up a sustainable environment that facilitates the adoption of healthy behaviours (see Figure 1.1).

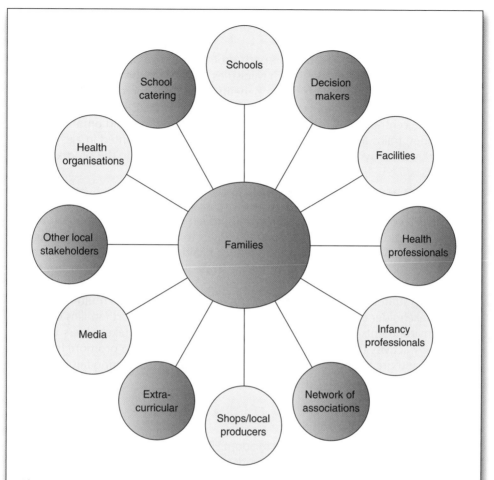

Figure 1.1 Stakeholders in the EPODE programme

The EPODE methodology relies on the importance of political support, aware-ness, willingness and involvement to set up and implement EPODE initiatives. The importance of political representatives' support for obesity prevention at their policy making level (national, regional or local) is key as they are best positioned to initiate and support cross-sectorial prevention dynamics in com-munities. The political representatives are well placed to encourage and build relationships with scientific experts, public and private partners (at national and local level) as well as with European and global political representatives to foster the set-up and implementation of further EPODE-type interventions

(Continued)

(Continued)

in other countries. The EPODE approach promotes the involvement of multiple stakeholders at a central level, from ministries, health groups and NGOs to private partners. The programme also benefits from the expertise and guidance of an independent expert committee. To put the EPODE methodology into practice, a central coordination team, using social marketing and organisational techniques, trains and coaches a local project manager appointed in each community by the mayor or another local leader able to champion the programme.

The social marketing based method

EPODE is a combined and coordinated approach with the application of marketing alongside other concepts and techniques to achieve specific behavioural goals to improve healthier habits and reduce health inequalities. Social marketing is incorporated into a wide range of strategies aimed at influencing the social and physical environments surrounding individuals. EPODE uses social marketing strategies to assist the development and delivery of a multi-level and multi-stakeholder approach to create the conditions to support families in their local environments. This approach aims to mobilise local stakeholders within their daily activity (teachers, local NGOs, catering services) to promote healthy lifestyles and greater physical activity in everyday life, empowering families and individuals in a sustainable way.

Impact

The pilot study of the first two towns to adopt EPODE, Fleurbaix Laventie Ville santé (FLVS), was initiated in 1992, aimed to understand the nutritional habits of children and their families and to study the effects of healthy nutritional information given in schools on the national habits of families. By taking a series of coordinated societal measures, it was possible to demonstrate the impact of EPODE on reducing obesity prevalence, improving children's lifestyle and decreasing health inequities.

Based on the lessons learned from this pilot study, the EPODE methodology was built and implemented in eight French pilot towns. In these towns, success to date is measured by a large field mobilisation. While recent data available in France at national level show an overall stabilisation in the prevalence of childhood overweight and obesity, results from the eight French EPODE pilot towns show a significant decrease of 9.86 per cent ($p < 0.01$; n= 23205 children) in overweight and obesity between 2005 and 2009. There are now similar projects in Belgium, Spain, the Netherlands, Greece, Ireland, Australia, Romania and the USA.

For more information see: www.epode-international-network.com/.

The organising potential of social marketing

Social marketing is the most comprehensive organising set of principles and concepts through which to strategically assess, design, deliver and evaluate social programmes that seek to influence behaviour for social good. Just like marketing in the for-profit sector, social marketing is a field of study that draws on theory, evidence and data from every discipline and then proceeds to synthesise all of this through systematic and transparent planning and implementation processes informed by principles that include value creation, exchange and relationship building, all of which are based on the sciences of behavioural influence and human interaction.

A new paradigm for social programme design is inevitable because we are now at a point in human history in many countries where a confluence of factors is occurring which means that existing approaches to social policy selection, design and application are no longer tenable. This situation has come about not just because of financial restrictions, emerging new evidence about what works, or because we know more about how behaviour can be influenced (Oliver, 2013), but also principally because there has been a fundamental power shift between states and the citizens they seek to govern and support (Clarke et al., 2007). This shift in power from small groups of powerful elites identifying and solving social problems to a more citizen empowered present has been brought about via a wide range of social, economic, scientific and technical developments.

These factors include but are not limited to the following:

- A realisation of the limitations of current social policy intervention approaches in a world of complex social problems, all of which have a large behavioural element together with a growing and accessible evidence base about what works and what does not (Australian Public Service Commission, 2007).
- The development of new understanding about how people make decisions and how their behaviour can be influenced (Dolan et al., 2010).
- A growing understanding of the key characteristics of effective social programmes and insight about how to select, test, develop, implement and evaluate social intervention programmes (Cabinet Office, 1999).
- The development of market research, citizen insight methodologies and the exponential growth and integration of 'Big Data' (Mayer-Schonberger and Cukier, 2013).

In addition, growing wealth and literacy levels and mass access to information and social networks are all serving to empower citizens. Although it varies considerably around the world, people generally trust governments, other civic institutions and professions much less than they used to and expect more from those in positions of authority. Clarke et al. (2007) have described the growth of the 'consumer citizen' as one of the key social phenomena of the last fifty years. As people become educated, empowered by liberal democracies and their wealth increases they experience more power as citizen consumers. This expectation of choice and power is transferred into expectations about how government and other not-for-profit institutions should behave and function.

Given impetus by these factors, social marketing has slowly begun to influence the social policy agenda. It has been given momentum by the growing recognition among policy makers about the limitations of traditional forms of state action (Oliver, 2013; Shafir, 2013). What is needed now, due to the growth of citizen power and improved understanding about how to develop and deliver more effective social programmes, are approaches to social policy that reflect a more equal distribution of social power and responsibility and more citizen insight informed social policy and programmes.

What this means in practice is converting citizens from being passive recipients of social programmes in systems that deny them both power and responsibility to being active co-creators of their own, and societal wellbeing.

In relation to environmental action it means engaging and enabling citizens to act in a sustainable way by creating policy, systems and services that encourage and reward positive environmental behaviour and not just nagging people to act. In the field of health it means empowering patients and care givers so that they can take a more active role in managing how healthcare services are provided and more joint decision making about treatment and care options. What we are now witnessing in many countries is the emergence of a new relationship between the state and citizens in which doing things 'with people' rather than 'to them' becomes a key factor in effective, efficient and acceptable social policy delivery. Such an approach is characterised by a relationship built on listening, dialogue and engagement. This respectful relationship building and solution generation process, if adopted, will result in interventions that apply the best available insights about citizen behaviour and their motivations, together with evidence about what works to develop social programmes that are effective and efficient and also valued by citizens and result in valued social benefit.

Such a change reflects citizen's expectations and acknowledges that citizens are more informed and inquiring. This emerging new paradigm signals a break from a situation where governing elites ruled and the ruled were grateful, and experts told people what to think and do and they did it. It also reflects modern conceptions of marketing practice that emphasise relationship building (Gummesson, 2002; Finne and Grönroos, 2009), and the dominance of quality service delivery (Lusch and Vargo, 2009) rather than just a focus on products or services.

Social marketing is a set of core organising principles, concepts and techniques that can be used to develop effective, efficient and citizen responsive social programme design. As Andreasen (2012) has argued we are potentially at a point in history where marketing comes to be seen as a field of application that is as dominant in the social sector as it is in the for-profit sector.

Big scary complex behavioural challenges

All societies face a number of significant social, health, economic and cultural challenges over the coming years. These include but are not limited to: massive growth in the burden of chronic disease, the consequences of global warming, environmental scarcities such as water and food, intolerance and discrimination, social service uptake and economic inequality. In addition most governments around the world are experiencing growth in social, welfare and healthcare spending as a percentage of GDP that will be difficult to sustain in the face of increasing demand. To tackle each of these problems governments and other civic institutions need to influence people's attitudes, beliefs and behaviours. However, many social change programmes have limited impact on these issues due to a number of systemic weaknesses in their conceptualisation, planning, implementation and evaluation:

1. Many social programmes that aim to change behaviour are constructed by policy makers, and then attempts are made to drive them through delivery agencies and professionals down into communities. This 'top down' and 'expert led' approach is often not informed by in-depth target audience understanding or insight. The frequent result is that interventions are misunderstood or viewed as irrelevant by the people who they are intended to help and end up having little impact.

2. Many behaviour change programmes are developed by politicians or experts as a means of demonstrating activity or concern around an issue high on the political or media agenda. Projects often have a 'short shelf life' and few interventions are sustained for a sufficient length of time to either develop effective interventions or have a sustained population level impact. Short-term awareness raising campaigns are often selected as a default response driven by a need for organisations or governments to demonstrate activity or manage political agendas rather than promoting real change. In addition many programmes are insufficiently funded to achieve their desired outcomes.

3. Many programmes either have vague, unquantifiable aims or at the other extreme have unrealistic goals. Many are also not adequately performance managed and lack clear performance metrics. Activity is focused around developing interventions, information or products such as social advertising, toolkits, training programmes, web services or the distribution of products. This focus on 'activity' and 'product' output results in programmes that are often not guided by insight data or theory, and also often do not have sufficient stakeholder engagement to enable sustainability.

4. There is often a lack of coordination and integration between programmes. This results in the development of competing interventions that provide contradictory advice and competing incentives or disincentives. Few programmes utilise a full intervention mix of education, information provision, design, support services and control measures.

5. Many programmes fail to take account of the complexity of causation of problems and the need for interdisciplinarity, and multiple interventions to tackle the determinants of social problems. Too often interventions depend on single or simplistic intervention strategies despite evidence that sustained interventions that simultaneously seek to influence several variables are more likely to be successful.

We also know that in many circumstances solutions to social problems such as obesity and global warming will not flow from untrammelled free markets or the unrestricted marketing of goods and services that produce net harm to citizens. In Chapter 14 we explore the issue of critical marketing, which we believe to be a key element in the strategic social marketing process.

The final driver for change comes in the form of economic imperatives. Many governments, as well as struggling with difficult economic circumstances, are under increasing pressure due to a demand for more transparent government to demonstrate value for money (VFM) and return on investment (ROI) from social programmes (Cabinet Office, 2009). The need to demonstrate that funding is having a positive effect and that money is being spent wisely is a positive and increasingly common situation.

These significant common programme and policy weaknesses can sometimes seem both complex and intractable. However, while these issues are complex the solutions are not always complicated. There is a growing body of evidence and many examples of good practice, some of which are captured as case studies in this book, which demonstrate that well planned and executed behaviour change programmes, based on social marketing principles and planning, can be highly effective in reducing the impact of current and future social challenges.

Taken together these factors result in the need for an approach to social policy development and implementation that is built on:

- a commitment to engagement and building value for citizens
- a deep understanding of citizens' beliefs and motivations
- an understanding of how to influence behaviour, social and cultural structures, and systems
- systematic planning and evaluation methodologies.

How we can embed these imperatives into the social policy and strategy development process and how marketing can assist with this process are explored in Chapters 2, 3 and 13.

Out of the shadows and into the policy spotlight

Social marketing is becoming an integral part of all public policy making and social programme design. However, to fully realise its potential as a force for social change it should not be viewed as an adjunct to social policy.

Social marketing's biggest contribution lies not simply in persuading people to behave in socially beneficial ways but by helping empower them to do so and enlisting their energy and support to promote and sustain socially beneficial behaviour in others. Improving health, reducing crime, promoting economic and social renewal cannot happen if society has to choose between either having an active state or having active citizens, as it requires both.

Social marketing began in the 1960s as a process (French, 2014) for ensuring that government and NGO campaigns were aimed at encouraging more people in both developed and developing communities to take up preventive health products and services such as increasing vaccination, the use of oral rehydration and contraception. Social marketing has subsequently developed into evidence and insight based approaches to social programme design focused on influencing behaviour. Social marketing has also developed into a philosophy of practice grounded in the belief that attempts to influence social behaviour should be built on ethical principles and a deep understanding of citizens' circumstances, needs, wants and beliefs. A core feature of social marketing is a commitment to a process that seeks to engage citizens and all relevant stakeholders in developing solutions to social challenges that are valued and are subject to broad civic support.

Social marketing is now supported by a number of policy makers, practitioners, specialist companies and academics, all of whom are focused on demonstrating its effectiveness and refining what we know about what works in influencing behaviour for social good. A small but growing number of governments and international agencies focused on solving the world's big social, economic, environmental, health and civil justice problems have now recognised the potency of social marketing in influencing positive civic and personal behaviour. Examples of these developments are explored in this book.

Conclusion

Social marketing, like every other field of study, progresses through a process of exploration, review, challenge and refinement. In this book we set out some challenges to the view that social marketing should only be considered when it comes to programme delivery. It is our hope that this book makes a helpful contribution to the field of social marketing by setting out an expanded view of its potential contribution to the selection, design, implementation and evaluation of social policy and strategy as well as its contribution to specific intervention programme design and delivery. Positioning social marketing as an integral part of the policy and strategic development process rather than just an element of operational planning and tactical delivery will, we hope, both raise the status of social marketing but more importantly improve the effectiveness and efficacy of social programmes designed to influence positive social behaviour.

By positioning the contribution that social marketing can make across the spectrum from policy development through to tactical project delivery we hope that this book will act as a helpful guide to practitioners and policy makers, as well as students, scholars and researchers.

Reflective questions

1. What are some of the main social and economic factors that are encouraging organisations and governments to incorporate social marketing into their social policy and programme development strategy?
2. What are some of the key weaknesses associated with current social policy and strategy aimed at influencing behaviour?
3. What added value can social marketing bring to social policy selection and the strategy development process?

Further reading

Australian Public Service Commission (2007) *Tackling Wicked Problems: A Public Policy Perspective*. Canberra: Australian Government. Available at: www.apsc.gov.au/publications-and-media/archive/publications-archive/tackling-wicked-problems (last accessed 18 November 2014).
Gordon, R. (2013) 'Unlocking the potential of upstream social marketing', *European Journal of Marketing*, 47 (9): 1525–1547.

References

Andreasen, A.R. (2002) 'Marketing social marketing in the social change marketplace', *Journal of Public Policy and Marketing*, 21 (1): 3–13.
Andreasen, A.R. (2006) *Social Marketing in the 21st Century*. Thousand Oaks, CA: SAGE.
Andreasen, A.R. (2012) 'Rethinking the relationship between social/nonprofit marketing and commercial marketing', *Journal of Public Policy and Marketing*, 31 (1): 36–41.
Australian Public Service Commission (2007) *Tackling Wicked Problems: A Public Policy Perspective*. Canberra: Australian Government. Available at: www.apsc.gov.au/publications-and-media/archive/publications-archive/tackling-wicked-problems (last accessed 18 November 2014).
Bullock, H., Mountford, J. and Stanley, R. (2001) *Better Policy Making*. London: Centre for Management and Policy Studies.
Cabinet Office (1999) *Professional Policy Making for the Twenty First Century*. Report by Strategic Policy Making Team Cabinet Office. London: Cabinet Office.
Cabinet Office (2009) *A Guide to Social Return on Investment*. London: Cabinet Office.
Clarke, J., Newman, J., Smith, N., Vidler, E. and Westmarland, L. (2007) *Creating Citizen Consumers: Changing Publics & Changing Public Service*. London: SAGE.
Dibb, S. and Carrigan, M. (2013) 'Social marketing transformed: Kotler, Polonsky and Hastings reflect on social marketing in a period of social change', *European Journal of Marketing*, 47 (9): 1376–1398.

Dolan, P., Hallsworth, M., Halpern, D., Kind, D. and Vlaev, I. (2010) *Mindspace: Influencing Behaviour through Public Policy*. Full Report Cabinet Office. London: Institute for Government.

Finne, A. and Grönroos, C. (2009) 'Rethinking marketing communication: from integrated marketing communication to relationship communication,' *Journal of Marketing Communications*, 15 (2/3): 179–195.

French, J. (2011) 'Why nudging is not enough', *Journal of Social Marketing*, 1 (2): 154–162.

French, J. (2014) 'The unfolding history of the social marketing concept', in D. Stewart (ed.), *Handbook of Persuasion and Social Marketing*. Thousand Oaks CA: SAGE, pp. 11–34.

Goldberg, M.E. (1995) 'Social marketing: are we fiddling while Rome burns?', *Journal of Consumer Psychology*, 4 (4): 347–370.

Gordon, R. (2011) 'Critical social marketing: definition, application and domain', *Journal of Social Marketing*, 1 (2): 82–99.

Gordon, R. (2013) 'Unlocking the potential of upstream social marketing', *European Journal of Marketing*, 47 (9): 1525–1547.

Gordon, R., McDermott, L., Stead, M. and Angus, K. (2006) 'The effectiveness of social marketing interventions for health improvement: what's the evidence?', *Public Health*, 120 (12): 1133–1139.

Gummesson, E. (2002) *Total Relationship Marketing: Rethinking Marketing Management: From 4Ps to 30Rs* (2nd edn). Oxford: Butterworth Heinemann.

Hastings, G. and Domegan, C. (2014) *Social Marketing: From Tunes to Symphonies* (2nd edn). London: Routledge.

Kahneman, D. (2011) *Thinking, Fast and Slow*. London: Penguin.

Lazer, W. and Kelley, E.J. (1973) *Social Marketing: Perspectives and Viewpoints*. Homewood: Richard D. Irwin.

Lefebvre, R.C. (2012) 'Transformative social marketing', *Journal of Social Marketing*, 2 (2): 118–129.

Lusch, R.F. and Vargo, S.L. (2009) 'Service-dominant logic – a guiding framework for inbound marketing', *Marketing Review St. Gallen*, 26 (6): 6–10.

Mayer-Schonberger, V. and Cukier, K. (2013) *Big Data*. St Ives: John Murry.

Oliver, A. (2013) *Behavioural Public Policy*. Cambridge: Cambridge University Press.

Russell-Bennett, R., Wood, M. and Previte, J. (2013) 'Fresh ideas: services thinking for social marketing', *Journal of Social Marketing*, 3 (3): 223–238.

Shafir, E. (ed.) (2013) *The Behavioral Foundations of Public Policy*. Princeton and Oxford: Princeton University Press.

Smith, A. and O'Sullivan, T. (2012) 'Environmentally responsible behaviour in the workplace: an internal social marketing approach', *Journal of Marketing Management*, 28 (3–4): 469–493.

Stead, M., Gordon, R., Angus, K. and McDermott, L. (2007) 'A systematic review of social marketing effectiveness', *Health Education*, 107 (2): 126–140.

Tapp, A. and Spotswood, F. (2013) 'From the 4Ps to COM-SM: reconfiguring the social marketing mix', *Journal of Social Marketing*, 3 (3): 206–222.

Thaler, R.H. and Sunstein, C.R. (2008) *Nudge: Improving Decisions about Health, Wealth and Happiness*. New Haven, CT and London: Yale University Press.

Womack, J. and Jones, D. (2007) *Lean Solutions*. London: Simon and Schuster.

Zainuddin, N., Previte, J. and Russell-Bennett, R. (2011) 'A social marketing approach to value creation in a well-women's health service', *Journal of Marketing Management*, 27 (3–4): 361–385.

2 THE NATURE OF SOCIAL MARKETING

Learning objectives

By the end of this chapter, readers should be able to:

- identify and understand key characteristics of social marketing
- differentiate social marketing from less comprehensive forms of social intervention such as behaviour change communication or social advertising
- understand the contribution that social marketing can make to the development, delivery and evaluation of social policy, including strategy development and operational delivery
- engage with some of the major criticisms of current social marketing practice, and the arguments for the development of a more strategic approach to social marketing.

Introduction

This chapter sets out what social marketing is, identifies what it is not, and discusses some of the issues and current criticisms of social marketing that create an imperative to move towards a more strategic application of social marketing. In this chapter we introduce our vision of strategic social marketing that is further elaborated in detail in subsequent chapters. We begin by briefly describing what social marketing is and present a short history, before examining some of the common mistruths, misconceptions and misunderstandings of social marketing. Case study examples of social marketing are used to illustrate our view of social marketing.

We discuss some common criticisms of social marketing, from within the field and also from external sources. Finally, we introduce the concept of *strategic social marketing* which is further developed in Chapter 4 with the aim of enhancing the understanding and application of social marketing as a strategic and holistic consumer-oriented marketing approach to social good.

What is social marketing?

The core to understanding all marketing including social marketing is that it is fundamentally about influencing human behaviour. Social marketing has recently been defined as follows:

> Social marketing seeks to develop and integrate marketing concepts with other approaches to influence behaviours that benefit individuals and communities for the greater social good. It seeks to integrate research, best practice, theory, participant and partnership insight, to inform the delivery of competition sensitive and segmented social change programmes that are effective, efficient, equitable and sustainable. (iSMA, ESMA, AASM, 2013)

Social marketing is a comprehensive, strategic and multi-faceted, marketing based approach to facilitate or maintain social good. It takes a citizen centred approach in which insight developed with participants and stakeholders informs the process. This 'participant orientation' of social marketing is a key part of the concept, and differentiates it from a traditional top-down expert-driven approach.

Key to understanding what social marketing is, and what it can achieve, is an understanding of what marketing is. The American Marketing Association (AMA, 2013) offers the following definition: '... marketing is the activity, set of institutions, and processes for creating, communicating, delivering, and exchanging offerings that have value for customers, clients, partners, and society at large'. This definition demonstrates how encompassing the marketing concept is; it is a big umbrella under which a host of activities, actors, frameworks and processes occur. Indeed, marketing affects everyone and engages everyone. At an ideological level social marketing is not, as some have argued, a stalking horse for uncontrolled free market economics to be applied to the supply and consumption of social goods. Nor is it simply the application of commercially derived marketing techniques to assist with social objectives. Rather social marketing seeks to reclaim the three fundamental human characteristics of mutuality, cooperation and reciprocity that have been appropriated by commercial marketing. These three fundamental characteristics can and should be used as powerful drivers to promote social development, and for most of human history they have been. Clearly, ever since groups of humans have existed, they have tried to influence each other. It has been argued by Ridley (2012) that trade and exchanges are fundamental aspects of what it is to be human. Exchange and trade are part of the social fabric of reciprocity that characterises humans and has enabled them to be a successful species. It could be argued that we are in fact *'Homosociomarketus'*, so deep rooted are the instincts to trade and exchange and through these processes we develop the collective good. This realisation can often come as a surprise to people who erroneously believe marketing is merely about advertising and communication in relation to the promotion of goods and services.

Dibb et al. (2012) have outlined the multi-dimensional nature of marketing:

- Marketing is performed by individuals and organisations.
- Marketing facilitates satisfying exchange relationships.
- Marketing occurs in a dynamic environment.
- Marketing involves products, distribution, places, promotion, pricing, people, policy, relationships, advocacy, lobbying, public relations, information, value creation and other activities.
- Marketing focuses on goods, services and ideas.

Discussion question

In addition to the list of features of marketing set out by Dibb et al. (2012) can you list any additional features of marketing that are either positive or negative?

The key difference between what we will call *commercial marketing* and social marketing is that in the commercial world the core objective of marketing is to deliver value to the owners and/or shareholders of a firm. In social marketing, the core objective is to support the development or continuation of social good, and through this create individual and social value.

Given the primary focus on creating social value, the conditions in which social marketing operates are often quite different from those for commercial marketing. For example, firms are likely to target primary customer segments that will provide them with the greatest volume of sales, or most profitable sales. In social marketing, participants (whether active or passive) in social programmes are segmented and engaged based on different criteria, including the significance and prevalence of the social problem, available resources, the ability to reach and influence the group, and a group's ability to change.

Competition – a key differentiator

Although both commercial marketing and social marketing recognise the importance of and make offerings relative to the competition, competitors are very different in nature between the two domains. In commercial marketing the competition comes in the form of alternative providers of goods and services or in competition for attention, loyalty and resources.

In social marketing competition involves biological, social, environmental, economic and systems factors that impact on behaviours and outcomes, as well as organisations and individuals that seek to influence target groups and individuals to behave in ways that create social or individual harm. Competition can also consist of:

- existing behaviours
- social, economic, environmental and systems barriers
- perceived benefits of existing behaviours
- a lack of clear incentives to change and incentives to sustain harm related behaviour
- the influence or lack of influence of others such as policy makers (unwilling to change the structural environment); peers (not providing social support for change); the media and commercial marketing (bombarding people with incentives to consume unhealthy products such as tobacco, alcohol or energy dense high fat foods or to drive inefficient cars).

Therefore, the nature of competition often makes the design and delivery of social marketing more complex than that of commercial marketing (Lee and Kotler, 2011). Consider the challenges faced when attempting to influence people to stop smoking (give up an addictive behaviour that is believed to relieve stress or control weight), reduce thermostat settings to limit energy consumption (change what is perceived as a comfortable lifestyle choice), give blood (fear of being uncomfortable and subjected to pain), or buy recycled paper (spend more money for what may be considered as a lower quality product).

The key to addressing the competition in both commercial and social marketing is to conduct robust competitive analysis and then develop strategies and tactics to reduce or eliminate the impact of the competition. These strategies and tactics are discussed in more detail in Chapter 14.

Competitive analysis forms an important part of marketing strategy in the commercial world (Wensley, 2003). In social marketing we need to recognise sources of competition and the factors that may inhibit our target audience from adopting the behaviours we are promoting. Clearly there will be various potential sources of competition to a social marketing programme intervention, which will depend on the specific behaviour being promoted and the specific target group.

One form of competition that we cannot ignore is the potential detrimental impact of commercial marketing on many of the social challenges in which we are trying to influence behaviour. For example, our ability to encourage and support children to eat a better diet will be vastly improved if we can tackle some of the wider commercial and environmental factors that are making it difficult for them to consume the kinds of foods that would promote health and reduce the risk of chronic disease. Encouraging policy makers and legislators to ban or restrict junk food advertising to children, or encouraging retailers to stock more healthy foods as opposed to highly processed foods or remove confectionary at check-outs, are just some examples of how we might achieve this. Scholars have identified how utilising *critical social marketing* research, which involves critically examining the impact of commercial marketing on society, and then using this knowledge to inform interventions, can form an important tool for competitive analysis (Hastings, 2010; Gordon, 2011a). Other strategies that remove the competition to social marketing, such as transmitting or increasing the benefits associated with change, and providing incentives and addressing barriers to change are also key components of a strategic social marketing approach that should be addressed in most social change programmes. We explore the contribution of critical competitive analysis and critical social marketing in more detail in Chapter 14.

Key principles of social marketing

Nevertheless, despite important differences between commercial marketing and social marketing, many of the underlying principles and activities are similar, or can be adapted to deliver social change. *Consumer* or *participant orientation* in the case of social marketing is key in both domains. All forms of marketing are about creating value, and marketers know that their offering – whether it is a product, service, idea or experience – will need to appeal to participants, solve a problem they face or satisfy needs and wants. In this respect the concept of *exchange theory* is often viewed as fundamental (Bagozzi, 1975). Participant groups must perceive benefits that justify them purchasing a product or service, or performing a behaviour. However, with respect to social marketing, one could move beyond exchange to argue that social marketing should ultimately be about delivering individual and social value. Exchange as a marketing concept can be uni- or bi-directional and focused on what is in it for the parties involved, whereas social marketing seeks to promote social good. Therefore, it may be posited that rather than being about creating motivational exchanges, social marketing should be about *creating individual value* and *societal/ social value*.

Marketing research is crucial to identify such insights on the specific needs, desires, beliefs, attitudes, and what moves and motivates participants as well as understanding about non-rational or cognitive decision making when emotional or biologically determined preferences will influence behaviour.

The segmentation, targeting and *positioning* of social marketing offerings based on representational insight are vital to ensure that strategies, interventions and activities are tailored to the unique needs, wants, values, resources, attitudes and behaviours of different participant segments. Market segmentation is a well-established business approach to identify and manage diverse customer/participant needs and to target marketing resources (Weinstein, 2004; Dibb and Simkin, 2009). The basic premise of segmentation is that heterogeneity in preferences can be managed by grouping similar groups of people into market segments, some of whom may become the focus of marketing efforts (Mahajan and Jain, 1978). Segmentation facilitates consumer/ participant orientation by enabling organisations to develop, *target, position* and maintain close links with their customers. This permits a more efficient use and allocation of marketing resources, and helps identify and better attune to how to serve particular customers' needs (Albert, 2003). Essentially segmentation recognises that people are different, and often want different things or will respond to different forms of engagement and interaction. This is important for social marketing, as we know that 'one size fits all' approaches to achieving social change are often ineffective. Segmentation can be performed based on a number of different characteristics and profiles (Eagle et al., 2013):

- demographics such as age, gender, marital status, employment, income, socio-economic status
- cultures/subcultures including ethnicity, religious beliefs, subcultures of consumption behaviours (e.g. night clubbers, bikers)
- attitudes such as acceptability towards smoking or drinking
- psychological including motivations, personality, interests and opinions
- value perceptions such as perceived functional, economic or social value of using energy efficiently
- psychographics such as lifestyle, knowledge, activities
- behavioural, for example, people who are gamblers, smokers or drinkers.

Using segmentation in social marketing requires balancing the benefits offered with available resources, as comprehensive segmentation strategies can be expensive and time consuming and involve difficulties in implementation (Dibb and Simkin, 2009). Simkin and Dibb (2011) identify that strategic planning but also detailed planning, internal marketing of segmentation strategy to gain organisational buy-in, tracking of implementation, monitoring of performance, clear allocation of resources, proactive response to barriers, engaging champions for strategy, and rewarding progress are key considerations to achieve successful segmentation. Packages and toolkits have also been developed to assist with a segmentation strategy such as the Values and Lifestyle Survey (VALS), grouping people according to their personal values and lifestyle choices (Della et al., 2009), or the UK Department of Health's 'Healthy Foundations' model, which identifies life stage, environment and attitudes towards health issues as three key dimensions linked with health behaviours (see Department of Health, 2008a). We discuss segmentation further in Chapter 10.

Targeting requires social marketers to utilise segmentation analysis to carefully consider which population segments to target and try to engage in social programmes. Target groups need to be large enough to warrant attention and to be viable in terms of allocation of resources (e.g. low income smokers are an example of a potentially viable target group as smoking prevalence is higher in low income populations). Target groups also need to be accessible and channels of communication and engagement need to exist. The target also needs to be one that is potentially responsive to social marketing efforts – there is no point engaging groups that do not need or do not want to be engaged on a given social issue (Hastings and Domegan, 2014).

Positioning in social marketing refers to what strategy to adopt to achieve goals such as raised awareness, brand recognition or reach of communications. Products, services, issues or ideas are positioned through the use of marketing mix strategies. Positioning also helps us present distinct offerings that stand out from the crowd and that are appealing, compared to the competition's (Trout and Rivkin, 1996). In many ways positioning is a concept in the mind of target segments, and how the consumer sees the product, service, or idea. In social marketing we sometimes need to consider repositioning social issues to highlight their importance, or reframe how people might perceive them. Examples include how smoke-free legislation in Scotland was repositioned from a purely public health issue to also be concerned with the civil rights of workers exposed to secondhand smoke (see Chapter 7 for a case study on this issue). Similarly, social marketers have proposed that gambling harm should be repositioned from a psychology of addiction problem to a public health and broader social issue (Gordon and Moodie, 2009; Gordon et. al. 2015).

Two further fundamental markers of effective social marketing are the application of a full breadth of strategies and activities in a *marketing intervention mix* and *robust systematic planning and evaluation strategies*. A successful social marketing programme will normally apply a mix of education and engagement, product or service delivery, information provision, environmental and systems change, and potentially control methods as well (see Chapter 3 for more details on this issue). A successful selection of the right weighted mix requires using research and if necessary pre-testing to determine which intervention mix strategy will be capable of bringing about an affordable and ethical programme capable of delivering the desired behavioural change. Comprehensive evaluation and the establishment of a learning culture are necessary to benchmark, measure and understand processes and outcomes, and develop an insight and understanding of how things can be improved. Although this book seeks to challenge and develop established thinking across some of these key components of the social marketing approach, the key principles outlined here offer a useful starting point.

The objective in social marketing is to use the principles, concepts, techniques and resources at our disposal to try to influence human behaviour for social good. Given that human behaviour is complex, multi-factorial, distinct and often irrational and unpredictable, marketers need to use a wide range of disciplinary approaches, theories, concepts, strategies and techniques to influence people. In the commercial world, the idea that comprehensive and systematic marketing strategies are required to influence human behaviour is well accepted. However, in the public and social policy arenas, such a strategic and nuanced approach has been somewhat lacking or has taken time to achieve acceptance as a useful approach. To fully understand what social marketing is, where it needs to go, and why we are calling for a move to what we call *strategic social marketing*, it is important to first consider the historical development of the concept.

A brief history of social marketing

The birth of social marketing can be traced to research psychologist for CBS Radio and lecturer in psychology at City College New York, G.D. Wiebe, who in his seminal article 'Merchandizing commodities and citizenship on television' (Wiebe, 1951) posed the question, can brotherhood be sold like soap? Although Wiebe was really referring to using social advertising to promote social ideas, his suggestion helped stimulate discourse within the marketing discipline about broadening the marketing concept to the social sphere. During the 1960s, marketing scholars began to solidify proposals to extend marketing beyond the firm–customer dimension to social issues (Kotler and Levy, 1969). Although examples of marketing applications beyond commercial gain have existed since the emergence of the academic discipline in the early twentieth century (Wilkie and Moore, 1999), the second half of the twentieth century saw the emergence of a dedicated sub-discipline of marketing social good, for example to promote merit goods, encourage a society to avoid demerit goods, and promote society's wellbeing as a whole. Kotler and Zaltman were the first to formalise a definition of social marketing as:

> the design, implementation and control of programs calculated to influence the acceptability of social ideas and involving considerations of product planning, pricing, communication, distribution and marketing research. (1971: 5)

Kotler and Zaltman's work emerged at a time in which the 'broadening the marketing concept' movement was in full swing. This movement involved scholars arguing for a wider conceptual and applied scope for marketing beyond the commercial domain, to the public and social sphere to market organisations, people and ideas (Kotler and Levy, 1969). This new application for marketing was developed by a number of people during the 1960s, including Paul Bloom, Karen Fox, Dick Manoff and Bill Novelli (MacFadyen et al., 1999). However, different ideas and conceptualisations existed (see Gordon, 2011a), and arguably what finally emerged was a relatively narrowly focused social marketing discipline (see Gordon and Gurrieri, 2014).

Early examples of social marketing involved the use of commercial marketing techniques applied to health education, and interventions and programmes in developing countries (Manoff, 1985; Ling et al., 1992). In Sri Lanka, family planning programmes moved away from clinical approaches to examine the distribution of contraceptives through pharmacists and small shops (Population Services International, 1977). Similarly, oral re-hydration projects in Africa began to take a more consumer focused approach to their development (MacFadyen et al., 1999).

Many of these programmes were predominantly exercises in community health, often dominated by approaches that emphasised social advertising or social communication and, especially in the developing world, the distribution of tangible products such as condoms. However, these early attempts to apply marketing thinking were important staging posts in the development of social marketing theory and practice. At the time it should also be remembered that some of these programmes were not being described as social marketing. However, reviews have shown that these programmes display characteristics of social marketing (Stead et al., 2007). The last 20 years have resulted in a considerable expansion and consolidation of theory and concepts that influence social marketing (Dann, 2010). Yet, there is no single identifiable and exclusive social marketing theory. Rather social marketing acts as a conceptual cluster of principles, concepts and techniques that together offer a structural framework for behaviour change and social good (Stead et al., 2007). Furthermore, social marketing is influenced by many other disciplines including sociology, psychology, economics, anthropology, behavioural theory, education, communications theory and design theory. Essentially marketing is interdisciplinary, and is what Peters and Hirst (1971) would call a field of applied study.

The common theme across the various definitions of social marketing is the use of marketing principles and practice to influence behaviour that results in personal and social good. Two key constructs in this process are consumer orientation, or in the case of social marketing participant orientation, and exchange theory. Consumer orientation is a central component of all forms of marketing. In social marketing, the aim is to ensure the citizen consumer is an active participant in the change process, and that a relationship and understanding are developed and maintained through formative, process and evaluative research. Marketing also requires two or more parties each with something to exchange (Kotler and Zaltman, 1971). In marketing, exchange is defined as an exchange of goods, services, resources or values between two or more parties with the expectation of some benefits that will satisfy needs (Bagozzi, 1975; Houston and Gassenheimer, 1987).

Normally an exchange will involve the exchange of goods or services for money, but can also involve, for example, a vote in return for a political policy that appears attractive, or acceptance of a vaccination in return for protection from a disease, or paying tax to ensure access to good roads and a clean water supply. In social marketing exchange is often voluntary and positive in nature, the emphasis is on voluntary behaviour change rewarded by some positive social advantage. However social marketing exchanges can also include approaches to influencing behaviour that use penalties and negative consequences if the desired behaviour is not complied with. Examples would be the use of fines or other legal sanctions to persuade people to act in a socially responsible manner. Fundamentally these exchanges reflect a collective agreement that such interventions are supported, and have ideally been brought into being through debate within democratic systems that have the support of communities and ultimately individuals. Obviously individuals can, and some do opt to defy legal sanctions and restrictions and choose to bear the consequences.

To encourage positive social exchange social marketers need to offer something people actually want and value. This can be difficult if the benefits are complex, abstract or are only realised in the long term and involve short-term costs. Examples include improved long-term health from living a healthy lifestyle, the benefits of active citizenship through voting in elections, or changes in behaviour to reduce global warming. Therefore, social marketers often have to develop innovative ways in which to promote positive social behaviour. Following this exchange approach, it is important to highlight immediate gains, the use of emotional drivers of behaviour, emotional appeals as well as rational ones, and the development of emotional as well as functional value. However, as introduced earlier, there is increasing debate on whether the concept of exchange is still relevant to modern day marketing and social marketing. While offering motivational exchanges may still form a relevant part of social marketing activity, as discussed earlier and as expanded upon in Chapter 6, contemporary discourse has moved towards a focus on delivering individual, social, and societal value.

Following the earlier work in the social marketing domain during the 1970s, academics in the 1980s and 1990s identified social marketing programmes as containing the following core elements:

- participant (consumer) orientation (Lefebvre and Flora, 1988; Andreasen, 1995)
- exchange (Leather and Hastings, 1987; Lefebvre, 1996)
- a systematic planning approach (Andreasen, 1995).

Alan Andreasen (2002) then further developed this list of characteristics and identified six benchmarks for good social marketing interventions:

1. behaviour change
2. consumer research
3. segmentation and targeting

4. the use of the marketing mix of product, price, place, and promotion
5. exchange
6. consideration of competition.

In the UK these criteria were later expanded to develop a set of what were termed 'benchmark criteria' by French and Blair-Stevens (2006): see Table 2.1.

Table 2.1 Social marketing benchmark criteria

Benchmark	Explanation
1. Sets behavioural goals	Social marketing programmes should have a clear focus on behaviour, based on a strong behavioural analysis, with specific behavioural goals.
2. Uses consumer research and pre-testing	Developing a clear understanding of the audience, based on consumer research using data from a variety of sources, helps develop a consumer-oriented approach.
3. Makes judicious use of theory	Programmes benefit from being based upon behavioural theory, and are informed by and should draw from an integrated theoretical framework.
4. Is insight driven	Focus should be on gaining a deeper understanding of what moves and what motivates the consumer. Identification of key factors and issues relevant to positively influencing behaviour allows actionable insights to be developed.
5. Applies principles of segmentation and targeting	Avoiding blanket approaches, segmentation and targeting allows interventions to be tailored to specific audience segments.
6. Makes use of the marketing mix beyond communications	Programmes consider the best strategic application of the marketing mix consisting of the four Ps of 'product', 'price', 'place' and 'promotion'. Other Ps might include 'policy change' or 'people', for example delivering training to intervention delivery agents.
7. Creates attractive motivational exchanges with the target group	Programmes consider what motivates people to engage voluntarily with the intervention and offers them something beneficial in exchange. The offered benefit may be tangible (e.g. rewards/incentives for participation or making behavioural changes) or intangible (e.g. personal satisfaction, improved health and wellbeing).
8. Addresses the competition to the desired behaviour	Forces competing with the desired behaviour change are analysed and the intervention considers the appeal of competing behaviours. Strategies that seek to remove or minimise the competition are used.

Source: adapted from French and Blair-Stevens, 2006; and Stead et al., 2007

Work is continuing in the area of benchmarking social marketing, with the iSMA, ESMA and AASM currently conducting a collaborative project to develop a set of enhanced and comprehensive social marketing benchmark criteria – with the project due for completion in late 2015. Proposals emanating from this work have identified that benchmarks of social marketing can potentially be categorised according to principles, concepts and techniques (see Figure 2.1).

Figure 2.1 presents a pyramid schema, with layer one, the *social marketing principle*, based on the core social marketing principle of facilitating social good and delivering individual and social value through exchanges, social offerings, experiences and structural change.

Layer two of the pyramid presents *social marketing concepts*, including social/ behavioural influence, participant/citizen/civic society orientation, social offerings (ideas, products, services, resources and experiences), relationship and network building, critical and reflexive thinking, and systems thinking.

Finally, the top layer of the pyramid presents *social marketing techniques*, including systematic planning and evaluation, participatory and representative research, insight driven segmentation, an integrated intervention mix, co-creation through social markets, and competition analysis and action. This layer also includes what we describe as a wide range of other social marketing tools and models such as branding and lobbying. These tools, techniques and strategies are explored more extensively in Chapter 4.

What this schema does is identify a hierarchy of relevance and importance with regard to the key attributes and distinguishing features of social marketing.

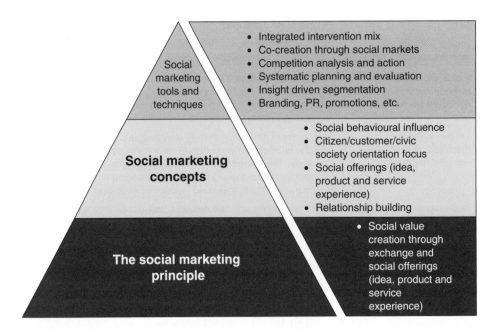

Figure 2.1 Social marketing principles, concepts and techniques hierarchy model

Source: French and Russell-Bennett, forthcoming

Previous social marketing benchmark criteria have not explicitly identified what criteria are essential and must be incorporated in a social marketing programme. However, Andreasen (2002) indicated that he felt some criteria were core (insight, exchange and behavioural focus) and by omission that some were less important, and he states: 'At this stage of the field's development, I do not argue that programs must have all six elements in strong measure to qualify for the label "social marketing"' (2002: 7).

The model proposed in Figure 2.1 distinguishes between core social marketing principles and concepts and then a broad set of techniques and tools that are not unique to social marketing but are often associated with it. We propose that this new model for social marketing criteria reflects some of the latest discourse and developments in the field, and can act as a useful guide for scholars and practitioners who may have grappled with the issue of equivalence and identifying what key criteria they must incorporate in social programmes. However, we do acknowledge that this model is not exhaustive or restrictive, and there should be the freedom to introduce, incorporate or even replace principles, concepts and techniques moving forward. Indeed, the authors invite social marketers to contribute to such debates.

Discussion question

Which social marketing criteria (principles, concepts or techniques) would you consider to be the most important markers of social marketing practice?

Expansion and growth in support of social marketing

As the value of social marketing as a behaviour influencing strategy has emerged, it has enjoyed a period of expansion worldwide since the 1960s. This growth has included increased funding and capacity for research, a stronger practitioner skills base, and the development of professional standards in social marketing under the auspices of the Marketing and Sales Standards Setting Body (White and French, 2010).

Social marketing has also engendered political support with the UK government embracing social marketing in the 'Choosing Health' white paper which espoused 'the power of social marketing and marketing tools applied to social good being used to build public awareness and change behaviour' (Department of Health, 2004: 21). Indeed, government support for social marketing in the UK culminated in the formation of the National Social Marketing Centre (NSMC), a collaboration between the Department of Health and Consumer Focus, designed to build capacity and skills in social marketing at strategic and operational levels. The UK government has since developed two successive social marketing strategies (Department of Health, 2008b; 2011).

In the United States, the Centres for Disease Control and Prevention (CDC) have endorsed social marketing as a core public health strategy (CDC, 2005). The US government's Healthy People 2020 strategy for the first time includes a commitment to develop the competencies of the public health workforce in social marketing (US Department of Health and Human Services, 2010). In Canada, Health Canada has been a long-term advocate of social marketing and has incorporated social marketing into its strategy since the 1970s (Lalonde, 1974). In Australia, social marketing has been influential in guiding tobacco control efforts, there are hubs of leading research and practice across the country, as well as the first national peak body in the field – the Australian Association of Social Marketing (AASM). In New Zealand, the Health Sponsorship Council (HSC) was founded in 1990 as a crown entity utilising social marketing to promote health and encourage health lifestyles – with its successor the Health Promotion Agency: www.hpa.org.nz. The World Health Organisation Europe has recently incorporated social marketing as one of its central components for the next phase of its strategy WHO 2020 (WHO, 2012). Social marketing has also been recently endorsed by the Indian government which is currently supporting a new working group to further develop its application and integration in social policy in the country (Ayyappan, 2013); and many other countries including Bangladesh, Pakistan and Indonesia have indicated strong commitment to the application of social marketing principles (New Indian Express, 2013; Deshpande and Lee, 2014).

Social marketing research and teaching centres have emerged in the UK at the University of Stirling, the Open University, the University of the West of England and Brighton University, among others. In the United States there are strong social marketing research groups at Georgetown University and the University of South Florida; in Canada at Carleton University and the University of Lethbridge; in Australia at Macquarie University, the University of Wollongong, QUT, Curtin University and Griffith University; and in New Zealand at the University of Otago. There has also been the emergence of a number of social marketing teaching programmes around the world and efforts to further embed social marketing within undergraduate and postgraduate marketing, public health and social policy programmes are continuing (Kelly, 2013).

As social marketing has generated attention, its scope and application have broadened beyond public health behaviour issues such as tobacco, alcohol, nutrition and physical activity. Indeed the ability for social marketing to demonstrate applicability beyond public health has been identified as one of the key tasks on the agenda for the future of the field (Gordon et al., 2008). A range of social issues to which social marketing can be applied has been examined, including climate change and sustainability (McKenzie-Mohr and Smith, 1999; Marcell et al., 2004; Gordon et al., 2011), energy efficiency (Kennedy et al., 2000), public transport use (Cooper, 2007), citizen engagement (Bhattacharya and Elsbach, 2002) and gambling (Messerlain and Derevensky, 2007; Powell and Tapp, 2008; Gordon and Moodie, 2009).

Some criticisms and identified weaknesses of social marketing

Undoubtedly, social marketing has demonstrated its utility as a behaviour influencing approach since its emergence in the middle of the twentieth century. However, there is growing commentary within the discipline about some of the shortcomings inherent within current frameworks and understanding of social marketing.

One such issue relates to the concept of *upstream social marketing*. Upstream social marketing emerged as a response to calls to focus beyond the narrower confines of individual behaviour change (Wallack, 1990; Novelli, 1996). During the 1990s there were also calls for a shift in emphasis within the social marketing discipline towards a focus on upstream applications (Wells, 1993; Andreasen, 1995; Goldberg, 1995). Social marketers acknowledged that rather than solely focus on downstream individual behaviour, social marketing could influence behaviour at the upstream level, targeting decision makers, policy makers, service providers and regulators. Operating upstream often involves research to inform regulation and policy, and involvement in media advocacy and lobbying. The example of tobacco offers a good demonstration of upstream social marketing. Research evidence was presented, tobacco control activists lobbied policy makers and regulators, public relations work was carried out in the media, and eventually policy change occurred.

Crucially, upstream social marketing requires recognition that managers, regulators and politicians are a legitimate target audience, with specific goals, influences, needs and motivations, just like anyone else. The electoral cycle, political agendas, the views of the electorate, good public relations and prestige are all areas of interest to policy makers, and upstream social marketing acknowledges these influences. Yet despite increasing recognition of the importance of moving beyond the individual (Wymer, 2010; Hoek and Jones, 2011), applications of social marketing have largely remained rooted at the individual behaviour change level. Therefore, despite recent works attempting to drive the upstream social marketing agenda (e.g. French, 2011; Gordon, 2013a), it is easy to understand why a common criticism of social marketing is that it ignores the influence of the wider structural environment on behaviour.

Another contemporary issue in social marketing relates to the use of out-dated, unsuitable or simplistic frameworks to achieve social change. By its very nature, human behaviour, social change and the considerable health, social and environmental challenges faced by contemporary societies are complex and multi-factorial. For too long, social marketing has readily embraced simple metrics and mantras such as the 4Ps marketing mix or a focus on being fun, easy and popular (Lee and Kotler, 2011). While such frameworks may be easy to understand, they often fail to acknowledge the complexity and realities of marketing social change, and the wealth of potential strategies and activities that can be utilised to achieve it (Gordon, 2012).

Therefore, what this book sets out to achieve, is to acknowledge the significant work that has been done to carry social marketing to where it currently is, but also that there is a need to move forward to the next stage of the development of social marketing – towards what we term *strategic social marketing*. This involves broadening the concept, scope and application of social marketing to unlock its true potential as a systematic evidence and data driven approach to social policy delivery. Having offered a brief synopsis of its history, it is important to understand some of the common mistruths, misconceptions and misunderstandings of social marketing that help justify our call for a move towards strategic social marketing.

Mistruths, misconceptions and misunderstandings of social marketing

One of the major difficulties for social marketing relates to commonly held misunderstandings and misconceptions of what it actually is.

Erroneous views of social marketing include that it is just social advertising or promotion, what our colleague Alan Tapp refers to as the SPLAT (Some Posters, Leaflets, Ads 'n' Things) view of social marketing, or that it is another name for marketing using social media. These views are held not only by the general public or those from other areas such as public health (see Grier and Bryant, 2005), but also people claiming to be working within social marketing (see Donovan, 2011) – witness the regular presentation of social advertising campaigns at social marketing conferences. This situation is further exacerbated by actions and beliefs held within the social marketing field that it is only concerned with individual voluntary behaviour change, and that it involves only using out-dated models such as the 4Ps marketing mix. Recognising these debates, scholars have commented on the 'mythunderstandings' of social marketing (Donovan, 2011).

As the social marketing discipline develops and matures it is important that these mistruths, misconceptions and misunderstandings of social marketing are robustly addressed. The danger is that a failure to address erroneous views of what social marketing is could lead to its marginalisation. Furthermore, a failure to grasp the true nature and potential of social marketing means that currently a lot of activities are poorly designed or executed and with improvement could achieve much more. Therefore, there is an imperative to be clear about what social marketing is, and what it is not (McDermott et al., 2005). To understand the reasons behind such levels of misunderstanding of what social marketing really is, we need to return to the 1970s, when it first emerged as a sub-discipline of marketing.

Following Kotler and Zaltman's (1971) initial definition of social marketing, considerable debate emerged on what its remit should be. Kotler and Zaltman defined social marketing as:

> the design, implementation and control of programs calculated to influence the acceptability of social ideas and involving considerations of product planning, pricing, communication, distribution and marketing research. (1971: 5)

While the field owes much to this definition, for some scholars the nature of this definition and its lack of clarity created confusion about what social marketing is (Andreasen, 2003). For some, social marketing involved selling products that could result in socially beneficial outcomes, such as contraception to reduce unwanted pregnancies or sexually transmitted diseases. Examples include the aforementioned marketing influenced family planning interventions run by organisations such as Population Services International in the 1970s in countries like Sri Lanka, involving the distribution of products (contraceptives), often at cost (Population Services International, 1977). At the time, this move away from clinical approaches to health interventions was considered revolutionary. A focus on the promotion and distribution of tangible products such as condoms and utilising channels such as existing retail outlets to market the health product was innovative. Although many of the early examples of social marketing influenced programmes were actually more like health promotion campaigns, the stage had been set for consumer-oriented marketing approaches to social change.

However, others took the view that social marketing was also about marketing ideas and values that could bring about socially beneficial change. This was especially the case in the developed world where the real challenge in many areas was to encourage behaviour change rather than the take-up of a health product like an anti-malaria bed net or oral rehydration salts. This attracted criticism from those in the commercial marketing field who believed that stepping away from tangible products and services to marketing ideas and values was a step too far (Luck, 1974). An argument was also made that social marketing should include considering the impact that commercial marketing has on society to provide control and a level of social audit (Lazer and Kelley, 1973). While some scholars have supported this view, and conducted research in this area (Hastings and Saren, 2003; Gordon, 2011a), others identify this with socially responsible or societal marketing, or critical marketing (Andreasen, 2003; Dann, 2010).

During the 1980s and more so into the 1990s some level of agreement on what social marketing constituted appeared to emerge. Essentially, social marketing emerged as a strategic planning framework for developing social change programmes comprising consumer research, use of behavioural theory, segmentation and targeting, objective setting and utilisation of the marketing mix (McDermott et al., 2005). In recent years as social marketing has matured, the level of debate has increased. Current debates in social marketing are centred on whether the focus should be solely on voluntary behaviour, what should constitute the social marketing intervention mix, which arenas of social policy social marketing should operate within, and whether it should be used midstream and upstream to alter the social environment.

Therefore, considerable ongoing debate continues about what social marketing is. Much of this confusion about social marketing emerges from its regular use in the public health arena. For some in this sphere, social marketing was essentially a rebadged form of health promotion (Buchanan et al., 1994). Given that social marketing is often used as an approach to social change by practitioners within the public health field, often with little or no informed understanding of core marketing theory, principles and practice, it is easy to identify where some of these issues emerge from.

Lindenberger (2001) has commented on how a lack of basic understanding of marketing has led to poor understanding and utilisation of social marketing. Tapp and Spotswood (2013) discuss the problem of *classic part-time marketers* who enter the social marketing field through other fields such as the health professions. While such people may consider themselves as social marketers, and have been involved in the management or delivery of social marketing interventions, they often have no background in marketing, and an incomplete understanding of what it entails. Others such as communication specialists may also be involved in the delivery of social marketing programmes but lack formal qualifications or training in marketing. While social marketing should encourage 'part-time' marketers to enter the field, proper training, education and support are required to ensure that stakeholders have an adequate understanding of marketing concepts and principles. Social marketing scholars have identified poor understanding of core marketing concepts such as market orientation, exchange, relationships, service logic, and a strategic planning process within these cohorts (Andreasen, 2006; Smith, 2011).

This confusion is further confounded when we consider those outside the social marketing discipline. Many working within the public health discipline (in which context social marketing has been used most often), have an incomplete understanding of social marketing (Grier and Bryant, 2005). Commonly held beliefs that social marketing is a more advanced form of health promotion, or relates to social advertising or health communication campaigns, persist (Hill, 2001). At the World Social Marketing Conference in Toronto in 2013 these misunderstandings were evident in many presentations of health communications or social advertising campaigns that were not

Figure 2.2

developed using comprehensive marketing conceptual frameworks. An example of this was a campaign about social smoking called 'Quit the Denial' funded by the Canadian Ministry of Health, and devised by the BBDO advertising agency (www.facebook.com/quitthedenial).

The advertising campaign humorously likened social smokers to 'social farters', ridiculing the female star of the ads for perceiving herself to not being a real farter but only a social farter. While the irreverent use of a metaphor for social smoking attracted attention and some laughs, it was clear to those with a more nuanced and complete understanding of social marketing that what was being presented to the conference was nothing more than a clever social advertising campaign. The fact that this campaign was delivered by a large advertising agency was also an interesting observation, and is something that we will return to later in this chapter.

Another smoking intervention, however, provides one of the best examples of a comprehensive, well-researched and well-executed strategic social marketing programme: the truth® programme (www.thetruth.com; see the following case study). The truth® programme demonstrates that moving beyond mere social advertising and using a comprehensive social marketing approach can be effective. Therefore, the importance of addressing the erroneous identification of social advertising as being social marketing is apparent.

CASE STUDY

The truth® campaign: www.thetruth.com

The campaign is a comprehensive youth anti-tobacco intervention that uses events, road shows, public relations and media relations activities, youth driven advocacy, branding, merchandising, support and advice services, mass media (including TV advertising, posters and billboards), digital and social media activities and various other strategies to help engage young people.

Crucially, the programme is informed by extensive formative consumer research with young people to identify what moves and motivates them, and test strategies that would engage them effectively in the issue of smoking control. Furthermore, the programme is based upon behavioural theory, particularly social exchange theory – which theorises that human relationships and behaviours are formed by the use of a subjective cost–benefit analysis and comparison of alternatives (Homans, 1961). A key theme in the truth® programme is the use of a counter marketing strategy, in which materials and activities focus on how the tobacco industry has lied, manipulated, stigmatised

(Continued)

(Continued)

and generally behaved unethically to recruit youth smokers. Communicating this to young people appeals to the rebellious nature and mistrust of older authority figures often held by teenagers.

Evaluation research of the impact of the truth® programme has demonstrated its effectiveness at reducing rates of youth smoking (Farrelly et al., 2005), and the intervention is still running to this day, more than ten years since it was first conceptualised.

Scholars such as Grier and Bryant (2005) and Tapp and Spotswood (2013) have identified how social advertising is conflated with social marketing in the large number of abstracts submitted to journals like *Social Marketing Quarterly* that describe their focus as being on social marketing, when in fact they present social advertising or communication activities. While newer journals like the *Journal of Social Marketing* encourage a more robust understanding, such problems persist. Yet conflating advertising with marketing is not a phenomenon restricted to the social marketing domain. Indeed, this is a common refrain in business and the wider world, and the failure to understand that marketing is much more than advertising has been discussed in considerable detail (Ames, 1970; Piercy, 2009). In particular Ames's (1970) seminal piece discusses how presidents of commercial organisations lamented the failure of their marketing efforts and then discussed how they had poured money into advertising and promotion campaigns, and failed to concentrate on embedding a strategic and comprehensive marketing framework within their companies. As such, it emerges that one of the core and basic principles in social marketing is to make sure that you understand what marketing is (see McKenna, 1991, or numerous textbooks on marketing management).

It should also be acknowledge that equivocating (social) advertising for marketing is also promulgated by the advertising industry itself. One only has to watch an episode of the television show *Mad Men* to witness advertising executive Don Draper discard consumer insights and strategic marketing planning, preferring to go on a hunch or focus solely on creative ideas to develop an advertising (not marketing) campaign. The 'Don Draper effect' is unfortunately still too often found in the advertising industry, and in the social marketing arena. There is no doubt that advertising can be and often is an important part of social marketing programmes; however, it is not and cannot be the most important or only show in town.

The fact that large advertising agencies are increasingly seeking work in the social change area may be linked to a gradual shift away from use of traditional advertising by commercial firms towards other forms of marketing such as use of social media platforms, online, ambient, mobile technologies and experiential marketing. Indeed, a large portion of overall marketing spend is now spent on non-advertising activities such as sponsorship, new media, branding, experiential marketing, stakeholder marketing and other such activities (Kotler and Armstrong, 2012). As an example, the UK alcohol industry spends around £800m per annum on alcohol marketing – with only approximately £200m of this amount spent on advertising (Prime Minister's Strategy Unit, 2003; AC Nielsen, 2006). As this marketing spend has shifted away from traditional advertising, advertising agencies have been required to seek other clients. It is perhaps unsurprising then that when approached by a social change client, advertising agencies will normally recommend advertising centred solutions, rather than comprehensive social marketing programmes. Therefore, the onus is on social change stakeholders to have a good understanding of their commissioning brief, what they are trying to achieve, and what they may be offered by contractors. Some of the issues relating to commissioning social marketing, and identifying indicators of competence and quality, are discussed in the online resources attached to this textbook.

While we have sought to address some of the myths and misunderstanding associated with social marketing, it is also important to recognise that it is not a panacea to the entire world's social problems, and that there are criticisms that should be acknowledged, before discussing how *strategic social marketing* may help address these.

Social marketing critiques

Unsurprisingly, given that it operates in a domain in which there are lots of contested ideas and power-control interactions, criticisms of social marketing have emerged from within the marketing discipline, the public health discipline and from other external sources. Some of these criticisms are valid, and should be acknowledged and carefully considered by those operating in the field. Other criticisms relate to misunderstandings or misinformation about what social marketing really is. Moreover, some complaints about social marketing can be addressed depending on what vision of social marketing one takes.

The view offered in this book is that a strategic and holistic social marketing approach could address some of the more prominent criticisms. However, criticism should not necessarily be viewed as a negative, but rather a sign of a healthy discipline in which critical debate and reflexivity are encouraged. Therefore, criticisms of social marketing should be viewed as providing opportunities for debate, reflection and the advancement of knowledge and practice in the field.

Stretching the definition of marketing too far?

One of the earliest criticisms of social marketing emerged during the broadening movement in marketing, when scholars like Kotler and Levy (1969) proposed that marketing should be concerned with selling not only products and services, but also ideas. The argument followed that churches, public sector organisations, governments and people could use marketing to influence their publics. However, for traditionalists within the marketing paradigm this was a step too far and they objected to the broadened concept, preferring a more orthodox view (Luck, 1969; Laczniak and Michie, 1979). For example, Luck (1974) argued that replacing products or services with ideas or values threatened the concept of economic exchange. Further, in the earlier days of its development social marketing was identified as lacking theory and rigour (Rothschild, 1979; Andreasen, 2003). Although work has been done to address these criticisms (see Bloom and Novelli, 1981; Hastings, 2007), this is an issue that still holds some truth today (Gordon, 2013b).

Ethics

There is also contested discourse on the ethical dimensions of social marketing. It has been argued that social marketing uses manipulative subterfuge to trick citizens into performing state desired behaviours without challenging the underlying causal influences (Buchanan et al., 1994). There have been specific criticisms of some of the social marketing programmes in the developing world, for example birth control interventions, which involve the distribution of free condoms, without tackling structural issues like exploring the underlying reasons for poor birth control such as the oppression and exploitation of women (Fraser and Restrepo-Estrada, 1998). Further, the ethics of using marketing to influence social issues and behaviours, especially those that are controversial, has been questioned. Laczniak et al. (1979) suggest that social marketing could be regarded as consisting of a form of thought control imposed by the elite, with marketers operating as 'neopropagandists' without consideration of ethical concerns. This leads to an important and somewhat abstract debate around when and whether it is right to intervene, and what constitutes 'social good' (Spotswood et al., 2012).

However, a limited or non-interventionist neo-liberal approach is not a vision shared by the authors. Rather, our view is that a socially progressive model of social marketing geared towards the amelioration of behavioural and social challenges and focused on value creation, mutualism, social welfare, social justice and social equality is required, and can provide benefits to society. Therefore, criticisms of an interventionist approach (see Laczniak et al., 1979) seem misguided by reinforcing an 'everybody for themselves' mentality. Our view is that provided it is done fairly, sensitively, reflexively and ethically, and is subject to transparency, public scrutiny and broad public support, the ends justify the means. This is particularly the case when society as a whole is supportive of interventions and the approaches they adopt. However, this does attach significant importance to applying standard ethical tests in social marketing.

The use of fear campaigns in some social marketing programmes has also been criticised as unethical (Hastings et al., 2004). In recent years there has been a gradual move away from the use of fear appeals in social marketing, particularly when targeting consumers who we know do not respond well to them such as adolescents (Stead and Gordon, 2010). Yet ethical dilemmas in social marketing still persist – for example Gurrieri et al. (2013) have identified unintended effects of stigmatisation of overweight people, and perpetuating social pressures that women may feel regarding their body image as a result of obesity social marketing programmes.

Therefore social marketers need to consider ethics in all that they do. That is, social marketing should be conducted as ethically as possible and ethics should form a central component of the approach. There are frameworks for ethics that can assist us in this. The literature on ethics largely focuses on two common frameworks: *deontology* (relating to intentions of actions), and *teleology* (relating to consequences of actions). As such a social marketing programme on obesity that was driven by good intentions, without consideration of whether it may create stigma, would be acceptable according to a deontology perspective, but would not be acceptable under teleological reasoning. However, it is also important to acknowledge the *relativist* perspective that there may be no universal framework for ethics, as interpretations of what is ethical and what is not may differ according to individual, cultural and social aspects. In such cases each group's ethical perspective should be acknowledged and hold equal value. Other frameworks such as the UN Charter have aimed to create *social contracts* governing basic rights that humans have such as health, shelter, food and water, etc. (see Chapter 11 for examples of this). However, under a social contract theory perspective, contracts are often implied, and this can mean there is little or no shared understanding of what rights and responsibilities apply to various parties. Therefore, a more holistic perspective may be to recognise the relevance of each of these ethical frameworks to build a more complete hybrid model of social marketing ethics that puts the focus on doing things with good intentions, but also being aware of the consequences of actions, and in doing so recognising the diversity of views and interpretations of ethical issues between individuals, social groups, organisations and cultures. Engaging in systems thinking, critical thinking and reflexive practice can help us adopt this bigger picture and multi-perspective view. General models of marketing ethics have been offered by scholars such as Hunt and Vitell (2006), which have aimed to acknowledge these various dimensions.

Chapter 14, focusing on critical social marketing, features a discussion on how critical thinking and engaging in reflexivity can help us think through whether what we are doing is ethical. As the discussions later in Chapter 11 identify, ethical decisions in social marketing can relate to what social issues warrant attention, what participant groups should be engaged, and what intervention tools and strategies should be used. We also discuss the relevance and importance of ethics in social marketing research in Chapter 9. What is important is that social marketers recognise that ethics is a complex and multi-faceted concept, and understanding and behaving ethically are critical for social marketing to be viewed as a legitimate approach to engendering social good.

Fortunately there are codes of ethics and also technical reports that can help social marketers understand ethics and assess if and how they can perform ethically. However, we would again encourage social marketers to think critically and reflexively about how they use these. Many marketing associations such as the American Marketing Association (AMA, 2007), or the Market Research Society (MRS, 2014) have codes of ethics. For example, the AMA code stipulates that marketers:

1. Must do no harm.
2. Must foster trust in the marketing systems (i.e. not mislead), good faith and fair dealing.
3. Must embrace, communicate and practise fundamental ethical values that will improve consumer confidence in the integrity of marketing. These basic values include honesty, responsibility, fairness, respect, openness and citizenship (Adapted from AMA, 2007).

However, while such codes may transmit good intentions, these are often just idealistic statements rather than containing any technical aspects of how codes of ethics will be implemented, and what the potential punishments are for transgressions. This has opened up debate about whether sectors like marketing should be self-regulated by codes such as the British Committee of Advertising Practice's UK Code of Advertising Practice (BCAP, 2010), or whether they should be statutorily regulated (see Gordon, 2011b). In some professions ethical transgressions are dealt with very severely – for example, doctors or lawyers may be struck off the register of practice. These same punitive measures are often not enforced for marketers. Codes such as BCAP (2010) may ask for unethical advertising or other marketing to be withdrawn and desisted. However, more severe penalties such as high financial penalties, bans on marketing activity, and withdrawal of licenses are not common. The public health sector has developed perhaps more informative ethical principles that may be relevant to social marketing:

*   Respect for the autonomy of individuals and communities, a need for consultation and agreement, and the absence of deceit.
*   Beneficence – the provision of net benefit to participant groups or patients.
*   An obligation to ensure no harm is caused by actions.
*   Justice in terms of the fairness of a distribution of resources, the respecting of rights and for morally accepted law. (Adapted from Gillon, 1994)

Increasing consideration of ethics in social marketing has generated proposed frameworks, checklists and codes of conduct for ethics (see Eagle, 2009). Donovan and Henley (2003) offer a potentially useful ethical checklist for social marketing programmes:

*   Ensure that the programme will not cause physical or psychological harm.
*   Does the programme give assistance where it is needed?

- Does the programme allow those who need assistance the freedom to exercise their entitlements?
- Are all actors treated equally and fairly?
- Will the choices made produce the greatest good for the greatest number of people?
- Is the autonomy of participants recognised? (Adapted from Donovan and Henley, 2003)

In terms of codes of ethics, Rothschild (2001) proposes the following:

- Do more good than harm.
- Favour free choice.
- Evaluate marketing with a broad context of behaviour management (considering other tools such as education and law).
- Select tools that are effective and efficient.
- Select marketing tools that fit the marketing philosophy and meet the needs of participants rather than the self-interest of the organisation.
- Evaluate the ethicality of a policy before agreeing to develop strategy. (Adapted from Rothschild, 2001)

Again, while these checklists and codes of ethics offer useful reference points for social marketing, what is crucial is that social marketers think holistically, critically and reflexively about how they interpret and apply these frameworks, and more broadly about how they ensure ethical practice in social marketing.

Disciplinary boundaries

Within the health promotion field, criticisms of social marketing include that it is essentially a form of health promotion re-badged (Buchanan et al., 1994; Hill, 2001), or that it re-labels practice in other fields (Tones, 1996). This last point is an important one when considering a broadened social marketing concept that encompasses the use of a wide range of marketing-oriented strategies at multiple levels to influence the behaviour of individuals, communities, stakeholders, organisations, policy makers, opinion formers, the media, the commercial sector, social norms and other influences on behaviour. As Gordon (2013a) discusses, it is important to acknowledge that this more strategic application of social marketing involves multidisciplinary approaches, and use of relational thinking, media advocacy, lobbying, public relations and political engagement – all activities or even disciplines that are well established and exist in their own right. Acknowledging the critique of Tones (1996), this may cause issues with territorialism and accusations that social marketing is re-badging existent approaches, or unwelcomingly laying claim to other disciplines (McKie and Toledano, 2008). Therefore, it is important to acknowledge that a *strategic social marketing* approach does not claim to reinvent these activities and approaches. Rather it seeks to acknowledge and apply the contribution of multiple fields of study and intervention and so add value. The key is to use the concepts and tools available to design effective and efficient social programmes capable of generating social change and social value. The application of a strategic marketing perspective also adds value through the requirement for an ongoing focus on citizens' beliefs, attitudes, needs, wants, behaviours, and practices. Taking a citizen centric approach together with the development of systemic solutions to social problems signals a commitment to constructing comprehensive intervention programmes. Delivering social programmes in such ways acknowledges the need to engage citizens in creating value and enabling them to exist in ways that are beneficial to them personally and to the wider society.

Lack of theoretical grounding and critical discourse

There is also debate on how social marketing has responded to criticism that suggests a defensive stance and a lack of critical reflexivity, which is arguably a marker of mature academic and practice disciplines. Critical marketers, who espouse rethought marketing systems to address inadequacies with existing marketing systems, have criticised social marketing for being too positivist (Dholakia and Dholakia, 2001), lacking a critical discourse and engagement with reflexivity (Tadajewski and Brownlie, 2008), and effectively being a self-serving adaptation of the dominant capitalist marketing system (Bettany and Woodruffe-Burton, 2009; Tadajewski, 2010). Leading on from this, external criticism of social marketing has identified it as a neo-liberal approach that puts the blame on individuals and ignores the effect of the wider environment on behaviour (Crawshaw, 2012; Langford and Panter-Brick, 2013). This reinforces our argument for a socially progressive model of social marketing to emerge.

The perceived lack of critical discourse in social marketing appears to offer some grounds for justified criticism. Certainly social marketers have vigorously emphasised the legitimacy of social marketing as a sub-discipline of marketing thought, and an approach to influencing behaviour for social good. At times, the potential and scope of social marketing have been hyperbolised. Social marketing is not a magic bullet – it cannot solve all of society's behavioural problems nor correct all of marketing's excesses. Rather it can provide a component of multi-faceted strategies for dealing with societal issues. Given a perceived lack of acceptance for social marketing within the marketing discipline, and scepticism within the public health field in which it has mostly operated, it is unsurprising that scholars have on occasion been protective of social marketing and espoused its virtues with a missionary zeal (Witkowski, 2005). The majority of marketing journals and marketing conferences within the discipline are not concerned with, or pay limited attention to, social marketing, and it remains somewhat marginalised. These misconceptions and antipathy have contributed towards the difficult environment in which social marketing has operated. Although attempts to develop critical discourse (Hastings and Saren, 2003; Gordon, 2011a) and encourage reflexivity (Spotswood et al., 2012; Gordon and Gurrieri, 2014) have emerged, as this book sets out, critical reflection in social marketing should be further developed and encouraged.

Despite these criticisms, social marketing has demonstrated its utility as an effective behaviour influence approach (Gordon et al., 2006; Stead et al., 2007). Nevertheless, our argument is that many of the root sources of criticism and current limitations of social marketing relate to the narrow definition, scope, interpretation and myopic applications that are largely prevalent. In this book, we set out how moving towards a socially progressive orientation of *strategic social marketing* can help address some of these criticisms, and truly unlock the potential of social marketing as a social change approach.

Conclusion: moving towards strategic social marketing

Our clarion call for social marketing is that it is time to move towards *strategic social marketing*, which we define as:

> The systemic, critical and reflexive application of social marketing principals to enhance social policy selection, objective setting, planning and operational delivery.

We argue that the time has come for social marketing to begin to operate at both a tactical level and a strategic level, helping to guide the selection and coordination of efforts to bring about social good, wellbeing and social cohesion. It is time to move beyond communication or persuasion or the narrow confines of legislation as the principle default responses to social development. We also need to shift the focus away from just individual responsibility to recognise and address the significant impact that the wider social, economic, cultural and structural environment has on social behaviour, and to acknowledge and embrace the complexity required to engineer social change. The foundations of *strategic social marketing* are concerned with these wider social issues. Moving forward, social marketing should aim to become a prominent approach to social policy selection and development. Strategic social marketing can offer a useful approach to the delivery of interdisciplinary, multi-faceted, multi-level, strategic and holistic, and long-term social change programmes. Strategic social marketing programmes should be based on research evidence, participant insight, joined-up thinking, judicious theory, multi-level segmentation, targeting and positioning, critical thinking, reflexivity and competitive analysis that utilise all the available cross disciplinary knowledge, tools, strategies and activities available to us. Such a shift in emphasis will involve a step change away from the narrow, individual 'voluntary' behaviour change interpretations of social marketing that are currently prevalent, and away from product or communications focused approaches (Gordon and Gurrieri, 2014).

While reducing social marketing and social change down to easy digestible formulas such as the 4Ps (see Gordon, 2012), and making it fun, easy and popular, may seem attractive (Lee and Kotler, 2011), in fact this simplistic framing of social marketing and social change is both disingenuous and ultimately counterproductive.

Social change, human behaviour and the role and influence of multiple forces on societies are complex phenomena. Yet some proclaim that narrow interpretations of social marketing offer a standardised, easy, bite-sized formula for tackling some of the greatest challenges faced by humankind. In doing so social marketing is exposed to rightful criticism of false claims and arrogance. Rather, the authors encourage social marketers to recognise and embrace complexity. By admitting and responding to the fact that the social issues to which social marketing are applied are extremely complex and challenging, we can then move on to systematically and strategically address these challenges. Indeed, complexity should not be considered a threat but an opportunity. Colleagues in social marketing have sometimes lamented that the field struggles to attract the best thinkers and the brightest minds. By embracing complexity, *strategic social marketing* can encourage the greatest minds and the best thinkers to research, apply and evaluate effective, equitable and just social change programmes.

Having outlined the imperative for moving towards *strategic social marketing* Chapter 3 explores what we know about influencing human behaviour and systems and how we can use marketing to enhance the development of both social policy and the delivery of a broad mix of interventions to improve human wellbeing. Chapter 4 then goes on to explore further the range of social marketing techniques and tools that make up the full social marketing intervention mix.

Reflective questions

- Make a list of what you consider to be the key markers of a social marketing programme.
- Make a list of all the criticisms you think can be levelled at current social marketing practice from both practical and ethical perspectives. What about theoretical perspectives?
- List the reasons why you think social marketing may need to adopt a more strategic and upstream approach to its practice. Illustrate your answers with some examples.

Further reading

Andreasen, A.R. (2003) 'The life trajectory of social marketing: some implications', *Marketing Theory*, 3 (3): 293–303.

Crawshaw, P. (2012) 'Governing at a distance: social marketing and the (bio) politics of responsibility', *Social Science and Medicine*, 75 (1): 200–207.

Gordon, R. (2011) 'Critical social marketing: definition, application and domain', *Journal of Social Marketing*, 1 (2): 82–99.

Gordon, R. (2013) 'New ideas, fresh thinking: towards a broadening of the social marketing concept?', *Journal of Social Marketing*, 3 (3): 200–205.

Spotswood, F., French, J., Tapp, A. and Stead, M. (2012) 'Some reasonable but uncomfortable questions about social marketing', *Journal of Social Marketing*, 2 (3): 163–175.

References

AC Nielsen (2006) *The Drink Pocket Book 2006*. Oxford: World Advertising Research Centre.

Albert, T.C. (2003) 'Need-based segmentation and customized communication strategies in a complex-commodity industry: a supply chain study', *Industrial Marketing Management*, 32 (4): 281–290.

AMA (American Marketing Association) (2007) *American Marketing Association Code of Ethics: Ethical Norms and Values for Marketers*. Available at: https://archive.ama.org/Archive/About AMA/Pages/Statement%20of%20Ethics.aspx (last accessed 9 December 2014).

AMA (American Marketing Association) (2013) 'Definition of marketing'. Available at: www. marketingpower.com/AboutAMA/Pages/DefinitionofMarketing.aspx (last accessed 12 November 2013).

Ames, B.C. (1970) 'Trappings vs substance in industrial marketing', *Harvard Business Review*, 48 (4): 93–102.

Andreasen, A.R. (1995) *Marketing Social Change*. San Francisco, CA: Jossey-Bass.

Andreasen, A.R. (2002) 'Marketing social marketing in the social change marketplace', *Journal of Public Policy and Marketing*, 21 (1): 3–13.

Andreasen, A.R. (2003) 'The life trajectory of social marketing: some implications', *Marketing Theory*, 3 (3): 293–303.

Andreasen, A.R. (2006) *Social Marketing in the 21st Century*. Thousand Oaks, CA: SAGE.

Ayyappan, M. (2013) *HLL Lifecare*. Proceedings of the Global Conference on Social marketing and social franchising, Kerala.

Bagozzi, R.P. (1975) 'Marketing as exchange', *Journal of Marketing*, 39 (3): 32–39.

BCAP (Broadcast Committee of Advertising Practice) (2010) *The UK Code of Advertising Practice*. London: Committee of Advertising Practice.

Bettany, S. and Woodruffe-Burton, H. (2009) 'Working the limits of method: the possibilities of critical reflexive practice in marketing and consumer research', *Journal of Marketing Management*, 25 (7/8): 661–679.

Bhattacharya, C.B. and Elsbach, K.D. (2002) 'Us versus them: the roles of organizational identification and disidentification in social marketing initiatives', *Journal of Public Policy and Marketing*, 21 (1): 26–36.

Bloom, P.N. and Novelli, W.D. (1981) 'Problems and challenges in social marketing', *Journal of Marketing*, 45 (2): 79–88.

Buchanan, D.R., Reddy, S. and Hossain, Z. (1994) 'Social marketing: a critical appraisal', *Health Promotion International*, 9 (1): 49–57.

Buss, D. (2004) *Evolutionary Psychology: The New Science of the Mind*. Boston, MA: Pearson.

CDC (Centers for Disease Control and Prevention) (2005). *Communication at CDC, Practice Areas: Social Marketing*. Atlanta, GA: CDC. Available at: www.cdc.gov/communication/prac tice/socialmarketing.html (last accessed 1 August 2013).

Cooper, C. (2007) 'Successfully changing individual travel behavior: applying community-based social marketing to travel choice', *Transportation Research Board Journal*, 2021: 89–99.

Crawshaw, P. (2012) 'Governing at a distance: social marketing and the (bio) politics of responsibility', *Social Science and Medicine*, 75 (1): 200–207.

Dann, S. (2010) 'Redefining social marketing with contemporary commercial marketing definitions', *Journal of Business Research*, 63 (2): 147–153.

Della, L.J., DeJoy, D.M. and Lance, C.E. (2009) 'Explaining fruit and vegetable intake using a consumer marketing tool', *Health Education and Behaviour*, 36 (5): 895–914.

Department of Health (2004) *Choosing Health: Making Healthier Choices Easier*, Public health white paper, Series No. CM 6374. London: The Stationery Office.

Department of Health (2008a) *Healthy Foundations: A Segmentation Model*. London: The Stationery Office.

Department of Health (2008b) *Ambitions for Health: Government Social Marketing Strategy*. London: The Stationery Office.

Department of Health (2011) *Changing Behaviour, Improving Outcomes: Social Marketing Strategy*. London: The Stationery Office.

Deshpande, S. and Lee, N. (2014). *Social Marketing in India*. New York: SAGE.

Dholakia, R.R. and Dholakia, N. (2001) 'Social marketing and development', in P. Bloom and G. Gundlach (eds), *Handbook of Marketing and Society*. Thousand Oaks, CA: SAGE, pp. 486–505.

Dibb, S. and Simkin, L. (2009) 'Implementation rules to bridge the theory/practice divide in market segmentation', *Journal of Marketing Management*, 25 (3): 375–396.

Dibb, S., Simkin, L., Pride, W.M. and Ferrell, O.C. (2012) *Marketing: Concepts and Strategies*. London: Cengage.

Donovan, R. (2011) 'Social marketing's mythunderstandings', *Journal of Social Marketing*, 1 (1): 8–16.

Donovan, R. and Henley, N. (2003) *Social Marketing Principles and Practice*. Melbourne: IP Communications.

Eagle, L. (2009) *Social Marketing Ethics: Report Prepared for the National Social Marketing Centre*. London: NSMC.

Eagle, L., Dahl, S., Hill, S., Bird, S., Spotswood, F. and Tapp, A. (2013) *Social Marketing*. London: Pearson.

Farrelly, M.C., Davis, K.C., Haviland, M.L., Messeri, P. and Healton, C.G. (2005) 'Evidence of a dose–response relationship between "truth" antismoking ads and youth smoking prevalence', *American Journal of Public Health*, 95 (3): 425–431.

Fraser, C. and Restrepo-Estrada, S. (1998) *Communicating for Development: Human Change for Survival*. New York: I.B. Tauris Publishers.

French, J. (2011) 'Business as unusual: the contribution of social marketing to government policy making and strategy development', in G. Hastings, K. Angus and C. Bryant (eds), *The SAGE Handbook of Social Marketing*. London: SAGE, pp. 359–374.

French, J. and Blair-Stevens, C. (2006) *Social Marketing Pocket Guide*. London: National Social Marketing Centre. Available at: www.nsms.org.uk (last accessed 1 July 2013).

French, J. and Russell-Bennett, R. (forthcoming) 'A hierarchical model of social marketing', *Journal of Social Marketing*.

Gillon, R. (1994) 'Medical ethics: four principles plus attention to scope', *British Medical Journal*, 309 (6948): 184.

Goldberg, M.E. (1995) 'Social marketing: are we fiddling while Rome burns?', *Journal of Consumer Psychology*, 4 (4): 347–370.

Gordon, R. (2011a) 'Critical social marketing: definition, application and domain', *Journal of Social Marketing*, 1 (2): 82–99.

Gordon, R. (2011b) 'Critical social marketing: assessing the cumulative impact of alcohol marketing on youth drinking', PhD thesis. Stirling: University of Stirling. Available at: https://dspace.stir.ac.uk/bitstream/1893/3135/1/Ross%20Gordon%20PhD%20FINAL%20SUBMITTED.pdf (last accessed 12 August 2014).

Gordon, R. (2012) 'Re-thinking and re-tooling the social marketing mix', *Australasian Marketing Journal*, 20 (2): 122–126.

Gordon, R. (2013a) 'Unlocking the potential of upstream social marketing', *European Journal of Marketing*, 47 (9): 1525–1547.

Gordon, R. (2013b) 'New ideas, fresh thinking: towards a broadening of the social marketing concept?', *Journal of Social marketing*, 3 (3): 200–205.

Gordon, R., Carrigan, C. and Hastings, G. (2011) 'A framework for sustainable marketing', *Marketing Theory*, 11 (2): 143–163.

Gordon, R. and Gurrieri, L. (2014) 'Towards a reflexive turn: social marketing assemblages', *Journal of Social Marketing*, 4 (3): 261–278.

Gordon, R., and Gurrieri, L., Chapman, M. (2015 in press). 'Broadening an understanding of problem gambling: the lifestyle consumption community of sports betting', *Journal of Business Research*.

Gordon, R., McDermott, L., Stead, M. and Angus, K. (2006) 'The effectiveness of social marketing interventions for health improvement: what's the evidence?', *Public Health*, 120 (12): 1133–1139.

Gordon, R., McDermott, L. and Hastings, G. (2008) 'Critical issues in social marketing: a review and research agenda', in A. Sargeant and W. Wymer (eds), *The Routledge Companion to Nonprofit Marketing*. London: Routledge, pp. 333–346.

Gordon, R. and Moodie, C. (2009) 'Dead cert or long shot: the utility of social marketing in tackling problem gambling in the UK?', *International Journal of Nonprofit and Voluntary Sector Marketing*, 14 (3): 243–253.

Grier, S. and Bryant, C.A. (2005) 'Social marketing in public health', *Annual Review of Public Health*, 26: 319–339.

Gurrieri, L., Cherrier, H. and Previte, J. (2013) 'Women's bodies as a site of control: inadvertent stigma and exclusion in social marketing', *Journal of Macromarketing*, 33 (2): 128–143.

Hastings, G. (2007) *Social Marketing: Why Should the Devil Have All the Best Tunes?* London: Butterworth-Heinemann.

Hastings, G. (2010) 'Critical social marketing', in J. French, C. Blair-Stevens, D. McVey and R. Merritt (eds), *Social Marketing and Public Health: Theory and Practice*. Oxford: Oxford University Press, pp. 263–280.

Hastings, G. and Domegan, C. (2014) *Social Marketing: From Tunes to Symphonies* (2nd edn). London: Routledge.

Hastings, G. and Saren, M. (2003) 'The critical contribution of social marketing: theory and application', *Marketing Theory*, 3 (3): 305–322.

Hastings, G., Stead, M. and Webb, J. (2004) 'Fear appeals in social marketing: strategic and ethical reasons for concern', *Psychology and Marketing*, 21 (11): 961–986.

Hill, R. (2001) 'The marketing concept and health promotion: a survey and analysis of recent health promotion literature', *Social Marketing Quarterly*, 7 (1): 29–53.

Hoek, J. and Jones, S.C. (2011) 'Regulation, public health and social marketing: a behaviour change trinity', *Journal of Social Marketing*, 1 (1): 32–44.

Homans, G. (1961) *Social Behavior: Its Elementary Forms*. New York: Harcourt Brace Jovanovich.

Houston, F.S. and Gassenheimer, J.B. (1987) 'Marketing and exchange', *Journal of Marketing*, 51 (4): 3–18.

Hunt, S.D. and Vitell, S.J. (2006) 'The general theory of marketing ethics: a revision and three questions', *Journal of Macromarketing*, 26 (2): 143–153.

iSMA, ESMA, AASM (International Social Marketing Association, European Social Marketing Association and Australian Association of Social Marketing) (2013) 'Consensus definition of social marketing'. Available at: www.i-socialmarketing.org/index.php?option=com_content&view=article&id=84:social-marketing-definition&catid=28:front-page#.VIoD0sKzV2s (last accessed 18 November 2014).

Jenkins, K. (Ed.) (1997) *The Postmodern History Reader*. London: Routledge.

Kelly, K.J. (2013) 'Academic course offerings in social marketing: the beat continues', *Social Marketing Quarterly*, 19 (4): 290–295.

Kennedy, R., Parker, P., Scott, D. and Rowlands, I.H. (2000) 'Social marketing of the residential energy efficiency project: effective community implementation of a national program', *Environments*, 28 (3): 57–72.

Kotler, P. and Armstrong, G. (2012) *Principles of Marketing*. New York: Pearson.

Kotler, P. and Levy, P. (1969) 'Broadening the concept of marketing', *Journal of Marketing*, 33 (1): 10–15.

Kotler, P. and Zaltman, G. (1971) 'Social marketing: an approach to planned social change', *Journal of Marketing*, 35 (3): 3–12.

Laczniak, G.R., Lusch, R.F. and Murphy, P.E. (1979) 'Social marketing: its ethical dimensions', *Journal of Marketing*, 43 (2): 29–36.

Laczniak, G.R. and Michie, D.A. (1979) 'The social disorder of the broadened concept of marketing', *Journal of the Academy of Marketing Science*, 7 (3): 214–232.

Lalonde M. (1974) *A New Perspective on the Health of Canadians: A Working Document*. Ottawa: Government of Canada.

Langford, R. and Panter-Brick, C. (2013) 'A health equity critique of social marketing: when interventions have impact but insufficient reach', *Social Science and Medicine*, 83: 133–141.

Lazer, W. and Kelley, E.J. (1973) *Social Marketing: Perspectives and Viewpoints*. Homewood: Richard D. Irwin.

Leather, D.S. and Hastings, G.B. (1987) 'Social marketing and health education', *Journal of Services Marketing*, 1 (2): 49–52.

Lee, N. and Kotler, P. (2011) *Social Marketing: Influencing Behaviors for Good*. New York: SAGE.

Lefebvre, R.C. (1996) '25 years of social marketing: looking back to the future', *Social Marketing Quarterly*, Special Issue: 51–58.

Lefebvre, R.C. and Flora, J.A. (1988) 'Social marketing and public health intervention', *Health Education Quarterly*, 15 (3): 299–315.

Lindenberger, K. (2001) 'Publishers notes', *Social Marketing Quarterly*, 7 (1): 2–3.

Ling, J.C., Franklin, B.A.K., Lindsteadt, J.F. and Gearion, S.A.N. (1992) 'Social marketing: its place in public health', *Annual Review of Public Health*, 13: 341–362.

Luck, D.J. (1969) 'Broadening the concept of marketing – too far', *Journal of Marketing*, 33 (3): 53–55.

Luck, D.J. (1974) 'Social marketing: confusion confounded', *Journal of Marketing*, 38 (4): 70–72.

MacFadyen, L., Stead, M. and Hastings, G. (1999). *A Synopsis of Social Marketing*. Stirling: Institute for Social Marketing. Available at: www.stir.ac.uk/media/schools/management/documents/social_marketing.pdf (last accessed 22 July 2013).

McDermott, L., Stead, M. and Hastings, G.B. (2005) 'What is and what is not social marketing: the challenge of reviewing the evidence', *Journal of Marketing Management*, 21 (5–6): 545–553.

McKenna, R. (1991) 'Marketing is everything', *Harvard Business Review*, 69 (1): 65–79.

McKenzie-Mohr, D. and Smith, W. (1999) *Fostering Sustainable Behavior: An Introduction to Community-based Social Marketing*. Gabriola Island, Canada: New Society Publishers.

McKie, D. and Toledano, M. (2008) 'Dangerous liaison or perfect match? Public relations and social marketing', *Public Relations Review*, 34 (4): 318–324.

Mahajan, V. and Jain, A.K. (1978) 'An approach to normative segmentation', *Journal of Marketing Research*, 15 (3): 338–345.

Manoff, R.K. (1985) *Social Marketing: New Imperatives for Public Health*. New York: Praeger.

Marcell, K., Agyeman, J. and Rapport, A. (2004) 'Cooling the campus', *International Journal of Sustainability in Higher Education*, 5 (2): 169–189.

Messerlain, C. and Derevensky, G. (2007) 'Social marketing campaigns for youth gambling prevention: lessons learned from youth', *International Journal of Mental Health and Addiction*, 4 (4): 294–306.

MRS (Market Research Society) (2014) *Code of Conduct: Celebrating 60 Years of Self Regulation*. Available at: www.mrs.org.uk/pdf/mrs%20code%20of%20conduct%202014.pdf (last accessed 14 December 2014).

New Indian Express (2013) *South East Asian Forum on Social Marketing Soon*. Chennai: The New Indian Express. Available at: www.newindianexpress.com/states/kerala/South-East-Asian-Forum-on-Social-Marketing-Soon/2013/12/07/article1932956.ece (last accessed 17 December 2013).

Novelli, W.D. (1996) 'Class presentation on the campaign for smoke-free kids', 24 April. Washington, DC: School of Business, Georgetown University.

Peters, R.S. and Hirst, P.H. (1971) *The Logic of Education*. London: Routledge and Kegan Paul.

Piercy, N. (2009) *Market Led Strategic Change*. Amsterdam: Elsevier.

Population Services International (1977) 'Preetni project: transferred to Sri-Lanka FPA', *PSI Newsletter* (November/December): 4.

Powell, J.E. and Tapp, A. (2008) 'The use of social marketing to influence the development of problem gambling in the UK: implications for public health', *International Journal of Mental Health and Addiction*, 7 (1): 3–11.

Prime Minister's Strategy Unit (2003) *Strategy Unit Alcohol Harm Reduction Project: Interim Analytical Report*. London: The Stationery Office.

Ridley, M. (2012) *The Rational Optimist*. London: Harper Collins.

Rothschild, M.L. (1979) 'Marketing communications in non-business situations or why it's so hard to sell brotherhood like soap', *Journal of Marketing*, 43 (2): 11–20.

Rothschild, M.L. (2001) 'Ethical considerations in the use of marketing for the management of public health and social issues', in A.R. Andreasen (ed.), *Ethics in Social Marketing*. Washington, DC: Georgetown University Press, pp. 17–38.

Simkin, L. and Dibb, S. (2011) 'Segmenting the energy market: problems and successes', *Marketing Intelligence and Planning*, 29 (6): 580–592.

Smith, W. (2011) 'Social marketing: a future rooted in the past', in G. Hastings, K. Angus and C. Bryant, C. (eds), *The SAGE Handbook of Social Marketing*. London: SAGE, pp. 419–424.

Spotswood, F., French, J., Tapp, A. and Stead, M. (2012) 'Some reasonable but uncomfortable questions about social marketing', *Journal of Social Marketing*, 2 (3): 163–175.

Stead, M. and Gordon, R. (2010) 'Providing evidence for social marketing's effectiveness', in J. French, C. Blair-Stevens, D. McVey and R. Merritt (eds), *Social Marketing and Public Health: Theory and Practice*. Oxford: Oxford University Press, pp. 81–96.

Stead, M., Gordon, R., Angus, K. and McDermott, L. (2007) 'A systematic review of social marketing effectiveness', *Health Education*, 107 (2): 126–140.

Tadajewski, M. (2010) 'Towards a history of critical marketing studies', *Journal of Marketing Management*, 26 (9/10): 773–824.

Tadajewski, M. and Brownlie, D. (2008) 'Critical marketing: a limit attitude', in M. Tadajewski and D. Brownlie (eds), *Critical Marketing: Issues in Contemporary Marketing*. London: John Wiley, pp. 1–28.

Tapp, A. and Spotswood, F. (2013) 'From the 4Ps to COM-SM: reconfiguring the social marketing mix', *Journal of Social Marketing*, 3 (3): 206–222.

Tones, K. (1996) 'Models of mass media: hypodermic, aerosol or agent provocateur?', *Drugs, Education, Prevention and Policy*, 3 (1): 29–37.

Trout, J. and Rivkin, S. (1996) *The New Positioning: The Latest on the World's #1 Business Strategy*. New York: McGraw-Hill.

US Department of Health and Human Services (2010) *Healthy People 2020*. Washington, DC: Office of Disease Prevention and Health Promotion.

Wallack, L. (1990) 'Media advocacy: promoting health through mass communication', in K. Glanz, F. Marcus Lewis and B.K. Rimer (eds), *Health Behavior and Health Education*. San Francisco, CA: Jossey-Bass, pp. 370–386.

Weinstein, A. (2004) *Handbook of Market Segmentation*. New York: The Haworth Press.

Wells, W.D (1993) 'Discovery-oriented consumer research', *Journal of Consumer Research*, 19 (4): 489–504.

Wensley, R. (2003) 'The basics of marketing strategy', in M.J. Baker (ed.), *The Marketing Book* (5th edn). Oxford: Butterworth-Heinemann, pp. 53–86.

White, P. and French, J. (2010) 'Capacity building, competencies and standards', in J. French, C. Blair-Stevens, D. McVey and R. Merritt (eds), *Social Marketing and Public Health: Theory and Practice*. Oxford: Oxford University Press, pp. 291–300.

WHO (World Health Organisation) (2012) *Health 2020: The Europe Policy for Health and Wellbeing*. Geneva: WHO. Available at: www.euro.who.int/en/what-we-do/health-topics/health-policy/health-2020 (last accessed 17 December 2013).

Wiebe, G.D. (1951) 'Merchandising commodities and citizenship on television', *Public Opinion Quarterly*, 15 (4): 679–691.

Wilkie, W.L. and Moore, S.E. (1999) 'Marketing's contributions to society', *Journal of Marketing*, 63 (Special Issue 1): 198–218.

Witkowski, T. (2005) 'Anti-global challenges to marketing in developing countries: exploring the ideological divide', *Journal of Public Policy and Marketing*, 24 (1): 7–23.

Wymer, W. (2010) 'Rethinking the boundaries of social marketing: activism or advertising?', *Journal of Business Research*, 63 (2): 99–103.

3   MARKETING SOCIAL GOOD

Learning objectives

By the end of this chapter, readers should be able to:

- understand the complexity of human behavioural intervention design and the options that are open to policy makers and planners that go beyond just focusing on individual change
- consider how social marketing can assist with the selection and implementation of all forms and types of social intervention
- identify some of the key principles of behavioural influence and tools in the social marketing mix and how they can be applied to social programme design.

Introduction

This chapter sets out some of the key insights and principles about why effective social behavioural design needs to incorporate a focus on behavioural influence, and the nature of the options available and what actually works.

Social interventions such as emotional appeals to not gamble, the establishment of default systems to encourage people to donate their organs in the event of their death, reducing choice of certain food types, or imposing fines to influence behaviour such as speeding can all be politically sensitive. The chapter therefore explores how social marketers, politicians and other stakeholders can build strategies that work with and are guided by what is known about how people make decisions and react to different approaches to encourage them to act in socially responsible ways. Social marketing can help inform intervention strategy selection by establishing whether citizens perceive interventions to be appropriate, fair and proportionate. Without this understanding social interventions run the risk of not only not working optimally but also causing backlashes or other unintended consequences. For example, imposing a tax that is seen to be both unfair and disproportionate can result in perverse consequences or even civil unrest. A practical example of such a situation is the imposition of high taxes on cigarettes that encourage smuggling and illegal sales, or the failure to impose or collect adequate taxes from companies that results in rioting by campaigners who oppose capitalism.

The chapter also explores why the application of a diverse intervention toolbox informed not only by evidence of what has worked in the past and what is efficient but also by what citizens believe are just, value, want and wish to engage with is a key factor in developing more effective social intervention programmes. The chapter considers the role that policy makers and planners can play in the selection of interventions based on what is known about how people make decisions, and consequently how their behaviour can be influenced. The limitations of 'rational economic man' theory and its related behavioural models are also considered, as is the role of the application of non-rational decision making intervention 'forms' such as 'nudging'. The chapter ends with the setting out of a map of 'forms' and 'types' of interventions that can be used in social marketing programmes together with selection criteria that can be used to develop an effective intervention mix. In Chapter 4 we explore in more detail other elements of the social marketing intervention mix.

The need for a big behavioural influence toolbox

Whether they like it or not politicians and public servants are in the business of influencing behaviour, be it individual behaviour, group behaviour or the causal conditions such as economics the built environment or social service provision that influence people's behaviour (House of Lords, 2011). The underlying premise of this chapter is that there is a need for an expanded behavioural toolbox that goes beyond the crafting and delivery of well planned and executed communication programmes focused on the transmission of scientifically accurate information or the application of legislation to compel people to act in certain socially desirable ways. This call echoes that made by Rothschild (1999) and many other social marketing advocates. In Chapter 8 we examine a number of other behavioural theories and models that further illustrate the broad range of possible ways to both conceptualise and plan interventions that impact on the behaviour of citizens.

Those concerned with the management of social policy need to understand that in addition to communication and legal strategies, applying other 'forms' and 'types' of interventions is necessary. What we mean by 'forms' and 'types' of intervention is defined later in this chapter. Key policy and political influences on decisions regarding programme selection and implementation increasingly depend on what Mulgan (2011) calls 'public permission' for state directed actions when issues concerned with the curtailment of personal freedoms and the role of personal responsibility are involved.

As citizens become more educated, wealthy and empowered, governments and other public organisations increasingly have to be driven by citizens' expectations and needs rather than being primarily directed by the views of experts and ruling elites. This shift in emphasis signals an inevitable and fundamental change in the power relationship between states and public organisations and the citizens they seek to represent and serve. This shift also necessitates the integration of social marketing as an embedded and consistent feature of social policy development and delivery because it is the discipline that is focused on developing an understanding of citizens and how they can be influenced and engaged in delivering solutions to social challenges.

We also know that many individual decisions and consequent behaviour related to social issues such as alcohol misuse, overeating and energy use are often influenced by unconscious and automatic thinking as well as a rational mindful consideration of issues (Dawnay and Shah, 2005). These decisions have both personal and social implications and are influenced by a range of evolutionary derived responses and heuristic systems that interplay with the specific emotional contexts, social influence, environmental prompts, and factors such as timing and our physiological state (Social Market Foundation, 2008; Prinz, 2012). Much of this new understanding about how to influence behaviour has for many years been used by the commercial marketing sector, often developed through a process of trial and error rather than deductive reasoning and controlled experimentation. What this new evidence-based understanding provides is numerous theoretical and intervention constructs, such as the application of default systems and interventions designed to use the power of social norming influence. These constructs can be used as part of future social interventions and their impact can be assessed in a more controlled and evaluated way than has been the norm in the past.

According to Nielsen the business community invested over $500 billion in 2013–14 in programmes to promote the uptake of goods and services. There is good evidence that business success is correlated with investment in this form of marketing and promotion work. The key factor in much of the success of commercial organisations is that they apply strategic marketing planning and research. They think long term and they select and execute strategy based on data and insights about their customers, the environment and the competition they face. They try to drive out guess work and reactive responses in favour of long-term strategic action.

At the heart of this success, the commercial sector over the last twenty or so years has increasingly focused on three key concepts that are called 'exchange' (Bagozzi, 1975), 'relationship marketing' (Gummesson, 1987), and 'service-dominant logic' (Vargo and Lusch, 2004). Engagement with these three concepts has moved the commercial sector away from a transactional relationship with clients and customers to a strategic position that seeks to build a valued relationship between the service or product provider and the customer based on trust, respect and good service. A considerable factor in this shift has been the need to apply much of the new understandings about how people can be influenced and how they make decisions, i.e. the need to move beyond the purely logical transaction model to one that influences the deeper and more profound influences on behaviour such as emotions and physiological and psychological fulfilment.

These concepts are the basis of many social marketing programmes and lead to measurable positive impact (McDermott et al., 2005). Social marketing programmes in the developing world, focused on issues such as oral rehydration, vaccination uptake and HIV prevention and other aspects of sexual health and population control, have had many successes through the application of such an approach.

CASE STUDY

The Social Marketing Company (SMC), Bangladesh

The concept of social marketing first came to Bangladesh in 1974 when Family Planning Social Marketing Project (FPSMP) was initiated to deal with rapid population growth by making contraceptive products widely accessible at a price affordable to the general population. It was initiated by a US-based not-for-profit organisation, Population Services International (PSI), in agreement with the Ministry of Health and Population (GOB), and with funding support from USAID. The Social Marketing Company or SMC is a not-for-profit, private, limited company that was set up as a family planning project in 1974 under an agreement between the government of Bangladesh, an international NGO and USAID. The project was established to engage the private sector in increasing access to and demand for family planning products and services through the application of social marketing. In 1986 the SMC was also asked by the government of Bangladesh to deliver the national oral rehydration salts (ORS) to assist with the challenge of reducing the then high infant mortality rate due to diarrheal induced dehydration. Over the years SMC has continued to expand its portfolio and now markets over 20 brands including four donated products in several product categories that include long acting family planning methods, nutrition and in the field of hygiene. A range of products is offered with different pricing options to different market segments. In 1990 the project became a not-for-profit company with a voluntary board.

SMC has three major operational wings. Business operations are driven to earn revenue from sales of products and services that are self-financed and fully sustainable without donor support. The manufacturing unit provides commodity security for ORS and creates opportunities to expand into new product areas. SMC's programme operations aim to achieve social good in line with SMC's mission, fully supported through grants from donors and surplus funds from the company's business operations. Through cross subsidy, earnings from sales of self-financed and profitable products help sustain markets created through the sale of low priced, subsidised commodities. Branding is critical in this effort to protect the marketing investment in the brands developed by SMC and to guard against a loss of revenue in the event of donors phasing out support. A well thought out pricing strategy has been instrumental in achieving full financial sustainability. SMC products are categorised into three different pricing categories as follows:

- Profitable brands are procured using SMC's own funds and provide significant contribution margins after meeting all of its direct cost.
- Break even brands are purchased from SMC's own funds and generate sufficient revenues to recover its commodity and packaging cost. Promotion is largely subsidised.
- Donated and subsidised brands are either donated or purchased from donations and sold at heavily subsidised prices only to recover their distribution cost.

SMC has one of the largest and most efficient distribution networks in Bangladesh, reaching out to over 250,000 pharmacy and non-pharmacy outlets each year. SMC implements a number of donor-funded projects through community mobilisation and behaviour change communication activities. SMC delivers training of private sector health providers in areas of family planning, reproductive health, TB, HIV/AIDS and diarrheal disease management. It also supports a large network of 6,000 functional franchise clinics called Blue Star in the private sector.

(Continued)

(Continued)

Unlike many of its counterparts in other countries who have applied social marketing to improve the uptake of health enhancing products and services, SMC has pursued a long-term strategy aimed at self-reliance and self-financing rather than relying on continued state or international donor funding. In 2013 SMC reached the milestone of full cost recovery for all non-programme related expenditures from its own sales proceeds.

Having achieved full financial sustainability, SMC is now pursuing a business strategy that will allow it to grow to its full potential. SMC has created a separate for-profit subsidiary company called SMC Enterprise which is owned fully by SMC non-profit holding. Dividends earned from SMC Enterprise are being invested to allow expansion into new social programme areas, support innovation and provide grants to other NGOs for social interventions.

The SMC model of social marketing has two components – multi-strata programmes for initiating the desired behaviour change, and the development and supply of affordable, readily accessible products and services for sustaining the desired behaviour. Market segmentation, effective positioning and brand development efforts also continue to be a major part of SMC's marketing strategies supported with brand-specific and generic advertising and promotion. SMC has extensively used mass media, including TV, radio, newspaper and outdoor advertising, all of which assist with promoting both awareness and the desired behaviour change. Other non-traditional media are used including mobile film programmes that mostly reach media dark areas, school-based programmes, telephone counselling and support and a wide range of other community-based programmes.

A national success story

SMC is a great example of a social enterprise that has developed a long-term strategic vision together with a comprehensive marketing informed strategy that is enabling it to achieve its stated strategic goals in a sustainable way.

SMC marketed contraceptives have so far protected over 77 million couples from an unwanted pregnancy. SMC currently represents 30 per cent of all contraceptive use nationally. It is the largest supplier of condoms, with a 61 per cent market share, and a major player in the oral contraceptive market with a 38 per cent share of use. SMC is also the largest manufacturer and distributor of ORS, selling over 400 million sachets annually. Since its introduction, SMC has sold over 3.2 billion ORS sachets, saving innumerable lives from diarrheal deaths.

For more details see: http://smc-bd.org/index.php/page/view/1.

The role and responsibility of politicians, public institutions and planners

It is now clear that it is insufficient to consider an individual's voluntary behaviour change in isolation from social and environmental influences on behaviour (Wilkinson and Pickett, 2009). The impact of social, economic and environmental factors has a large influence on people's ability to behave in certain ways and their motivation to do so (WHO, 2008). The behaviour of others and the general, economic, cultural and social environments expressed though notions of social capital (Putman, 1995) and community resilience also need to be considered and targeted if individuals are to be helped to sustain a positive social behaviour or modify damaging behaviour (Woolcock, 2001).

Governments and other agencies concerned with influencing behaviour to achieve social objectives often focus on information, education and a 'voluntary' behaviour change. However, in some circumstances governments will need to use other policy tools to create supportive environments in which positive social behaviours and social change can be achieved. These tools include legislation, penalties and incentives, as well as the design of systems, services and environments, for example in the field of road safety fines for speeding and road system designs that encourage people to slow down at crossing points. When a risk and threat are great and highly probable governments may need to use different tools to influence people to be compliant with social policy, including incentives and sanctions. Governments can also use systems and policy design interventions that incorporate elements of enforced change.

It is probable that in most circumstances in both the developed and developing world to succeed in designing optimally effective, efficient and acceptable social programmes the marketing concepts of value creation, exchange and relationship building will all need to be used to design social programmes. These core marketing concepts focus on building social policy and intervention strategies through collaborative and consensus building, incorporating effort aimed at the genuine engagement and empowerment of citizens in the policy selection and implementation process. The development of social strategy based on both value creation and citizen engagement also leads to the application of a longer-term strategic approach and a more diverse range of intervention 'types' and 'forms' being applied. This is because when citizens are engaged and listened to they generate policy responses and intervention solutions that go beyond the narrow confines of legislation enforcement and information provision. Adopting a listening and engagement approach also forces organisations and governments to adopt an intervention selection system that is more extensive and neutral in its stance.

By 'neutral stance' we mean that those responsible for selecting interventions should not start out with a solution, such as a media campaign to increase awareness or a pre-defined solution, without first having determined that such an intervention is supported by evidence of its efficacy and also by insight research derived from the intended target group, which indicates that it will both resonate with them as a useful and justifiable intervention and meet their and wider social needs.

The more subtle behaviour change approaches are, the more they may provoke public and political concern. Behavioural approaches that embody a line of thinking which moves from the idea of an autonomous individual making rational decisions to a decision maker, much of whose behaviour is automatic and influenced by their choice environment, raise the question of who decides on and can influence this choice environment? One of the key challenges that face social policy planners who seek to use non-rational approaches to influencing behaviour is how the permission to use these approaches will be given and legitimised in order that a backlash of public opinion does not result in accusations such as trickery and unconscious manipulation.

Clearly few behaviours are ever fully rational and few choices are fully voluntary. We also know that structural, environmental and systems are important influences on behaviour. Therefore policy makers need to also create supportive structures and environments that influence behaviours. What is clear is that politicians and public officials, if they are to succeed in tackling many of the big social challenges faced by all societies, need to seek ways to influence behaviour, be it through a focus on assisting individual decision making or by the provision of social structural and environmental prompts to encourage desired behaviours.

Politicians and public officials, however, also need a popular mandate via the ballot box or, in countries where there are less developed democratic structures, popular consent to act. However, this consent is by itself probably not sufficient to legitimise action. An additional set of criteria also need to be considered before a state, or one of its agencies or NGOs acting to support its policies, decides to institute a behavioural intervention that includes interventions designed to influence non-rational or rapid cognition.

Discussion question

What kinds of intervention tactics are used to influence people's behaviour by not-for-profit and government organisations?

Table 3.1 sets out a checklist designed to assist decision making about when it is appropriate for a government or agency to deploy a range of behavioural influencing interventions that, to at least some extent, go beyond appeals to just reasoned decision making to achieve a positive social goal. Additional selection criteria are explored related to the effectiveness and efficiency of such interventions later in this chapter.

It is probable that governments and public agencies will always use some interventions that are not fully supported by strong evidence (Lindblom, 1959). However, a culture of systematic planning and evaluation should be encouraged to enable transparent reporting on the impact and efficiency of all behavioural programmes, as

Table 3.1   Criteria for non-rational appeal behavioural intervention selection

1. When there are severe and highly probable risks to individuals and communities if nothing is done.
2. When many people are at risk or will be if no action is taken.
3. When there is a clear popular mandate for action using such approaches.
4. When the intervention design is culturally and ethically acceptable to a majority of citizens.
5. When there are popular acceptable trade-offs between the benefits of the intervention and negative side effects of the intervention.

emphasised and explored in Chapter 10. Such an approach will also help with developing the evidence base for effective and efficient social intervention strategies (Cabinet Office Behavioural Insight Team, 2011). It is also the case that not all citizens will universally support interventions. Individual governments and agencies will need to determine, based on local laws, circumstances and traditions, what level of popular support is necessary for specific behavioural interventions. On occasion, however, there will be substantial popular public opinion that is resistant to government interventions intended to influence behaviour in the face of evidence that the intervention will result in positive social outputs.

A good example is the resistance that often precedes the introduction of congestion charging to restrict car use in big cities. In these situations, despite there being good evidence that such schemes, which typically involve charging motorists to drive into city centres at certain times, actually work in terms of reducing traffic congestion, citizens will resist them. In such situations governments and public service agencies should not simply give way to public opinion but focus on the value that will be created, and then communicate this in the knowledge that after a period of settling in such schemes will not only be accepted by the public but will also be valued. Sometimes governments need to govern, set the agenda and lead the debate.

Why positioning social marketing centrally in social programme planning is key to success

This chapter and book make the case that there is a significant cultural and technical shift required within governments and specialist not-for-profit agencies to move towards a more citizen focused marketing approach to social policy development and delivery, and a fully integrated partnership between marketing professionals and policy and delivery professionals if a more optimum set of social outcomes are to be achieved from social policy interventions. Figure 3.1 sets out a simplified model of a typical expert driven approach to social programme design and delivery.

In the past many social programmes have been developed on the basis of their fit with the prevailing political, economic, ideological and moral sensibilities of societies. Alongside these considerations there has also been a focus on evidence and efficiency

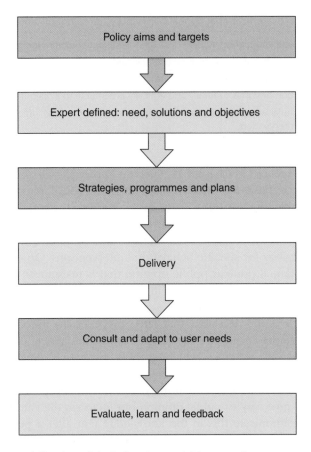

Figure 3.1 Expert defined model of planning social interventions

based policy making and social programme delivery. This approach is informed by undertaking systematic evidence reviews and gathering evidence about what works through the setting up of demonstration projects and pilots. The data collected are then analysed by expert committees to decide what the 'evidence' indicates about what works and what should be invested in. Of course at other times polices are developed based on other trigger factors such as reactions to disasters or if a policy might win votes at an upcoming election. This 'expert defined' model of social programme selection has many strengths but it lacks one essential ingredient: the 'expert' knowledge of the people who are experiencing the issue and an understanding of what they think would help them and what would not.

Applying social marketing as an integral part of the selection, design, implementation and evaluation of social programmes begins with a commitment to building solutions around citizens' expressed needs and wants. Developing propositions and interventions that are valued by citizens requires an additional commitment to investing in understanding their knowledge, attitudes and beliefs, and using this insight to help select and structure interventions designed to impact on the selected social issue. Creating value for citizens is not about abdicating responsibility for defining what constitutes social good by just responding to what people say they need and want. It is about understanding, listening and engaging people as partners in defining the nature of problems and in the selection and delivery of solutions. Social marketing is a respectful and democratic process. Figure 3.2 sets out an alternative value for a citizen based approach to social intervention planning and delivery.

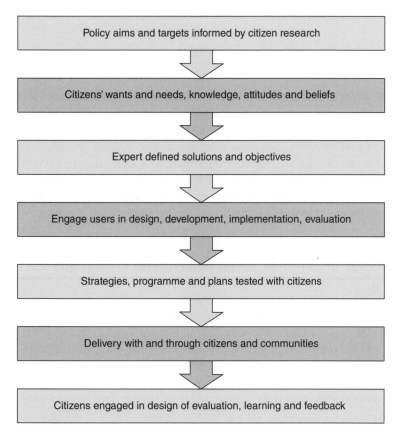

Figure 3.2 Value for a citizen model

The key difference in the two approaches is that a marketing focused approach seeks the engagement of citizens throughout the policy, planning, delivery and evaluation processes. Such an approach does not disregard expert opinion and wider political considerations. Rather it seeks to enhance these streams of intelligence by adding citizen insight, engagement and value creation into the planning and delivery mix.

Social marketing often exists as a bolted on adjunct to the influence of technical and topic experts' advice in the public policy and strategy development process. Social marketers and those responsible for influencing behaviour often operate in an environment where policies are developed prior to and independent of any input from consumer/marketing specialists. This often leads to a technical expert dominated or producer led selling and promotional approach to social change, i.e. a focus on broadcasting evidence based messages about risk reduction and compliance with expert opinion. Examples of this kind of bolting on, and misinterpretation of marketing, have been compounded by authors such as Michie et al. (2011) and Hendriks et al. (2013), who continue to foster the misconception that marketing is only concerned with communication. They state that:

'Communication and marketing' involves using print, electronic media, telephone or broadcast media. (Hendriks et al., 2013: 6)

This misinterpretation of marketing fails to recognise the vast literature about the real nature of marketing or its wider role in both the commercial and not-for-profit sectors. Michie et al. (2011) and Hendriks et al. (2013) hold a linked view that social policy development and delivery, including behavioural intervention design, is defined and driven by experts and policy makers rather than, as social marketers would advocate, a system that is equally driven by citizens' needs and wants and engages them fully in the development process. Michie's *behaviour change wheel*, which seeks to deliver a totalising model of behavioural influence, is further critiqued in Chapter 5.

The challenge of complex social behavioural challenges

Influencing behaviour is clearly not without profound ethical and political considerations (Oliver, 2013). Issues such as: at what level of risk should behavioural influence approaches be applied that compel people to behave in a certain way? Or what level of risk should be present to trigger a government to go beyond the provision of just information to strategies focused on influence or compulsion? Work in this field is also complex because it seeks to influence behaviour related to risks that are often difficult to convey and quantify and risks that are likely to change rapidly over time, for example during pandemic events or during natural disasters (Shafir, 2013).

What is clear is that one of the main challenges of most big social problems is that they exhibit a number of specific features that have led Rittel and Webber (1984 [1973]) to called them 'wicked problems'. The term 'wicked' in this context is used not in the sense of evil or doing harm. Rather Rittel and Webber used this description to encapsulate the large number of social challenges and planning problems that cannot be successfully treated with traditional linear, analytical approaches and simple informational or legislative responses. Rittel and Webber used the label 'wicked problems' to describe these challenges and contrasted them with 'tame problems'.

'Tame problems' are not necessarily simple: they can be very technically complex, but the problem can be tightly defined and a solution fairly readily identified or worked through based on a limited number of variables that can be controlled. Solutions are primarily developed based on natural science or engineering solutions that can be empirically developed and monitored. 'Wicked problems', however, are more complex, difficult to define and often involve many intersecting variables. The nature and extent of the problem also depend on who has been asked to define it and possible solutions. Different stakeholders often have different interpretations of what the problem is and how to deal with it and in what order of priority. Rittel and Webber set out the following characteristics of 'wicked problems' (Australian Public Service Commission, 2007a):

- 'Wicked problems' have many interdependencies and are often multi-causal.
- Attempts to address 'wicked problems' often lead to unforeseen consequences.
- 'Wicked problems' are often not stable.
- 'Wicked problems' usually have no clear solution.
- 'Wicked problems' are socially complex.
- 'Wicked problems' hardly ever sit conveniently within the responsibility of any one organisation.
- 'Wicked problems' involve changing behaviour.

In addition to these characteristics, Rittel and Webber make the case that 'wicked problems' can only be tackled if a full range of stakeholders is engaged in both defining the problem and the search for and delivery of solutions. Yet a further complexity relates to bringing about changes in the way people behave, as this cannot always be easily imposed in advanced democracies for reasons of ethics and public acceptability in terms of fundamental civic rights and respect for personal freedoms. We also know that behaviours are also more likely to change if issues such as risk and how to behave to reduce risks are widely understood, and owned by the people whose behaviour is being targeted (see Chapter 6). Solving a 'wicked problem' is fundamentally a social process. A starting point is stakeholder and citizen engagement. To this end the OECD (2001) identifies three levels of government-citizen relations in this context:

1. *Information*: government disseminates information on policy making or programme. Design and information flow from the government to citizens in a one-way relationship.
2. *Consultation*: government asks for and receives feedback from citizens on policy making and programme design. In order to receive feedback, government defines whose views are sought and on what issues. Receiving citizens' feedback also requires government to provide information to citizens beforehand. Consultation thus creates a limited two-way relationship between government and citizens.

3. *Active participation or citizen engagement*: this occurs where citizens actively engage in policy and decision making processes. Citizens may propose policy options and engage in debate on the relative merits of various options, although the final responsibility for policy formulation and regulation rests with the government. Engaging citizens in policy making and programme design requires that both governments and citizens engage in the process. It represents more than just a simple two-way dialogue, rather all citizens, community groups, organisations and government have a responsibility to reach out and engage in a systemic way with potential stakeholders, partners and target groups so that every social asset and stream of insight can be used to develop solutions to social problems.

The OECD has endorsed some basic principles as set out by Canada's Institute on Governance (1998), upon which active participation (or citizen engagement) is based. These include:

- shared agenda-setting for all participants
- a relaxed time frame for deliberation
- an emphasis on value-sharing rather than debate
- consultative practices based on inclusiveness, courtesy and respect.

Discussion question

Think about a behavioural programme that you have been are or would like to be involved in. Is the problem a 'wicked problem' or a 'tame problem'?

Tackling the complex web of social behaviour

Human behaviour is often influenced by a complex web of factors. Consequently influencing behaviour is a multi-faceted field of study and application that draws on a wide range of disciplines, research, theory and experience. The effectiveness of traditional social policy approaches to influencing behaviour may be limited, however, without additional tools and an understanding of how to engage citizens and public sector staff in developing cooperative and valued behavioural interventions. Many governments have a growing policy interest in engaging citizens to achieve sustained behavioural change to assist in tackling 'wicked problems'. For example, the UK government established in 2010 a 'Behavioural Insight Team' led by the Cabinet Office focused on developing new approaches to policy delivery based on insights and emerging research from fields such as behavioural economics, evolutionary biology, social psychology and design thinking.

In a similar manner the Australian Public Service Commission (2007b) published a discussion chapter, *Changing Behaviour: A Public Policy Perspective*, which outlines the key theories and empirical evidence about behavioural change and draws out the implications for improving policy making and programme implementation. The Australian government also in 2014 set up a behavioural influencing team within government. The US government has engaged Thaler and Sunstein, the authors of the popular book *Nudge* (2008), to act as advisors on several policy areas.

The Canadian government has also been actively interested in the area of behavioural change and has produced a set of guidelines known as the 'Tools of Change' for altering public behaviour in relation to 'wicked problems' in the environmental and health areas (see: www.toolsofchange.com/en/home/).

What is clear is that given the complex nature of public policy making when dealing with 'wicked problems' and the complexity involved in both understanding and developing intervention programmes that can achieve positive behavioural responses, a basic understanding is required of key individual, organisational, social and environmental determinants of behaviour.

The limitations of traditional behavioural theory and its impact on social behavioural planning and programme management

Policy makers have tended to assume that human behaviour can be influenced in the way suggested by neo-classical economics models and derived social psychological models such as the theory of planned behaviour (Azjen, 1985). This stance assumes that humans are rational beings that, when isolated from one another, behave logically and react to financial and social incentives and disincentives. The phrase 'rational economic man' approach is often used as shorthand for this set of beliefs. The 'rational economic man' set of theories postulates that people undertake a form of cost–benefit analysis, dispassionately weighing up the costs and benefits, or pain and pleasure, of choices and then select the option that will maximise the net benefit for them. Poor choices according to these theories often spring from a lack of relevant or important information. Classical economists often talk in this regard of 'information asymmetry' distorting markets and decision making. This view and many of the social psychological models of behaviour, reviewed in the Chapter 6, work on the assumption that human behaviour is intentional, considered and consistent with our beliefs and attitudes based on the information we have at our disposal.

These assumptions often result in linear views of behaviour, such as those in which beliefs lead to attitudes, which inform intentions, which result in behaviours. This way of thinking about influencing behaviour often reinforces information dominated interventions, which aim to change attitudes, on the assumption that attitude change will lead to a change in behaviour. However, research has shown that this assumption has not always been shown to be the case, for example most people know that smoking is bad for them but they still do it. This is what is known as the attitude–behaviour gap, a common phenomenon in many social policy areas.

Traditional economic theory does not make any value judgements about the validity of people's preferences. It is not interested in trying to explain where those preferences come from. Therefore it does not take into account internal decision processes or the way we interact with others, i.e. the direct influence of others' behaviour, reciprocation, and the emotions that others provoke in us, such as envy. Also the impact of environmental and physiological factors on our decisions is often not considered. Once people have a set of preferences, these are assumed to be relatively fixed over time. In this way, rewards or incentives are assumed and expected to encourage behaviour, while disincentives, be they financial or emotional such as fear, are expected to discourage behaviours. Examples of incentives and sanctions being used in this way include fines for driving too fast in cities, or conditional cash payments for taking children to school in the developing world.

It is clear then that the 'rational economic man' approach that underpins neo-classical economic theory and much of social policy has a fundamental weakness in that it ignores the complexities of human nature and decision making. In reality people do not always have access to a full range of relevant information, and even if they do, are not always capable of systematically processing this information in order to make the most rational choice. People are also influenced by other factors such as the behaviour of peers, emotions, habits and their own physiological state. The risk of relying on an approach that does not take into account these complexities is that it may lead to unrealistic analysis of what a policy intervention is capable of or investment in interventions that are doomed to fail.

Traditionally, the focus for many public policies has been to seek to change behaviour using external drivers. Such drivers include information provision, financial incentives and regulation. Obviously such traditional external approaches will always be important policy tools but the effectiveness of policy interventions is also dependent on understanding and reflecting on what is known about the internal processes for decision making and action, much of which lies outside the rational domain.

Developments in economic and behavioural theory are providing new insights about how many decisions are made in non-rational ways and how this new understanding can be used to build more effective and efficient programmes. This has highlighted the need to pay more attention to how non-rational decision making processes (desires, habits, emotions, etc.) and the range of external social influences (e.g. economic pressures, interpersonal relationships, social norms and culture) shape behaviour.

The contribution of behavioural economics

A cross disciplinary field called 'behavioural economics' has emerged as a challenge to neo-classical economic theory. Behavioural economics accepts that people are sometimes irrational but believes that this irrationality can be understood and predicted and therefore used in the design of social programmes. Behavioural economics has been defined as:

> The combination of psychology and economics that investigates what happens in markets in which some agents display human limitations and complications. (Mullainathan and Thaler, 2000: 1)

Interestingly, behavioural economics theory has been underpinned by two people who are not economists, but have won Nobel prizes in the field. Herbert Simon (1979), a political scientist, developed the concept of 'bounded rationality' that puts forward the suggestion that rational thought alone cannot explain decision making. Daniel Kahneman (Kahneman et al., 2003), a psychologist, developed 'prospect theory', an analysis of decision under risk. Prospect theory is focused on how people handle decisions about rewards and risks when alternative outcomes are known with some certainty. According to prospect theory it is the ways in which alternatives are perceived and framed, not just their relative value, that influence decisions. People also assess the potential value of losses and gains rather than just the final outcome. The theory also explains how people evaluate potential losses and gains using a number of heuristics, cognitive manoeuvres and mental short cuts.

In 2000, Stanovich and West added their description of two distinct systems of cognition that influence decision making based on emerging experimental studies. They describe these systems as: 'System One' and 'System Two'. System One is more intuitive, reactive, quick and holistic. When using System One thinking, we rely on a number of heuristics, situational prompts, readily associated ideas and vivid memories to arrive at fast and confident decisions. System One thinking is particularly helpful in routine situations when time is short and immediate action is necessary. However, while System One is functioning, another powerful system is also at work, unless people specifically shut it down by, for example, drinking a lot of alcohol. System Two is the more reflective thinking system that people use for making judgements when they find themselves in unfamiliar or complex situations and also have more time to weigh the options, cost and benefits of a particular choice or course of action. It allows us to process abstract concepts, to deliberate, to plan ahead, to consider options carefully, to review and revise our work in the light of relevant guidelines or standards or rules of procedure.

However, System Two thinking is exhausting and difficult and people tend not to use this form of thinking very much. System Two is described by Kahneman as 'our lazy controller'. System Two decisions are more deliberative, however they are still influenced by heuristics that impact on System One. System Two, however, relies on well-articulated reasoning and more fully developed evidence. It uses reasoning based on what people have learned through analysis, evaluation, explanation and self-correction. This is the system which people rely on to think carefully through complex, novel, high-stakes and highly integrative problems.

For most of the time according to Stanovich and West, we prefer to operate in System One mode. This model has been expanded by Kahneman (2011) in his popular book *Thinking, Fast and Slow*, in which he rehearses not only the basic findings in relation to prospect theory but also how these two systems operate, how they influence each other and how they can be influenced. Kahneman gives many examples backed by research studies that illustrate how factors such as cognitive ease, social norms, anchoring, availability, emotion, the impact of recent events and framing all impact on decision making.

Behavioural economics uses insights from experimentation and observation in building new explanations about human decision making and behaviour. Additions to the neo-classical model of understanding include:

- People exhibit bounded rationality, they are not always rational.
- People often make systematic mistakes.
- People have limited willpower, which gets rapidly used up if continuously challenged.
- People avoid making complicated decisions.
- People often make choices that are inconsistent over time.
- People prefer fairness and are willing to pay for it.
- People are influenced by how choices are 'framed'.
- People tend to be over-confident and over-optimistic.
- People are risk averse.

Behavioural economics recognises that people are inconsistent, flawed decision makers and make decisions based on 'unreliable facts', such as previous personal experience and beliefs about the trustworthiness of sources of information.

Useful summaries of key behavioural economics tactics

A great deal of other work has been undertaken by behavioural psychologists, brain scientists and biologists in recent years that has expanded our understanding about what influences non-rational or rapid decision making. Major works in this area are those by Goldstein et al. (2007), Ciladidi (1994), Ariely (2009), and Brafman and Brafman (2009).

For example, Ciladidi sets out a list of six principles of persuasion that are based on emergent understanding about influences on non-rational choice or System One thinking. These are:

1. *Liking*: we are influenced by people we feel we can relate to.
2. *Authority*: we are more open to being influenced by a person who can demonstrate, or we perceive to have, impressive credentials, experience and knowledge.
3. *Scarcity*: we all want what is scarce.
4. *Consistency/commitment*: we like to think of ourselves as being consistent; when we commit to a belief or action we tend to stick with it.
5. *Reciprocity*: we all like to return favours, if we are offered something we will give something back.
6. *Social proof*: we are influenced by our perceptions and observations about what others are doing.

Two key review documents have been produced that give helpful summaries of key strategies and tactics that can be derived from behavioural economics thinking. These are from the New Economics Foundation (2005) and the UK government's Behavioural Insight team's MINDSPACE review (Dolan, 2010).

The New Economics Foundation's (2005) summary of behavioural economics distils seven key principles for policy makers, as set out in Table 3.2.

These biases all show us that people don't always act in their own 'best interest' and aren't always rational when taking decisions.

Table 3.2 New Economics Foundation's summary of behavioural economics principles

1. Other people's behaviour matters

Behaviour of individuals is strongly influenced by other people's behaviours, from friends and family to community groups and classmates.

2. Habits are important

When we do something out of habit, we don't use much cognitive effort. Behaviour moves from being internally guided through attitudes and intentions to being controlled by environmental cues through habit.

3. People are motivated to 'do the right thing'

Individuals routinely forego narrowly conceived self-interest for the sake of altruistic motives.

4. People's self-expectations influence how they behave

People want their behaviours and attitudes to match. They are motivated to seek consistency between their beliefs, values and perceptions.

5. People are loss averse

People will go out of their way to avoid loss but will not go out of their way to gain.

6. People are bad at computation

People are bad at calculating probabilities and have internal bias. Decisions made are impacted by how a problem is presented which is influenced by a number of internal heuristic biases that include: fear of loss, over-optimism, preference for immediate rewards, etc.

7. People need to feel involved and effective to make a change

If people feel helpless and out of control they are often incapable of doing anything to change their situation. Control of a situation can bring motivation.

The MINDSPACE review

The MINDSPACE review (Dolan et al., 2010), a UK review of how behavioural economics and social psychology can be used to develop better public policy aimed at influencing behaviour, states that policy tools such as incentives and information are intended to change behaviour by 'changing minds', for example incentives and information need to be supplemented by approaches based on 'changing contexts' – the environment within which people make decisions. The report makes the case that there is potential to bring about significant changes in behaviour at relatively low cost by applying some of the principles of behavioural economics to shaping many new social policy interventions (see Table 3.3). The report makes it clear, however, that when applying MINDSPACE in practice it should not simply be seen as an alternative to existing methods.

Table 3.3   What the MINDSPACE mnemonic stands for

Messenger
We are heavily influenced by who communicates information.
Incentives
Our responses to incentives are shaped by predictable mental shortcuts such as strongly avoiding losses.
Norms
We are strongly influenced by what others do.
Defaults
We go with the flow of pre-set options.
Salience
Our attention is drawn to what is novel and seems relevant to us.
Priming
Our acts are often influenced by sub-conscious cues.
Affect
Our emotional associations can powerfully shape our actions.
Commitments
We seek to be consistent with our public promises, and reciprocate acts.
Ego
We act in ways that make us feel better about ourselves.

The fact that these two reports which seek to distil the essence of behavioural economics come up with slightly different sets of key principles illustrates the diverse nature of behavioural economics and its unfolding interpretation. However, many of the concepts are shared and these concepts, such as inertia and the path of least resistance, are helpful in developing a better understanding of how to encourage people to behave in socially responsible ways.

Nudging

In the 1980s Richard Thaler, an economist, began importing this new thinking into economics. This work was later captured in his popular book with Cass Sunstein, *Nudge* (2008). *Nudge*, like a number of similar books, brings together in an easy to digest way some of the neo-libertarian philosophy promoted by Thaler and Sunstein, together with a number of case studies about how redesigning systems using some of the theory of behavioural economics and social psychology can make it easier for more people to make positive social choices, albeit choices that do not always require them to fully engage with a decision.

Nudges are a key mechanism for an approach to social transformation called 'liberal paternalism'. A central tenant of this position is that there is now a growing body of evidence that people do not always act in a logically way, e.g. we do not always act in a way designed to maximise our own advantage. Many decisions are processed by what Thaler and Sunstein call the 'automatic' mental system, or as described earlier, what Stanovich and West call System One thinking. This leads to what Thaler and Sunstein call 'mindless choosing'.

Thaler and Sunstein describe a set of concepts that can help those with the responsibility for developing choice situations set up choices that use prompts which influence non-rational elements of our decision making. The hallmark of this kind of 'paternalism' is a focus not on tackling the determinants of social problems or punishing 'bad' behaviour by interventions, such as nagging people about what they should do. Rather the focus is on incentivising positive choices and creating the conditions or systems in which people feel able to and want to make constructive choices for their own and their families' benefit, or constructing choices that require little or no effort, which result in a positive personal and social benefit. Thaler and Sunstein describe 'choice architecture' as the process of designing such systems and services. Choice architecture results in good social and personal choice and behaviours being made easy and rewarding. A classic example is that of establishing an organ donor scheme that automatically enrols every citizen unless they take action to opt out. In such schemes typically over 95 per cent of citizens remain in the scheme. In contrast, with schemes that require action on the part of citizens to seek out and apply to be part of a scheme typically less than 30 per cent sign up (Welsh Government, 2008).

A key part of the nudge agenda is to find low cost interventions that produce high value returns. Thaler and Sunstein's concept of 'nudging' people into different behaviours encompasses interventions that are easy and cheap to avoid. Nudges are not mandates. Putting fruit at eye level counts as a nudge. Banning junk food does not.

Libertarian paternalism as advocated by Sunstein and Thaler (2003) seeks a middle ground between a state dominated coercive paternalistic approach to creating social change and a more liberal approach that emphasises free choice and the power of the market as the key driver. They argue that nudges are a practical representation of this middle ground. These developments are also being driven in many parts of the world by the need to develop more cost effective and sustainable forms of social intervention. Nudges can be characterised as:

- positive, i.e. they give positive rewards or only minor penalties
- voluntary
- avoidable
- passive/easy, i.e. they require little effort, and work on mindless choosing
- low cost, to both the person targeted and to the government or organisation utilising them (consequently they are highly cost effective).

Nudges can be seen as a helpful part of many social intervention strategies but are not a universal magic bullet.

Why 'nudging' is not enough

A weakness of the behavioural economics approach is that while a large number of observed phenomena about human preferences have been documented, there seems to be little research or understanding about the interaction between the different principles, specifically where they might work against each other or how they can be combined. The risk of not knowing the interplay of the different principles is that policy makers may place more weight/significance on one principle, or alternatively equal weight on all principles, which may lead to interventions that are not targeting the key behavioural triggers. This suggests further research is required or that when principles of behavioural economics are applied the relevant effect and contribution of each principle need to be carefully evaluated.

From an ideological perspective 'nudging' can also be criticised for adopting a neo-liberal, paternalistic approach rather than an approach that seeks to maximise personal decision making and community empowerment (French, 2011). This kind of nudge paternalism is top down. Nudges are designed by 'choice architects' and not by the people themselves, they are directive and they are controlling. In this sense the application of a nudge based approach to public policy runs counter to some of the newer public policy drives for a more citizen directed, whole society response to issues such as pandemic events.

Nudges are paternalistic in that the people who are selecting and designing interventions are still experts rather than citizens and are seeking to use their expert understanding of human behaviour to manipulate people, all be it in a benign way, into a pre-selected behavioural response. A further problem is that liberal paternalism is focused not on tackling the determinants of issues such as obesity or crime. This approach locates responsibility for actions not only with individuals but also with providers of public services, NGOs and private organisations, to create the choice architecture that will nudge people in the 'right' direction.

It is also clear that in many circumstances 'nudging' people will seldom be enough to result in population level improvements because in many situations, evidence and experience make it clear that there is a need for other forms of intervention that address the causes of problems. This conclusion was reached by the House of Lords review into behaviour change in public policy, which reported in 2011. The report, which reviewed how concepts such as behavioural economics were being used in government and the evidence for their effectiveness, came to the conclusion that it is important to consider the whole range of possible interventions when policy interventions are designed. The report stated that:

> We place particular emphasis on this conclusion because the evidence we received indicated that the Government's preference for non-regulatory interventions has encouraged officials to exclude consideration of regulatory measures when thinking about behaviour change. Though there is a lack of applied research on changing behaviour at a population level, there is other available evidence that the Government need to use to better effect. (House of Lords, 2011)

In general the report found that to date there were few strong examples where behavioural economics had delivered substantial measurable improvements in interventions and that more effort should be put into gathering such evidence.

The need to develop and apply comprehensive behavioural strategies

'Nudging', and the application of other principles of behavioural economics as an approach to policy development and tactical implementation, are being implemented by many governments. However, rather than adopt interventions that emphasise positive rewards and mindless choosing as the default preferred intervention mode, those responsible for public behavioural interventions should be informed by citizen insight alongside evidence from research about what works and how efficiently it works when selecting interventions.

Positive rewards and mindless choosing will not work in all situations, and critical reflection and judgement are also often needed when making many complex decisions to change (Grist, 2010). The crux of the matter is how to discern, based on theory, citizen insight and evidence, what forms of social programme interventions will work in which situation, with a specific target audience. This is the essence of the contribution of social marketing processes to social policy planning and delivery.

The concepts of exchange, value creation and relationship building are central to social marketing. Exchange is based on the premise that we tend to change our behaviour when we perceive that it is in our interests to do so and the effort and cost are worth the result. We are also normally seeking value, things that make us feel better, safer or more respected, etc. We are also deeply influenced by our relationships, both interpersonal and with ideas, beliefs, services, products and brands.

To apply these fundamental marketing concepts in social programmes we need to first focus on developing a deep understanding about what people believe, say they want and value. We can then use this insight to develop interventions, systems, products or services that people will want to engage with or use, or interventions that do not require conscious engagement but nevertheless work with people's expressed or observed preferences.

In some cases if the data we collect tell us it is necessary we may need to use exchanges that are negative in nature. For example, it may be necessary to impose a fine for littering if our research tells us this would incentivise people not to drop litter and such an intervention has broad public support. Negative social exchanges such as fines for driving too fast are, however, still collectively positive in that they are designed to have a net positive social effect. Fining individuals for driving too fast reduces the overall impact of road deaths on society as a whole as well as saving individual lives.

A key factor is to ensure that whatever is decided on as the basis of an exchange is valued positively or seen as a meaningful and fair deterrent or cost by the specific target audience that it is designed to influence and also society as a whole. For example, imposing a penalty fine that is set at a rate that the audience does not consider high enough, or where they believe that there is little chance of being caught, will probably not bring about change. However, if the rate of a fine is too high, or is imposed at what is considered to be too low a threshold point, citizens will oppose the use and collection of such a fine.

The following value/cost exchange matrix (French, 2011) is a way to represent these four 'forms' of social exchange – active, passive, positive and negative – that can be used in social marketing interventions. The social marketing exchange matrix can be used as a conceptual tool for analysing what 'forms' of intervention have been, are or could be used across a programme designed to influence behaviour.

Social programmes aimed at influencing behaviour can select one of four primary 'forms' of intervention. These forms of intervention are defined by two main factors. First, will the intervention use rewards or some form of punishment to encourage a particular behaviour? Second, will the approach need considered cognitive decision making or will it seek to influence unconscious decision making? By combining these two factors, four options are possible, which can be called: *hug*, *nudge*, *shove* and *smack*.

1. *Hug*: high cognitive engagement with a positive reward.
2. *Nudge*: low cognitive engagement with a positive reward.
3. *Shove*: low cognitive engagement with a penalty.
4. *Smack*: high cognitive engagement with a penalty.

All of these four 'forms' of exchange are legitimate strategies and often a combination of approaches will be indicted from both literature reviews of what works and what is acceptable to citizens. The four 'forms' of exchange are set out in Figure 3.3 illustrating the social marketing value/cost exchange matrix. As with any matrix the four 'forms' of exchange should be viewed as continuums rather than absolute categories.

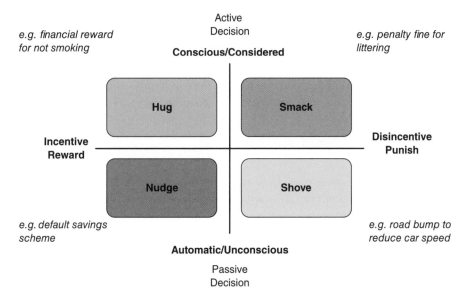

e.g. financial reward for not smoking

e.g. penalty fine for littering

Figure 3.3 The social marketing value/cost exchange matrix

Source: French, 2011

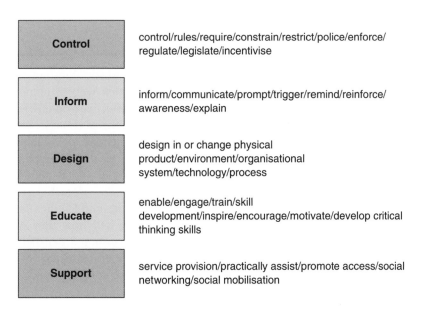

Figure 3.4 The basic five types of intervention clusters (the deCIDES) framework

Source: French, 2011

In addition to these four 'forms' of exchange social marketing planners seek to apply an appropriate mix of intervention 'types' to achieve the behavioural goals of the programme. A range of different approaches is examined and evidence, citizen insight, acceptability assessment and field testing are used to establish the most effective and efficient mix of interventions. The basic five 'types' of intervention clusters that organisations have at their disposal are depicted in Figure 3.4.

These tools can be understood as follows:

1. *Control*: using the power of the law and regulations as a body of rules and having binding force to incentivise and penalise the behaviour of individuals, organisations and markets for social good.
2. *Information and persuasion*: inform and communicate facts and attitudes and may seek to persuade and suggest behaviours.
3. *Education*: informs and empowers critical decision making, creates awareness about benefits and develops skills for change and personal development.
4. *Design*: creates the environment and procedures that support self and community development, and safety.
5. *Support*: state and other collectively funded goods and services provided to support mutually agreed social priorities.

Conclusion

This chapter has explored the challenges for governments and social institutions when seeking to influence behaviour for social good. The complex web of influences on behaviour and the complexity associated with developing effective and efficient interventions have also been explored. The current tendency in many countries to rely on simplistic information transmission and legal and fiscal sanctions to influence social behaviour can reduce the impact of social programmes. In this chapter we have looked at how scientists and others working in the field of behaviour influence have developed a growing body of behavioural research.

This chapter has sought to draw out some of the key issues and features associated with the development of behavioural economics thinking and how they might be applied in the field of social policy. This chapter has demonstrated that behavioural economics and the concepts that underpin it have important implications for the development of social interventions. This new understanding is now generating interest among many policy makers and planners in government organisations. This new work confirms and makes accessible the understanding that a much wider range of human motivations exists that just rational self-interest based on logical information processing.

This new understanding makes clear the need for strategies that go beyond the transmission of factually accurate logical information as the main way to influence behaviour. The challenge now for social planners is to develop intervention programmes based on our understanding of both passive and active decision making. This means developing social programmes and interventions that are valued by citizens. Ideally these programmes should also be delivered through civic relationships which demonstrate that citizens have been appropriately engaged in the selection, design, delivery and evaluation of interventions.

The conceptual models set out in the chapter are suggested tools for reviewing and deciding on how social marketing can be used to influence social policy development and which interventions might be included in an effective and efficient mix in any given situation. Given that there is only emerging evidence about behavioural interventions based on concepts such as behavioural economics, it is important to apply a systematic approach to developing and selecting potential interventions. This process needs to include, as argued in this chapter, a sustained dialogue with the specific target audiences of interventions and wider civil society to ensure that a deep level of insight about the acceptability and appropriateness of interventions is used to select and design interventions and also that all available public assets are recognised and deployed to bring about the desired public behaviour. Social marketing principles can be used to ensure that the creation of citizen defined value sits at the heart of this process.

Reflective questions

- List the reasons why social policy planners and social marketers need to apply a broad range of behavioural interventions to tackle social challenges.
- What are some of the factors that politicians and planners should take into consideration when deciding if a behavioural intervention should be attempted?
- Using the conceptual tools in the chapter, assess which mix of 'types' and 'forms' of interventions is being used in a social intervention you are familiar with. Use the social marketing cost/value exchange matrix to map the mix of interventions that is being applied.

Further reading

Dolan, P., Hallsworth, M., Halpern, D., Kind, D. and Vlaev, I. (2010) *Mindspace: Influencing Behaviour through Public Policy*. Full Report Cabinet Office. London: Institute for Government.

French, J. (2011) 'Why nudging is not enough', *Journal of Social Marketing*, 1 (2): 154–162.

References

Ariely, D. (2009) *Predictably Irrational: The Hidden Forces That Shape Our Decisions*. London: HarperCollins.

Australian Public Service Commission (2007a) *Tackling Wicked Problems: A Public Policy Perspective*. Canberra: Australian Government. Available at: www.apsc.gov.au/publications-and-media/archive/publications-archive/tackling-wicked-problems (last accessed 18 November 2014).

Australian Public Service Commission (2007b) *Changing Behaviour: A Public Policy Perspective*. Canberra: Australian Government. Available at: www.apsc.gov.au/publications-and-media/archive/publications-archive/changing-behaviour (last accessed 18 November 2014).

Azjen, I. (1985) 'From intentions to actions: a theory of planned behaviour', in J. Kuhl and J. Beckman (eds), *Action Control from Cognition to Behaviour*. New York: Springer-Verlag, pp. 11–39.

Bagozzi, R. (1975) 'Marketing as exchange', *Journal of Marketing*, 39 (3): 32–39.

Brafman, O. and Brafman, R. (2009) *Sway: The Irresistible Pull of Irrational Behaviour*. London: Virgin.

Cabinet Office Behavioural Insight Team (2011) *Applying Behavioural Insight to Health*. London: Cabinet Office.

Ciladidi, R. (1994) *Influence: The Psychology of Persuasion*. London: Collins.

Dawnay, E. and Shah, H. (2005) *Behavioural Economics: 7 Principles for Policymakers*. London: New Economics Foundation.

Dolan, P., Hallsworth, M., Halpern, D., Kind, D. and Vlaev, I. (2010) *Mindspace: Influencing Behaviour through Public Policy*. Full Report Cabinet Office. London: Institute for Government.

French, J. (2011) 'Why nudging is not enough', *Journal of Social Marketing*, 1 (2): 154–162.

Goldstein, N., Martin, S. and Cialdini, R. (2007) *Yes: Fifty Secrets from the Science of Persuasion*. London: Profile Books.

Grist, M. (2010) *Steer: Mastering Our Behaviour through Instinct, Environment and Reason*. London: RSA. Available at: www.thersa.org/__data/assets/pdf_file/0017/313208/RSA-Social-Brain_WEB-2.pdf (last accessed 14 March 2011).

Gummesson, E. (1987) 'The new marketing – developing long term interactive relationships', *Long Range Planning*, 20 (4): 10–20.

Hendriks, A.M., Jansen, M., Gubbels, J., De Vries, N., Paulussen, T. and Kremers, S. (2013) 'Proposing a conceptual framework for integrated local public health policy, applied to childhood obesity – the behavior change ball', *Implementation Science*, 8 (46). doi: 10.1186/1748-5908-8-46.

House of Lords (2011) *Behaviour Change*. Science and Technology Select Committee Report. London: The Stationery Office. Available at: www.publications.parliament.uk/pa/ld201012/ldselect/ldsctech/179/179.pdf (last accessed 18 November 2014)

Institute on Governance (1998) *A Voice for All: Engaging Canadians for Change*. Report (including Summary of Findings) of the Conference on Citizen Engagement, Ottawa, 27–28 October. Available at: http://iog.ca/publications/a-voice-for-all-engaging-canadians-for-change (last accessed 18 November 2014).

Kahneman, D. (2011) *Thinking, Fast and Slow*. London: Penguin.

Kahneman, D., Diener, E. and Schwarz, N. (2003) *Well-being: The Foundations of Hedonic Psychology*. New York: Russell SAGE Foundation

Lindblom, C. (1959) 'The science of "muddling through"', *Public Administration Review*, 19 (2): 79–88.

McDermott, L., Stead, M., Hastings, G., Angus, K., Banerjee, S., Rayner, M. and Kent, R. (2005) *A Systematic Review of the Effectiveness of Social Marketing Nutrition and Food Safety Interventions-Final Report-Prepared for Safefood*. Stirling: Institute for Social Marketing.

Michie, S., van Stralen, M.M. and West, R. (2011) 'The behaviour change wheel: a new method for characterising and designing behaviour change interventions', *Implementation Science*, 6 (42). doi: 10.1186/1748-5908-6-42.

Mulgan, J. (2011) *Behavioural Insight Team First Year Annual Report*. London: Cabinet Office.

Mullainathan, S. and Thaler, R. (2000) 'Behavioural economics', Working Paper 7948. Cambridge MA: National Bureau of Economic Research.

New Economics Foundation (2005) *Behavioural Economics*. London: The New Economics Foundation. Available at: www.neweconomics.org/publications/entry/behavioural-economics (last accessed 18 November 2014).

OECD (2001) *Citizens as Partners: Information, Consultation and Public Participation in Policy-making*. Paris: OECD.

Oliver, A. (2013) *Behavioural Public Policy*. Cambridge: Cambridge University Press.

Prinz, J. (2012) *Beyond Human Nature: How Culture and Experience Shape Our Lives*. London: Allen Lane/Penguin.

Putman, R. (1995) 'Bowling alone: America's declining social capital', *Journal of Democracy*, 6 (1): 65–79.

Rittel, H. and Webber, M. (1984 [1973]) 'Dilemmas in a general theory of planning', *Policy Sciences*, 4: 155–169, reprinted in N. Cross (ed.), *Developments in Design Methodology*. Chichester: J. Wiley and Sons, pp. 135–144.

Rothschild, M. (1999) 'Carrots, stick and promises: a conceptual framework for the management of public health and social behaviours', *Journal of Marketing*, 63: 24–37.

Shafir, E. (ed.) (2013) *The Behavioral Foundations of Public Policy*. Princeton and Oxford: Princeton University Press.

Simon, H. (1979) *Models of Thought*, Vols. 1 and 2. New Haven, CT: Yale University Press.

Social Market Foundation (2008) *Creatures of Habit. The Art of Behaviour Change*. London: Social Market Foundation.

Stanovich, K. and West, R. (2000) 'Individual differences in reasoning: implications for the rationality debate?', *Behavioural and Brain Sciences*, 23: 645–726.

Sunstein, C. and Thaler, T. (2003) 'Libertarian paternalism is not an oxymoron', *The University of Chicago Law Review*, 70 (4): 1159–1202.

Thaler, R.H. and Sunstein, C.R. (2008) *Nudge: Improving Decisions about Health, Wealth and Happiness*. New Haven, CT and London: Yale University Press.

Vargo, S. and Lusch, R. (2004) 'Evolving to a new dominant logic for marketing', *Journal of Marketing*, 68 (1): 1–17.

Welsh Government (2008) *Opt-out Systems of Organ Donation: International Evidence Review*. Government Social Research (GSR), Social Research Summary Number: 44/2012, Cardiff.

WHO (World Health Organisation) (2008) *Closing the Gap in a Generation: Health Equity through Action on the Social Determinants of Health*. Final Report of the Commission on Social Determinants of Health. Geneva: World Health Organisation.

Wilkinson, R. and Pickett, K. (2009) *The Spirit Level: Why More Equal Societies Almost Always Do Better*. London: Allen Lane.

Woolcock, M. (2001) 'The place of social capital in understanding social and economic outcomes', *Canadian Journal of Policy Research*, 2 (10): 11–17.

PART II
WHAT?

4 THE SOCIAL MARKETING MIX

Introduction

This chapter is focused on the social marketing mix – the range of intervention techniques and tools that can be selected and used in delivering social programmes to engender social good. In this chapter we identify that limited and restrictive older models of the social marketing mix have dominated the literature, and that this has led to somewhat formulaic use of the same limited number of tools and techniques in many programmes. Therefore, we discuss some of the key debates in the marketing and social marketing literature around the marketing mix concept, and identify some key limitations of the traditional and dominant 4Ps framework. We then introduce discussions on alternative models to the 4Ps marketing mix from commercial marketing, and specifically from the social marketing literature. We make the argument that social marketers should not be restricted to a limited and narrow range of intervention tools or techniques. Rather we make the case that social marketers should be creative, strategic and holistic with their selection and application of the social marketing mix.

We review and explain a range of the relevant social marketing techniques and tools that can be used in social programmes, and also identify where some other relevant tools are discussed elsewhere in this book. Importantly, we make the point that the techniques and tools mentioned here are not an exhaustive list, and encourage social marketers to think broadly and creatively about what strategies may be used in programmes. We then discuss the critical importance of pre-testing intervention tools with target participant groups, and with other relevant stakeholders, as a means to identify issues related to acceptability and impact, and to refine or change approaches before the roll-out of programmes. We conclude by recapping on what is covered in this chapter, by again identifying that the social marketing mix should be a broad, adaptive and creative collection of tools that can be used in various combinations in social programmes, and by encouraging social marketers to move away from restricting themselves to using limited frameworks such as the 4Ps.

The marketing mix

As we discussed in Chapter 2, social marketing has often relied heavily on borrowing concepts, principles and practices from its mainstream marketing progenitor in relation to the range of interventions techniques and tools we can use to bring about social good. To date adaptations of the commercial marketing mix have been predominantly used in social marketing (see Gordon, 2012). Neil Borden first formally referred to the concept of the marketing mix when he gave his American Marketing Association presidential address in 1953. Borden then developed the proposal in his 1964 article entitled 'The concept of the marketing mix' (Borden, 1964). In proposing the concept of the marketing mix, Borden reflected upon how his associate James

Culliton (1948) had described the role of a marketing manager as a sort of chef – a mixer of ingredients who can use recipes created by others, adapt recipes using ingredients (tools) and techniques available to hand, or even invent new ingredients and new recipes that nobody has ever used before. What Culliton and Borden were suggesting is that marketers should be creative, and use or develop whatever combinations of tools and strategies are required to get the job done.

However, following the introduction of the concept of the marketing mix, Jerome McCarthy (1960) proposed a fairly restrictively defined marketing mix framework that has become to be known as the 4Ps of *product*, *price*, *place* and *promotion*.

- *Product*: a physically tangible object or an intangible service produced and offered to consumers in the marketplace.
- *Price*: what a consumer pays for the product or service – usually focused on the economic cost but can also include intangible costs such as time and effort expended to uptake the offering.
- *Place*: refers to the location (physical or virtual/online) in which a product or service is offered for purchase, and also the process by which it is distributed to the purchase point (the distribution channel).
- *Promotion*: the range of communications used by marketers to promote offerings to consumers in the marketplace, for example advertising, public relations, personal selling and sales promotion.

In introducing a narrowly defined and prescriptive marketing mix it could be argued that McCarthy (1960) missed the whole point of the marketing mix concept proposed by Culliton (1948) and Borden (1964). Culliton and Borden proposed that the marketing mix should be open to creative formulation and use a variety of tools, strategies and combinations of ideas currently in existence as well as new ideas. McCarthy (1960) seems to have ignored or misinterpreted this encouragement of creativity and innovation, and instead created a myopic, prescriptive and managerial 4Ps marketing mix that has dominated marketing for many years (Arndt, 1980; Grönroos, 1994).

This 4Ps marketing mix was adopted by distinguished marketing academic Philip Kotler (1967) and has become the dominant framework for teaching, understanding and applying marketing tools ever since (Grönroos, 1994). It has also emerged as the dominant model relating to the intervention toolkit in social marketing (Hastings, 2007). Indeed, Kotler and Zaltman's (1971) first formal definition of social marketing referred to each of the four components of the 4Ps marketing mix: 'Social marketing is the design, implementation and control of programs calculated to influence the acceptability of social ideas and involving considerations of *product* planning, *pricing*, *communication*, *distribution* and marketing research' (Kotler and Zaltman, 1971: 5, emphasis added). Early examples of social marketing such as sexual health and family planning programmes in developing countries followed this 4Ps framework quite closely.

The 4Ps in social marketing

The application of the 4Ps marketing mix to social marketing emerged to become the dominant interpretation of what and how intervention tools are used to market social change. See Table 4.1 for an explanation of how the 4Ps are applied to social marketing.

Table 4.1   The 4Ps social marketing mix

Product	In social marketing product represents the behavioural offer made to participants and often involves intangibles such as the adoption of an idea or behaviour. Tangible product offerings such as condoms to encourage safe sex can also be present.
Price	In social marketing price relates to the costs that participants have to pay and the barriers they have to overcome to adopt the desired behaviour, and these costs can be psychological (e.g. loss of the de-stressing effect from smoking), cultural, social (e.g. the peer pressure to drink), temporal, practical (e.g. cancelling the school run to reduce car use), physical and financial (e.g. the cost of joining a gym to get fit).
Place	Place in social marketing is the channel by which behaviour change is promoted and the places in which change is encouraged and supported.
Promotion	In the social marketing context promotion is the means by which behaviour change is promoted to participants, for example advertising, media relations, direct mail and interpersonal.

Source: adapted from Gordon, 2012

Indeed, in identifying key benchmark criteria of components of social marketing programmes, Andreasen (2002: 2) stated that they should 'use all four Ps of the traditional marketing mix'. Furthermore, much of the contemporary social marketing literature reflects this predominance of the 4Ps – with recent popular textbooks still largely deferring to this model (see Lee and Kotler, 2011; Hastings and Domegan, 2014).

Although the 4Ps mix arguably provides a useful starting point for identifying and applying intervention techniques and tools to market social good, when we look more closely at Table 4.1 we begin to see some inconsistencies and issues with restricting ourselves to its use. For example, in the commercial marketing sphere there is most often a tangible product, or a service, whereas in the social marketing domain one or sometimes both may not be present. This has caused social marketers to identify auxiliaries or alternatives for each of the 4Ps when a direct translation from the commercial context does not seem to work. An example is the concept of *augmented products* – features that might encourage the take-up of a social marketing product or service. For example, in relation to encouraging uptake of a Chlamydia screening test, websites and information phone lines may be used to facilitate that uptake. Price in the social marketing context often is translated to refer to tangible economic and intangible physical, psychological, emotional, social and cultural costs to a participant for engaging in a social marketing programme. Therefore, we can see that in the social marketing domain, considerable reinterpretations and adaptations of the commercial 4Ps marketing mix are often used. Furthermore, reviews of the social marketing literature have identified that social programmes often use a range of other intervention tools, techniques and strategies that do not directly fit in the 4Ps model or are not featured at all – examples include policy change or training people (Stead et al., 2007).

During the 1980s and 1990s the development of social marketing was influenced by ideas from public health, psychology, sociology, anthropology and political science. This focus on multidisciplinarity introduced perspectives including environmental issues, community engagement and development, social justice and international development, alongside marketing. This created a divergence between commercial marketing and social marketing, put simply the tools and strategies used and needed to engender social good are broader, more varied and often different from those used in commercial marketing (Gordon, 2012). This suggests that the 4Ps marketing mix alone is not powerful enough to explain, and offer, the range of intervention techniques, tools and strategies required in social marketing.

Some traditionalist social marketers have rejected these arguments, positing that the 4Ps remain the best and most relevant intervention mix framework today (Lee and Kotler, 2011). However, some other social marketing scholars who have recognised the limitations of the 4Ps model, have guarded against unthinkingly and directly transferring commercial marketing concepts and models to social marketing, and have called for debate and a rethink of the social marketing mix (Peattie and Peattie, 2003; Gordon, 2012; Tapp and Spotswood, 2013).

The limitations of the 4Ps

If we examine the commercial marketing literature we can find that the debate on the suitability and relevance of the 4Ps marketing mix has been ongoing for a number of years. A number of other weaknesses with the marketing mix have been identified. One is that it encourages a narrow focus on a short-term, transactional interpretation of marketing and fails to value strategic, long-term relational thinking and concepts like brand equity (Rafiq and Ahmed, 1995). The 4Ps mix also tends to put a major focus on short-term evaluation of the effects of marketing such a sales, rather than longer-term concepts such as lifetime customer satisfaction, value co-creation and brand equity. Such concepts are not readily represented through interrogating sales figures. This short-term orientation for the 4Ps is especially problematic in the social marketing domain given that social change and facilitating social good often require long-term commitments, relational thinking and building brand equity (Evans and Hastings, 2008).

The 4Ps model has also been identified as proffering a bias towards time specific media channels such as television advertising rather than other forms of promotion that are less easily modelled for 'audience' effects such as sponsorship, viral marketing or social media marketing. This means that the 4Ps can be poor in accounting for temporal effects (the effect of time). Scholars have also identified that the 4Ps framework is too simplistic and lacking in breadth to encompass the wide range of tools and strategies used in modern marketing (Rafiq and Ahmed, 1995; Gordon, 2012). This means the 4Ps may not always tell us what are the best forms of promotional channel to use (Doyle, 2000). The emergence of new paradigms in marketing since the 1960s, such as services marketing, relationship marketing, business to business marketing and macromarketing, has also encouraged a reconsideration of the suitability of the 4Ps.

Alternatives to the 4Ps

A number of alternative commercial marketing mix models have been presented including an extended 7Ps – adding process, physical evidence and people to the core product, price, place and promotion (Booms and Bitner, 1981). Shizimu (1973) offered the 4Cs and 7Cs compass model incorporating corporation and competitor, commodity, cost, channel, communication, consumer and circumstance. Lauterborn (1990) devised the 4Cs framework with a stronger consumer orientation: consumer (wants and needs), cost, communication and convenience. Later, the emergence of relationship marketing recognised a broader scope for marketing beyond firms and consumers featuring various stakeholders or actors, whose various goals and objectives need to be met, and who operate within different structures and systems. Grönroos (1989, 1994) proposed that in relationship marketing mutual exchange, fulfilling promises, satisfaction, trust and value creation are important components. These relational ideas also found traction in social marketing (see Hastings, 2003), given the complexity and multi-actor nature of social marketing issues (see Chapter 7 for more on social marketing systems).

As services marketing became more prominent in marketing in the 1990s and 2000s, further models such as solutions, information, value and access (SIVA) have been conceptualised in recognition that marketing should be about meeting needs and wants, tackling problems, providing solutions, and creating and offering value (Dev and Schultz, 2005a, 2005b). This more consumer-oriented, relational and value creation orientation of the marketing mix has synergies with reflexive social marketing (Domegan, 2008; Desai, 2009).

What these discussions identify is that the basic 4Ps marketing mix model is simplistic and reductive. It may offer some semblance of a starting point for understanding tools and strategies available to us, but it is more often used restrictively, and practitioners may often lack the imagination or judgement to reinterpret or identify other tools not easily identifiable in the 4Ps. As such, some social marketers have called for a rethought and retooled social marketing mix. For example, Gordon (2012) offered an intervention mix model to act as a stimulus for debate on creating a framework fit for purpose in twenty-first-century social marketing (see Figure 4.1).

This model identifies important tools and strategies such as consumer (or participant) orientation, co-creation of value, citizen engagement and empowerment, relational, strategic and holistic thinking, and use of a number of operational tactics beyond the 4Ps including advocacy, lobbying, public relations and policy change. It also recognises multiple levels of influence and action that may be present or required in relation to social issues. Similarly, Tapp and Spotswood (2013) offered a new social marketing mix model COM-SM – based on the motivation, opportunity, capability model – which may be applied across different activity clusters: promotion, nudge techniques, rewards and exchanges, service and support, and relationships and community.

French (2011) offers a similar matrix to Tapp and Spotswood (2013), identifying that the fours 'forms' of behavioural interventions – *hug*, *smack*, *nudge* and *shove* (see

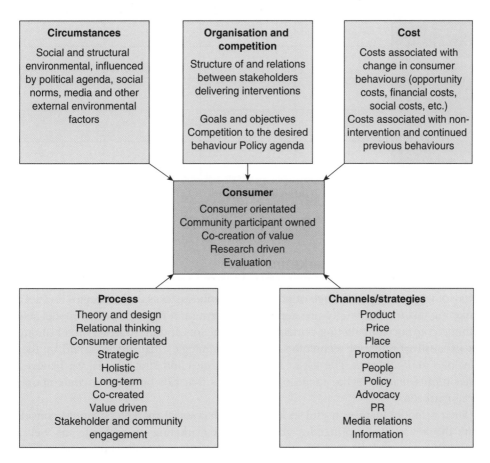

Figure 4.1   Gordon's (2012) rethought and retooled social marketing mix

Source: Gordon, 2012

Chapter 3 for more detail) – can be combined with the five intervention 'types' – *control, inform, design, educate* and *support* – to map 20 possible intervention approaches that can be used in different combinations. These options are set out in Figure 4.2 – the social marketing behavioural intervention matrix. This matrix can also be used to assess current strategies and plan new programmes.

It is important to acknowledge that in many social programme/change situations multiple combinations of these intervention approaches will be necessary; and different mixes are need with different participants/stakeholders target groups.

Behavioural Intervention Matrix
Value/Cost Exchange

	Hug	Nudge	Shove	Smack
Control				
Inform				
Design				
Educate				
Support				

Figure 4.2   The social marketing intervention matrix

Source: French, 2011

Broadening the social marketing mix

A way of representing the range of potential techniques, tools and strategies in a social marketing mix for the twenty-first century is presented in Figure 4.3. This model starts with the core social marketing principles and concepts and illustrates a broad (though not exhaustive) range of techniques, tools and strategies that are informed by these principles and concepts. The list of tools, techniques and strategies is, we believe, a better representation of the range of approaches that can be used in contemporary social marketing.

Such a model may be useful in identifying that social marketers should consider more the key strategic principles guiding social marketing programmes, as well as creatively using and mixing a broad and holistic range of intervention techniques, tools and strategies. Like any model or framework, the one presented in Figure 4.3 is not intended to be exhaustive or definitive; it does help, however, to illustrate the extent of the techniques, tools and strategies available in the social marketing toolkit.

Furthermore, acknowledging Culliton's (1948) and Borden's (1964) original ideas, newly conceived tools or original combinations of tools may supplement such a model and be used in social programmes. What we hoped to have identified here is that it is important that social marketers recognise the serious limitations of the traditional 4Ps model and are less restrictive, and more creative, holistic and strategic in their use of intervention tools and strategies.

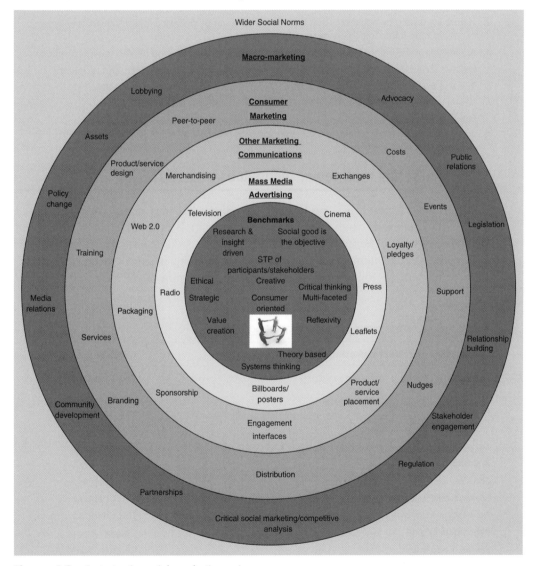

Figure 4.3   A strategic social marketing mix

Source: adapted from BMA, 2009; Gordon, 2011

It is probable that in most social marketing programmes a combination of approaches will be used. Table 4.2 sets out the criteria that should be used to guide the selection of the particular mix of interventions, types and forms.

Table 4.2 Selection criteria for social marketing interventions

1. Intervention is supported by evidence of effectiveness from published and unpublished literature.
2. Plausibility testing demonstrates that the intervention can be delivered and sustained over the necessary time-frame to achieve results.
3. An analysis of the insight data from target groups demonstrates a good fit with the intervention.
4. Positive acceptability analysis can be demonstrated with funders, stakeholders and recipients.
5. Risk and reward analysis demonstrates positive outcomes, cost-benefit, ROI and VFM.
6. Intervention passes required ethical tests and complies with relevant legislation.
7. The intervention is consistent and additive to the overall policy and strategy objectives.

Social marketing mix: tools, techniques and strategies

So far in this chapter we hope to have identified that it is important to be broad minded and reflexive when selecting intervention tools and strategies in the social marketing mix. Throughout this book we also examine, discuss and provide examples of how the aforementioned tools, and strategies techniques can be used. To act as a guide to readers, we identify in Table 4.3 where a selection of the tools can be found in this book.

Table 4.3 Chapter guide for social marketing mix tools

Component of social marketing mix	Chapter
Product	This Chapter
Price	This Chapter
Place	This Chapter
Promotion	This Chapter
Social Media	This Chapter
Branding	This Chapter
Services	This Chapter
Media/Public Relations	This Chapter
Advocacy and lobbying	This Chapter
Benchmark criteria	Chapter 2
Research and insight	Chapters 9 and 10
Theory	Chapters 3 and 8
Systems/strategic thinking	Chapters 5, 7 and 11

Component of social marketing mix	Chapter
Policy and legislation	Chapters 1, 3, 11 and 13
Critical thinking and reflexivity	Chapter 14
Ethics	Chapters 2 and 9
Stakeholder engagement	Chapters 7, 11 and 12
Regulation	Chapters 3 and 14
Community development	Chapter 7

However, we must again reiterate that this list of tools in this chapter and indeed this book is not exhaustive, and using Culliton's (1948) and Borden's (1964) analogy – there may be other tools and new tools that can be used and developed.

In the remainder of this chapter we will examine some of the key tools in the toolkit, including *product, price, place, promotion* – but broadening the scope of tools to include *social media, branding, services, public and media relations*, and *advocacy and lobbying*.

Product

In social marketing the initial step in creating a product concept is to identify and clarify the product attributes. In the commercial world these include tangible characteristics such as taste, shape, size, packaging and performance, and intangible characteristics like image, status and brand. Products in the social marketing domain may be physical and tangible, such as a screening test kit for chlamydia or a condom for family planning and sexual health, and therefore have tangible characteristics. However, social marketing products are often intangible, and often encompass complex behaviours that are being marketed – such as being physically active. This means it can be difficult for social marketers to create simple and meaningful product constructs (MacFadyen et al., 2003). Examples of such intangible products may include adoption of an idea, adoption, adaption or maintenance of behaviour(s), or avoidance/non-engagement with competing ideas and behaviours (Hastings and Domegan, 2014). To help us think about how such social marketing behavioural products may be formulated, MacFadyen et al. (2003) identified strategies for identifying and clarifying their attributes. These include:

- *Trialability*: can the behaviour be piloted and tested out before continuous adoption (e.g. wearing safety goggles)?
- *Ease*: how easy or difficult is it to adopt the desired behaviour that will create social good (e.g. wearing a seatbelt versus doing regular physical activity)?
- *Risks*: what are the risks associated with adoption of the behaviour?
- *Image*: is the behaviour perceived to be attractive or unattractive?

- *Acceptability*: is the behaviour socially accepted by peers, colleagues, the community and society?
- *Duration*: is the behaviour to be performed one time only or repeated? Is it to be sustained over the short or the long term?
- *Cost*: does the behaviour incur a financial cost or not (e.g. joining a gym to stay or become physically active)?

In the social marketing sphere Kotler et al. (1999) have distinguished between *actual products* (either tangible or, as above, behavioural), *augmented products* (things supporting the behaviour change – as discussed earlier in this chapter), and *core products* (the social good resultant from behaviour change). However, as we can see from this exploration of product, in social marketing considerable leaps in interpretation are required which may explain the criticisms of the 4Ps from some social marketers (Peattie and Peattie, 2003). That is, it may be difficult to assume that all social marketing practitioners will be able to interpret and adapt the concept of product to social marketing domains.

Price

Social marketing programmes often do not involve tangible products that carry an economic price. Price in social marketing is often considered from a broader perspective, and relates to the costs associated with behaviour change, or acting in a way that facilitates social good. These may involve the costs that participants have to pay and the barriers they have to overcome to adopt a desired behaviour. These costs may be financial, for example if there are tangible social marketing products or services to purchase like condoms to protect sexual health or facilitate family planning, or the cost of joining a gym to get fit. In the social marketing domain we might consider charging for products or services as anathema given the core orientation towards engendering social good. This becomes even more of a consideration when we are dealing with vulnerable or low-income groups. However, as Hastings and Domegan (2014) point out there is a close relationship between price and value – citing the example of condom social marketing in India, where free condoms were not treated with respect, but when a small charge was introduced perceived value was increased and subsequently condom use increased (Dahl et al., 1997). Therefore, although it may seem counter intuitive, financial costs can help engage participants.

Other costs may be psychological (e.g. loss of the de-stressing effect from smoking), cultural, social (e.g. peer pressure to drink), temporal (loss of valuable time to visit a recycling depot), practical (e.g. cancelling the school run to reduce car use), or physical (feeling sore after doing fitness classes). In social marketing, much of the focus is often placed on trying to reduce or mitigate costs and perceived barriers to change, while accentuating the benefits. Rangun et al. (1996) offer a useful matrix for

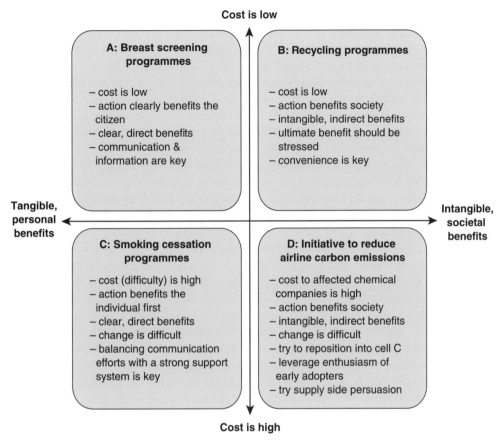

Figure 4.4 A matrix of price in social marketing

Source: Rangun et al., 1996: 44–45

understanding price in social marketing and what strategies may be used (see Figure 4.4). Hastings and Domegan (2014) identify that change is easier when costs are low and there are personal benefits to participants (e.g. wearing a seatbelt).

Place

Place in social marketing refers to the distribution channels (physical, virtual, interpersonal, social, cultural) by which behaviour change is promoted, and the places in which change is encouraged and supported (e.g. workplaces, schools, homes, communities, health centres). This means that place variables such as channels of distribution, cost, timing, reach and coverage (Lee and Kotler, 2011), location and logistics (Eagle et al., 2013), and accessibility (Cowell, 1994) are all important. An example is the BreastScreen Queensland cancer screening service that reduces the costs and barriers of attending by considering place-based variables of time, distance and convenience by offering a mobile screening van service at varied times (Zainuddin et al., 2011).

Furthermore, social marketing programmes often involve a number of actors and implementers including government employees, health professionals, pharmacists, educators and community workers, who act as distribution channels for social market- ing messages and materials and who may also act as advocates for behaviour change. As an example, community Doctors are often given the responsibility of influencing their patients' smoking or drinking behaviours (Hastings and Domegan, 2014). In such cases issues such as accessibility (how often patients may visit the community Doctors and whether they can do so easily) and appropriateness (whether community Doctors are the best people to discuss these issues with citizens) are important to consider. When social marketing actors have more complex roles such as youth workers deliv- ering an alcohol media literacy curriculum, place variables such as source visibility, credence, attractiveness and power relations are often relevant (Eagle et al., 2013). Taking the example of alcohol media literacy programmes, there is considerable debate in the literature over whether teachers, youth workers, academics, peers or law enforcement agencies are the best people to deliver content to students and who young people will be most likely to listen to and engage with. Therefore in social marketing the source of the message is vital. In the truth® campaign, place-based mar- keting was focused on young people themselves being delivery agents and distribution channels through which programme messages and the behavioural objectives to stop young people smoking or from starting to smoke were disseminated.

Social marketing programmes often rely on the engagement and support of a range of actors to help engender socially beneficial outcomes. This is especially the case when programmes concern sensitive issues such as drug abuse, or with vulnerable groups such as children or old aged pensioners – where there is often a requirement to engage not only participants but also other actors such as teachers, parents, social workers, care providers and politicians. Often these actors are gatekeepers and can control or at least influence the distribution channels and messages to participants, or are important stake- holders who want to have a say on the activities in social programmes (McGrath, 1995). If a social marketing programme is to be effective it is important that place-based mar- keting is done ethically, sensitively and strategically to ensure that the needs not only of participants, but also other relevant actors, are met. We consider the roles of stakehold- ers and actors in social marketing programmes further in Chapter 7.

Promotion

Promotion in social marketing refers to the means by which behaviour change is pro- moted to participants, for example advertising, price promotions, direct mail or interpersonal communications. Promotion can also be conceptualised to include social media communications, branding and public/media relations. Social marketing promotions should be designed to support rather than act as the core pillar of social change programmes. Research suggests that advertising and communications alone are unlikely to lead to change (Wakefield et al., 2010). Identifying the relevant forms of promotion that should be used in programmes should be based on scoping and research with participant groups to identify sources of information, the types of information (e.g. visual, audio, written), and the most appropriate mediums that people prefer and give credence to. For example, a programme for oral and bowel cancer screening targeting lower income adults aged 45 and over used formative research to identify that newspaper adverts to encourage people to attend a screening service were a good strategy (Eadie and MacAskill, 2008). Ensuring that promotional communications are ethical, acceptable to the participant audience, and that they are legible and can be interpreted clearly is also an important consideration. Eagle et al. (2013) draw attention to the importance of using simple language, clear fonts, appropriate colours and formatting, and clever designs in social marketing materials. Importantly, such materials should be pilot tested with participants in the relevant segments relating to social marketing programmes, to identify any issues and permit changes to be made before implementation. It is also important to acknowledge that people draw information from a variety of sources, therefore concentrating on only one form and medium for social marketing promotional activity can be ineffective. Pro-social promotional and media messages can help create normative effects and an environment in which social good can be facilitated, but it is important to remember that these are only one tool in the toolkit.

Social media

Social media are the social interaction between individuals and groups involving the creation, sharing and exchanging of information and ideas in Web 2.0/Web 3.0 virtual/online communities and networks. Although social media originated as a way in which citizens can communicate, marketers and social marketers eagerly try to harness the potential of social media as a marketing tool (Dooley et al., 2012). The emergence of social media has dramatically altered communications between organisations, communities and individuals (Kietzmann and Hermkens, 2011). In social media users often generate or co-create content – which has changed the way organisations and marketers relate to consumers from a passive one-directional process, to an active and multi-dimensional virtual social process. There are multiple types of social media, illustrated in Figure 4.5.

The advantages of using social media in social marketing are that it offers greater reach, and a better opportunity to segment and target specific groups, and to co-create value and engage participants in long-term relationships with social change issues (Thackeray et al., 2012). Social media present a range of platforms through

Figure 4.5   Social media forms

Source: Solis and Thomas, 2014

which social marketing actors can identify, have conversations, share content, create relationships, foster reputations, and form groups and communities. This offers great potential – for example, creating support groups around smoking cessation, engaging young people in physical activity programmes such as VERB™ and encouraging them to come up with ideas for activities online (Huhman, 2008), or creating blogs about healthy lifestyles among fashion conscious women aged 40–60 (Taubenheim et al., 2008). Unsurprisingly social marketers have identified and called for the use of social media in social programmes (Bernhardt et al., 2012). Yet challenges remain – social media are not a panacea, they are merely one tool in the social marketing mix, and there can be difficulties in finding resources and generating appropriate content (Dooley et al., 2014). Thackeray et al. (2012) assert that the potential of social media in social marketing has been so far relatively untapped but propose a four-step process for considering its use:

- *Step one* involves describing the participant groups you wish to engage, discovering which social media they use and how they use these (are they posting blogs or just reading content, do they read reviews but never write any?).
- *Step two* involves identifying the objectives for wanting to engage with participants – is it to deliver information, gain feedback or invite new ideas? Other objectives may be to encourage people to talk to others about a social issue and share stories, ideas and experiences. This can help create brand advocates – people who will share knowledge and ideas about a social issue with others and encourage them to engage. Another objective may be to provide social support networks such as online forums of advice and encouragement to increase physical activity or reduce energy dense food consumption. Engagement with participants may also be desired to facilitate co-creation – getting people to design products, services and communications.
- *Step three* involves generating a specific strategy to engage target participants and achieve the objectives outlined in step two. This involves allocating resources to ensure engagement with participants is ongoing and responsive, making sure that interactions are mutually beneficial (for example, are there incentives, rewards or social benefits from participating?), creating clear and fully disseminated and understood organisational policies on using social media, and devising a realistic and measurable evaluation plan.
- *Step four* involves choosing the technology based on insight and objectives identified in steps one and two, and the resources available from step three. This means being smart about what platforms to use and making sure that you identify where people are or want to be engaging and interacting with the organisation and with a social issue. Often this means tapping into existing social media platforms, for example creating a Facebook profile page to run a wellness programme at work, rather than creating new social media platforms that people might not want to use (Thackeray et al., 2012). Importantly, any social media social marketing content that is created has to be relevant, meaningful, important, appropriate and ethical to target participants.

Branding

A brand has been defined as 'a name that symbolises a long-term engagement, crusade or commitment to a unique set of values, embedded into products, services and behaviours, which make the organisation, person or product stand apart and stand out'

(Kapferer, 2012: 12). The concept of a brand is multi-dimensional, and relates to various entities that identify a product, service or organisation (such as name, term, sign, symbol or design, or combination of them) and how it relates to key actors such as customers/participants, staff, partners, funders, etc. Brands can be a marketer's most powerful emotional tool. They often symbolise and reinforce the functional and emotional value of an offering, and encourage engagement, consumption and loyalty from consumers (de Chernatony, 1993). Brands can also supply signals to consumers about the quality of a product or service (Janiszewski and van Osselaer, 2000), as well as helping to gain consumers' attention (Ray and Batra, 1983), and encourage deeper processing of messages (Dutta and Kanungo, 1975). Branding can also help to establish meaningful connections and even a sense of community with consumers through the signalling of mental associations and emotions (Kapferer, 2012).

Brands can possess psychological characteristics and be associated with thoughts, feelings, perceptions, images, experiences, beliefs and attitudes. This can be symbolised through the concept of *brand personality*, which can be defined as the set of human characteristics associated with a brand. Research has found that brand personality plays an important role in influencing people's attitudes and behaviours (Sirgy, 1982; Aaker, 1997). Brands can also possess an experiential component consisting of the sum of all points of contact with the brand – often referred to as the *brand experience*. The brand experience is a brand's action perceived by a person. How a brand is perceived psychologically and experientially has an effect on the *brand image*. Brand image is a symbolic construct consisting of consumers' information and expectations associated with a product, service or the organisations providing them. A brand that has a high level of *brand awareness* is said to possess *brand recognition*. Brand recognition is demonstrated by people being able to identify the brand without exposure to the name, but through visual signifiers like logos, slogans and colours. Brands are also a good way to build relationships and loyalty with customers.

Many of the social issues to which social marketing is applied, such as obesity or using energy efficiently, require long-term relationship building and strategic approaches to influence behaviours to improve health and society. Given the effect branding can have on consumer attitudes and behaviours, social marketers have identified the potential of branding in social marketing (Evans and Hastings, 2008) but highlight that this often remains underdeveloped and largely unrealised (Gordon et al., 2013; Hastings and Domegan, 2014).

Hastings (2007) identified the potential of branding to foster long-term strategic engagement in social marketing yet highlights examples such as 'Be all you can be' – a health brand in Scotland that utilised some commercial brand strategy ideas. After four years the brand was scrapped and more traditional didactic health campaigns returned. Another example of the lack of strategic branding in social marketing is the body responsible for health behaviour change programmes in Scotland being rebranded four times in the past twenty-five years, thereby limiting the development of brand recognition, relationships and loyalty (Gordon et al., 2008).

The truth® and VERB™ programme brands

Nevertheless, some examples of strong branding in social marketing do exist. The truth® social marketing programme developed by the American Legacy Foundation featured the creation of a powerful brand designed to compete with the evocative image of smoking portrayed by tobacco brands such as Marlboro, to discourage youth from smoking. The truth® brand (see Figure 4.6 for the logo) was carefully developed following formative research and engagement with young people, and appealed to the rebelliousness of youth, and encouraged adolescents to take control by using counter marketing to explicate the manipulative and exploitative marketing tactics of Big Tobacco. Work by Evans et al. (2005) utilised Aaker's (1996) ten dimensional model of brand equity, identifying that truth® achieved high brand equity among young people, and was perceived to be of high quality. This powerful branding of truth® helped the programme achieve a reduction in smoking prevalence among adolescents (Farrelly et al., 2005).

Figure 4.6 The truth® brand logo

Source: American Legacy Foundation, 2014

Similarly, the Centers for Disease Control and Prevention used branding in their VERB™ public health programme encouraging children aged 9–13 years to be physically active. Extensive formative research, consultation with brand experts and agencies such as Saatchi and Saatchi, and a process of engagement and co-creation with participant groups helped develop a comprehensive brand strategy (Asbury et al., 2008). The VERB™ brand (see Figure 4.7 for the brand logo) was created with the attributes of inclusiveness, playfulness, having fun while playing with friends, and accessibility (Asbury et al., 2008).

Evaluation research of the VERB™ programme identified that tweens who recognised the VERB™ brand and understood its message were more physically active than those who were not aware (Huhman et al., 2007). A study also found that high VERB™ brand equity was linked with increased positive attitudes towards physical activity, and that the perceived brand personality of VERB™ was a strong predictor of attitudes to physical activity. Therefore the high potential of creating social marketing brands that have high awareness, high brand equity, attractive brand personalities and that engage participants and facilitate relationships in long-term social change programmes has been established (Hastings and Domegan, 2014).

Figure 4.7   VERB™ brand logo

Source: Centers for Disease Control and Prevention, 2014

Yet McDivitt (2003) has identified that to use branding successfully in social marketing will require a move beyond focusing on messages, persuasion and transactional orientations in programmes, to acknowledge the relevance of relational thinking, longevity, and co-creation and co-ownership of brands with participants. Branding is something that the commercial sector does well – evocative and powerful brands such as Apple and Harley Davidson have been so successful that they have invoked strong consumer responses to the point where consumption communities have formed around them (Schembri, 2009). Often our competitors in the social marketing domain use powerful branding to engage people to consume harmful products. For example, a study in the USA identified that 30 per cent of children aged three years and 91.3 per cent of children aged six years recognised and could match the Old Joe Camel brand logo with a cigarette (Fischer et al., 1991). Recent research in the UK found associations between high engagement with alcohol brands and youth drinking (Harris et al., forthcoming).

Branding is an important area for social marketing research and practice. Creating and managing successful brands require considerable effort, the development of brand strategy based on research, insight, the engagement of brand experts, and engaging participants in a co-creation process for social marketing brands. It also means recognising that a brand is more than a logo or a name, but is a psychological, emotional and experiential concept that marks and influences a person's engagement with an organisation. Recent social programmes such as Change4Life in the UK have cleverly used brand strategy – applying the 4life brand to different behaviours such as cycling and walking. Furthermore, Change4Life has facilitated the co-creation of the brand, with Figure 4.8 presenting a brand montage created by a Facebook fan of Change4Life, Rachael Benham, which is available on the programme website and social media pages. Change4Life also takes a strategic approach to health behaviours by engaging people in healthy lifestyle concepts as well as specific issues (such as reducing fat intake) – see www.nhs.uk/change4life/Pages/change-for-life.aspx.

Branding undoubtedly holds massive potential for social marketing, but more research is needed. Work in Australia (Gordon et al., 2013) is exploring how social marketing brand personality (Guens et al., 2009) and brand personality appeal

Figure 4.8 Change4Life brand montage

Source: Benham, 2012

(Freling et al., 2011) may influence people's attitudes and behaviours. Early findings from this inquiry suggest that creating appealing social marketing brand personalities can have positive effects on attitudes and behavioural outcomes. This suggests that social marketers should focus on brand strategy and seek to create powerful, engaging and appealing brands to engage citizens in social programmes. However, further research on, and application of branding in social marketing is required to truly unlock its potential.

Services

Service thinking has become a prominent perspective in the mainstream marketing literature, recognising that marketing is a process focused on value creation among organisations, citizens, stakeholders and society. The service-dominant logic proposes that all marketing offerings are bundles of services (Vargo and Lusch, 2004), and that value is created not delivered to people (Grönroos, 2013). Services are often an important component of social marketing programmes (Lefebvre, 2012; Russell-Bennett et al., 2013), whether it is a smoking cessation service to help people quit smoking, a cancer screening service to help with the early detection and treatment of breast cancer, or recycling services to help reduce waste and promote environmental sustainability. Furthermore, services marketing research in social marketing have identified that the way services are designed and delivered, and how they engage participants, can have a significant effect on socially beneficial outcomes (see Zainuddin et al., 2013).

Therefore, services thinking and understanding how to design and implement high quality services that provide satisfaction to citizens is an important consideration for social marketing. Service thinking can be conceptualised as a midstream approach to social marketing – focusing on the intersection between individuals and public policy and decision makers that fund services (Russell-Bennett et al., 2013).

Russell-Bennett et al. (2013: 227) identify four key principles of services marketing:

1. place the service experience as central,
2. the service employee as a critical interface,
3. identifies service quality and customer value as key drivers of behaviour, and
4. views the customer as active (though not always) rather than passive.

In the social marketing paradigm, it follows that a positive service experience is important for facilitating and sustaining a desired behaviour (for instance, if a diabetic has a positive experience attending their annual checkup clinic they are more likely to monitor their blood and diet effectively and also return to the clinic). The service employees and front-line staff are critical touch points between social marketing organisations and citizens. Therefore service staff need to be highly engaged, motivated, personable and rewarded for good performance. From the services marketing literature we know that perceived service quality and customer value are key predictors of customer behaviour. Furthermore, as we discuss in Chapter 6, customers/citizens are active participants in the value creation process at all stages before, during and after services are delivered (Russell-Bennett et al., 2013). Russell-Bennett et al. (2013: 231) offer a useful matrix of challenges and strategies for applying service thinking in social marketing (see Table 4.4). Engaging with service thinking and services marketing principles holds the potential to benefit the delivery of effective social marketing programmes.

Table 4.4 Challenges and recommended strategies for implementing service thinking

Issues	Challenges	Recommended strategies/ guidelines
Language and terminology	To understand the service recipient as a customer and active participant.	Training, multi-stakeholder engagement/ workshops including service users to achieve mutual understanding and a common language.
Regulatory and institutional frameworks	To identify the appropriate institutions and level of governance needed to change environmental forces that negatively impact customer behaviours.	Conduct market scanning and research to identify appropriate service institutions and delivery processes that encourage voluntary behaviours in target audiences and support the achievement of social marketing outcomes.
Job rules/identity	To challenge workers' beliefs and attitudes that social marketing-like practices will undermine professional status and expertise.	Introduce staff training programmes that encourage open discussion of the problems and challenges to be addressed in introducing standardised services processes.
		Encourage staff reward programmes that acknowledge the service contribution made by staff across the full servicescape from administration/reception through to professional/clinical service provision.
Defining social marketing as a strategic approach	To educate those public service professionals who may equate social marketing with promotions and communications alone.	Social marketing training has proved to be effective in presenting a broader, strategic view of marketing.
Power/control	To encourage customer involvement and participation in service and other marketing activities. Support customer participation.	Changes in policy, staff development processes and the use of role-playing and drama techniques can facilitate a shift in mindset. Professionals should be sold the benefits of customer involvement, i.e. happier customers and more fulfilling jobs.

Source: Russell-Bennett et al., 2013: 231

Public relations

Public relations (PR) refers to the management and dissemination of information between individuals or organisations, and public citizens (Grunig and Hunt, 1984). Public relations is influenced by perspectives from communications theory, psychology, phenomenology, semiotics, sociology and cultural studies (see Chapter 8), systems thinking (see Chapter 7) and critical thinking (see Chapter 14) (Macnamara, 2012).

Some scholars identify PR (and advocacy, branding and social media) as forms of promotion and thus falling within the 4Ps framework (Lee and Kotler, 2011). However, we take the view here that it is somewhat distinct and it is better to be explicit about the existence of these social marketing tools, as we cannot always assume practitioners will discern that promotion can include activities such as PR and advocacy.

The Public Relations Society of America (PRSA, 2012) offers the following definition: 'Public relations is a strategic communication process that builds mutually beneficial relationships between organisations and their publics'. From this definition we can identify the relevance to social marketing, given that organisations and public citizens are involved in communication and value creation processes when engaging in social programmes. Indeed, scholars have identified strong synergies between PR and social marketing (McKie and Toledano, 2008), with Macnamara (2012: 325) identifying that social marketing programmes 'often rely heavily on public relations'.

An example is the smoke-free Scotland case study in Chapter 7, where a coalition in support of the proposed legislation used public relations to build support for the measure among citizens. Public relations can involve an organisation or individual gaining exposure to relevant audiences using topics of public and social interest and news items (Seitel, 2007). Often this does not require direct payment for exposure, unlike commercial or even social advertising. The objective of public relations is to engage and persuade public citizens, prospective customers or clients, investors, partners, employees and other relevant stakeholders to develop or maintain a certain point of view about a topic, the source organisation and its leadership and offerings, or of political decisions (Macnamara, 2012). It is important that PR is undertaken strategically and ethically, and involves critical reflection on activities.

A range of specific tools is often used in PR activity including strategic advice/counsel, working with the press, supplying content for news programmes, blogs, newspapers and magazines, publishing feature articles on topics, or arranging interviews with expert spokespersons. Such strategies are often useful for gaining public, political and stakeholder attention to certain issues – for example, organisations like Greenpeace have used PR to draw attention to the threats posed by climate change. Other strategies often employed in PR include speaking at conferences, and internal/employee level communications. Within the public relations paradigm, there are three sub-disciplines that are of particular interest to social marketing – government relations, media relations and internal communications.

Government relations

Government relations refers to engagement with government departments and public bodies to influence public policy. The main way by which organisations perform government relations is through the use of lobbying (discussed later in this chapter). Ensuring that there is government support, political buy-in, and a supportive policy environment for social change and/or social good is essential.

Media relations

Media relations refers to the relationships and interactions that stakeholder organisations develop with journalists (Johnston, 2008). Due to the way in which news media operate, organisations cannot ultimately control which stories are disseminated. Therefore, organisations must look to foster effective relationships with the media as an ongoing practice. Working with the media allows social marketing organisations such as government departments, public health bodies or environmental sustainability groups to raise citizen awareness about them and social issues. Media relations can also be fairly segmented and targeted, or used to engage wider audiences. In the social marketing sphere effective media relations can help build public support and mobilise public opinion (Johnston, 2008). However, Macnamara (2012) warns that working with the media must be undertaken with caution as sometimes media coverage can lead to misrepresentations of issues, or even be counterproductive towards stakeholder relationships. This requires good communications, building trust and strong partnerships with the media, and being reflexive on when media relations is an appropriate tool to use in social marketing.

Internal communications

Internal communications within organisations are also an important consideration for social marketing. Ensuring that there is a high level of engagement and buy-in from managers and front-line staff involved in the delivery of social programmes is often critical to their success (Stead et al., 2007). Ensuring that internal communication is done to a high standard, is co-participatory, regularly carried out and is engaging, is critical to maintain buy-in and to provide a platform for commentary, feedback and critical reflection. The process of internal communications can be related to internal social marketing – ensuring that employees, managers and front-line staff are engaged with social change processes. Smith and O'Sullivan (2012) have identified how it is important to use internal social marketing to engage, empower and facilitate employees within organisations to be participants in social change efforts such as increasing the environmental friendliness of a company. They identify that applying social marketing principles to market environmentally responsible behaviours to staff and creating incentives to do so, while removing barriers to pro-environmental behaviour, can be effective. This sort of internal communication effectively represents internal PR.

Advocacy and lobbying

Advocacy is a political process undertaken by individuals, groups or organisations that aims to influence public policy and resource decisions within political, economic and social systems and institutions. Advocacy can involve a number of activities including running mass media campaigns, public speaking, commissioning and disseminating research, carrying out public opinion polls, or lobbying. Lobbying is a form of advocacy in which stakeholder groups directly approach policy makers and decision makers (such as civil servants) regarding an issue. With the advent of social media, advocacy groups are increasingly using these platforms to mobilise people, facilitate civic engagement and take collective action (Obar et al., 2012).

Advocacy

Scholars have long recognised the relevance of advocacy to influencing social issues, particularly through change in the upstream (policy/structural/legislative) environment (Wallack et al., 1993; Hastings, 2007; Gordon, 2013). For example, much of the work on tobacco control involved advocacy to change the legal, regulatory and policy environment surrounding tobacco, leading to bans on tobacco marketing and the introduction of smoke-free legislation (see Chapman, 2001, 2007). Gordon (2013) identifies how media advocacy was used by public health and tobacco control groups to raise awareness of, and generate support for, the introduction of smoke-free legislation in Scotland. Similarly, advocacy has been used to build support and make the case for the introduction of a minimum unit price for alcohol to help tackle the considerable health and social harms caused by harmful alcohol consumption (Hagger et al., 2011). See the case study below from Jeff Jordan on youth engagement programmes (YEPs) on tobacco control in the USA that features advocacy work.

Advocacy can take many forms and come from a variety of perspectives, but in the social marketing sphere this often has a public health, social justice or environmental sustainability orientation. For example, advocacy for social good that takes a social justice perspective often focuses on power relations and considers how issues can be highlighted and action taken to alter the structural environment and change 'what is' to 'what should be' (Cohen et al., 2001). The relevance to social marketing here is clear, as participant groups may be under-represented, and have a lack of information, resources or power to change things. Therefore, organisations involved in advocacy seek to represent citizens to bring about a change in the dynamics and effects of a situation. Advocates often engage in reflexive practice to frame what may need to be done, and consider various characteristics of existing systems to build fairer and just societies. Advocates:

- question the way policy is administered
- engage with and participate in agenda setting and raise significant issues

- target political systems when they are not serving or responding to people's needs
- are inclusive and engaging
- propose policy solutions
- create space for public augmentation.

Advocacy has often been identified as part of the *upstream social marketing* paradigm (Andreasen, 2006; Gordon, 2013). For some, advocacy may be considered as a form of promotional activity (Lee and Kotler, 2011), but however we conceive it, it does offer an important and relevant tool in the social marketing mix. Indeed, if we examine marketing in the commercial sector, many corporations undertake advocacy work to shape the legal, political and social environment to create more favourable conditions for business (Waltzer, 1988). This can potentially pose competition for social marketing (for example, political advocacy by the tobacco industry to be permitted to market their products), but it also tells us that advocacy is a potentially effective tool. In the social marketing domain in addition to tobacco and alcohol issues advocacy has also been used to tackle other social issues such as road safety (Stead et al., 2002).

CASE STUDY

Applying social marketing to youth engagement programmes to achieve policy change

Figure 4.9

The US Centers for Disease Control have identified youth engagement programmes (YEP) as a best practice to achieve policy change, particularly when the policy in question affects youth, such as tobacco control policies. However, YEP models vary significantly and the characteristics of effective and efficient YEPs are, to date, unclear. This case study explores the application of the social marketing framework to develop specific strategies for both efficient and effective YEPs.

For the purposes of this case study, we define YEPs as programmes that provide young people with the opportunity to engage in semi-autonomous

(Continued)

(Continued)

actions that tangibly contribute to changing a policy that positively affects behaviour(s) in their community. This strategy became particularly popular among tobacco control programmes in the USA in the early 2000s and has since spread in the United States and abroad to policies related to behaviours affecting obesity, alcohol, voting and environmental conservation among others. Each implementation of a YEP is unique, with both effectiveness and efficiency varying widely across implementations. As such, we examine YEPs through the lens of social marketing principles to establish high standards for the practice.

Citizen orientation

Social marketing programmes typically have a single group of citizens of interest. YEPs, however, almost always have at least two groups. The first group is the youth advocates themselves. YEPs must be designed to appeal to youth advocates to recruit and retain engagement. The second audience is the adults with decision making power regarding a policy, including political leaders, voters and/or stakeholders. YEPs often focus on only one of these citizen groups, inadvertently alienating the other. For example, some YEPs focus on youth, making all materials and strategies youth-oriented. While this keeps youth volunteers excited, adults rarely take notice and behaviour change is not achieved. Other YEPs focus exclusively on adults, which often is not interesting to youth, so volunteers quit the programme or never join. The solution is to target both citizen groups: develop youthful recruitment strategies and adult-oriented outreach strategies. Each strategy or material should have only a single audience, which must be defined before anything is developed. Since youth engagement is the unique concept YEPs bring to the practice of policy change, we will focus on the youth audience for the remaining social marketing principles.

Behaviour/theory/insight

The behaviour targeted by YEPs is often unclear. Some YEPs claim that the behaviour is the one targeted by the policy change effort, such as tobacco prevention or recycling. Others claim not to target a behaviour at all. Neither of these are correct. When considering youth involvement in these programmes, the behaviour is actually volunteerism itself. In order to reach adults with the power to change policy, YEPs must first recruit and retain youth engagement. Additionally, volunteers are likely to support the cause they are volunteering for, and thus it is unlikely that these volunteers are a target audience for the behaviour change that the policy aims to address. For example, it is unlikely that teens who use tobacco would volunteer for tobacco policy change YEPs. Attempting to recruit at-risk youth into YEPs is an unnecessary distraction to the policy change purpose of the programme, and not an evidence-based strategy to change behaviours among at-risk youth. Instead, YEPs should gather insights to engage willing youth volunteers and keep them engaged over the long term since high turnover in YEPs can lead to significant reductions in effectiveness and efficiency.

Exchange/value/competition

Understanding that the targeted youth behaviour is volunteerism clarifies our application of the exchange, value and competition principles in YEPs. First, YEPs must realise that the intrinsic value of volunteerism is high for youth who want to volunteer. However, the intrinsic value is not realised until an outcome is realised. Fortunately, this outcome does not need to be the finalisation of a policy change, which can take significant time and effort, but can be the feeling youth experience when they successfully reach community members. Consequently, YEPs should make these opportunities frequent and quantifiable for youth. For example, some YEPs require many months of volunteering to complete a single project or event. Since the reward is the outcome of the volunteerism and not the volunteerism itself, this approach requires youth to have a high tolerance for delayed gratification. This approach is driven by a 'purist' youth engagement perspective that requires youth to make every decision in the planning process, which significantly lengthens planning. Since young people are particularly known to expect immediate gratification, this approach is not recommended. Instead, YEPs should help youth accelerate planning with expert adult involvement that creates a planning environment where youth are semi-autonomous rather than fully autonomous. With support from expert adults, shortened planning will give youth more frequent opportunities to engage with the adult decision makers and feel gratification for their effort. Secondly, any tangible outcomes during outreach activities, such as petitions, surveys and/or pledges, would quantify the youth volunteer's impact, which increases the value of the experience. Finally, rewards should be used to reinforce these outputs. For example, rather than give all youth participants free t-shirts and backpacks, create a rewards structure that allows youth to get these items after completing certain outreach activities or milestones. This will reinforce the value of policy change outreach efforts, which will increase youth's own focus on these activities.

(Continued)

(Continued)

Segmentation

With multiple audiences and behavioural objectives, YEPs have many different segmentation variables to consider. From a youth perspective, YEPs should segment based on likely interest and commitment to volunteerism. If a certain group of young people are more difficult to maintain in the programme than others, segmentation should help avoid them. As mentioned above, it is not advised to try to recruit at-risk youth that would be affected by the policy change effort as they are unlikely to be interested in the programme. However, effectiveness reaching adults is an important second factor to consider in youth recruitment. For example, targeted adults might respond better to youth from their own neighbourhoods or from the neighbourhoods the policy would impact, among other factors. Factors affecting both the youth and adult behaviours should be understood and considered as part of a segmentation model.

Methods mix

With a clearer understanding of the audience, behaviour, exchange and segmentation, more effective methods for the recruitment and retention of youth volunteers can be considered for YEP implementation. For example, recruitment materials can include more persuasive messages, and communication channels can be selected based on the segmented audience.

Figure 4.10   Students in Virginia, USA, presenting their policy issues to local stakeholders as part of a local youth engagement programme

Source: RescueSCG, 2014

YEPs can contribute significantly to policy change efforts, but only if youth actually join and effectively volunteer. By analysing the youth engagement strategy from a social marketing perspective, practitioners can use this model to achieve effective and efficient outcomes in their programmes.

For more information see: CDC Guide to Youth Engagement – http://stacks.cdc.gov/view/cdc/5628.

RescueSCG – rescueSCG.com.

Evolvement, a RescueSCG Youth Engagement Programme – theevolvement.org.

A video about Evolvement's Approach – http://youtu.be/sjSvK2Zi1UM.

Acknowledgements to Jeff Jordan, President of RescueSCG, and Mayo Djakaria, Behaviour Change Officer at Rescue SG, for this case study.

Lobbying

Lobbying refers to the act of attempting to influence decisions made by those in government, usually policy makers/politicians or civil servants, or members of regulatory bodies. Various groups, including the private sector, corporations, political parties, or public health and social advocacy groups, can undertake lobbying. Lobbying can be a controversial tool if used to promote unethical or socially damaging objectives, and it can also serve to create elite and exclusive power relations through which only the interests of the few are represented. However, lobbying that is conducted from a social justice perspective and is oriented towards engendering social good can often help represent minority interests or those who are disempowered or disengaged (Fitzgerald, 2006). Examples of lobbying in social marketing include influencing policy makers to change legislation relating to tobacco control (Mackay et al., 2012), or the example of the Bootheel Heart Health Project in the USA, which included lobbying of decisions makers that led to the proposal and construction of a network of walking paths in low income communities to facilitate physical activity (Brownson et al., 1996). As Gordon (2013) identifies, lobbying is another relevant tool for the social marketing mix, but what is important is that it is done ethically, honestly, fairly, and meets relevant codes of conduct.

Discussion questions

- Read through the case study on youth engagement programmes in relation to tobacco use. Which tools in the social marketing mix can you identify as being used in these? List as many as you can.
- Imagine you have been asked to tackle youth smoking in your area using a social marketing approach. Which intervention tools would you use? Why?

The importance of pre-testing intervention tools

Whatever social marketing tools are used in programmes, what is important is that appropriate combinations are used based on scoping and research with target populations. Furthermore, any selection of tools should be informed by pre-testing research. Social marketers have identified that pre-testing is a critical component of social marketing (McKenzie-Mohr, 2011; Hastings and Domegan, 2014). Pre-testing social marketing mix intervention tools enables social marketers to pilot programme activities with members of target participant groups to test the appropriateness, acceptability and responses. This may involve testing new services, products, communication messages, materials, branding, or engaging participants to assess whether they believe activities like peer-to-peer networking or advocacy and lobbying are appropriate and whether there are the required assets and resources to do this.

There are two main reasons for pre-testing. Firstly, it allows us to refine ideas that are identified and designed in the scoping phase and that have now been further developed. These can be tested with target participants so that they can be enhanced and be made more specific to their needs. Also, pre-testing can help us identify problems and change the approach. Essentially, pre-testing offers a good way of assessing whether there are any issues with the proposed intervention tools for a social marketing programme, and offers the opportunity to change, adapt and/or refine the approach. This helps us avoid costly mistakes, for example errors may have been made in interpreting the existing literature on a social issue, or we may have misunderstood the motivations and needs of target populations. Furthermore, other factors such as the policy environment or social norms may have changed over time meaning different approaches are required. By undertaking pre-testing it is possible to identify such issues and highlight problems before a programme is fully launched and substantial resources are committed.

To undertake pre-testing it is first of all important to identify what exactly is to be tested and develop a strategic pre-testing and piloting plan. Often in social programmes resources are limited. If there is a rich literature suggesting a given tool is well proven and effective, then it may make more sense to test other components where there is less evidence or questions over acceptability or effects. The less knowledge there is about a particular approach from social marketing practitioners and target participants then the more risk this incurs, and the more important conducting pre-testing becomes. Having open, honest and critically reflexive discussions with project staff and relevant stakeholders is important to build consensus on pre-testing strategy and what should be tested. Although engaging target participants is critical in pre-testing, other groups could and often should also take part in this process. For example, stakeholders such as those responsible for service delivery or experts on branding may be engaged. Considering what data collection and evaluation methods will be used is also important (French et al., 2010).

Test delivery might involve a limited roll-out of programme components. For example, new health clinic services might be delivered in one clinic rather than across a whole region, new physical activity programmes could be tested in one workplace, or new approaches to reducing energy use could be tested in one specific geographical region. The way social marketers carry out pre-testing is through using research, for example asking people in the participant group to take part in focus groups to discuss a social marketing brand, or surveying people on what kind of programme strategies they would like and what gaps in existing social services they perceive. We discuss how research can be used for pre-testing in social marketing in Chapter 10.

Because smaller numbers are usually involved it is important when undertaking pre-testing that social marketers are cautious about extrapolating results to a wider population. Furthermore, pre-testing can be undertaken in the field, or in an experimental laboratory, and there are strengths, weaknesses and resource implications to each approach which must be considered. Furthermore, citizens and some stakeholders may perceive that pre-testing is unfair or unethical if some groups receive interventions or services before others.

Following a process of pre-testing it is important that the results and any reports or briefing notes are discussed reflexively by relevant stakeholders to interpret what is going on, and what refinements or changes may be required. The process of pre-testing should offer a better understanding of the likely responses of target participants to the proposed social marketing programme (or elements of it), and help make decisions as to whether to modify, drop, or go ahead and fully launch.

Conclusion

In this chapter we examined the topic of the social marketing mix – that is the range of intervention tools that can be utilised in social programmes to facilitate socially beneficial outcomes. We started out in this chapter by discussing some of the important debates concerning the marketing mix from the commercial and social marketing literature. We identified that social marketing has been dominated by the use of restrictive and narrow models of intervention tools, particularly the 4Ps. We argued that this has led to the somewhat formulaic use of the same or similar tools in many programmes. In reviewing contemporary debates on the marketing mix, we were able to identify some key limitations of the traditional and dominant 4Ps framework. We then introduced debate and some ideas for alternative models to the 4Ps marketing mix from commercial marketing, and specifically from the social marketing literature.

Although these newer and broader models offer a useful platform for thinking about and applying social change tools in programmes, we feel it is important to reiterate that these can only act as a guide and not a rigid and restrictive formula. We would encourage social marketers to think and act creatively, strategically and holistically when it comes to using the intervention toolkit. Following this examination of debates on the social marketing mix, we introduced and discussed the application of a selected range of tools in the social marketing context. The tools examined in this chapter, and indeed throughout this book, offer a broader selection than traditional models such as the 4Ps. However, we argue that this should only act as a stimulus for further debate, consideration and the application of tools to social marketing pro- grammes. After reviewing some social marketing mix tools, we then identified how important it is to pre-test strategies with the target participants and relevant stakeholders. This is vital to identify issues concerning acceptability and assess likely impacts. It also serves to identify errors, issues and problems that might require refinement or a change to approaches before the roll-out of social marketing programmes. We hope to have made clear to readers the relevance of and our support for the emergence of a broad, adaptive and creative collection of tools that can be used in various combina- tions in social programmes by social marketers in a strategic, holistic and critically reflexive manner. We would argue that doing so can help social marketing progress as a discipline, but more importantly can also help develop a more appropriate, responsive and better approach to engendering social good.

Reflective questions

- Do you agree with the critics of the 4Ps model? Do you think it is important that there are easy formulas to think about how we do social marketing, or are you comfortable with the idea of being creative in using intervention tools? List some reasons for your answers.
- Imagine you are running a social marketing programme to encourage low- income older residents to use energy efficiently, and also to live comfortably in terms of temperature in their homes. Which social marketing mix tools would you use to engage participants and how would you inform your decisions?
- What do you think would be the most difficult to use social marketing mix tool that is discussed in this chapter? Why?

Further reading

Borden, N.H. (1964) 'The concept of the marketing mix', *Journal of Advertising Research*, 4 (2): 2–7.

Gordon, R. (2012) 'Re-thinking and re-tooling the social marketing mix', *Australasian Marketing Journal*, 20 (2): 122–126.

Grönroos, C. (2007) *Service Management and Marketing: Customer Management in Service Competition* (3rd edn). Chichester: John Wiley and Sons.

Kietzmann, J.H., Hermkens, K., McCarthy, I.P. and Silvestre, B.S. (2011) 'Social media? Get serious! Understanding the functional building blocks of social media', *Business Horizons*, 54 (3): 241–251.

McKie, D. and Toledano, M. (2008) 'Dangerous liaison or perfect match? Public relations and social marketing', *Public Relations Review*, 34 (4): 318–324.

Peattie, S. and Peattie, K. (2003) 'Ready to fly solo: reducing social marketing's reliance of commercial marketing theory', *Marketing Theory*, 3 (3): 365–385.

Russell-Bennett, R., Wood, M. and Previte, J. (2013) 'Fresh ideas: services thinking for social marketing', *Journal of Social Marketing*, 3 (3): 223–238.

References

Aaker, D.A. (1996) 'Measuring brand equity across products and markets', *California Management Review*, 38 (3): 102–120.

Aaker, J.L. (1997) 'Dimensions of brand personality', *Journal of Marketing Research*, 34 (3): 347–356.

American Legacy Foundation (2014) Truth Brand Logo. Available at: www.thetruth.com (last accessed 10 March 2014).

Andreasen, A.R. (2002) 'Marketing social marketing in the social change marketplace', *Journal of Public Policy and Marketing*, 21 (1): 3–13.

Andreasen, A.R. (2006) *Social Marketing in the 21st Century*. Thousand Oaks, CA: SAGE.

Arndt, J. (1980) 'Perspectives for a theory on marketing', *Journal of Business Research*, 9 (3): 389–402.

Asbury, L.D., Wong, F.L., Price, S.M. and Nolin, M.J. (2008) 'The VERB™ campaign: applying a branding strategy in public health', *American Journal of Preventive Medicine*, 35 (6): S183–S187.

Benham, R. (2012) Montage of Change4life images. Available at: www.nhs.uk/Change4Life/Pages/what-is-change-for-life.aspx (last accessed 15 August 2014).

Bernhardt, J., Mays, D. and Hall, A.K. (2012) 'Social marketing and the right place and right time with new media', *Journal of Social Marketing*, 2 (2): 130–137.

BMA Board of Science (2009) *Under the Influence: The Damaging Effect of Alcohol Marketing on Young People*. London: British Medical Association.

Booms, B.H. and Bitner, M.J. (1981) 'Marketing strategies and organization structures for service firms', in J.H. Donnelly and W.R. George (eds), *Marketing of Services*. Chicago, IL: American Marketing Association, pp. 47–51.

Borden, N.H. (1964) 'The concept of the marketing mix', *Journal of Advertising Research*, 4 (2): 2–7.

Brownson, R.C., Smith, C.A., Pratt, M., Nilsa, E.M., Jackson-Thompson, J., Dean, C.G., Dabney, S. and Wilkerson, J.C. (1996) 'Preventing cardiovascular disease through community based risk reduction: the Bootheel Heart Health Project', *American Journal of Public Health*, 86 (2): 206–213.

Centers for Disease Control and Prevention (2014) VERB Brand Logo. Available at: www.cdc.gov/verb/ (last accessed 1 March 2010).

Chapman, S. (2001) 'Tobacco control advocacy in Australia: reflections on 30 years of progress', *Health Education and Behavior*, 28 (3): 274–289.

Chapman, S. (2007) *Public Health Advocacy and Tobacco Control: Making Smoking History*. London: Wiley-Blackwell.

Cohen, D., de la Vega, R. and Watson, G. (2001) *Advocacy for Social Justice*. Bloomfield, CT: Kumarian Press.

Cowell, D.W. (1994) 'Marketing of services', in M. Baker (ed.), *The Marketing Book* (3rd edn). Oxford: Butterworth Heinemann, pp. 456–466.

Culliton, J.W. (1948). *The Management of Marketing Costs, Division of Research, Graduate School of Business Administration*. Boston, MA: Harvard University.

Dahl, D.W., Gorn, G.J. and Weinberg, C.B. (1997) 'Marketing, safer sex and condom acquisition', in M.E. Goldberg, M. Fishbein and S.E. Middlestadt (eds), *Social Marketing: Theoretical and Practical Perspectives*. Mahwah, NJ: Lawrence Erlbaum Associates, pp. 169–185.

de Chernatony, L. (1993) 'Categorizing brands: evolutionary processes underpinned by two key dimensions', *Journal of Marketing Management*, 9 (2): 173–188.

Desai, D. (2009) 'Role of relationship management and value co-creation in social marketing', *Social Marketing Quarterly*, 15 (4): 112–125.

Dev, C.S. and Schultz, D.E. (2005a) 'A customer focused approach can bring the current marketing mix into the 21st century', *Marketing Management*, 14 (1): 18–24.

Dev, C.S. and Schultz, D.E. (2005b) 'Simply SIVA', *Marketing Management*, 14 (2): 36–41.

Domegan, C.T. (2008) 'Social marketing: implications for contemporary marketing practices classification scheme', *Journal of Business and Industrial Marketing*, 23 (2): 135–41.

Dooley, J.A., Jones, S.C. and Iverson, D. (2012) 'Web 2.0: an assessment of social marketing principles', *Journal of Social Marketing*, 2 (3): 207–221.

Dooley, J.A., Jones, S.C. and Iverson, D. (2014) 'Using Web 2.0 for health promotion and social marketing efforts: lessons learned from Web 2.0 expert', *Health Marketing Quarterly*, 31 (2): 178–196.

Doyle, P. (2000) *Value Based Marketing*. Chichester: Wiley.

Dutta, S. and Kanungo, R.N. (1975) *Affect and Memory*. New York: Pergamon Press.

Eadie, D. and MacAskill, S. (2008) 'Symptom awareness and cancer prevention: exploratory findings from an at-risk population', *Health Education*, 108 (4): 332–345.

Eagle, L., Dahl, S., Hill, S., Bird, S., Spotswood, F. and Tapp, A. (2013) *Social Marketing*. London: Pearson.

Evans, W.D. and Hastings, G. (eds) (2008) *Public Health Branding: Applying Marketing for Social Change*. Oxford: Oxford University Press.

Evans, W.D., Price, S. and Blahut, S. (2005) 'Evaluating the truth® brand', *Journal of Health Communication*, 10 (2): 181–192.

Farrelly, M.C., Davis, K.C., Haviland, M.L., Messeri, P. and Healton, C.G. (2005) 'Evidence of a dose–response relationship between "truth" antismoking ads and youth smoking prevalence', *American Journal of Public Health*, 95 (3): 425–431.

Fischer, P.M., Schwartz, M.P., Richards, J.W. Jr, Goldstein, A.O. and Rojas, T.H. (1991) 'Brand logo recognition by children aged 3 to 6 years: Mickey Mouse and Old Joe the Camel', *Journal of the American Medical Association*, 266 (22): 3145–3148.

Fitzgerald, J. (2006) *Lobbying in Australia: You Can't Expect Anything to Change If You Don't Speak Up*. Kenthurst: Rosenberg.

Freling, T.H., Crosno, J.L. and Henard, D.H. (2011) 'Brand personality appeal: conceptualization and empirical validation', *Journal of the Academy of Marketing Science*, 39 (3): 392–406.

French, J. (2011) 'Why nudging is not enough', *Journal of Social Marketing*, 1 (2): 154–162.

French, J., Blair-Stevens, C., McVey, D. and Merritt, R. (eds) (2010) *Social Marketing and Public Health: Theory and Practice*. Oxford: Oxford University Press.

Gordon, R. (2011) 'Critical social marketing: assessing the cumulative impact of alcohol marketing on youth drinking', PhD thesis. Stirling: University of Stirling. Available at: https://dspace.stir.ac.uk/bitstream/1893/3135/1/Ross%20Gordon%20PhD%20FINAL%20SUBMITTED.pdf (last accessed 12 August 2014).

Gordon, R. (2012) 'Re-thinking and re-tooling the social marketing mix', *Australasian Marketing Journal*, 20 (2): 122–126.

Gordon, R. (2013) 'Unlocking the potential of upstream social marketing', *European Journal of Marketing*, 47 (9): 1525–1547.

Gordon, R., Hastings, G., McDermott, L. and Evans, D.W. (2008) 'Building brands with competitive analysis', in D.W. Evans and G. Hastings (eds), *Public Health Branding: Applying Marketing for Social Change*. Oxford: Oxford University Press, pp. 73–90.

Gordon, R., Zainuddin, N. and Powell, S. (2013) *Unlocking the Potential of Branding in Social Marketing*. World Social Marketing Conference, Toronto, April.

Grönroos, C. (1989) 'Defining marketing: a market-oriented approach', *European Journal of Marketing*, 23 (1): 52–60.

Grönroos, C. (1994) 'From marketing mix to relationship marketing: towards a paradigm shift in marketing', *Management Decision*, 32 (2): 4–20.

Grönroos, C. (2013) 'Forward', in R. Fisk, R. Russell-Bennett and L. Harris (eds), *Serving Customers: Global Services Marketing Perspectives*. Melbourne: Tilde University Press, pp. ix–xiii.

Grunig, J.E. and Hunt, T. (1984). *Managing Public Relations* (6th edn). Orlando, FL: Harcourt Brace Jovanovich.

Guens, M., Weijters, B. and De Wulf, K. (2009) 'A new measure of brand personality', *International Journal of Research in Marketing*, 26 (2): 97–107.

Hagger, M.S., Lonsdale, A.J., Baggott, R., Penny, G. and Bowen, M. (2011) *The Cost of Alcohol: The Advocacy for a Minimum Unit Price Per Unit in the UK*. Nottingham: University of Nottingham.

Harris, F., Gordon, R., MacKintosh, A.M. and Hastings, G. (forthcoming) 'Consumer socialization and the role of branding in adolescent drinking', *Psychology and Marketing*.

Hastings, G. (2003) 'Relational paradigms in social marketing', *Journal of Macromarketing*, 23 (1): 6–15.

Hastings, G. (2007) *Social Marketing: Why Should the Devil Have All the Best Tunes?* London: Butterworth-Heinemann.

Hastings, G. and Domegan, C. (2014) *Social Marketing: From Tunes to Symphonies* (2nd edn). London: Routledge.

Huhman, M. (2008) 'New media and the VERB campaign: tools to motivate tweens to be physically active', *Cases in Public Health Communication and Marketing*, 2: 126–139.

Huhman, M.E., Potter, L.D., Duke, J.C., Judkins, D.R., Heitzler, C.D. and Wong, F.L. (2007) 'Evaluation of a national physical activity intervention for children: the VERB™ campaign 2002–2004', *American Journal of Preventive Medicine*, 32 (1): 38–43.

Janiszewski, C. and van Osselaer, S. (2000) 'A connectionist model of brand quality associations', *Journal of Marketing Research*, 37 (3): 331–350.

Johnston, J. (2008) *Media Relations: Issues and Strategies*. Sydney: Allen and Unwin Academic.

Kapferer, J.N. (2012) *The New Strategic Brand Management: Advanced Insights and Strategic Thinking* (5th edn). London: Kogan Page.

Kietzmann, J.H., Hermkens, K., McCarthy, I.P. and Silvestre, B.S (2011) 'Social media? Get serious! Understanding the functional building blocks of social media', *Business Horizons*, 54 (3): 241–251.

Kotler, P. (1967) *Marketing Management: Analysis, Planning and Control*. Englewood Cliffs, NJ: Prentice Hall.

Kotler, P., Armstrong, G., Saunders, J. and Wong, V. (1999) *Principles of Marketing* (2nd European edn). London: Prentice Hall.

Kotler, P. and Zaltman, G. (1971) 'Social marketing: an approach to planned social change', *Journal of Marketing*, 35 (3): 3–12.

Lauterborn, B. (1990) 'New Marketing Litany: Four Ps passé: C-words take over', *Advertising Age*, 61 (41): 26.

Lee, N. and Kotler, P. (2011) *Social Marketing: Influencing Behaviours for Good*. New York: SAGE.

Lefebvre, R.C. (2012) 'Transformative social marketing: co-creating the social marketing discipline and brand', *Journal of Social Marketing*, 2 (2): 118–129.

MacFadyen, L., Stead, M. and Hastings, G.B. (2003) 'Social marketing', in M.J. Baker (ed.), *The Marketing Book* (5th edn). Oxford: Butterworth-Heinemann, pp. 694–725.

Mackay, J.M., Bettcher, D.W., Minhas, R. and Schotte, K. (2012) 'Successes and new emerging challenges in tobacco control: addressing the vector', *Tobacco Control*, 21 (2): 77–79.

Macnamara, J. (2012) *Public Relations: Theories, Practices, Critiques*. French's Forest: Pearson.

McCarthy, E.J. (1960) *Basic marketing: a managerial approach*. Homewood: Irwin.

McDivitt, J. (2003) 'Is there a role for branding in social marketing?' *Social Marketing Quarterly*, 9 (3): 11–17.

McGrath, J. (1995) 'The gatekeeping process: the right combinations to unlock the gates', in E. Maibach and R.C. Parrott (eds), *Designing Health Messages: Approaches from Communication Theory and Public Health Practice*. Thousand Oaks, CA: SAGE, pp. 199–217.

McKenzie-Mohr, D. (2011) *Fostering Sustainable Behavior: An Introduction to Community-based Social Marketing* (3rd edn). Gabriola Island, Canada: New Society Publishers.

McKie, D. and Toledano, M. (2008) 'Dangerous liaison or perfect match? Public relations and social marketing', *Public Relations Review*, 34 (4): 318–324.

Obar, J.A., Zube, P. and Lampe, C. (2012) 'Advocacy 2.0: an analysis of how advocacy groups in the United States perceive and use social media as tools for facilitating civic engagement and collective action', *Journal of Information Policy*, 2: 1–25.

Peattie, S. and Peattie, K. (2003) 'Ready to fly solo: reducing social marketing's reliance of commercial marketing theory', *Marketing Theory*, 3 (3): 365–385.

PRSA (Public Relations Society of America) (2012) *What Is Public Relations? PRSA's Widely Accepted Definition*. PRSA: New York. Available at: www.prsa.org/aboutprsa/publicrelationsdefined/ (last accessed 14 August 2014).

Rafiq, M. and Ahmed, P. K. (1995) 'Using the 7Ps as a generic marketing mix: an exploratory survey of UK and European marketing academics', *Marketing Intelligence and Planning*, 13 (9), 4–15.

Rangun, V.K., Karim, S. and Sandberg, S.K. (1996) 'Do better at doing good', *Harvard Business Review*, 81 (12): 46–54.

Ray, M.L. and Batra, R. (1983) 'Emotion and persuasion in advertising: what we do and don't know about affect', in R.P. Bagozzi and A.M. Tybout (eds), *Advances in Consumer Research*. Ann Arbor, MI: Association for Consumer Research, pp. 543–548.

Russell-Bennett, R., Wood, M. and Previte, J. (2013) 'Fresh ideas: services thinking for social marketing', *Journal of Social Marketing*, 3 (3): 223–238.

Schembri, S. (2009) 'Reframing brand experience: the experiential meaning of Harley-Davidson', *Journal of Business Research*, 62 (12): 1299–1310.

Seitel, Fraser P. (2007) *The Practice of Public Relations* (10th edn). Upper Saddle River, NJ: Pearson/Prentice Hall.

Shizimu, K. (1973) *Symbiotic Marketing Strategy*. Japan: Souseisha Book Company.

Sirgy, J.M. (1982) 'Self-concept in consumer behaviour: a critical review', *Journal of Consumer Research*, 9 (3): 287–300.

Smith, A.M. and O'Sullivan, T. (2012) 'Environmentally responsible behaviour in the workplace: an internal social marketing approach', *Journal of Marketing Management*, 28 (3–4): 469–493.

Solis, B. and Thomas, J. (2014) *The Conversation Prism*. Available at: https://conversationprism.com/ (last accessed 16 August 2014).

Stead, M., Gordon, R., Angus, K. and McDermott, L. (2007) 'A systematic review of social marketing effectiveness', *Health Education*, 107 (2): 126–140.

Stead, M., Hastings, G.B. and Eadie, D. (2002) 'The challenge of evaluating complex interventions: a framework for evaluating media advocacy', *Health Education Research Theory and Practice*, 17 (3), 351–364.

Tapp, A. and Spotswood, F. (2013) 'From the 4Ps to COM-SM: reconfiguring the social marketing mix', *Journal of Social Marketing*, 3 (3): 206–222.

Taubenheim, A.M., Long, T., Smith, E.C., Jeffers, D., Wayman, J. and Temple, S. (2008) 'Using social media and internet marketing to reach women with the heart truth', *Social Marketing Quarterly*, 14 (3): 58–67.

Thackeray, R., Nieger, B.L. and Keller, H. (2012) 'Integrating social media and social marketing: a four step process', *Health Promotion Practice*, 13 (2): 165–168.

Vargo, S. and Lusch, R. (2004) 'Evolving to a new dominant logic for marketing', *Journal of Marketing*, 68 (1): 1–17.

Wakefield, M.A., Loken, B. and Hornik, R.C. (2010) 'Use of mass media campaigns to change health behaviour', *The Lancet*, 376 (9748): 1261–1271.

Wallack, L., Dorfman, L., Jernigan, D. and Themba, M. (1993) *Media Advocacy and Public Health*. Newbury Park, CA: SAGE.

Waltzer, H. (1988) 'Corporate advocacy advertising and political influence', *Public Relations Review*, 14 (1): 41–55.

Zainuddin, N., Previte, J. and Russell-Bennett, R. (2011) 'A social marketing approach to value creation in a well-women's health service', *Journal of Marketing Management*, 27 (3–4): 361–385.

Zainuddin, N., Russell-Bennett, R. and Previte, J. (2013) 'The value of health and wellbeing: an empirical model of value creation in social marketing', *European Journal of Marketing*, 47 (9): 1504–1524.

5 STRATEGIC SOCIAL MARKETING

Learning objectives

By the end of this chapter, readers should be able to:

- understand the nature and components of strategic planning within the context of social programme design
- describe, identify and define the contribution and added value that social marketing can make to the development of social programmes aimed at influencing behaviour
- give examples about how social marketing can help to optimise the selection and delivery of social programmes in terms of their effectiveness and efficiency.

Introduction

Marketing in the commercial sector is not solely about creating demand for products and services that people do not necessarily need or want. As we have discussed so far in this book, contemporary marketing is often focused on value creation, service delivery, brand loyalty and relationship building – delivered and facilitated through a process of mutually beneficial exchange. These core marketing principles are ones that can be used to positive effect in the not-for-profit and social programme sectors. For those interested in advocating the use of marketing in the governmental and wider not-for-profit sectors, these principles also have the potential to enhance the development and delivery of more effective and efficient social interventions. However, this revolution in contemporary commercial marketing thought and practice has hardly been reflected in any social marketing textbooks or programmes to date. Many books still advocate a model of social marketing that is based on marketing theory and practice that date back to McCarthy's (1960) ancient and outmoded 4Ps model (Eagle et al., 2013; Hastings and Domegan, 2014; see Chapter 4 for a fuller review of the social marketing mix).

As discussed in Chapter 2, much of social marketing practice and many practitioners are stuck in the past, using a limited and limiting set of principles and conceptual tools to analyse, develop, implement and evaluate social challenges. This problem is further magnified by the fact that the vast majority of social marketing effort to date has been focused on downstream or tactical project delivery rather than on influencing upstream social policy. This limited approach together with a status quo bias in favour of existing approaches to social policy development, which does not recognise the potential contribution from marketing, has resulted in social marketing being confined to a largely tactical role within social policy delivery. However, academics and practitioners have begun to advocate that social marketing should go beyond just a focus on developing effective social behavioural interventions to embrace and make a contribution to social policy selection and development. Social marketing, it is argued, has a bigger contribution to make to informing and shaping the overall policy and strategic planning of social programmes aimed at making a positive impact on social, cultural and economic problems (Dann, 2006; Lee and Kotler, 2011). This argument has been characterised by calls to focus upstream on developing strategies that tackle the casual conditions of social problems, and ensuring the development of more comprehensive and coordinated intervention programmes (Gordon, 2013) rather than just focusing on downstream responses delivered through operational projects and campaigns. The complex challenges faced by countries around the world, ranging from infectious and chronic diseases, aging populations and water shortages, to global warming and economic, social and cultural inequality, will not be fixed by short-term project interventions alone. What is required is long-term, sustained and coordinated action focused on unambiguous measurable goals. This implies the need for a more strategic approach to social programme selection, coordination and delivery, a process that can be greatly enhanced by the application of social marketing principles, concepts and techniques.

Social marketing is essentially 'focused on developing and applying marketing principles, concepts and techniques to create value for society and individuals through the integration of research, evidence and theory' (iSMA, ESMA and AASM, 2013). Strategic social marketing has the potential then to be used to select and implement behavioural interventions aimed not only at citizens but also at politicians, policy makers, community leaders and organisations. Social marketing can assist overall policy selection and strategy development by influencing the selection and mix of interventions that might be applied in tackling any given social behavioural challenge by ensuring that understanding about citizens' views, beliefs and needs has a direct impact on which interventions are selected and how they are delivered. Social marketing, just like marketing in the for-profit sector, has a contribution to make to the process of strategy review, analysis and formulation.

Defining marketing strategy

There are many reasons why organisations tend to avoid or at least not fully adopt a strategic approach to defining their priorities, understanding their operating environment and developing coherent integrated interventions to deliver their identified organisational or social goals. Bowman (1990) has identified seven reasons why organisations in both the for-profit and not-for-profit sectors do not tend to apply strategic thinking and analysis:

1. Lack of awareness about the true situation of the organisation.
2. Senior management delude themselves about the organisation's position.
3. Some managers have vested interests in sticking with the status quo.
4. Managers get locked into operational problem solving and management.
5. Past success can make people blind to current or future threats and opportunities.
6. Changing direction can be seen as an admission that what was done before was a mistake.
7. Lack of awareness within senior management about quite why the organisation is successful.

All of these reasons can individually or collectively conspire to reduce strategic thinking, management and planning.

There is no single, universally accepted definition of marketing strategy. Strategy is a contested concept but it is mainly viewed (Wensley, 2003) as a process that is focused on agreeing a clear mission and set of objectives for an organisation that is then, via a set of analytical steps, developed into a short-, medium- and long-term intervention plan informed by evidence and data. Strategy typically consists of three main clusters of actions and decisions, as depicted in Figure 5.1.

First is the process of strategic analysis to understand the operating environment and internal capabilities and goals of the organisation, next comes a set of choice processes to select the most appropriate strategic approach, and finally strategy also involves the development, execution, coordination and review of the strategy. All three of these tasks are iterative in nature rather than being undertaken in a simple mechanistic linear fashion.

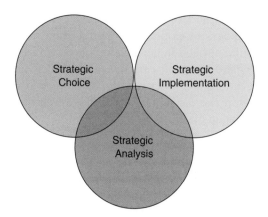

Figure 5.1   The three key strategy processes

In terms of implementation, strategy can also be seen as the process of developing a detailed plan for achieving the stated goals of the organisation, in a social programme context this might be the eradication of absolute poverty or the attainment of a certain level of youth employment. Strategy can also be viewed as a stream of significant decisions taken over time that are focused on the development of a consistent approach to achieving an organisational or social objective.

As Kotler and Armstrong (2008: 29) state, strategic planning sets the stage for the rest of the planning:

> We define strategic planning as the process of developing and maintaining a strategic fit between the organisation's goals and capabilities and its changing opportunities. It relies on developing a clear company mission, supporting objectives, a sound business portfolio and coordinated functional strategies.

Marketing strategy starts with articulating business goals, or in the case of social programmes, the social mission and goals that are to be achieved. Critically this involves decisions about which business to be in, or when focused on social issues which social issues to focus on.

In the case of social challenge a key strategic choice involves decisions about which social problems are capable of being influenced, their relative priority and to what extent effective, sustainable and affordable interventions exist. The next stage in the strategy process is the generation and selection of the optimal mix of methods to achieve these goals.

A key part of the marketing strategy process is an assessment of external environments and trends and internal organisational strengths and weaknesses. Strategy also considers an organisation's ability to develop and take advantage of market or social opportunities or respond to existing or probable threats. Marketing strategy is a continuous process that runs over the long term. However, it also is influenced by and influences short- and medium-term planning and delivery cycles. Marketing strategy in the commercial sector is essentially about ensuring a continued competitive advantage; in the social sector marketing strategy is about ensuring an optimal impact and return on investment related to specific social challenges.

Marketing strategy consists of the seven sets of actions depicted in Table 5.1. For more details on each of these steps see Chapter 11. Strategy is not something that is developed and then set on a shelf while delivery takes over. Rather strategy is an iterative process of reflection focused on ensuring that the right goals and objectives are being pursued and the right mix of interventions and tactics is deployed to deliver the goals that have been agreed.

Table 5.1   The seven strategic processes

---

1. Determine the mission, aims and objectives of the social programme.
2. Analyse the current intervention strategy and assess its strengths and weaknesses.
3. Assess current and future external and internal threats and opportunities.
4. Generate new options, analyse each against conclusions from internal and external analysis and mission goals and objectives.
5. Agree the criteria and apply those for selecting any new strategy.
6. Summarise the results of analysis and conclusions and articulate a new strategy.
7. Plan and deliver the new strategy through selected operational and tactical approaches.

As stated above, strategy is a continuous process rooted in the gathering and feedback of data about the success or failure of the mix of interventions deployed to achieve the strategy. These seven processes can also be thought of as a cyclical process involving feedback and iterative development, as set out in Figure 5.2.

The strategic mindset

Strategy is essentially about future-proofing organisations and allowing them to prepare and be ready for unfolding new challenges, threats and opportunities. In the case of social programmes being able to predict, spot and develop plans to prevent harm associated with trends such as a massive growth in dementia or the adverse consequences of food insecurity, this enables responsible organisations to put in place strategies that perform better than ones based on a reactive response.

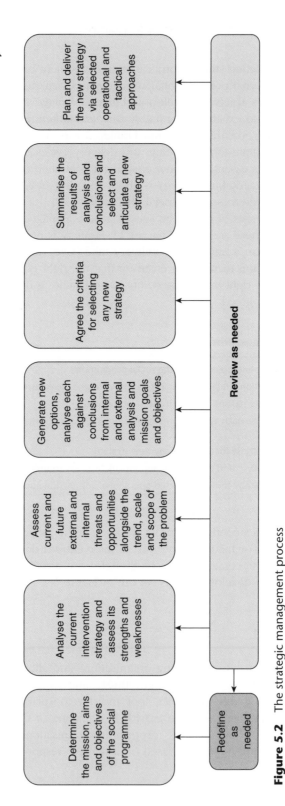

Figure 5.2 The strategic management process

Source: adapted from Thompson and Strickland, 1993

Just like strategic marketing there is no single definition of what constitutes strategic thinking or what characteristics and competencies can be observed as representing strategic thinking (Hussey, 2001). What is agreed by many marketing experts is that strategy is more than just the formulaic application of a set of standardised processes (Chussil, 2005). Strategy, it is argued, is more about responsive, critical and creative problem solving, augmented by a number of systematic processes for analysing and making decisions about the optimum strategy that should be selected and delivered. McKeown (2011) makes the point that what is needed are strategic thinkers who can accurately assess future trends, as well as existing circumstances, and develop new and creative strategies that do not simply react to environmental conditions or social challenges but rather aim to proactively shape such future environments and challenges. However, according to Johnson and Scholes (1989) there are a number of characteristics associated with strategic thinking and decision making, and these include the following:

- A focus on the scope of an organisation's activities.
- Matching the activities of an organisation to the environment in which it operates.
- Seeking to match the organisation's activities to its resource capability.
- Consideration of the resource implications of various potential strategies for an organisation.
- Strategic decisions are likely to affect operational decisions, and set off waves of lesser decisions.
- Strategy will be affected not only by environmental forces and resource availability, but also by the values and expectations of those who have power in and around the organisation.
- Strategic decisions are likely to affect the long-term direction of an organisation.

The development of organisational strategy is closely linked in the commercial sector to the development of its marketing strategy. As discussed above, strategy consists of three major tasks; strategic analysis, strategic decision making and strategic implementation. All of these tasks have a number of specific elements such as competition and SWOT (strengths, weaknesses, opportunities and threats) analysis. These processes are set out in Chapter 11 alongside their relevance and application as part of a social marketing approach. Strategy development is an iterative process primarily concerned with ensuring in the for-profit sector that companies continue to thrive in new circumstances. In the social policy arena strategy is focused on the development of programmes that will be capable of tackling both existing and future threats to health and wellbeing in the most cost effective and publically acceptable way.

———— Discussion question ————

Consider the organisation where you work or an organisation that you know. How strategic is it in terms of applying the seven strategic processes set out above?

Defining strategic social marketing

Before the full potential of social marketing can be realised in the development and implementation of social policy it needs to be acknowledged that there is still a major under-utilisation and misinterpretation of marketing and social marketing by many governments and not-for-profit institutions. Social marketing is often viewed as a second order task in many public sector policy and strategy development circles. So before social marketing can bring value to the policy table it is necessary to consider how it can best be embedded into the policy making and strategy development process. Chapter 13 is focused on how this can be achieved.

Without an acceptance of the added value of applying the concepts, principles and techniques of social marketing, the social marketer is forever playing a game of peripheral influence and disconnected project delivery. While it is not a bad thing to attempt to convince organisations on a project-by-project basis to apply a social marketing approach, this is a recipe for getting stuck in a reactive or 'add on' mode of operation. The probable impact of such an approach is that the potential of social marketing's contribution to social policy and strategy delivery will be greatly diminished.

The case for applying strategic social marketing, as defined in this book, is not new, as others have called for such an approach and described it in terms of macro-social marketing (Domegan, 2008; Wymer, 2011; Kenny and Parsons, 2012) and upstream social marketing (Stead et al., 2007). In essence all these authors and many others make the case for applying a more strategic approach and moving beyond social marketing being viewed as a second order operational delivery component to being seen as a core part of all social policy and strategy.

A strategic social marketing approach is focused on both the selection of which social changes to address and shaping the nature of the social policy and subsequent strategy as well as making a contribution to the coordination and evaluation of operational delivery. Much of the social marketing literature and examples of practice currently lie at the 'operational social marketing' end of the spectrum, where social marketing programmes or campaigns are developed to address specific topics, such as condom use or water conservation. A strategic social marketing approach, in contrast, needs to be developed to look at ways in which a stronger citizen understanding and insight approach, aligned with more strategic audience segmentation work and whole systems planning, can inform issue selection, policy development and strategic planning. As Craig Lefebvre (2008: 12) suggested:

> We need social marketers to be at the policy table when options are being discussed and presented, not just sat at the side-lines. There are glimmers visible of people in policy areas asking for social marketing viewpoints for policy analysis and creation stages. We need to ensure they know and understand the social marketing viewpoint – be part of the discussions. This is about having an upstream focus, not just advising for the policy status. Change needs to be part of the discussion.

A key challenge for social marketing then is to focus upstream to influence policy that in turn can impact on factors that affect people's behaviour such as fiscal policy, food policy and transport policy.

Lazer (2013: 329–330) has stated in a recent reappraisal of his famous article 'Marketing's changing social relationships' (1969) that:

> Social marketing is more than a technology or a set of problem solving tools. It is more than the marketing of social programmes ... social marketing views marketing activities through social lenses just as previous marketing approaches utilized institutional, commodity and functional lenses. As the 1969 article noted marketing is indeed a key element in understanding and influencing lifestyles around the world.

A clarity of focus on what social issues to target at government and other social resources is key to the development and implementation of effective government and broader social policy. As Osborne and Gaebler (1992) have argued for many years one of the most important aspects of effective social policy delivery is a focus on selecting the right mission or, as they call it, 'mission driven government' rather than bureaucratic government. Social marketing has a role to play in ensuring not only that social programmes are effective and efficient but also that the right social challenges and intervention programmes are selected in the first place. The selection of those social challenges where there is both a good chance of success and a reasonable return on investment sits at the heart of the added value of what social marketing can bring to the social policy selection and development process. In essence strategic social marketing seeks to influence corporate level strategy that in the private sector would be focused on the question 'What business should we be in and how do we manage it?' When considering social programmes the question can be reframed as 'What social issue is key and how do we tackle it?'

Andreasen (1995) first wrote about strategic social marketing and defined it as 'A strategy is the broad approach that an organisation takes to achieve its objectives'. Andreasen lists 'Six key stages that make up the strategic social marketing task':

1. Listening.
2. Planning.
3. Structuring (establishing a marketing organisation, procedures, etc.).
4. Pre-testing.
5. Implementing.
6. Monitoring.

Andreasen goes on to set these six tasks out in a continuous cycle of progressive reflection. He also states that there are two key features of the strategic process: first the process is continuous and second the 'customers are central'. By customers Andreasen means citizens who are to be influenced in terms of their attitudes, knowledge or behaviour. In Andreasen's view strategic social marketing is essentially a planning process designed to ensure that effective programmes are developed. Andreasen does not consider the application of social marketing principles to the development of wider social issue selection and policy development; however, in later works he does stress the potential contribution of social marketing to these tasks (Andreasen, 2006).

The authors of this volume believe that the strategic social marketing process is not confined to ensuring that social marketing programmes and projects are systematically constructed with long- as well as short-term perspectives as advocated by Andreasen. The real added value of applying social marketing in a strategic as well as an operational way to the selection of social issues and the development of policy and strategy flows from the application of marketing principles in informing the development of an organisation's overall mission and goals, reviewing its operating core and environment, and developing and selecting the right mix of interventions that may or may not involve direct marketing activity to bring about positive social development.

In this sense social marketing is not seen as a discreet, standalone activity that sits alongside other approaches to policy development and implementation. Rather strategic social marketing is concerned with making a contribution to all social policy development regardless of any direct marketing activity that may be associated within it. Conceived in this way strategic social marketing can be defined as:

> The systemic, critical and reflexive application of social marketing principals to enhance social policy selection, objective setting, planning and operational delivery.

As can be inferred from the above definition, strategic social marketing is concerned with informing policy selection, development and strategic goal setting, selecting effective interventions, assisting with the process of determining how success will be measured and ensuring that the mix of interventions selected is managed and coordinated.

Social marketing also has a critical role to play in ensuring that understanding and insights about the beliefs, values and needs of target groups for any social intervention, such as citizens, community leaders, politicians and professionals, are captured, analysed and fed into the policy selection and development process. The added value of applying a social marketing approach to social policy selection and development is directly related to its:

- strategic and operational focus on creating social value for communities and individuals, based on respect and a willingness to engage in the co-creation and delivery of solutions
- focus on mutuality, exchange and reciprocity as positive social goods in their own right and as key enablers of social development and more effective and efficient social programme delivery
- a reflexive learning orientation that encompasses both logical positivism and social reflexivity and takes account of social, economic, cultural and environmental influences on the human condition and behaviour.

It is helpful to think about social marketing influencing policy, strategy, tactics and operational delivery levels of social programmes, as depicted in Figure 5.3. In order to facilitate consistency of language we use the phrase 'strategic social marketing' to encompass the added value that social marketing can bring to all of these levels of social programme design. We use the term 'operational social marketing' to cover tactics and operational project management issues only. The overlap in the area of tactical selection is influenced by both the need for constancy with policy and strategic decisions and consideration of operational issues such as the skills and competences of the staff delivering the tactics selected.

The first and most important level is the selection and articulation of the social challenge. Adding value at this policy level is about informing decisions about which social challenge is to be tackled, what needs to be achieved and how success in terms of influencing behaviour and its causes will be defined and measured.

The second strategic level is focused on analysing internal capability and external factors, alongside evidence, data and trends related to the social challenge. The outcome of this second strategic level is the development and final selection of the optimum mix of interventions that meet agreed selection criteria and together form a credible array of interventions capable of having measurable impact on the social challenge selected.

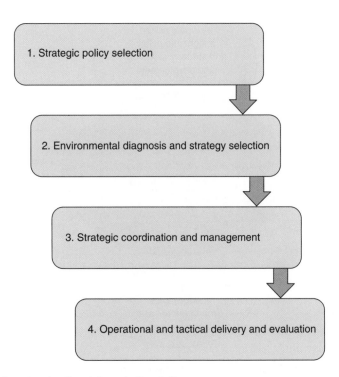

Figure 5.3 Four levels of social marketing influence

The third level of strategy is the development and coordination of the selected tactical intervention mix. At this level the key tasks are to ensure that all those responsible for delivering and evaluating the mix of interventions agreed are clear about their responsibilities and contribution to the strategy and that they have the capability and capacity including all necessary resources to deliver their part of the strategy.

The fourth level is related to operational management issues associated with delivery and review. At this level the focus is on the effective management, implementation, risk management and coordination of specific interventions and tracking the interventions' impact in support of the overall mission, aims and goals of a programme. Social marketing can and should be applied at all of these four strategic levels.

How social marketing adds value to social policy selection, development delivery and evaluation

Figure 5.4 sets out the four key contributions that social marketing can make within the social policy selection, development and implementation process.

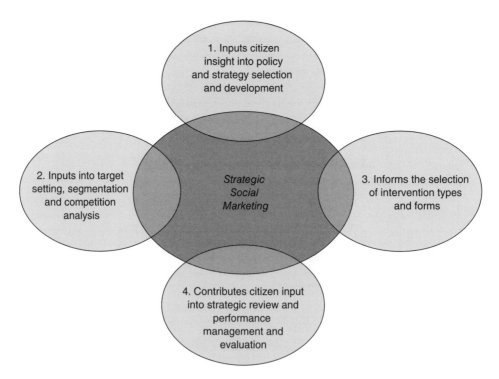

Figure 5.4 The contribution of social marketing to social policy selection and strategy development and implementation

Figure 5.4 illustrates how social marketing can help the social policy development and the strategy selection process. The input of citizens' views about what policy imperatives exist and how to prioritise among these is a process that most politicians use when developing their manifestoes. Social marketing can assist at this formulation stage but also with the refinement of political or other forms of public commitments into more developed working policy proposals. As indicated earlier in this chapter, one of the key weaknesses of many social policies is the lack of clear objectives and congruent behavioural evaluation targets. As illustrated in Figure 5.4, social marketing can assist with the collection and analysis of citizen understanding, views, needs and behaviour. Through this process social marketing can assist the development of achievable behavioural objectives using behavioural modelling and competition analysis based on theory, insight data, situational analysis, evidence and assessments of existing practice. Social marketing can help policy makers with the development of targeted intervention strategies consisting of the optimum mix of interventions. Social marketing also has a role to play in assisting with ongoing policy and strategy development through an impact evaluation and assessment of the return on social investment. Table 5.2 provides further examples about how social marketing can assist the social issue selection process and the policy and strategy development process.

All social marketing is centred on an approach to problem definition and solution generation that is built around understanding and creating value for citizens, rather than a process that is just dominated by expert narrative about what should be tackled

Table 5.2 How social marketing assists social issue selection, policy and strategy development

1. Setting clear, measurable policy objectives and targets.
2. Collection and analysis of citizen behaviour, and causes of behaviour, understanding views and needs about potential social behavioural challenges.
3. Situational and environmental analysis including, PESTLE (Political, Environmental, Social, Technological, Legal, Economic) and SWOT (Strengths, Weaknesses, Opportunities, Threats) and competition analysis.
4. Gathering citizens' views on the evidence regarding the acceptability, costs and value of possible policy and potential tactics to influence behaviour.
5. Stakeholder, partnership and assets analysis and management.
6. Informing programme design and highlighting potential intervention approaches based on theory and evidence reviews, user experience and feedback.
7. Development, prototyping and pre-testing of services, products, campaigns and other interventions.
8. Audience and stakeholder insight and segmentation development.
9. Understanding and formulating the most cost effective and acceptable mix of behavioural influence strategies and tactics.
10. Modelling and measuring impact, outcome costs and gains including ROI, VFM and cost-benefit analysis.

and how success should be delivered. A strategic approach also recognises that there are multiple 'types' and 'forms' of intervention that can be applied (see Chapters 3 and 4). Taking a strategic social marketing approach also recognises that action will be required to be directed at the causal conditions of social behaviours as well as the provision of direct support for individuals and families to assist them personally to adopt or sustain positive social behaviours.

A strategic approach to social marketing is built on the foundations of research, data, evidence and target group insight and environmental scanning, which includes competition, stakeholder and environmental analysis. A strategic approach to social marketing is informed by theory that includes both marketing theory and theory from other related and relevant fields focused on the human condition and behaviour, such as behavioural economics, sociology, psychology and anthropology. A strategic social marketing approach is fundamentally defined by its systematic, transparent analytic processes together with a pragmatic assessment of the political and social acceptability of potential social policy initiatives. At its core strategic social marketing seeks to influence social policy selection, development and programme delivery to reflect citizens' wants, needs and values.

Social marketing can be used in this way to ensure that understanding about participants' behaviour and preferences directly informs the identification and selection of appropriate social issues, policy and interventions.

Any social policy seeking to influence citizen behaviour that does not have the broad support of the public and does not meet the needs of the target audiences is unlikely to be successful. There is a need then, if successful social programmes are to be developed, to engender a sense of ownership among the intended recipients. Delivering any social policy also needs the involvement of the widest possible coalition of interests if a sense of ownership is to be created and if all available expertise and resources are to be used to inform the development and delivery of the policy. Social marketing has a role to play in creating this sense of ownership and buy-in to social policies. Social marketing can also help politicians and public officials to test potential policies and refine them through a process of target audience engagement and consultation as well as through a process of market research. The use of focus groups, surveys, interviews, observational studies and other forms of gathering citizens' views can be a powerful tool for ensuring that policy and strategy are developed in such a way that they will be supported and taken up by those whom they are designed to help. However, such policy/strategy/intervention testing is still comparatively rare in many countries despite the obvious advantages to policy makers of testing and refining potential interventions using marketing research and marketing principles to engage and gather citizens' views. The application of this kind of citizen focused approach to the development and testing of policy and strategy will need to be use more often by governments and political parties to help them develop manifestoes and social programmes that carry popular support and are feasible.

CASE STUDY

Social marketing and the health policy development process in the United States

The dream of creating a national public health policy that both recognises and promotes social marketing in the United States began many years ago. It started in the 1980s when social marketing took on a central role in the design of two large community-based cardiovascular disease prevention programmes in Rhode Island and California. The work of the Pawtucket, RI Heart Health Program and the Stanford Five City Project was captured in one of the seminal social marketing and public health articles (Lefebvre and Flora, 1988). The authors established a key point – that social marketing provided a critical strategic planning framework for designing and implementing programmes aimed at achieving population-wide behaviour change (risk behaviour reduction).

During that same period, public health leaders began the process for creating national disease prevention and health promotion objectives for the next several decades, i.e. Healthy People 2000: Objectives for the Nation, where Crain Lefebvre participated as a reviewer of the initial set of objectives.

In essence, our objective was to encouraged public health policy makers to think 'big change', and not be satisfied with clinical encounters and small group programmes for behaviour change.

Over the following decade many local and state public health programmes embraced marketing and mass communications. Following on from this work the new Healthy People 2010 health strategy for the first time included a discussion and definition of social marketing: 'The application of marketing principles and techniques to program development, implementation, and evaluation to promote healthy behaviours or reduce risky ones' (United States Department of Health and Human Services, 2010).

However, the application of social marketing continued to be developed and deployed in a disjointed way. The major reasons appeared to be the reluctance of the Healthy People policy team to explicitly or implicitly endorse a social marketing approach to disease prevention and promotion over other methods. However, during the course of the next decade, this reluctance eased as the practice and evidence base for social marketing continued to grow. That process set the stage for the development of a specific Healthy People 2020 objective to increase the use of social marketing in health promotion and disease prevention programmes.

A new openness towards establishing a specific strategic social marketing objective by policy makers led to a group of social marketers working to develop

(Continued)

(Continued)

a consensus about what a formal social marketing objective or objectives might focus on in the new health strategy. Three major areas of agreement evolved: (1) objectives for using social marketing principles in federally funded public health programmes, (2) increasing access for current and future public health professionals to training opportunities in social marketing, and (3) promoting increased investments in applied prevention research and demonstration projects. The Healthy People policy work group and steering committee reviewed these objectives and encouraged further action to refine ideas. A revised set of objectives was developed and submitted for consideration:

- Increase the number of programmes that use evidence-based social marketing for health promotion and disease prevention.
- Increase undergraduate/graduate training in schools of public health.
- Increase continuing education for public health practitioners.
- Increase evidence-based research in prevention research centres and schools of public health, business and other related disciplines.

These objectives were made available for public comment. Robert J. Marshall and R. Craig Lefebvre orchestrated a concerted effort by social marketing advocates to promote these objectives among social marketers and others in the public health community. This work included extended personal outreach to officers in national public health organisations including the Association of State and Territorial Health Officers (ASTHO), the National Association of Chronic Disease Directors (NACDD), the National Public Health Information Coalition (NPHIC), the Society for Public Health Education (SOPHE) and others. These organisations, as well as many state health departments and individuals, submitted letters in support of the social marketing objectives. The comments included:

> We must address the critical need for social marketing as a 'gold standard' approach to planning and executing health communications.

> By adding an objective to HP2020 that specifically recognises social marketing, we will be able to spread the use of this paradigm and have a greater impact in improving the health of the public in the next decade.

> We believe that social marketing, along with the many other programmes, disciplines and professions already included in HP2020, will play an essential role over the next decade to create a healthier population at every phase of the lifespan. Please help us assure that the practice, training opportunities and research basis of social marketing continue to be a valued component of our national strategy.

The 'truth' is that social marketing is a successful tool in developing healthy people. Much sadness will be in the neglect of using what we have already learned from social marketing programmes. Please do not allow this to be an opportunity missed, include social marketing in the 2020 objectives.

Now is the time to take the lessons and evidence-based experience of the last decade (and longer) to recognise the key role that social marketing can play in achieving a healthier population.

Increase social marketing in health promotion and disease prevention.

1. Increase the proportion of state health departments that report using social marketing in health promotion and disease prevention programmes.
2. Increase the proportion of schools of public health and accredited MPH programmes that offer one or more courses in social marketing.
3. Increase the proportion of schools of public health and accredited MPH programmes that offer workforce development activities in social marketing for public health practitioners.

A final challenge was raised before these objectives could be accepted for inclusion in the new Healthy People 2020 strategy; namely, how would progress towards these objectives be measured, and what are their baselines? This led us to confer with colleagues at NPHIC and the Florida Prevention Research Centre (PRC) at the University of South Florida about how we might design and sustain surveys that could provide baseline, mid-decade and end-of-decade data points for each of the sub-objectives. Until such data could be provided, the objectives would be considered 'developmental' and subject to periodic reviews to determine if they would remain in Healthy People (i.e. was progress being made on measuring them?).

Fortunately, both NPHIC and the PRC agreed to identify resources, opportunities and sampling plans to make the baseline assessments happen. Briefly, the surveys documented that eight of the 50 state health departments surveyed reported using social marketing in at least one or more of their disease prevention and health promotion programmes. In a separate survey, four out of 50 schools of public health reported offering a graduate-level social marketing course, and six others offered a combined health communication/social marketing course. Only two schools offered any postgraduate professional education opportunities in social marketing (Biroscak et al., 2014).

With the availability of the new baseline data, the Federal Interagency Workgroup for National Health Objectives for 2020 reviewed and approved

(Continued)

(Continued)

proposed changes to objective a, which now reads: 'Increase the number ("proportion" in the earlier version) of state health departments that report using social marketing in health promotion and disease prevention pro-grammes'. The Workgroup also approved moving the objective from its previous 'developmental' status to a measurable one, and set the proposed target for 2020 to 50 (or all) state health departments.

Acknowledgements to Robert J. Marshall and R. Craig Lefebvre for this case study.

How social marketing can assist with policy coherence and integration

Social marketing is focused on creating social value and in so doing contributing to the development of social good. This can involve action to bring about behaviour change, but also action to influence social norms, change attitudes, change structural, systems and physical environments or the maintenance of positive behaviours/atti-tudes/norms/structures.

It is vital that social policy that seeks to influence social good is developed and implemented in a way that encourages coordinated contributions from all relevant agencies, stakeholders and partners, as well as citizens (see Chapter 7 on systems thinking and social marketing). Most behavioural challenges facing governments will require the development of delivery coalitions with private sector organisations and NGOs and citizens to ensure that sufficient weight of effort and resources can be brought to bear on the issue over a sustained period of time. A multi-faceted approach, where a number of sections of government or departments together with stakeholders and partners develop a joint vision of what they want to achieve, has a much higher chance of success than single initiatives developed in silos (Perri 6, 1997).

It is always critical to ensure policy coherence as there are numerous examples of programmes across government which have contradictory aims and objectives. For example, health departments encouraging vegetable consumption while at the same time agricultural departments remove subsidies for growing them. There is rarely a single intervention or remedy that can fix complex clusters of behavioural patterns in society. As we have learned from our experience with tobacco, it requires a prolonged commitment of skills and resources in a multi-setting, multi-factor, multi-strategy approach to achieve success (Ministry of Health Planning, 2003).

The most successful interventions in reducing smoking rates have involved com-binations of policies, including price increases, advertising restrictions, smoking site restrictions, consumer education and smoking cessation therapies (Goodman and Anise, 2006).

All successful behavioural programmes utilise a combination of strategies across government/NGOs/stakeholder organisations to achieve change. Part of this approach is the development of stakeholder coalitions. It is 'vital that any behaviour change programme should be developed in partnership with stakeholder organisations' (NICE, 2007). Working with external stakeholders can provide:

- useful insight into consumer behaviours – for example, the development of the obesity social marketing strategy in the UK involved many retail organisations who contributed valuable insight into the behaviours of key groups of consumers/target groups
- strategic advice and support within the wider political environment – often stakeholders circumnavigate the hierarchical processes of government by their direct access to ministers
- organisations close to the target group acting as 'main message givers' – for example, UK tobacco campaigns fronted by charities to avoid the perception of 'stop smoking', and in the Netherlands a 'Fat watch' campaign run in partnership with supermarkets and other private sector allies brought favourable changes in the consumption of saturated fats.

We know that in any area of policy where there is a strong knowledge base, and broad consensus about what to do, a high degree of central policy specification can work, so long as it focuses on a few key priorities. However, where there is less knowledge about what works, management by setting out broad policy objectives is more likely to succeed, leaving more freedom for front-line managers and staff to develop and test new approaches (Prime Minister's Strategy Unit, 2006).

We also know that involving practitioners in policy making and ensuring that their knowledge is used early in the policy development process will improve the efficiency and effectiveness of interventions. Both of these areas of policy understanding lend themselves to the application of social marketing with respect to setting agreed behavioural objectives and to engaging people and service delivery workers in the development of programmes of action. We also know that effective policy making results when horizontal networks are developed to assist in the capture and sharing of best practice (Prime Minister's Strategy Unit, 2006). Effective policy making involves the following eight characteristics:

1. Policy should be designed around outcomes.
2. Policy should be informed by end user wants and needs.
3. Policy should be, and be seen to be, inclusive and fair.
4. Policy should be evidence based.
5. Policy should avoid laying unnecessary burdens on delivery agencies or other sectors.

6. Policy making should involve all the relevant stakeholders.
7. Policy making should be forward and outward looking.
8. Policy should have systems in place to learn from experience.
   (Adapted from Mulgan and Lee, 2001 and Bullock et al., 2001)

This core policy making process is essentially about understanding the problem, the context and the stakeholders who are affected by the issue and who might be part of the solution, and then going on to develop solutions based on a deep understanding of the evidence and experience that exist. On the basis of this knowledge the next phase of the policy making process is to formulate and test possible interventions and combinations against agreed criteria and risks. Next follows the selection of strategies and agreeing achievable objectives and how they will be measured. As discussed above, social marketing concepts and principles can be used strategically to ensure that a strong citizen focus informs the identification and selection of appropriate issues and interventions to address them. Social marketing can also assist with all eight of the effective policy making characteristics listed above.

Developing policy that can have an impact on many of the big behavioural challenges faced by governments also requires simultaneous short-, medium- and long-term strategic planning centred on at least eight levels of action, as indicated in the policy matrix in Table 5.3 (French, 2011).

Table 5.3 Policy level and duration matrix

	Short (1–2 years)	Medium (2–5 years)	Medium to Long (5–10 years)	Long (>10 years)
Indvidual				
Group				
Community				
Locality				
Regional, State or Province				
National				
International Region (IE EU)				
Global				

Source: French, 2011

This framework demonstrates the need to develop policy and strategy spanning different levels of intervention and over differing time-frames. In addition to developing and sustaining a consistent and coherent policy there is a need for the policy to be supported by congruent strategies, programmes and projects. This requirement sets out considerable challenges for national governments and even more challenges for international organisations. It requires the development of a long-term vision and the tenacity to stick with it often over time-frames that span more than one political administration or ministerial term in office.

Given the nature of politics in democratic countries governments will change and policy directions will shift. However, to tackle complex social challenges, shift ingrained social norms and support behaviour change at a population level requires the development of a consensus about what the evidence and market research indicate is the correct strategy. This represents a challenge to politicians for it requires the building of as much cross-party consensus as possible. Such consensus is possible and has been achieved in areas such as energy supply and transportation and health protection involving long-term projects such as nuclear building programmes, but this is not an easy task. A broad consensus still allows for different political approaches to be developed and enacted at the level of strategy development and implementation. For example, the World Health Organization has done much to build a consensus about the policy for health while still leaving individual countries to develop their own interpretations of this broad policy. Social marketing can assist with this broad consensus development process about the best way to tackle large behavioural issues by helping to bring together the concerns and understanding from target audience insights, evidence about what works and is possible, stakeholder concerns and wider political imperatives.

Conclusion

Adopting a strategic social marketing approach results in the development of a strategic marketing plan to support a specific social programme that is being developed. In Chapter 12 the process of developing and delivering an operational social marketing plan is set out. Ideally operational planning should be commenced within the context of and preferably after the development of a strategic plan to tackle a specific social challenge. The process for developing a strategic social marketing plan is set out in Chapter 11.

In this chapter we have sought to define the nature of social marketing's contribution to the policy strategy development process. Strategy can be thought of as both a set of processes to ensure that there is clarity of purpose within an organisation and the development of congruent intervention tactics. Strategy can also be conceived as a series of decisions that seek to ensure that organisations are prepared to address changing social and environmental circumstances. In the case of social issues, the development of a strategy is intended to ensure that future challenges and opportunities are predicted and plans put in place that are capable of minimising social harm and promoting maximum social wellbeing.

Social marketing has to date made a significant contribution to developing more effective and efficient social projects and interventions designed to influence behaviour across a wide range of topics and groups within societies all over the world. It also has the potential to add to this success story by ensuring that marketing principles, concepts and techniques are applied to the selection and development of social policy and strategy. This chapter has sought to demonstrate that through its focus on data gathering and building programmes that reflect citizens' needs, beliefs and attitudes, social marketing has a significant contribution to make to the social policy, strategy and delivery process.

Reflective questions

- Describe how strategy can be defined and its key features.
- Discuss the consequences for social programme selection and design of adopting a more strategic social marketing approach.
- List the main ways that social marketing can add value to policy selection, development, implementation and evaluation.
- What are some of the ways that social marketing can add value to policy and strategy making and delivery processes?

Further reading

French, J. (2011) 'Business as unusual: the contribution of social marketing to government policy making and strategy development', in G. Hastings, K. Angus and C. Bryant (eds), *The SAGE Handbook of Social Marketing*. London: SAGE, pp. 359–374.

Gordon, R. (2013) 'Unlocking the potential of upstream social marketing', *European Journal of Marketing*, 47 (9): 1525–1547.

Kenny, A. and Parsons, A. (2012) 'Macro-social marketing and social engineering: a systems approach', *Journal of Social Marketing*, 2 (1): 34–51.

References

Andreasen, A.R. (1995) *Marketing Social Change: Changing Behaviours to Promote Health, Social Development and the Environment*. San Francisco, CA: Jossey-Bass.

Andreasen, A.R. (2006) *Social Marketing in the 21st Century*. Thousand Oaks, CA: SAGE.

Biroscak, B.J., Lefebvre, R.C., Schneider, T., Marshall, R.J., McDermott, R.J. and Bryant, C.A. (2014) 'Assessment of social marketing education, training, and application public health settings', *International Review on Public and Non-Profit Marketing*. doi: 10.1007/s12208-013-0111-y.

Bowman, C. (1990) *The Essence of Strategic Management*. London: Prentice Hall.

Bullock, H., Mountford, J. and Stanley, R. (2001) *Better Policy Making*. London: Centre for Management and Policy Studies.

Chussil, M. (2005) 'With all this intelligence, why don't we have better strategies?', *Journal of Business Strategy*, 26 (1): 26–33.

Dann, S. (2006) *Social Marketing in the Age of Direct Benefit and Upstream Marketing*. Third Australasian Non-profit and Social Marketing Conference. August 10–11.

Department of Work and Pensions (2009) *Communicating with Customers*. London: Department of Work and Pensions.

Domegan, C. (2008) 'Social marketing implications for contemporary marketing practices classification scheme', *Journal of Business and Industrial Marketing*, 23 (2): 135–141

Eagle, L., Dahl, S., Hill, S., Bird, S., Spotswood, F. and Tapp, A. (2013) *Social Marketing*. London: Pearson.

French, J. (2011) 'Business as unusual: the contribution of social marketing to government policy making and strategy development', in G. Hastings, K. Angus and C. Bryant (eds), *The SAGE Handbook of Social Marketing*. London: SAGE, pp. 359–374.

Goodman, C. and Anise, A. (2006) *What Is Known about the Effectiveness of Economic Instruments to Reduce Consumption of Foods High in Saturated Fats and Other Energy-Dense Foods for Preventing and Treating Obesity?* Copenhagen: WHO Regional Office for Europe. Available at: www.euro.who.int/document/e88909.pdf (last accessed 18 November 2014).

Gordon, R. (2013) 'Unlocking the potential of upstream social marketing', *European Journal of Marketing*, 47 (9): 1525–1547

Hastings, G. and Domegan, C. (2014) *Social Marketing: From Tunes to Symphonies* (2nd edn). London: Routledge.

Hussey, D. (2001) 'Creative strategic thinking and the analytical process: critical factors for strategic success', *Strategic Change*, 10 (4): 201–213.

iSMA, ESMA and AASM (International Social Marketing Association, European Social Marketing Association and Australian Association of Social Marketing) (2013) 'Consensus definition of social marketing'. Available at: www.i-socialmarketing.org/index.php?option=com_content& view=article&id=84:social-marketing-definition&catid=28:front-page#.VIoD0sKzV2s (last accessed 18 November 2014).

Johnson, G. and Scholes, K. (1989) *Exploring Corporate Strategy* (3rd edn). London: Prentice Hall.

Kenny, A. and Parsons, A. (2012) 'Macro-social marketing and social engineering: a systems approach', *Journal of Social Marketing*, 2 (1): 37–51.

Kotler P. and Armstrong G. (2008) *Principles of Marketing* (5th edn). London: Prentice Hall.

Lazer, W. (1969) 'Marketing's changing social relationships', *Journal of Marketing*, 33: 3–9.

Lazer, W. (2013) 'Marketing's changing social relationships: a retrospective', *Journal of Social Business*. 3 (4): 325–343.

Lee, N. and Kotler, P. (2011) *Social Marketing: Influencing Behaviours for Good*. New York: SAGE.

Lefebvre, R.C. (2008) Interview for the National Social Marketing Centre, February 27.

Lefebvre, R.C. and Flora, J.A. (1988) 'Social marketing and public health intervention', *Health Education Quarterly*, 15 (3): 299–315.

McCarthy, E.J. (1960) *Basic Marketing: A Managerial Approach*. Homewood, IL: Richard D. Irwin.

McKeown, M. (2011) *The Strategy Book: How to Think and Act Strategically for Outstanding Results*. London: FT/Prentice Hall.

Ministry of Health Planning (2003) 'Prevention that works: a review of the evidence regarding the causation and prevention of chronic disease' (consultation draft). Victoria, BC: Prevention and Wellness Planning, Population Health and Wellness, Ministry of Health Planning.

Mulgan, G. and Lee, A. (2001) 'Better policy delivery and design: a discussion paper'. London: Performance and Innovation Unit, Cabinet Office.

NICE (National Institute for Health and Clinical Excellence) (2007) *Behaviour Change at Population, Community and Individual Levels: Reference Guide*. London: NICE.

Osborne, D. and Gaebler, T. (1992) *Reinventing Government: How the Entrepreneurial Spirit Is Transforming the Public Sector*. Reading, MA: Addison-Wesley.

Perri 6 (1997) *Holistic Government*, DEMOS. London.

Prime Minister's Strategy Unit (2006) *The UK Government's Approach to Public Service Reform*. London: Cabinet Office.

Stead, M., Hastings, G. and McDermott, L. (2007) 'The meaning, effectiveness and future of social marketing', *Obesity Reviews*, 8 (Suppl. 1): 189–193.

Thompson, A. and Strickland, A. (1993) *Strategic Management. Concepts and Cases*. Illinois: Irwin Professional Publishing.

United States Department of Health and Human Services (2010) *Healthy People 2020*. Washington, DC: Office of Disease Prevention and Health Promotion.

Wensley, R. (2002) 'Marketing strategy', in S. Dibb, L. Simkin, W. Pride and O. Ferrell (eds), *Marketing Concepts and Strategy* (5th edn). Boston: Houghton Mifflin.

Wensley, R. (2003) 'The basics of marketing strategy', in M.J. Baker (ed.), *The Marketing Book* (5th edn). Oxford: Butterworth-Heinemann, pp. 53–86.

Wymer, W. (2011) 'Developing more effective social marketing strategies', *Journal of Social Marketing*, 1 (1): 17–31.

6 CREATING VALUE IN SOCIAL MARKETING

Learning objectives

By the end of this chapter, readers should be able to:

- identify the importance of creating value as a core objective of social marketing
- identify different domains in which value can be perceived by citizens, including *value-in-exchange*, *value-in-use* and *value-in-behaviour*
- understand and apply different dimensions of value including but not limited to functional, economic, emotional, social and ecological perceived value to social marketing
- identify the relevance and importance of individual citizen perceived value *and* societal value in social marketing
- consider how value can be created passively, actively, co-created, destroyed and co-destroyed.

Introduction

Debate exists within the field as to what is the overarching objective of social marketing (Spotswood et al., 2012). Wiebe (1951) proposed the use of social advertising to promote ideas and social issues. Later, scholars in the marketing discipline advocated the use of broader and more comprehensive marketing approaches to promote social issues and engender social good (Kotler and Zaltman, 1971; Fine, 1981). Other marketing scholars argued that the emerging concept of social marketing could be used not only to market social good, but also to provide control and social audit of commercial forces (Lazer and Kelley, 1973). Later, scholars in the public health paradigm stated the case for social marketing to be oriented towards the protection of public health (Lefebvre and Flora, 1988), or the solution of health and social problems (MacFadyen et al., 1999). These mostly earlier works offered a fairly broad perspective on the core objectives of social marketing that permitted the inclusion of changing ideas, attitudes or language as well as behaviour.

In the early 1990s, Andreasen (1994) called for social marketing to focus specifically on voluntary behaviour change achieved through offering motivational exchanges, to tackle criticism that it lacked focus. Subsequently, the majority of definitions of social marketing have focused on behaviour change as a core objective – usually oriented towards resultant social change or social good (Dann, 2010). However, this narrower focus on behaviour change, although perhaps appropriate when the field lacked focus in the early 1990s, may no longer be appropriate. As Spotswood et al. (2012) identify, changing ideas, values, attitudes, language and social norms are often precursors to behaviour change. Furthermore, should behaviour change be the sole focus, when perhaps the primary objective is to achieve social good and positive social outcomes, whether that is through the change or maintenance of existing realities? We argue here that the time has come for social marketing to develop a broader focus – towards marketing for social good through the myriad of mechanisms through which this can be achieved – not just through a focus on individual behaviour change. In addition, we propose here that an important precursor or mechanism for social good is the creation of value. While not advocating a singular focus on value creation, we make the case that if social marketing is oriented towards creating value – this can assist with achieving positive social outcomes and creating social good.

Accordingly, in this chapter we argue for one of the core objectives for social marketing to be orientated towards value creation. We also propose that it is important to promote a broader conceptualisation of value – traditionally presented within the marketing literature as consumer or citizen perceived value, and usually towards goods or services. Here, we advocate for citizen perceived value to be conceptualised not only in relation to *value-in-exchange* and *value-in-use* of goods and services, but also towards *value-in-behaviour* (see Zainuddin and Gordon, 2014). In doing so, we examine five important dimensions of value: *functional value, economic value, emotional value, social value* and *ecological value*.

Moreover, moving beyond individuals we make the case that social marketing should be oriented towards the creation of citizen value, stakeholder value and *societal value*. We consider the role and function of these broader conceptualisations of value. In examining the concept of value, we also consider how value can be actively and passively created, co-created, destroyed and co-destroyed by actors within the value creation process. We conclude by summarising the crucial role we believe value creation could and should play in contemporary social marketing. We argue that value creation forms an important part of a socially progressive strategic social marketing perspective that is focused on value creation, mutualism, social welfare, social justice and social equality.

Value as a core objective in social marketing

Traditional orientations of social marketing have incorporated a central premise of offering motivational exchanges to consumers to achieve a socially beneficial behaviour change. The exchange concept has thus been central to traditional social marketing thinking (Bagozzi, 1975; Lee and Kotler, 2011). Furthermore, this exchange concept is largely, though not completely, centred on motivational exchanges for the individual – what is in it for them. The argument follows that if the exchange is attractive enough, participants will engage. However, what if the exchange is not attractive? This is often the case in social marketing. In these cases, the implications of engaging in a social marketing exchange are considerable and not very attractive. Traditionally, social marketing has focused on trying to accentuate the positives in such exchanges, and to mitigate or underplay the negatives (Lee and Kotler, 2011). However, such considerations remain quite limited in focus – largely on the implications for individuals based on a rational cost–benefit analysis.

We argue that social marketing should not just focus on exchanges, but also move towards a focus on creating or maintaining value. Indeed, contemporary commercial marketing has shifted somewhat away from a core focus on the exchange, towards the creation of value (Grönroos and Voima, 2013). Exchange was included in the 1985 American Marketing Association (AMA) definition of marketing – 'Marketing is … to create exchanges that satisfy individual and organisational goals' (AMA, 1985) – but was replaced by the time of the 2005 definition with 'value creation'. Sheth and Uslay (2007) contend that this was a positive development, arguing that a focus on exchange in marketing has been limiting, and has reduced the focus onto a buyer and seller perspective, ignoring other relevant parties such as the producer, the consumer, the user and the financier. Furthermore, Zafirovski (1999: 10) argues that applying a marketing lens and seeing all human interaction as exchange 'involves an untenable reductionism that grossly violates the real-life complexity by proceeding on the delusion of discovering simplicity in a complex socio-economic world'. These are strong words, but identify a common theme in marketing and indeed social marketing: the reduction of complex phenomena and human behaviours down to prescriptive formulas and frameworks.

Value presents a bigger picture concept that moves beyond the more immediate positive and negative exchange-oriented implications of engaging in a process or practice. For example, a focus on value creation with respect to giving up smoking may incorporate accentuating not only the health benefits to an individual, but also the economic value (more money to spend on other things rather than expensive cigarettes), and emotional value (such as a sense of achievement from a successful quit attempt). Furthermore, the social value from quitting (reducing the strain on family members concerned about a person's smoking and/or improved social standing from being a non-smoker) could also be acknowledged. Similarly, there may be ecological and/or societal value (reducing the burden on social systems potentially emanating from health problems relating to smoking). While such exchanges and motivational incentives are already included or at least implied in many social marketing programmes (see Stead et al., 2007), value offers a more contemporary and broader lens for understanding and applying this thinking.

Focusing on the systemic creation of value also carries with it the advantage of moving beyond the limiting concept of exchange, by encouraging a more 360 degree view of the implications of decisions, processes, practices, and external factors that are relevant not only to the individual, but also to families, communities, stakeholders and societies. Given our consistent argument that social marketing needs to move towards a more systemic approach, the benefits of shifting the focus towards value creation become clear. We propose a move away from a restrictive focus on exchange. Indeed, rather than just proposing that creating or maintaining value can provide a more progressive operational function in social marketing than exchange, we believe value has a more fundamental and central role in social marketing.

We submit that creating or maintaining functional, economic, emotional, social, ecological and societal value among multiple actors, including individuals, families, wider social groups, organisations and institutions, should be a core objective of social marketing to help engender social good.

Defining value

Broadly, value can be defined as 'the regard that something is held to deserve, the importance, worth, or usefulness of something' (*Oxford English Dictionary*, 2013). Traditional conceptualisations of value in marketing originate from the value chain framework (Porter, 1985), and emanate from an industrial and supply-chain perspective. This approach views firms as value determinants, creators and deliverers; and consumers as value consumers and destroyers. Value is an important theoretical concept in marketing, and specifically social marketing. This is reflected in the latest American Marketing Association definition of marketing as 'the activity, set of institutions and processes for creating, communicating, delivering, and exchanging offerings that have *value* for customers, clients, partners, and society at large' (AMA, 2013, emphasis added). This definition also acknowledges that marketing is a social and societal process (Dann, 2008). Recognising the synergy between marketing, social marketing and value, Lee and Kotler define social marketing as a 'process that applies marketing principles and techniques to create, communicate, and deliver *value* in order to influence target audience behaviors that benefit society (public health, safety, the environment and communities) as well as the target audience' (Lee and Kotler, 2011: 8, emphasis added). These definitions demonstrate the relevance of value in social marketing. Yet, only recently has a stream of value literature emerged in the social marketing domain (Zainuddin et al., 2011, 2013; Domegan et al., 2013).

Domains of value

Much of the existing work in operationalising value in marketing has been geared towards goods (e.g. Sweeney and Soutar, 2001) and has used a *value-in-exchange* perspective that is outcomes-oriented (Vargo and Lusch, 2004). This primarily takes an economic approach to value, and considers the process through which consumers measure value as an outcome of an evaluation of costs against benefits (Zeithaml, 1988). This *value-in-exchange* approach (Porter, 1985) often tends to be goods-based – for example, what is the value in purchasing a washing machine? While there may be both extrinsic and intrinsic benefits in *value-in-exchange*, primarily this tends towards extrinsic benefits. The *value-in-exchange* concept is especially relevant to commercial marketing, where the outcomes orientation tends to be profit for the organisation through delivery of value to the customer. At the core here is that value is derived during the exchange. In marketing, exchange is defined as an exchange of goods, services or resources between two or more parties with the expectation of some benefits that will satisfy the needs of these parties (Bagozzi, 1975; Houston and Gassenheimer, 1987). Thus *value-in-exchange* relates to the value derived by the consumer and firms in such exchanges. However, while *value-in-exchange* may be useful for understanding consumer perceived value towards the consumption of goods, this approach on its own does not encompass all of the dimensions of consumer value as we discuss later in this chapter.

In the social marketing context, *value-in-exchange* may be a useful rubric in social programmes that involve the distribution of goods, for example condoms or screening kits in sexual health interventions (Population Services International, 1977). However, social marketing often does not involve the kind of tangible or economic exchanges found in commercial marketing. Normally an exchange will involve the exchange of goods or services for money, but in social marketing this can often involve the exchange of non-tangibles such as the promise of a healthier life if you exercise regularly. Social marketers have attempted to tackle the limitations of the commercial conceptualisation of exchange, by proposing a broader idea of exchange that offers participants something beneficial in exchange for taking part in social programmes. In such cases, benefits offered may be tangible (e.g. rewards/incentives for participation or making behavioural changes) or intangible (e.g. personal satisfaction, improved health and wellbeing) (French and Blair-Stevens, 2006). However, as some social marketing scholars have noted (see Peattie and Peattie, 2003; Stead et al., 2007), the exchange concept, and therefore *value-in-exchange*, does not always sit comfortably in social marketing due to the commercial origins of the concept and because of its focus on tangibles and rational decision making.

More recently, an experiential approach to investigating value has emerged in the marketing literature. Experiential value considers value to be an interactive and relativistic preference experience related to the total experience of consuming goods *and services* (Holbrook, 2006). This uses a *value-in-use* approach (Holbrook, 2006) that is process-oriented and has largely emanated from the services marketing paradigm. Value-in-use proposes that consumer value is realised during the consumption experience, rather than being embedded within goods or services (Sandström et al., 2008). For example, *value-in-use* may be the value the consumer perceives towards the overall experience of using a banking service in store – such as how long they waited in the queue, how friendly the staff were, the benefits attached to the financial services they were offered and so on. While there are both extrinsic and intrinsic benefits in this consumption context, the benefits tend to lean more heavily towards intrinsic benefits due to the difference in the nature of this consumption context. As such, this perspective can be more suitable in social marketing, where the outcome orientation is not financial profit to the organisation, but behaviour change for individuals who may use a service. Social marketing scholars have utilised the *value-in-use* concept to explore participants' perceived value towards cancer screening programmes (Zainuddin et al., 2013), and blood donation services (Russell-Bennett et al., 2012). Importantly, this work has found that participants do identify *value-in-use* towards social marketing services, and that these value perceptions have an impact on attitudes and behaviours. Work in this area has begun to demonstrate the utility of value in social marketing, particularly in relation to the components of social marketing programmes that involve service delivery such as smoking cessation services. This focus on services in relation to *value-in-use* also forms part of the increasing scholarly attention given to *midstream social marketing* – consideration of the role and impact the more immediate environment (workplaces, schools, local communities and service organisations) has on behaviour and social change (Russell-Bennett et al., 2013). It follows that focusing on services and participant value in social marketing can help facilitate behaviour change and achieve objectives in social programmes. Yet, this service orientation of value in social marketing through *value-in-use* remains somewhat limiting as it can only apply in contexts in which there is service delivery. Furthermore, scholars such as Wright and Russell (2012) have identified limitations and some criticisms of perceiving marketing through the service-dominant logic espoused by Vargo and Lusch (2004). Specifically, these criticisms are that perceiving everything in marketing as focused on service is reductionist, and forms a tautological argument that is not testable, and not all social marketing programmes, and not all elements of programmes, involve service delivery. Indeed, McCosker et al. (2014) identified that there are many social marketing contexts in which citizens perform behaviours independently, with limited or no direct interaction with service organisations and systems.

Therefore, while both *value-in-exchange* and *value-in-use* have relevance to social marketing in cases where participants in social programmes may use goods, or services, more recent work has focused on whether and how citizens may perceive value in the actual behaviour(s) and practices required to facilitate social good. Zainuddin and Gordon (2014) have proposed moving from a goods orientation housed in economic exchange theory, towards not only an experiential orientation, but also a behaviour orientation towards value in social marketing. *Value-in-behaviour* builds upon the value-in-use concept, and expands this towards participant value that is, or is not, realised through the performance of behaviour. Indeed, scholars have argued that behaviour change is an active, rather than a passive, activity (Dann, 2010). Therefore, it seems reasonable to propose that people do perceive value in performing behaviours, not just using goods and services. This proposal can help add further insight to understanding behaviour and behaviour change by adding additional perspective.

This broader scope for value can therefore incorporate all the dimensions of value a participant may perceive towards the performance of behaviours such as quitting smoking or exercising more. These *value-in-behaviour* perceptions, just like *value-in-exchange* and *value-in-use*, may exist across several dimensions including *functional value, economic value, emotional value, social value* and *ecological value*. We will discuss these dimensions in the next section of this chapter. This view overlaps with the understanding that individuals provide their own contributions or inputs towards an activity (McColl-Kennedy et al., 2012), which can result in the achievement of social marketing goals (Zainuddin et al., 2013). This lends support to the proposal that there is a need to move forward in our conceptualisations of value, to consider value as an outcome of a behaviour. While the current understanding of value has evolved from a goods orientation to a service orientation there is limited existing work being done to understand it from a behaviour orientation. Table 6.1 presents a summary comparison between these three domains of value.

Recent thinking on *value creation* proposes that value is a process in which multiple actors provide inputs at various stages of a consumption experience or the performance of practices. Most research exploring value creation is situated within the services marketing paradigm. This has contributed to the dominant service orientation of value and the rise of service-dominant logic (Vargo and Lusch, 2004). What links most of the current thinking on value in marketing is the focus primarily on the individual and the firm. Kotler and Armstrong (2008) identify two main perspectives here: *consumer perceived value* (i.e. value for the consumer), and *consumer lifetime value* (value, normally monetary, to a firm from a consumer's lifetime purchases). Given that social marketing, unlike commercial marketing, is not usually oriented towards encouraging purchasing behaviours, the predominant focus has been on consumer or what we term here *participant (or citizen) perceived value*.

Table 6.1 Summary comparison table between economic, experiential and behavioural perspectives of value

	Economic approach	**Experiential approach**	**Behavioural approach**
Value definition	An outcome of an evaluation of costs against benefits (Zeithaml, 1988)	An interactive relativistic preference experience (Holbrook, 2006)	A holistic and multi-dimensional appraisal of value in performing behaviour(s) (Zainuddin and Gordon, 2014)
Value type	Value-in-exchange	Value-in-use	Value-in-behaviour
Orientation	Outcomes-oriented	Process-oriented	Behaviour-oriented
Context	Goods-based	Services-based	Behaviour-based
Benefits	Predominantly extrinsic to self	Predominantly intrinsic to self	Intrinsic and extrinsic to self and others
Marketing domain	Commercial marketing	Social marketing	Social marketing

Source: adapted from Zainuddin, 2011; Zainuddin and Gordon, 2014

Participant perceived value

As we have identified, participants in social marketing can perceive value in engaging in behaviours and in processes and practices resulting in social good. Therefore, similar to commercial marketing, it is reasonable to propose *participant perceived value* exists in the social marketing context. Consumers in the commercial marketing context may perceive value derived from consumption of products and services across a number of dimensions – for example, a new winter jacket keeps a person warm (functional), may have been purchased in a sale (economic value), may make the purchaser feel good about themselves (emotional value), may attract compliments from friends and colleagues (social value), and may have been produced sustainably and ethically (ecological value). The argument follows that participants in social marketing programmes may derive similar forms of value from using products and services in social marketing programmes or, as we argue in this chapter, from engaging in behaviours, processes, and practices (e.g. shifting attitudes, changing social norms, performing lifestyle rituals) in social marketing. In further understanding how citizens derive value it is worthwhile considering the dimensions of value that are currently identified in the literature.

There are often various sources of consumer perceived value towards goods or services that may be present during various stages of the consumption experience. These sources of value may include information, interaction, the environment, services, customer co-creation processes and social mandate (Smith and Colgate, 2007; Russell-Bennett et al., 2009). Scholars have also identified that similar sources of value are often present in the social marketing context. Studies in this area have categorised three broad sources of value in social marketing.

The first are organisational sources of value: *information* (such as a reminder letter to attend a cancer screening appointment), *interaction* (citizens' experience of interacting with organisational staff, systems and processes – for example, receptionists, doctors, nurses and technical staff in a health clinic), and *environment* (such as waiting areas or screening rooms in a clinic). A person's experiences of each of these organisational sources will influence the value they perceive from the process.

The second are participant sources of value: *cognitive inputs* (mental effort – for example, remembering to organise an appointment with a GP after receiving a reminder letter), *behavioural inputs* (such as following the instructions of staff during an annual eyesight test), and *affective inputs* (emotional effort – for example, not worrying too much about what the result of a pap smear test may be) (Zainuddin et al., 2013).

However, in social marketing there are other actors and institutions involved in social processes beyond organisations and consumers/citizens. The following case study by Nadia Zainuddin, Jo Previte and Rebekah Russell-Bennett, focusing on the BreastScreen Queensland (BSQ) cancer screening service, explores the concept of value in social marketing, and specifically what factors may act as sources of value.

CASE STUDY

BreastScreen Queensland (BSQ): exploring the influence of third party sources of value in social change management

Strategic and policy context for the intervention

Population cancer screening services are provided to Australian citizens as part of a government preventative health strategy to encourage living well in the older years, as well as disease management and treatment. BreastScreen Australia is a well-established programme within the government's preventative health strategy. The programme targets women aged 50–74 years, with no symptoms of breast cancer, to have a mammogram once every two years and aims to achieve a national participation rate of 70 per cent. Current participation rates are low at 54.9 per cent (Department of Health, 2013), despite the fact that the service is free to eligible women. The problem remains that a significant proportion of the population remain unscreened, leaving them susceptible to detecting breast cancer at the later stages, and decreasing their likelihood of successful treatment. To address this problem, the state-based BreastScreen Queensland (BSQ) adopted a social marketing strategy, engaging in consumer research, internal market orientation and branding, among other marketing strategies, in order to encourage participation among its target audience. The provision of public health services forms an important part of achieving social marketing goals and objectives of influencing individuals,

(Continued)

(Continued)

communities, structures and societies in order to bring about positive social change. The focus on services forms part of the growing interest and research in social marketing at the midstream level, which considers the effects of social marketing at the group, community or service level (Russell-Bennett et al., 2013). Cancer screening services, in particular, have been the focus of recent work in the social marketing area that uses a service approach (e.g. Zainuddin et al., 2011, 2013), identifying dimensions as well as sources of value relevant to value creation in social marketing.

Aim and objectives

The aims of this case study are two-fold:

1. Demonstrate service thinking progress that enhances social marketing applications in public health.
2. Explore the role of third parties – experts, mass media, peer groups, etc. – and their impact in a social marketing service experience.

The case objective is to outline the evidence on third-party involvement in social change and make recommendations to inform future social marketing service strategies.

Contribution of research to strategic goals

The research presented in the following case discussion illustrates the value of research in informing health service strategic goals, such as BSQ. It acknowledges the impact third party sources can have on BSQ clients' service experiences that affect customer value perceptions. Research drawing on alternative marketing principles, such as 'third party practices' and the concepts of value co-creation, adds value to marketing planning and the evaluation of services. Research and evaluation are fundamental when planning social marketing programmes and evaluations. In this sense, the investment in research services and participation of key decision makers in research activities contribute to BSQ's preventative health goals to increase women's participation in screening programmes.

Existing research in social marketing has examined the value creation process in public health services, as target audiences are understood to only engage in behaviour if they perceive value in doing so (Zainuddin et al., 2013). Sources of value emanating from both the organisation and clients were identified, and this insight is useful for highlighting service quality dimensions that cancer screening services should emphasise, as well as emphasising the need for customer education and empowerment. However, this research has predominantly focused on the point of engagement at the service interface (i.e. getting a mammogram), as this is the stage at which the organisation and client come together to co-produce a service. This is also the stage at which the organisation has the greatest control over the value creation process via the exchange through provision of organisational resources linked to administration, technical and interpersonal expertise (Dagger et al., 2007). Yet customers' value perceptions can change before, during and after a service experience (Woodruff, 1997). There has been little consideration from social marketing researchers about the sources that influence customer perceived value at the pre- and post-consumption stages. The following discussion demonstrates the additional influencers on participants' experiences with a social marketing service, which subsequently impact on their overall value perceptions of the experience. These insights are important in social marketing as decision makers need further evidence to guide and inform their approaches to managing sustainable health practices, such as regular cancer screening well into older age.

Participants

The participants in this case study were key decision makers in cancer screening services, as the purpose of this case study was to influence the thinking of internal social marketing planners to inform strategies that target women aged 50–74 years.

Methodology

Individual in-depth interviews with 25 women were conducted face-to-face across a variety of locations including those of the women's own choosing (e.g. in their homes), as well as at three different BSQ service locations.

Findings

Reports from women interviewed indicated that information from an interaction with third parties was influential for their experiences with BSQ and breast screening.

Influencing initiation

Many of the women identified experts in the medical field as being significant influencers on their experiences with breast screening and BSQ. General practitioners (GPs) had a particularly important role in assisting the

(Continued)

(Continued)

achievement of the behavioural goal of BSQ, which was for women to have a breast screen. These experts played a particularly important role in the initiation stage of the behaviour, as they were viewed by the women as trusted and reliable sources of information. Women further reported that they commenced breast screening early (before 50 years old) based on the recommendation of a medical expert. As one of the women commented during the interview: 'I was recommended by my GP. She just suggested I should get into a programme like this. It was free and reliable and it was a good idea and something I should consider doing' (Respondent 11, 54 years old, six years' experience).

While the effect of medical experts appeared to be limited to the initiation stage, they had minimal effect on keeping the behaviour top-of-mind for the women interviewed. The data suggested that other third party sources were more effective in maintaining the salience of breast screening. This is particularly important, given the long time-lapse between recommended screens (two years), resulting in the likelihood that women may forget that they are due for a screen.

Keeping screening top-of-mind

Breast cancer related events and media coverage on breast cancer, breast screening and journalist reporting on BSQ in the news were the most common types of third party sources of influence that impacted the salience of breast screening for the women interviewed. Events such as Breast Cancer Awareness Month, the Mothers' Day Classic fun run, and Pink Ribbon Day, were examples of breast cancer related events that were useful in keeping the issue of breast cancer and breast screening top-of-mind for the women interviewed. The women tended to relate to these events positively, as they focused on positive aspects of breast cancer such as raising awareness for prevention, or raising funds for research to find a cure.

In contrast, journalist news coverage on BSQ and the reporting on survivor stories or the incidence of breast cancer in the population had the potential to be both positive and negative. For some women, seeing media coverage of local celebrities who had been diagnosed with breast cancer, such as Kylie Minogue, or those who were diagnosed and later passed away, such as Belinda Emmett and Jane McGrath, saddened them and reinforced the prevalence and threatening nature of breast cancer. While the negative nature of such stories did not deter the current sample from having breast screens, the women did note that this might discourage other women who were non-users from having breast screens, out of fear of a cancer diagnosis.

Impact

The findings highlight that third parties are a category of sources which can create value opportunities for the maintenance of behaviours (i.e. regular breast screening), in addition to organisational and consumer sources identified in previous research (see Figure 6.1). In the case of public health services, doctors are likely to create positive value for target audiences, while the media can create both positive and negative value. Furthermore, the social marketing experience is one that extends beyond the one-to-one service exchange and is enduring over time. Key influences from stakeholders – other private health screening services, the media, experts in the field and social networks – all contribute to sustainable practices in target audiences. The evidence presented in this case study illustrates the effect of these external stakeholders, known as 'third parties', and the impact they can have on the value creation process that social marketing participants and organisations engage with.

Lessons learnt

The key lesson for decision makers is that value and value creation are not only controlled by the service organisation. Rather, other stakeholders create

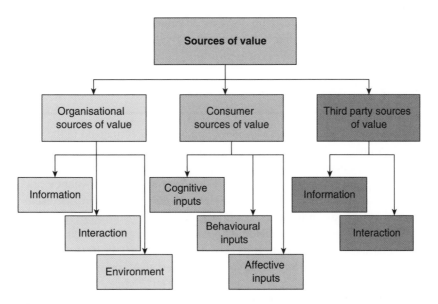

Figure 6.1   Sources of value in a social marketing breast screening service context

(Continued)

(Continued)

opportunities for value co-creation or co-destruction. Social marketing research has identified not only organisational sources of value, which were informed by services thinking (Dagger et al., 2007), but also consumer sources of value that reflect the cognitive, behavioural and affective contributions participants provide towards value creation in their experiences (Zainuddin et al., 2013). Evidence from research with customers indicates third parties are an additional category of sources of value that directly and indirectly influence the value co-creation or co-destruction in participants' experiences with social marketing behaviours.

For more information see: www.health.qld.gov.au/breastscreen/.

Acknowledgements to Dr Nadia Zainuddin, lecturer at the University of Wollongong, Dr Josephine Previte, lecturer at the University of Queensland, and Professor Rebekah Russell-Bennett of Queensland University of Technology for this case study.

It is important to acknowledge that value research is in its relative infancy in social marketing, and there may be additional or different sources of value depending on the context. Further research in this area will be important to add to the knowledge base here. In addition to identifying sources of value, it is also relevant to consider the different dimensions of value (i.e. the types of value) that a person may perceive towards using goods and services, or performing behaviour(s).

Dimensions of value

Several dimensions of value have been identified and conceptualised in the commercial marketing literature including *functional value, economic value* (sometimes included within functional value), *emotional value* (sometimes termed *hedonic value*), *social value* and *ecological value* (Sheth et al., 1991; Holbrook, 1994; Sweeney and Soutar, 2001; Koller et al., 2011). Other suggested dimensions include *altruistic value*, which entails concerns from an individual over how their own consumption behaviour affects others when the experience is viewed as a self-justifying end-in-itself – for example, donating to charity when the virtue is its own reward (Holbrook, 1994; Holbrook, 2006) and, as we argue for later, *societal value*. It is argued that some of these dimensions are independent of one another (e.g. Sheth et al., 1991), while others have been validated as interrelated dimensions (e.g. Sweeney and Soutar, 2001). It is also important to acknowledge that there are differences in how scholars model dimensions of value – for example, some consider functional value to include economic value. Until recently there was very little research even into whether these value dimensions existed in the social marketing context (Zainuddin, 2011). However, recent studies – for example that have assessed participants' perceived value towards using cancer screening services – have identified that dimensions such as *functional value* and *emotional value* do exist in social marketing (Zainuddin et al., 2013). Further research is required regarding the applicability of other value dimensions in social marketing. Currently a research study in Australia on citizen/participant value towards using energy efficiently is investigating whether other dimensions such as social and ecological value are relevant, and may add to the knowledge base (see http://globalchallenges.uow.edu.au/ news/UOW156636.html). The dimensions of value that may be relevant for social marketing are summarised in Table 6.2.

It should also be acknowledged here that there are limitations to value perspectives. The value literature in marketing makes assumptions that human behaviour is based on extrinsic or intrinsic motivations, and does not take into account other social forces such as structures – as argued by Giddens (1984) in structuration theory. Indeed, recent research on interactions between individuals and structures and institutions in the case of alcohol has suggested that structures can have a powerful influence on behaviour in the social marketing context (Cherrier and Gurrieri, 2014). Therefore, we advocate social marketers to consider the potential utility of value in social marketing, but not to unthinkingly accept and apply concepts and ideas without critically thinking about other forces that may be relevant in understanding and influencing behaviours. Furthermore, scholars advocating a Social Practice Theory (SPT) approach have identified how broadening out from a singular focus on behaviour, towards a focus on practices (Reckwitz, 2002): i.e. the performances and rituals of mind, body, things, knowledge, language, structures, agents, and place can offer greater insight for social marketing (Gordon et al. forthcoming).

Functional value

Functional value (also incorporating *economic value* by some scholars) is extrinsically motivated (perceived as a means to an end), and is for the benefit of the self rather than others (Holbrook, 2006). It is focused on the performance and functionality of a product, service, behaviour, or practice (Sheth et al., 1991; Sweeney and Soutar, 2001; Russell-Bennett et al., 2009). This can include economic benefit (usually in a commercial context), or the utility provided by the consumption of a product or service (Tellis and Gaeth, 1990). Zainuddin (2011) has argued that the functional value dimension is relevant with regard to the delivery and participants' experiences of using social marketing services such as breast screening – for example, consistency in the quality of the screening service, being well delivered, and being of an acceptable standard of quality. Therefore, in terms of functional value in the social marketing paradigm, the use of goods, services or performance of behaviours and practices serves as a means to the participant's own objectives (Holbrook, 2006), which in the context of breast screening is the maintenance of good health.

Table 6.2 Dimensions of value in social marketing

Dimension of value	Functional*	Economic*	Emotional	Social	Ecological	Societal
Motivation	Extrinsic	Extrinsic	Intrinsic	Extrinsic	Intrinsic	Extrinsic and intrinsic
Focus	Performance Functionality Responsiveness Tangibility	Financial benefit Price Cost-benefit ratio	Value derived from the experience such as pleasure, confidence, or anger and fear	Value derived from association with others/groups, and/or impact on self-worth	Value relating to impact on environment/ ecological concerns, impact on self-worth	Value for society at large
SM example	Consistency in quality of a breast screening service	A smoking cessation service that is free to users	Reduced anxiety from attending a health clinic	Attending gym classes to fit in with friends who do the same	Using energy efficiently to make a contribution towards reducing climate change, and be perceived as 'green' by peers	Stopping smoking to reduce the potential burden on a national health service from smoking related illness**

* Note that functional value and economic value are often presented as in the same dimension.

** As at least one of the reasons for quitting among others.

Economic value

As noted, economic value can often be integrated within the functional value dimension. However, there may be cases in which economic value may not be relevant – for example, when no economic exchange takes place. Also, there may be instances when functional value and economic value may be distinct from one another. Therefore, other scholars present economic value as a separate dimension (e.g. Payne and Holt, 1999; Koller et al., 2011). Using research techniques such as factor analysis from survey data can help discern whether in certain contexts, people perceive functional value and economic value as distinct. In the context of social marketing, we take the view that economic value is indeed a separate construct from functional value. Economic value is intrinsically motivated, and focused on price, and also cost–benefit analysis from consuming goods and services, or from performing behaviours and practices. This can include considerations of whether something is reasonably priced, whether it offers value for money, and whether it is economical to use or perform. In the social marketing context examples include whether using energy efficiently offers value for money, or if the price of gym membership to help increase physical activity is reasonable.

Emotional value

Emotional value is intrinsically motivated (an end in itself) and self-oriented whereby products are consumed for the emotional experience and for no other end-goal (Holbrook, 2006). This value is related to different affective states that can be positive (e.g. confidence and pleasure), negative (e.g. anger and fear) (Sánchez-Fernández and Iniesta-Bonillo, 2007), or even neutral (e.g. ambivalence). Utility in emotional value is derived from the feelings or affective states generated or aroused by the consumption of a product or service (Sheth et al., 1991; Sweeney and Soutar, 2001). Similarly, in the context of say marketing health services, participants could be expected to experience some form of emotion, particularly when it relates to personal health and wellbeing. For example, people may perceive reduced tension or anxiety from attending a sexual health clinic, or may feel nervous about attending a smoking cessation service for the first time.

Social value

Social value is also extrinsically motivated – however, it is directed at others (Holbrook, 2006). This type of value focuses on influencing other people as a means to achieving a desired goal, such as status or influence within groups (Russell-Bennett et al., 2009). Utility in social value is acquired from a product or service's association with social groups (Sheth et al., 1991) as well as its ability to enhance an individual's self-concept (Sweeney and Soutar, 2001). In social marketing, this value dimension may also be potentially relevant as participants may choose to perform socially desirable behaviours and engage in practices in order to fit in socially or to influence others to perform the same behaviours. For example, a father may choose to quit smoking if many of his friends do not smoke so that he fits in better when out socialising with them, or he may choose to quit smoking to set a good example to his children. Social value is often sought when individuals wish to shape the response of others (Gallarza and Saura, 2006; Holbrook, 2006). This is also relevant to a social marketing context as people often seek congruence (similarity) with the norms of friends and associates during consumption practices (Sánchez-Fernández and Iniesta-Bonillo, 2007), or when performing behaviours (Cialdini and Goldstein, 2004).

Ecological value

Ecological value is intrinsically motivated, and recognises the increasing importance that citizens place on the impacts of their consumption behaviours and experiences on the natural environment (Koller et al., 2011). This type of value derives utility from the perceived impacts on environmental/ecological issues and concerns, and also from its ability to enhance or impact on an individual's self-concept. For example, consumers may perceive ecological value in purchasing and using a Toyota Prius car as it consumes a lower amount of carbon than purely petrol driven vehicles. They may also perceive ecological value in how owning a Prius makes them feel about themselves – for example, that they are acting 'green'. Indeed, in the commercial sphere, marketers have recognised the potential in appealing to green consumers by transmitting ecological value in green marketing efforts (see Gordon et al., 2011). In the social marketing context, an example of perceived ecological value may be using energy efficiently to make a contribution towards reducing climate change, and also being perceived as 'green' by friends.

The future of value in social marketing

The relevance and importance of firstly understanding and secondly seeking to influence dimensions of value in social marketing are only beginning to emerge (Zainuddin, 2013). However, work in this area is growing and studies may be able to offer additional insight and understanding on the value for social marketing. In particular research considering value dimensions in non-health related contexts would be welcomed. For example, research under way in Australia is exploring participants' perceived *experiential value* in using mobile games in social marketing contexts (Mulcahy et al., 2014). Furthermore, there has been no exploration of perceived ecological value in a social marketing context, for example in programmes to reduce energy use or to encourage recycling. Therefore, there are numerous areas for future research on value in social marketing. However, we should also make clear that the ideas on value in social marketing presented here are not meant to be definitive, and it may be that there are other domains, sources and dimensions of value that are relevant to our field.

However, the extant research in this area, and our discussions here and in other social marketing textbooks (see Hastings and Domegan, 2014), do suggest an important role for value in social marketing. One observation we make about existing work in the value area is that the focus is relatively narrow. As outlined earlier in this chapter, value theory has focused on consumption experiences (whether of goods or services), and not on behavioural experiences – an extension we propose here. In addition, the focus of value theory tends towards individuals and firms, although dimensions such as social value and ecological value have started tending towards bigger picture thinking. Indeed, scholars in the value area have begun to discuss value as a social construction that relates to social structures, social systems, roles, positions, interactions and networks (Edvardsson et al., 2011). In this book we seek to extend even further the concept of value in social marketing by proposing an additional dimension of value: *societal value*, and argue why it is relevant for social marketing.

Societal value

The limitations of creating shared value (CSV)

As we have identified, much of the work on value theory from commercial marketing has retained a fairly narrow focus – on individuals and firms, largely based around consumption experiences. More recently, and perhaps recognising the limitations of this, Porter and Kramer (2011) proposed the concept of 'creating shared value' (CSV). The central premise of CSV is that the competitiveness and performance of a firm and the health, sustainability and viability of the communities and societies around it are mutually dependent. According to CSV, by recognising and capitalising on the connections between societal and economic progress, corporations and stakeholders have the power to facilitate the next phase of global growth and development and to redefine capitalism (Porter and Kramer, 2011). To do so would require corporations to focus on creating shared value – creating economic benefits for themselves in a way that also creates value for societies by addressing their shared challenges and needs. Porter and Kramer (2011) have argued that corporations need to align their business practices and social practices together to help achieve this. While this bigger picture thinking on business does hold some promise, critics have pointed out that the concept is still largely based on economic rationality, defers to ever continuing innovation, growth and development, and celebrates a form of capitalism that has been heavily criticised and discredited following the global financial crisis (Beschorner, 2013).

Critics of Porter and Kramer have argued that focusing on economic rationality and counting on firms to create shared value is at the very least naïve, if not disingenuous, and redolent of a 'one trick pony approach' (Beschorner, 2013). Furthermore, the concept of CSV tends to focus on win-wins, and cases of when businesses do good things, ignoring the negative impact that corporatism has had on societies (Crane et al., 2014): we discuss this in more detail in Chapter 14. Given the massive failure in capitalist systems experienced in recent years, it may be a bit of a reach to suggest that the answer lies in firms themselves to solve societies' problems. Indeed, Crane et al. (2014)

point out that the concept of CSV still retains a principal objective of creating economic value for a firm – as long as it can also create shared value for society. This first principle is in conflict with what others see as more important – addressing societal problems first, and not thinking about making money first. They also point out that CSV has the strong whiff of a rebadged corporate social responsibility (CSR), and that attempts to supersede CSR with CSV prompt scepticism (Crane et al., 2014). It is worth considering that contemporary definitions of CSR centre on corporate benefit (Vaaland et al., 2008). Furthermore, CSR practice is often geared towards the same objective as shown in the comment by Niall Fitzgerald, former CEO of Unilever, that 'Corporate social responsibility is a hard-edged business decision ... [We do it] ... not because it is a nice thing to do or because people are forcing us to do it ... [but] ... *because it is good for our business*' (Elliott, 2003, emphasis added). These criticisms identify the limitations and potential dangers of allowing commercial forces to set the agenda for social change and social good, which we discuss later in Chapter 14. Therefore, we reject the notion of *creating shared value* in this book as being too limited and still too focused on commercial gain. Instead we propose and argue the case for the concept of *societal value*.

Societal value – the concept

We define *societal value* as value in human endeavour for the benefit of society more broadly. This moves beyond the largely individual or firm orientation of much of the existing work on value, towards recognising that processes, behaviours, practice and experiences may be carried out with a view towards collective benefit and societal level value. The idea of societal value in doing something is perhaps by no means new, rather this is framing some of the motivations or rationale for doing things using value theory and marketing language. However, the relevance for proposing this concept for social marketing is clear. We know that human behaviour is very complex, and there are often multiple forces at play when trying to understand why people hold attitudes, views or perform behaviours and engage in practices. Research on value has identified that understanding and trying to influence how citizens perceive value towards doing something (whether that be buying a product, using a service or performing a behaviour) can make discernible impacts. Yet, the current literature on value largely ignores that people may do things because they believe it can have an effect on the bigger picture, that it can contribute to societal good, and that it can be oriented towards the collective benefit (Moore, 1912). Humans are social animals, and despite the predominance of individualism (Albrecht, 2012) – and Margaret Thatcher famously having the quote claiming that 'there is no such thing as society' attributed to her (Keay, 1987) – collective ideas and social interactions are not yet dead (Berkman and Kawachi, 2000). However, as has been widely discussed in the social marketing literature, a major challenge with a societal value concept is who perceives what provides value to society as a whole, and how and why (Gordon, 2011; Spotswood et al., 2012). This suggests that identifications and interpretations of societal value are likely to differ and be contested depending on the perspectives of individuals, groups, organisations and institutions. Here, we take a socially progressive perspective, but neo-liberals may obviously take a very different view on what societal value may be. However, given the dominance of neo-liberal world views in recent years, and the social problems that have been generated, we submit that ideas such as societal value which emanate from progressive sources are required to facilitate a move towards more equitable, sustainable, healthier and happier societies.

Discussion question

Do you agree with the above proposal for a societal value concept? Do you think people ever do anything for the greater good?

We argue here that it is important to recognise, particularly in the social marketing context, that citizens may do things because they perceive there to be societal value in doing so. It is important to note here that societal value (value benefiting society at large), differs from social value (value relating to how an individual is perceived by others). Examples may include picking up other people's litter, or boycotting unethically produced clothing to try to influence companies to stop using slave labour. Marketing scholars have suggested a concept of *altruistic value* (Holbrook, 1994; Zainuddin et al., 2011) that may have some overlaps with this proposed concept of societal value. Yet the altruistic value concept remains largely rooted in perceived value relating to how others may perceive the individual consumption experiences of a person. As Holbrook (2006: 723) describes, altruistic value relates to 'consumption experiences prized for their own sake because of relationships to the responses of others'. Furthermore, Rothschild (1999) argues that in marketing contexts there is no such thing as altruism, and that everyone acts in their own self-interest. Therefore, we make the case that conceptual framing for the idea of value that can be created for the greater good, for the benefit of society at large, does not lie within existing marketing thought, but in our proposed societal value concept. We therefore call for consideration and exploration of this concept of a societal value dimension to identify how it may relate to social marketing theory and practice.

We conclude these arguments by also proposing that if we are to consider the broader dimensions of perceived value, then we should also perhaps consider that not only individuals and firms/organisations hold value perceptions. Groups, stakeholders and societies or at least sections of societies may also feasibly hold value perceptions. Therefore, it would be encouraging to see value research move into these areas to consider a broader focus beyond just how individuals perceive value. The importance of thinking of the bigger picture is something we will return to later in this chapter and further in Chapter 7, when we consider the importance of systems thinking in social marketing not only to create value, but also to engender social good. Having now considered dimensions of value, we shall briefly look at how value is created.

How value is created

Passive value

Our final area of focus for value in social marketing is on how value is created. The original conceptualisation of value from a supply chain perspective (see Porter, 1985) relating to *value-in-exchange* suggests that value is created by means of a passive process. According to this view, consumers (and other supply chain actors) experience passive value reactively in response to the consumption of an object, service or experience (Holbrook, 1994). This implies that consumers are largely passive in their consumption experience and their experiential value perceptions are based on a 'distanced appreciation' of aspects of the product, service, or behaviour (Mathwick et al., 2001: 41). Passive value has relevance in situations in which the level of involvement from a citizen is low, or when a person does not wish to engage actively in value creation, for example they may feel ambivalence or, as is often the case, people are operating in a passive non-rational mind-state (see Chapter 3).

Active value

In contrast, active value implies a heightened collaboration between the consumer and producer/facilitator of goods, services or even behaviour change efforts. This concept is also known as *participative value* (Mathwick et al., 2001). This involves citizens participating more actively in their consumption or behavioural experience and their experiential value perceptions are based on direct usage of goods or services, or from performing behaviours, as they have deliberately sought a service exchange or interaction (Mathwick et al., 2001; Zainuddin, 2011). In the social marketing context, an example may include a participant actively setting aside time and making the effort to have a breast screening examination. The following quote is from research with women attending a breast screening service, conducted by Zainuddin (2011: 114):

> I make time to do it. If it's important enough, you make time to do it … I don't think you're ever too busy to do anything, it just depends on how important it is to you and what sort of priority you give it. (Respondent 5, aged 56, eight years' experience, employed)

Active value therefore proposes that people collaborate in processes and help create experiences.

Co-created value

Our discussion on active value leads us to consider that consumers (in the commercial context) or participants (in the social context) may actually be involved in the co-creation of value. Value co-creation has attracted significant attention in recent years, since emerging just over a decade ago (Prahalad and Ramaswamy, 2004). A first principle in thinking about value co-creation is that consumers actively participate in processes (Dabholkar, 1990). Indeed, there has been a monumental shift in the commercial marketing literature towards acceptance that consumers create value *with* the organisation, as opposed to the organisation creating value *for* the consumer (Lengnick-Hall, 1996; Vargo and Lusch, 2004). Subsequently, Prahalad and Ramaswamy (2004) proposed the concept of *co-creation of value*, whereby the consumer not only jointly creates value with the organisation, but also co-constructs the experience to suit their context and situation (see Figure 6.2 for a schema of how value may be co-created). We propose that this concept of co-creation needs to be expanded beyond the organisational-customer focus prevalent in commercial marketing, to recognise the role other actors play in value creation in the social context. However, it is important

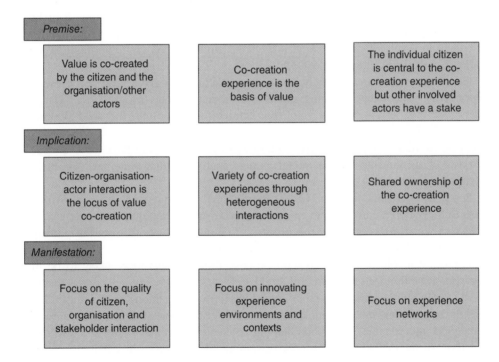

Figure 6.2 Process of value co-creation in the social marketing context

Source: adapted from Prahalad and Ramaswamay, 2004

to acknowledge that value may not always be co-created, nor may citizens always wish to actively co-create value, and it is also important that social marketers are cognisant of this fact. For example, Fiona Spotswood's ethnographic work in deprived communities in Northern England (see the case study in Chapter 10) explored how participants viewed physical activity and identified that citizens had much bigger priorities and concerns in their lives. Quite simply they did not want to actively participate in co-creation of value in relation to physical activity as they had bigger concerns (Spotswood and Tapp, 2013). However, as we discuss later in this chapter, these insights may be valuable in a process of *co-discovery of value*, by identifying the social issues citizens actually do care more strongly about.

In many ways the sense of active participation will be familiar to many who have worked in the social marketing field for a number of years, as there has long been an acceptance that social change can only be brought about by effectively engaging and collaborating with participants (Hastings, 2007). Therefore, value co-creation does not necessarily offer something new in itself, as many social programmes do involve active participation from citizens (Cottam and Leadbeater, 2004). However, this is not universal, and some scholars and practitioners may still defer to a more passive and transactional model of delivery (Weinrich, 2010). Furthermore, recognising and engaging with the concept of co-creation of value can help offer a more formalised framework for participation in social programmes that could perhaps avoid the inconsistencies in levels of engagement, active participation and empowerment in social marketing (Audit Commission, 2003).

Given that social marketing scholars and practitioners have long recognised the importance of actively engaging citizens in social change programmes (Hastings, 2007), the idea of co-creating value has attracted attention in the field (Domegan et al., 2013). Indeed, concepts such as *community-based social marketing* (CBSM) that marry social marketing ideas with community engagement, and have been conceptualised and applied to tackle social issues such as environmental sustainability (McKenzie-Mohr, 2011).

Research by Zainuddin et al. (2013) has found that participants in social marketing programmes often are involved in co-creating value, and importantly that there is a range of factors which may influence the process of co-creation – both from the participant perspective and also the organisational perspective. Furthermore, research suggests that if people are involved in a co-creation process, they are also more likely to be more engaged and influenced (O'Hern and Rindfleisch, 2010). These are key considerations in social marketing given that it often involves long-term commitments and changes. Therefore, if organisations involved in social marketing ensure that staff are well trained and have good interpersonal skills, thus helping co-create emotional value, and also ensure that they maintain high standards of operation and delivery, thus helping co-create functional value, this can result in positive outcomes (Zainuddin et al., 2013).

If organisations do not take care of these things, then there is the danger that instead of creating or co-creating value, that *value will be destroyed or co-destroyed.*

Indeed, this is an important wake-up call for social marketers, as recent work on value has identified that just as value can be created by actions, interactions and social systems, it can also be destroyed (Plé and Cáceres, 2010; Grönroos, 2011). This can be through a process of destruction solely by the organisation, or more readily through a process of co-destruction, in which resources, services or experiences are misused, misappropriated, and citizens disengage or do the opposite of what may have been intended (Plé and Cáceres, 2010; Echeverri and Skålén, 2011). Therefore, inertia in social marketing is something that needs to be guarded against, as the implications from not engaging in trying to create value for stakeholders involved in social marketing processes are serious. For example, if value is co-destroyed in a breast screening service due to poor standards of quality, poor training and poor interpersonal skills from staff, or from an unwelcoming physical environment, then people may stop coming to use the service. Indeed, Hastings and Domegan (2014) use the example of young people aged 18–35 with Type 1 Diabetes who are notorious for missing annual health checks. They identify that this is unsurprising given the 'value barriers' or how value has been destroyed – with 'waiting rooms that smell like operation theatres, no free Wi-Fi access and no privacy for people with distressing symptoms' (Hastings and Domegan, 2014: 278).

Value co-discovery

Involving participants in social marketing programmes in value co-creation can and should involve active participation at all stages of the process – from *co-discovery*, to *co-design*, to *co-delivery* (Domegan et al., 2013; Hastings and Domegan, 2014), and perhaps moving even further to *co-evaluation*, *co-interpretation* and *co-representation*. Scholars in the social marketing field have long recognised that programmes that are designed and delivered by participants are far more likely to succeed than those that are designed and delivered solely by external agents and passively 'received' by citizens (Bryant et al., 2000). Therefore, in social marketing the concept of value co-discovery suggests that citizens should be engaged and empowered to decide what their own priorities are, and what social changes or social good they wish to see happen. These ideas have significant overlap with the community development paradigm (Minkler and Wallenstein, 2008), in which members are encouraged to collectively identify issues and generate solutions to common problems. The example of the highly successful truth® campaign: (www.thetruth.com) is a good example of co-discovery, where the engagement and active participation of young people in trying to tackle the issue of youth smoking led to the identification and development of a counter marketing campaign that highlighted how the tobacco industry had manipulated young people into smoking. Another example is the aforementioned ethnographic research conducted by Fiona Spotswood among deprived communities in Northern England around physical activity, which identified that members had a range of other problems and focus on other social interests and dynamics, which meant that traditional models for influencing behaviours lacked resonance (Spotswood and Tapp, 2013). The co-discovery of value, through the identification of relevant issues for community members, provided valuable insight on how social programmes may be conceptualised and delivered, although this only acts as a starting point.

Value co-design

Indeed, engaging citizens in a process of value co-discovery in relation to social issues, social problems and desired social outcomes is all well and good, but it is largely meaningless unless they are active participants and the driving force behind the next steps. Value co-design involves active participation and leadership from citizens in terms of designing products, services, activities and experiences that may be offered in social marketing programmes. Co-design and indeed all steps in co-creating value in social marketing programmes can generate a number of benefits, including ensuring that they are culturally and socially appropriate, potentially reduce costs, and facilitate a process of engagement and empowerment in communities (Bryant et al., 2007; Stead et al., 2013). Examples of how citizens have acted as *design agents* in social marketing programmes have emerged in the literature more recently. For example, the Community Healthy Lifestyles programme in Edinburgh also featured participants as design agents, including a community food store taking part in a component to promote healthy home cooking, designing and producing recipe cards and billboards (Stead et al., 2013). A picture storybook was produced by local school children accentuating the positive aspects of living in the local community and advocating and helping normalise healthy activities such as outdoor play and eating fruit by featuring them in the stories (Stead et al., 2013).

Value co-delivery

A natural progression from involving participants in designing social programmes is to facilitate their active participation in delivering them. In essence, participants become front-line staff in delivering programmes, and are actively involved in rolling out, monitoring and evaluating activities. This can take a number of forms including having programme steering and advisory committees, peer-to-peer networking, having community champions and opinion leaders as project employees, and involving citizens in policy development, technical and technological delivery, infrastructure and media activities among others things. Indeed, in an ideal world, citizens would be actively involved in co-delivering all components and activities involved in the delivery of social marketing programmes – and whatever tools in the social marketing mix are used (see Chapter 4). By citizens, and indeed other stakeholders and actors, actively participating in a process of value co-delivery, a systems approach to social marketing can be realised – in which broader social forces coalesce to generate social change and social good. We discuss these ideas further in Chapter 7. Moreover, we could conceivably take this line of thinking on co-creating value further by encouraging citizens to actively participate in interpreting and representing meaning emanating from social marketing programmes – by being involved in evaluation, sharing learning and dissemination activities. These ideas have already been discussed in relation to the co-interpretation and representation of consumer culture research (Arnould and Thompson, 2005).

Conclusion

In this chapter we have considered the central role of *value* and *value creation* in social marketing, arguing that it should replace the more limited concept of exchange as a central pillar of the social marketing process. Furthermore, we argued that creating value for individual citizens, stakeholders and societies should be one of the core objectives of social marketing as it can help engender social good. We identified the important differences between commercial and social conceptualisations of value – arguing that social marketers need to consider carefully how value applies to social marketing, often in different or new ways compared to established thinking in the commercial marketing sector. We then identified and explored different domains in which value can be perceived by citizens – *value-in-exchange* from consuming goods and services that follows a transactional, firm–customer and economic perspective; to *value-in-use* that acknowledges an experiential and more service driven approach to understanding value from consuming goods and services; to a very new proposition of *value-in-behaviour* in which citizens may perceive different dimensions of value in relation to the behaviours they perform (Zainuddin and Gordon, 2014). We then examined various dimensions of value including *functional value, economic value, emotional value, social value* and *ecological value*, and distinguished the relevance of these to social marketing theory and practice. We also proposed an additional dimension for value – *societal value* – in which citizens perceive the benefits to society at large from engaging in processes and performing behaviours. Finally, we considered how value can be created passively (*passive value*) and actively (*active value*), and explored the concepts and processes of *co-creation of value* involving *co-discovery, co-design* and *co-delivery* (Hastings and Domegan, 2014). In paying close attention to the topic of value in this chapter, we hope to have transmitted to readers the important role, and significant relevance that value has in the social marketing domain, but also to have highlighted some of the areas where future work is needed to test ideas and gain further insight and understanding of how value can help social marketing facilitate social good.

Reflective questions

- Which of the dimensions of value – *functional value, economic value, emotional value, social value, ecological value* and *societal value* – do you think is most important and relevant for social marketing? What rationale do you have for your decision? Are there other value dimensions that you think are important or relevant?
- Can you think of an experience you have had of using a social programme or social services in which you feel there was value destruction? Why do you think this was the case, and what could have been done to avoid this?
- How easy do you think it is in practice to engage citizens in *co-creation of value* in social marketing programmes through a process of *co-discovery, co-design* and *co-delivery*?

Further reading

Dagger, T.S., Sweeney, J.C. and Johnson, L.W. (2007) 'A hierarchical model of health service quality: scale development and investigation of an integrated model', *Journal of Service Research*, 10 (2): 123–142.

Domegan, C., Collins, K., Stead, M., McHugh, P. and Hughes, T. (2013) 'Value co-creation in social marketing: functional or fanciful?', *Journal of Social Marketing*, 3 (3): 239–256.

Plé, L. and Cáceres, R.C. (2010) 'Not always co-creation: introducing interactional co-destruction of value in service-dominant logic', *Journal of Services Marketing*, 24 (6): 430–437.

Zainuddin, N., Russell-Bennett, R. and Previte, J. (2013) 'The value of health and wellbeing: an empirical model of value creation in social marketing', *European Journal of Marketing*, 47 (9): 1504–1524.

References

Albrecht, J.M. (2012) *Reconstructing Individualism: A Pragmatic Tradition from Emerson to Ellison*. New York City: Fordham University Press.

AMA (1985) *American Marketing Association: Definition of Marketing*. Chicago, IL: American Marketing Association. Available at: http://marketingpower.com/AboutAMA/Pages/Definitionof Marketing.aspx (last accessed 6 August 2014).

AMA (2013) *American Marketing Association: Definition of Marketing*. Chicago, IL: American Marketing Association. Available at: http://marketingpower.com/AboutAMA/Pages/Definitionof Marketing.aspx (last accessed 6 August 2014).

Andreasen, A.R. (1994) 'Social marketing: its definition and domain', *Journal of Public Policy and Marketing*, 13 (1): 108–114.

Arnould, E.J. and Thompson, C.J. (2005) 'Consumer Culture Theory (CCT): twenty years of research', *Journal of Consumer Research*, 31 (4): 868–882.

Audit Commission (2003) *User Focus and Citizen Engagement, Learning from Comprehensive Performance Assessment: Briefing*. London: Audit Commission.

Bagozzi, R.P. (1975) 'Marketing as exchange', *Journal of Marketing*, 39 (3): 32–39.

Berkman, L.F. and Kawachi, I. (eds) (2000) *Social Epidemiology*. Oxford: Oxford University Press.

Beschorner, T. (2013) 'Creating shared value: the one-trick pony approach', *Business Ethics Journal Review*, 1 (17): 106–112.

Bryant, C.A., Forthofer, M., McCormack Brown, K., Landis, D. and McDermott, R.J. (2000) 'Community-based prevention marketing: the next steps in disseminating behavior change', *American Journal of Health Behavior*, 24 (1): 61–68.

Bryant, C.A., McCormack Brown, K.R., McDermott, R.J., Forthofer, M.S., Bumpus, E.C., Calkins, S.A. and Zapata, L.B. (2007) 'Community-based prevention marketing: organizing a community for health behavior intervention', *Health Promotion Practice*, 8 (2): 154–163.

Cherrier, H. and Gurrieri, L. (2014) 'Framing social marketing as a system of interaction: a neo-institutional approach to alcohol abstinence', *Journal of Marketing Management*, 30 (7–8): 607–633.

Cialdini, R.B. and Goldstein, N.J. (2004) 'Social influence: compliance and conformity', *Annual Review of Psychology*, 55: 591–621.

Cottam, H. and Leadbeater, C. (2004) *Red Paper No. 1 Health: Co-creating Services*. London: The Design Council.

Crane, A., Palazzo, G., Spence, L.J. and Matten, D. (2014) 'Contesting the value of "creating shared value"', *California Management Review*, 56 (2): 130–153.

Dabholkar, P. (1990) 'How to improve perceived service quality by improving customer participation', in B.J. Dunlap (ed.), *Developments in Marketing Science*. Cullowhee, NC: Academy of Marketing Science, pp. 483–487.

Dagger, T.S., Sweeney, J.C., Johnson and L.W. (2007) 'A hierarchical model of health service quality: scale development and investigation of an integrated model', *Journal of Service Research*, 10 (2):123–142.

Dann, S. (2008) 'Adaptation and adoption of the American Marketing Association (2007) definition for social marketing', *Social Marketing Quarterly*, 14 (2): 92–100.

Dann, S. (2010) 'Redefining social marketing with contemporary commercial marketing definitions', *Journal of Business Research*, 63 (2): 147–153.

Department of Health (2013) *BreastScreen Australia Program: Key Statistics*. Available at: www.cancerscreening.gov.au/internet/screening/publishing.nsf/Content/key (last accessed 4 August 2014).

Domegan, C., Collins, K., Stead, M., McHugh, P. and Hughes, T. (2013) 'Value co-creation in social marketing: functional or fanciful?', *Journal of Social Marketing*, 3 (3): 239–256.

Echeverri, P. and Skålén, P. (2011) 'Co-creation and co-destruction: a practice-theory based study of interactive value formation', *Marketing Theory*, 11 (3): 351–373.

Edvardsson, B., Tronvoll, B. and Gruber, T. (2011) 'Expanding understanding of service exchange and value co-creation: a social construction approach', *Journal of the Academy of Marketing Science*, 39 (2): 327–339.

Elliott, L. (2003) 'Cleaning agent'. Interview: Niall FitzGerald, Co-Chairman and Chief Executive, Unilever. *The Guardian*, 5 July: 32.

Fine, S. (1981) *The Marketing of Ideas and Social Issues*. New York: Praeger.

French, J. and Blair-Stevens, C. (2006) *Social Marketing Pocket Guide*. London: National Social Marketing Centre. Available at: www.nsms.org.uk (last accessed 1 July 2014).

Gallarza, M.G. and Saura, I.G. (2006) 'Value dimensions, perceived value, satisfaction and loyalty: an investigation of university students' travel behaviour', *Tourism Management*, 27 (3): 437–452.

Giddens, A. (1984) *The Constitution of Society: Outline of the Theory of Structuration.* Cambridge: Polity Press.

Gordon, R. (2011) 'Critical social marketing: definition, application and domain', *Journal of Social Marketing*, 1 (2): 82–99.

Gordon, R., Carrigan, M. and Hastings, G. (2011) 'A framework for sustainable marketing', *Marketing Theory*, 11 (2): 143–163.

Gordon, R., Butler, K., Waitt, G., Roggeveen, K. and Cooper, P. (forthcoming) 'The site of the social in social marketing', Working paper. Sydney: Macquarie University.

Grönroos, C. (2011) 'Value co-creation in service logic: a critical analysis', *Marketing Theory*, 11: 279–301.

Grönroos, C. and Voima, P. (2013) 'Critical service logic: making sense of value creation and co-creation', *Journal of the Academy of Marketing Science*, 41 (2): 133–150.

Hastings, G. (2007) *Social Marketing: Why Should the Devil Have All the Best Tunes?* London: Butterworth-Heinemann.

Hastings, G. and Domegan, C. (2014) *Social Marketing: From Tunes to Symphonies* (2nd edn). London: Routledge.

Holbrook, M.B. (1994) 'The nature of customer value: an axiology of services in the consumption experience', in R.T. Rust and R.L. Oliver (eds), *Service Quality: New Directions and Theory and Practice*. London: SAGE, pp. 21–71.

Holbrook, M.B. (2006) 'Consumption experience, customer value, and subjective personal introspection: an illustrative photographic essay', *Journal of Business Research*, 59 (6): 714–725.

Houston, F.S. and Gassenheimer, J.B. (1987) 'Marketing and exchange', *Journal of Marketing*, 51 (4): 3–18.

Keay, D. (1987) 'AIDS, education and the year 2000: an interview with Margaret Thatcher', *Women's Own*, 31 October.

Koller, M., Floh, A. and Zauner, A. (2011) 'Further insights into perceived value and consumer loyalty: a "green" perspective', *Psychology and Marketing*, 28 (12): 1154–1176.

Kotler, P. and Armstrong, G. (2008) *Principles of Marketing*. (5th edn). London: Prentice Hall.

Kotler, P. and Zaltman, G. (1971) 'Social marketing: an approach to planned social change', *Journal of Marketing*, 35 (3): 3–12.

Lazer, W. and Kelley, E.J. (1973) *Social Marketing: Perspectives and Viewpoints.* Homewood: Richard D. Irwin.

Lee, N. and Kotler, P. (2011) *Social Marketing: Influencing Behaviors for Good.* New York: SAGE.

Lefebvre, R.C. and Flora, J.A. (1988) 'Social marketing and public health intervention', *Health Education Quarterly*, 15 (3): 299–315.

Lengnick-Hall, C.A. (1996) 'Customer contributions to quality: a different view of the customer-oriented term', *The Academy of Management Review*, 21 (3): 791–824.

MacFadyen, L., Stead, M. and Hastings, G. (1999) *A Synopsis of Social Marketing*. Stirling: Institute for Social Marketing. Available at: www.stir.ac.uk/media/schools/management/documents/social_marketing.pdf (last accessed 22 July 2013).

Mathwick, C., Malhotra, N. and Rigdon, E. (2001) 'Experiential value: conceptualization, measurement and application in the catalog and internet shopping environment', *Journal of Retailing*, 77 (1): 39–56.

McColl-Kennedy, J.R., Vargo, S.L., Dagger, T.S., Sweeney, J.C. and van Kasteren, Y. (2012) 'Health care customer value co-creation practice styles', *Journal of Service Research*, 15 (4): 370–389.

McCosker, A., Zainuddin, N. and Tam, L. (2014) 'Consumers as value creators: exploring value self-creation in social marketing'. Paper presented at the International Social Marketing Conference, Frankston, July.

McKenzie-Mohr, D. (2011) *Fostering Sustainable Behavior: An Introduction to Community-based Social Marketing* (3rd edn). Gabriola Island, Canada: New Society Publishers.

Minkler, M. and Wallenstein, N. (2008) *Community-based Participatory Research for Health: From Process to Outcomes.* Hoboken, NJ: John Wiley

Moore, G.E. (1912) *Ethics.* London: Williams and Norgate.

Mulcahy, R. and Kuhn, K.A. (2014) 'Social marketers playing to win? Experiential value creation in social marketing mobile games'. Paper presented at the International Social Marketing Conference, Frankston, July.

O'Hern, M.S. and Rindfleisch, A. (2010) 'Customer co-creation: a typology and research agenda', *Review of Marketing Research,* 6: 84–106.

Oxford English Dictionary (2013) Oxford: Oxford University Press.

Payne, A. and Holt, S. (1999) 'A review of the "value" literature and implications for relationship marketing', *Australasian Marketing Journal,* 7 (1): 41–51.

Peattie, S. and Peattie, K. (2003) 'Ready to fly solo: reducing social marketing's reliance of commercial marketing theory', *Marketing Theory,* 3 (3): 365–385.

Plé, L. and Cáceres, R.C. (2010) 'Not always co-creation: introducing interactional co-destruction of value in service-dominant logic', *Journal of Services Marketing,* 24 (6): 430–437.

Population Services International (1977) 'Preetni project: transferred to Sri-Lanka FPA', *PSI Newsletter* (November/December): 4.

Porter, M.E. (1985) *Competitive Advantage: Creating and Sustaining Superior Performance.* New York: The Free Press.

Porter, M.E. and Kramer, M.R. (2011) 'The big ideas: creating shared value – rethinking capitalism', *Harvard Business Review,* 89 (1/2): 62–77.

Prahalad, C.K. and Ramaswamy, V. (2004) 'Co-creation experiences: the next practice in value creation', *Journal of Interactive Marketing,* 18 (3): 5–14.

Reckwitz, A. (2002) 'Towards a theory of social practices: a development in culturalist theorizing', *European Journal of Social Theory,* 5 (2): 243–263.

Rothschild, M.L. (1999) 'Carrots, sticks, and promises: a conceptual framework for the management of public health and social issue behaviours', *Journal of Marketing,* 63 (4), 24–37.

Russell-Bennett, R., Hartel, C., Russell, K. and Previte, J. (2012) 'It's all about me! Emotional ambivalence Gen-Y blood donors', in J. Mickelsson and A. Helkkula (eds), *Proceedings from the AMA SERVSIG International Service Research Conference,* Helsinki, Finland: Hanken School of Economics, p. 43.

Russell-Bennett, R., Previte, J. and Zainuddin, N. (2009) 'Conceptualising value creation for social change management', *Australasian Marketing Journal,* 17 (4): 211–218.

Russell-Bennett, R., Wood, M. and Previte, J. (2013) 'Fresh ideas: services thinking for social marketing', *Journal of Social Marketing,* 3 (3): 223–238.

Sánchez-Fernández, R. and Iniesta-Bonillo, M.Á. (2007) 'The concept of perceived value: a systematic review of the research', *Marketing Theory,* 7 (4): 427–451.

Sandström, S., Edvardsson, B., Kristensson, P. and Magnusson, P. (2008) 'Value in use through service experience' *Managing Service Quality,* 18 (2): 112–126.

Sheth, J.N., Newman, B.I. and Gross, B.L. (1991) 'Why we buy what we buy: a theory of consumption values', *Journal of Business Research,* 22 (2): 159–170.

Sheth, J.N. and Uslay, C. (2007) 'Implications of the revised definition of marketing: from exchange to value creation', *Journal of Public Policy and Marketing,* 26 (2): 302–307.

Smith, J.B. and Colgate, M. (2007) 'Customer value creation: a practical framework', *Journal of Marketing Theory and Practice,* 15 (1): 7–23.

Spotswood, F., French, J., Tapp, A. and Stead, M. (2012) 'Some reasonable but uncomfortable questions about social marketing', *Journal of Social Marketing*, 2 (3): 163–175.

Spotswood, F. and Tapp, A. (2013) 'Beyond persuasion: a cultural perspective of behaviour', *Journal of Social Marketing*, 3 (3): 275–294.

Stead, M., Arnott, L. and Dempsey, E. (2013) 'Healthy heroes, magic meals, and a visiting alien: community-led assets-based social marketing', *Social Marketing Quarterly*, 19 (1): 26–39.

Stead, M., Gordon, R., Angus, K. and McDermott, L. (2007) 'A systematic review of social marketing effectiveness', *Health Education*, 107 (2): 126–140.

Sweeney, J.C. and Soutar, G.N. (2001) 'Consumer perceived value: the development of a multiple item scale', *Journal of Retailing*, 77 (2): 203–220.

Tellis, G.J. and Gaeth, G.J. (1990) 'Best value, price-seeking, and price aversion: the impact of information and learning on consumer choices', *Journal of Marketing*, 54 (2): 34–45.

Vaaland, T.I., Heide, M. and Grønhaug, K. (2008) 'Corporate social responsibility: investigating theory and research in the marketing context', *European Journal of Marketing*, 42 (9/10): 927–953.

Vargo, S.L. and Lusch, R.F. (2004) 'Evolving to a new dominant logic for marketing', *Journal of Marketing*, 68 (1): 1–17.

Weinrich, N.K. (2010) *Hands-on Social Marketing: A Step-by-step Guide to Designing Change for Good*. Thousand Oaks, CA: SAGE.

Wiebe, G.D. (1951) 'Merchandising commodities and citizenship on television', *Public Opinion Quarterly*, 15 (4): 679–691.

Woodruff, R. (1997) 'Customer value: the next source for competitive advantage', *Journal of the Academy of Marketing Science*, 25 (2): 139–153

Wright, M. and Russell, D. (2012) 'Some philosophical problems for service-dominant logic in marketing', *Australasian Marketing Journal*, 20 (3): 218–223.

Zafirovski, M.L. (1999) 'A socio-economic approach to market transactions', *Journal of Socio-economics*, 28 (3): 309–334.

Zainuddin, N. (2011) 'Value co-creation in social marketing wellness services', PhD thesis. Brisbane: Queensland University of Technology.

Zainuddin, N. (2013) 'The concept of value in social marketing', *AASM Viewpoint*, 2 (4): 16–18.

Zainuddin, N. and Gordon, R. (2014) 'Social marketing, value, and behaviour: some important considerations', Paper presented at the International Social Marketing Conference, Frankston, July.

Zainuddin, N., Previte, J. and Russell-Bennett, R. (2011) 'A social marketing approach to value creation in a well-women's health service', *Journal of Marketing Management*, 27 (3–4): 361–385.

Zainuddin, N., Russell-Bennett, R. and Previte, J. (2013) 'The value of health and wellbeing: an empirical model of value creation in social marketing', *European Journal of Marketing*, 47 (9): 1504–1524.

Zeithaml, V.A. (1988) 'Consumer perceptions of price, quality and value: a means-end model and synthesis of evidence', *Journal of Marketing*, 52 (3): 2–22.

PART III

HOW?

7 SYSTEMS THINKING AND SOCIAL MARKETING

Introduction

Acknowledging the common theme of thinking strategically and holistically that is found throughout this book, this chapter considers the important role of systems thinking in social marketing as a means for creating value and for engendering social good. Systems thinking emanates from *general systems theory*, which was advanced by Ludwig von Bertalanffy in the 1940s (see Bertalanffy, 1949), and further developed by Ross Ashby and others in the 1950s and 1960s (Ashby, 1964).

Systems thinking offers a way of thinking about, understanding and potentially tackling complex problems. Given the common complexity of social marketing problems, we consider how systems thinking may be defined, what it involves and how it is relevant for social marketing. We then consider how systems thinking in social marketing may be operationalised, including providing a checklist of the habits of a systems thinker. We also consider some approaches to engaging in systems thinking, and how this can enhance social marketing theory and practice. In particular we add to the whole systems theory that is explored in Chapter 3, an exploration of assemblages theory and specifically actor-network theory – a rubric that has recently emerged within the social marketing literature. We provide a case study example of how assemblages understood through actor-network theory can help us synthesise and analyse social marketing problems. We consider how frameworks such as assemblages theory, and more broadly systems thinking ideas, offer utility for social marketing. We conclude by summarising the crucial role we believe systems thinking should play in contemporary strategic social marketing.

Defining systems thinking

Systems thinking can be defined as the study and gaining of understanding of how systems behave, interact and influence one another. Systems thinking can also be applied to solving problems, by considering problems as constituent parts of overall systems. Importantly, systems thinking recognises that the usual way of understanding things through a process of analysis involving the deconstruction of problems into individual components, which we then study individually, is often ineffective for understanding complex issues (Boulding, 1956; Bertalanffy, 1968). Essentially this form of analysis is unable to answer the 'why' questions about things. For example, you can singularly focus on the study of the pieces of a clock for eternity but never understand why a minute is as long as it is (Ackoff, 1974). Gene Bellinger (2014), an expert in this area, provides a useful video that explains the basic premise of systems thinking on the following website: www.systemswiki.org/index.php?title=Systems_Thinking

What does systems thinking involve?

Systems thinking has emerged over the past sixty years as a high level or mega theory to try to gain an understanding of how complex systems operate and what influences them. A system is an entity that maintains its existence through the mutual interaction of its constituent parts (Bertalanffy, 1968). A system also interacts with the environment it is in. The process of mutual interaction in a system is key, as it is through these interactions that things occur and that system level effects are felt. Furthermore, a system displays characteristics not created by any subset of its parts, and a system exhibits discernible behaviours over time. Systems thinking also permits us to acknowledge that systems may be relatively stable and in a state of equilibrium; but that they may also often be relatively transient, unstructured, incoherent, oscillating, chaotic or exponential (Checkland, 1981).

By using systems thinking, it may be possible not only to think about events that have already happened reactively, but also to think anticipatively about patterns and trends, i.e. what has been happening and what might happen. Furthermore, using systems thinking means we can learn about system structures (what are the multiple forces that may contribute to these patterns and trends), and to think transformatively about why situations or problems persist and how they could potentially be tackled.

The relevance of systems thinking for social marketing therefore becomes apparent. Social marketing is often used to tackle complex social problems that involve individual citizens, groups, communities, institutions, structures, systems and environments, all of which interact and influence each other. Systems thinking offers social marketing a way to think about and tackle complex problems, and embrace the complexity of the social issues we discussed in Chapter 2. Indeed, taking any complex social marketing issue in a given context and location, we could conceptualise it as a system.

Systems thinking advocates analysis and synthesis. Therefore, it is just as important to attempt to understand and synthesise the nature of a system, how things fit together and how a system operates and relates to the environment, in addition to undertaking analysis of the elements of a system and the nature of their interaction.

This helps us to understand the how and the why. The idea is that this understanding can then inform the development of strategy that can improve the situation, while also mitigating unintended consequences – an issue that social marketing has struggled with up to now (see Gurrieri et al., 2013). As systems thinking has developed over the past sixty years, scholars have acknowledged that there can be struggles when dealing with extreme complexity, that there have been adverse effects from a conservative bias, and that there are challenges associated with dealing with multiple perceptions of reality (Beer, 1975; Checkland, 1981; Ulrich, 1983).

This has led to the development of critical systems thinking (Senge, 1990; Flood and Jackson, 1991), that according to Bammer (2003: 1):

> aims to combine systems thinking and participatory methods to address the challenges of problems characterised by large scale, complexity, uncertainty, impermanence, and imperfection.

A critical approach to systems thinking recognises the limits of knowledge and explores the restrictions and assumptions made about hard systems (well-defined and quantifiable) and soft systems (ill-defined and not easily quantified). Therefore multi-perspective, multi-methodology approaches that combine techniques and tools to systems thinking are encouraged (Flood and Jackson, 1991; Ulrich, 2003). Critical systems thinking also recognises ethical, political and coercive dimensions and the role of systems thinking in society (Simon, 2003). Critical systems thinking unifies different streams of systems thinking, identifying that different approaches may be used depending on the nature of an issue. See Table 7.1 for Jackson's (2003) framework on which systems thinking approaches may be used dependent on the problem.

Table 7.1 Jackson's systems thinking matrix

Systems	Participants		
	Unitary	**Pluralist**	**Coercive**
	Participants have similar values, beliefs, and interests. Share a common purpose. All involved in decision-making	Basic interests are compatible. Don't share common values. Debate, disagreement and conflict occur. Compromises required	Few common interests, conflicting values and beliefs. Compromise is not possible. Decisions based on who holds power
Simple	**Hard systems thinking** defined, quantifiable, produces single scientific/technical solutions	**Soft systems thinking** complex, ill defined, involves psychological, social and cultural elements	**Emancipatory systems thinking** oriented towards ensuring fairness
Complex	**Dynamic systems thinking** oriented towards improved goal seeking and viability	**Soft systems thinking** complex, ill defined, involves psychological, social and cultural elements	**Postmodern systems thinking** promotes holism and diversity

Source: adapted from Jackson, 2003

Therefore, systems thinking forms a crucial component of thinking and acting strategically, and tackling complex problems. In relation to social marketing it is important to understand the nature and context of the systemic environment in which social issues occur, and then also consider and analyse specific problems and issues. From this insight and understanding we can then decide upon strategic as well as operational activities to try to facilitate social good.

Why is systems thinking important for social marketing?

As discussed in Chapter 1 and Chapter 3, social marketing is often used as an approach to tackle what are known as *wicked problems* (Churchman, 1967) – problems that are difficult or impossible to solve due to incomplete, contradictory or changing interactions and obligations, and/or multiple causal factors. Examples include obesity (PLOS Medicine Editors, 2013), climate change (Levin et al., 2012), and health inequalities (Petticrew et al., 2009). Tackling such problems requires us to acknowledge and embrace complexity, and to develop strategic, multi-component programmes for social change.

The relevance of systems thinking in tackling such problems is becoming increasingly recognised. The application of systems thinking has been espoused to deal with issues including workplace health and safety (Goh et al., 2014), infectious diseases (Diez Roux, 2011), health promotion (Naaldenberg et al., 2009; Best, 2011), healthcare service delivery (Gerst, 2013), population health (Aslanyan et al., 2010; Aslanyan et al., 2013), natural disasters (Leischow et al., 2008), conservation planning of coastal/marine areas (Cleland and Wyborn, 2011; Kløcker Larsen, 2011), and sustainable consumption (Conroy and Allen, 2010).

These are all social issues that social marketing has and may be applied to. Indeed, Conroy and Allen (2010) have already identified the synergies between systems thinking and social marketing to tackle sustainability, calling for further work in this area. This suggests to us that systems thinking and social marketing are synergistic.

Figure 7.1 presents an illustration of how complex the systems may be that relate to social problems. The diagram presented here in relation to obesity could conceivably represent a web of actors, institutions and interactions present in a social marketing context. As we have stated throughout this book, it is important that social marketers acknowledge and embrace such complexity, and use this to first understand and then develop coordinated strategic and operational responses to address the social challenge that is presented. We have also argued for a broader and strategic focus in social marketing. This requires expansive thinking, seeing the bigger picture and developing strategic responses that both address causal factors and support individuals and groups to act in such a way that net social good is achieved. Much of the work and writing in social marketing to date has focused on operational issues. Our call for an increased focus on strategic social marketing leads us to consider how marketing can influence policy development and structures. This has clear synergies with systems thinking. Furthermore, our focus in Chapter 6 on value at the individual and societal level also demonstrates the relevance of systems thinking. As outlined earlier in this chapter, systems thinking encourages us not only to think at the micro and macro level of analysis relating to constituent parts of problems, but also to understand and synthesise the whole. What is more, systems thinking not only helps us to develop strategies, but also as Levin (1994) identified it can be employed as an approach to action research (see Chapter 9 for more on action research). Therefore,

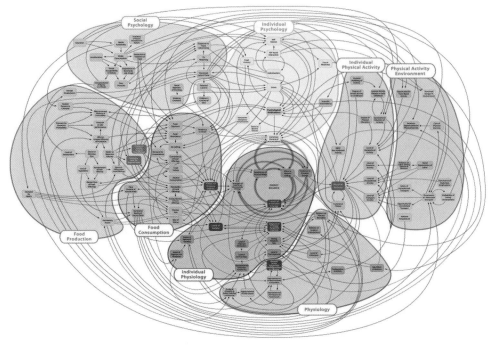

GO-Science, Foresight

Figure 7.1   A complex system

Source: Butland et al., 2007

systems thinking can aid us in moving beyond a narrow and simplistic focus, to understand and consider the various actors and stakeholders involved in social processes.

Understanding and influencing social processes is key in social marketing, as although we may seek to influence individuals, the ultimate objective is to influence societies and to engender social good. To do so requires individual and collective action, stakeholder engagement, interactions, the creation of links, partnerships and networks, and co-created approaches to social change. Scholars in social marketing have discussed the importance and relevance of multi-faceted and multi-level approaches to social change (Collins et al., 2010; Wymer, 2011; Gordon, 2013), advocating action at the micro, meso, macro and exo level described in the social ecological model (Bronfenbrenner, 1974, 1976, 1977, 1979). The advocacy of such an approach highlights the importance and utility of systems thinking.

Indeed, examples of where social marketing has contributed to multi-level action and social good – such as with environmental sustainability (see McKenzie-Mohr, 2011) and tobacco control (Kennedy and Parsons, 2012; Gordon, 2013; Gordon and Gurrieri, 2014) – demonstrate the value of understanding and applying system approaches.

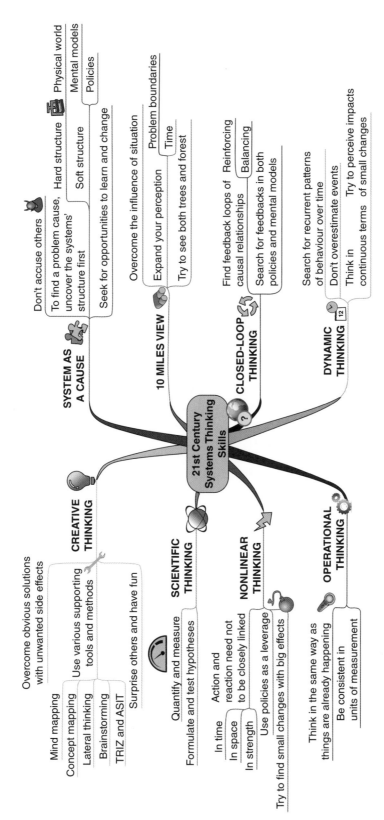

Figure 7.2 Systems thinking skills

Source: Vojtko, 2008

In such cases attempts were made to understand complex systems and levels of interactions to develop strategic approaches to tackle the problem of tobacco control. The case study on the introduction of smoke-free legislation in Scotland later in this chapter illustrates this point. Having outlined what systems thinking is, and why it is relevant and important for social marketing, we now consider how we may engage and *do* systems thinking.

Doing systems thinking – ways of thinking

Systems thinking requires people *to think*! As we have argued throughout this book, social marketing has developed and been predominantly focused on questions related to what *should be done*. This follows a very *operational thinking* perspective – focusing on simple cause and effect relationships and on processes of action (Richmond, 1998). Social marketing has also tended towards simplistic rational deductive thinking – focusing on quantifying, measuring, and formulating and testing hypotheses. This may be in part as a result of the dominance of positivist marketing management schools of thought in social marketing (Gordon and Gurrieri, 2014), and the aspiration within the mainstream marketing discipline to be considered more of a science than an art (Bass, 1993). While these are important objectives for recognising interdependencies and webs of relationships, they are not ends in themselves and in fact do not reflect postmodern scientific thinking. Merely engaging in operational and simplistic cause and effect thinking alone cannot offer a more complete understanding of social issues and processes. Indeed, we believe that doing this is erroneous. Social marketing is often used in situations demonstrating considerable complexity. Therefore, as Figure 7.2 illustrates, multiple approaches to thinking are often required to build a more complete understanding.

As we have discussed in Chapters 1 and 2, social issues and challenges facing societies are complex and multi-faceted. Human knowledge, attitudes, values, norms, behaviours, practices, and socialisation are also massively complex. Therefore, social marketing requires us to think before we act, as we act and after we have acted. Given our critique of simplistic formulas for social marketing, we do not proclaim here to cover the intricacies of doing systems thinking. However, the extant literature does offer some useful ideas and suggestions about how we can see the bigger picture, and be more reflexive, critically minded and systemic in our thinking, so that we can develop more effective and comprehensive social marketing informed strategies to address the many complex social challenges that we face.

A good start would be to broaden the scope of our thinking beyond operational matters. *Creative thinking* describes a way in which we as social marketers can start to break restrictive operational thinking shackles. Mind mapping, concept-testing, being progressive in your ideas, applying lateral thinking to issues, and using a wide range of supporting tools and techniques, as we argue for in Chapter 4, are just some ways in which we can engage in creative thinking (Jackson, 2003).

Non-linear thinking puts a focus on recognising that human thought can be characterised by development in many directions, and there may be multiple starting points to understand and tackle problems (Georgiou, 2006). Engaging in non-linear thinking can also help us think more broadly, strategically and systemically. In doing so we should consider the effects of time, space and power relations when considering social problems and recognise that the world we live in and the situations we face and experience are ever fluid, ever changing, multi-dimensional, and may be interpreted and understood in multiple ways. This links with the discussion in Chapter 9 on the interpretivist research paradigm that argues there is no one single truth, but multiple realities. Non-linear thinking can also help us break away from the step-by-step, linear process driven thinking that social marketing has largely deferred to. Engaging with non-linear thinking may mean acknowledging that there may be no direct pathways between actions and reactions. Encouraging this line of thinking involves moving beyond the predominant positivist mindset in social marketing (Dholakia and Dholakia, 2001; Brennan et al., 2011).

Dynamic thinking can also assist us to think strategically and systemically. For example, trying to identify recurrent patterns in behaviours over time, thinking in concurrent terms, or making sure you do not over-estimate effects are examples of dynamic thinking (Richmond, 1997a).

Thinking objectively, also known as taking *a 10-mile view* or *forest thinking*, is another form of thought process relevant to systems thinking. This involves trying to see the big picture and avoiding thinking and acting in silos. Examples here may include trying to take a step back to expand your perceptions, and trying to overcome the influence of the situation. Thinking about problem boundaries and the temporal effects is another example. Taking a 10-mile view also involves trying to see the wood and the trees, thinking at the micro and macro level at the same time (Richmond, 1997b). These suggestions have lots of synergies with the social ecological approaches discussed in Chapter 8, the critical and reflexive thinking ideas set out in Chapter 14, and decision making related to strategic prioritisation and choice set out in Chapter 11.

This also has links with our discussion in Chapter 5 and indeed throughout the book about how structures and systems can influence social problems and responses (see Giddens, 1984). Thinking like this may involve not accusing others of poor decisions or inaction but considering hard structures such as the physical environment, or soft structures such as mental models and policies as having a significant influence on events. This perspective involves viewing a system's behaviour as the result of the systems within it. Therefore, the system is under the control of decision makers (Richmond, 1997c). To understand and tackle social problems it is important to first understand the systems structures relating to the problem.

Finally, *closed loop thinking* can also help us to think systematically. This involves thinking about cause and effect as a loop, or perhaps even more reflexively as an iterative phenomenon of multiple connected feedback loops. This involves finding feedback loops and causal relationships and understanding how these may be reinforced and balanced (Richmond, 1997d). It can also involve searching for feedback in policies and mental models.

Systems thinking and thinking, teaching and learning in social marketing

The ideas about *how to think* that have been expressed here are not new, but have not witnessed much engagement within social marketing. We argue that this should change, and that social marketing scholars, practitioners, agents and institutions should consider how they think and engage with systems thinking in the ways we have proposed. It is important to acknowledge here that encouraging and teaching people *how* to think about things (as opposed to imposing on them how they should think about things), can be very challenging. Social systems, education systems and institutional systems do not always encourage people to think critically, certainly not at the more strategic level (Barnett, 1997). Indeed, scholars have argued that the predominant neo-liberal world order discourages citizens from thinking critically and strategically (Bourdieu, 1998; Chomsky, 2002; Frauley, 2012; Wilkins, 2012). Therefore, for systems thinking in social marketing to be achieved this may require people being bold in proposing and communicating these ideas. This may also require changes in how social marketing is taught and researched, moving away from a purely operational field to a thinking field in which critique, reflexivity and strategic orientation are facilitated.

How to engage with systems thinking

Drilling down a bit further into how we may engage with systems thinking, Gene Bellinger (2014) offers a useful checklist of characteristics relating to systems thinking

Table 7.2 Habits of a systems thinker

1. Systems thinkers … look at the big picture – they think strategically, which has a strong resonance with our calls for social marketing to get strategic.
2. They think about the interactions in a system.
3. They look for the keys to a system.
4. They examine how things fit together.
5. They consider the implications of things.
6. They think and talk about ideas and listen to the ideas of others.
7. They ask others what they think – harnessing the potential of multiple views on things.
8. They are patient when things get confusing or complicated as they often can.
9. They check results and make changes if needed to try to achieve incremental improvements.
10. They look at things from different sides – thinking critically and reflexively and from multiple perspectives.
11. They think about change over time – avoiding immediacy and short-termism.
12. They consider how our established thinking affects what happens.
13. They distinguish how connections cause changes over time.
14. They look for ways to assist the system to work better.
15. They figure out the effect of actions.

Source: adapted from Bellinger, 2014

that may help people start to engage in this area. However, we wish to guard here against being reductive, and argue that there may and likely will be other considerations and strategies that can help people and actors think systemically.

Discussion question

Consider the characteristics of systems thinking set out above: how many of these characteristics are applied to understanding social challenges within organisations that you have worked with?

Figure 7.3 Habits of a systems thinker

Source: Waters Foundation, 2010

What is important to identify with Bellinger's (2014) checklist is that it does not map out a step-by-step process or formulaic approach. Rather, critical systems thinkers take an iterative approach to trying to understand and tackle issues. This is illustrated in Figure 7.3.

Understanding systems and tackling complex problems

In terms of using systems thinking to tackle problems, scholars in this area argue that by understanding the whole we can make better judgements on how interactions operate and how we can influence those situations (Jackson, 2001). Therefore, systems thinking does not just involve doing some thinking, but also then using this understanding and insight gained to try to influence the problem. Therefore, in the social marketing context, a systemic perspective may involve engaging in the processes set out in Table 7.3.

Table 7.3   A sample systems thinking process

1. Begin with a situation/issue/problem.
2. Understand patterns of behaviour associated with that issue over time and space.
3. Understand the interactions that are responsible for that behaviour.
4. Establish boundaries around a system or systems to help understand who the stakeholders/ participants are, and what things they are responsible for.
5. Consider what the system that is to be addressed entails and what part of the environment it interacts with.
6. Ensure that stakeholders understand the issue and are encouraged to reflexively consider, understand and where appropriate challenge the assumptions that they have made in terms of understanding the issue.
7. Look for the leverage points that may alter the network of interactions in such a way that it will improve the situation. These leverage points essentially come together to aid the development of strategy then adopted by stakeholders to improve the situation.

See also the following iterative diagram provided by Gene Bellinger (2014): http:// insightmaker.com/insight/1366

Now that we have looked more closely at what is involved in systems thinking, and how we might go about it, we will consider examples and potential further developments of this in the social marketing context.

Social marketing: current approaches and perspectives on systems thinking

Proposals to introduce systems thinking in social marketing are not new (see Conroy and Allen, 2010; Kennedy and Parsons, 2012). Yet, systems thinking in social marketing has not really taken hold and become embedded at a strategic level. However, ideas that are approaching systems thinking have been introduced into the field as mechanisms to help facilitate participant, community and stakeholder engagement and empowerment, and partnerships (Hastings and Domegan, 2014).

One example of such an approach to social marketing is community-based social marketing (CBSM) (McKenzie-Mohr, 2011). McKenzie-Mohr (2000) identifies CBSM as a pragmatic approach to social change that utilises core social marketing principles including identifying barriers to desired behaviours, designing appropriate strategies using behaviour change tools, piloting strategy within the community, and evaluating a programme once it has been implemented. The community orientation of CBSM goes beyond more predominant individual level focused social marketing approaches, and thus can be identified as taking a somewhat more systematic approach. Through engagement and understanding and fostering interactions with community stakeholders, strategies can be more informed and reflect the multiple perspectives inherent. CBSM has primarily been applied to environmental issues such as energy efficiency, use of public transport, recycling and conservation (McKenzie-Mohr, 2011). It has also been identified as an effective approach to broader social change (Bryant et al., 2000; McKenzie-Mohr, 2011). However, CBSM has some limitations depending on the interpretation of what a community is, and what the boundaries are around a community. While community level action is important, change at other levels including not only the individual level, but also the macro-policy level, may also often be required. More complete systems thinking approaches to issues such as conservation would require understanding interactions and developing strategies beyond the community level, and even beyond national level to include international level agreements and systems, such as international agreements on carbon emissions or the restriction of trade on certain products such as ivory. Furthermore, although CBSM espouses thinking about various issues at community level, it does not specifically prescribe systems thinking synthesis and analysis.

Community-led assets-based social marketing (Stead et al., 2013) similarly focuses on community level engagement and empowerment, but with a somewhat different model. Under this approach, social programmes focus on the assets inherent within communities such as resources, skills, talents and ideas to help facilitate change (Kretzman and McKnight, 1998). This is viewed as a priority over identifying needs or deficits within communities (Stead et al., 2013). Where community-led assets-based social marketing perhaps goes further than CBSM is that it identifies that assets can be individual, material, social and cultural, and can include knowledge, skills, creativity, resources, services, infrastructure and organisations (Sharpe et al., 2000). Furthermore, this approach to social programmes promotes citizens to be drivers of change programmes themselves, and the agents of co-design and co-delivery that we discussed in Chapter 6. Therefore, by thinking systematically about the assets located within communities, these can be harnessed to engage and empower citizens to design and implement social programmes. Such approaches begin to unlock the potential of systems thinking in social marketing. However, similar to CBSM, the community-led assets-based social marketing approach may have some limitations in that the boundaries around a community may restrict or limit action at a more systemic and structural change level.

Engagement and *empowerment* are important concepts in social marketing as there is increasing recognition in the field that the real experts on social change are often citizens themselves – and the true role of social marketers is to act as facilitators. True engagement and empowerment would involve making sure that all relevant actors (individual citizens, organisations and institutions) are engaged, form partnerships, and have a stake in social processes, and that they are empowered economically, politically, socially, educationally and culturally.

In areas such as public health there has been increasing recognition that social problems can only be effectively tackled through full engagement, and mobilisation of citizens to become actively involved in social change processes (Wanless, 2004; Ouschan et al., 2006). Doing so involves working hard to map who the relevant stakeholders are, building trust and relationships with them, providing appropriate forums for interaction, debate, forming coalitions and identifying areas of consensus that lead to strategy development. Examples of efforts to engage people are beginning to emerge – for example the Scottish government introduced the Community Empowerment (Scotland) Bill in 2011, featuring a raft of legislative, service level and material activities to harness community energy, creativity and talent and to maximise potential (Scottish Parliament, 2011).

Empowerment can involve things such as ensuring political representation, fostering advocacy and forums for citizens to engage politically, providing high quality universal education, healthcare and employment opportunities, addressing income disparities and fostering access to social and cultural capital.

Currently in most societies there are massive inequalities and inconsistencies in the levels of engagement and empowerment with citizens, organisations and institutions. Social marketers need to be cognisant of this, and seek to include strategies to foster engagement and empowerment in social programmes.

Doing so successfully can be challenging. Citizen and community participation can be difficult and time consuming. Fostering trust and building relationships and partnerships between stakeholders with vastly different views of the world can be challenging (Blanchard et al., 1996). Social marketers need to put in careful, long-term efforts that engage with critical and reflexive practice, and strategic thinking to foster engagement and empowerment, and the creation of partnerships (Sowers et al., 2005).

Other social marketing scholars have called for socio-ecological approaches to social marketing (Collins et al., 2010; Gordon, 2013; Lindridge et al., 2013). *Socio-ecological social marketing* involves taking action at multiple levels to influence and tackle social issues. An example where this has been undertaken is tobacco control, where multi-faceted interventions have helped reduce smoking rates and denormalise tobacco (O'Connor et al., 2001). For example, smoking cessation services help individuals and community groups to stop smoking, anti-smoking social marketing programmes have helped encourage young people to stop smoking or not start smoking, regulation and bans on tobacco marketing have reduced the effect of commercial forces on smoking behaviours, and smoke-free legislation has helped denormalise smoking in work-places, public places and more generally in society. Socio-ecological social marketing certainly starts to move us towards systems social marketing in terms of the scope and domain for action. However, up to now there has been little on how we may think about and implement systemic social marketing approaches. Therefore, engaging in systems thinking may provide the missing link to be able to synthesise and analyse complex social systems and social problems that can then be tackled through the development of socio-ecological social marketing strategies.

Kennedy and Parsons (2012) in their support for *macro-social marketing* foster similar ideas. They argue that social marketing can act in conjunction with other interventions such as regulation, legislation, taxation, community mobilisation, research, funding and education to form a systems approach to social change and social good. They identify macro-social marketing as being government led, and seeking macro levels of change at the societal level rather than the individual level (Domegan, 2008; Kennedy and Parsons, 2012). Kennedy and Parsons provide the example of the years of stakeholder engagement and macro-level policy change that went into the Canadian government's anti-smoking campaign as a prime example of macro-social marketing. However, as we have argued in this book, tools such as regulation, taxation, community mobilisation and research are potential components of a fuller social marketing intervention mix and activities that can be enhanced by the application of social marketing (Gordon, 2012; 2013). Furthermore, while it is undoubtedly important that social marketing and social marketers focus on the macro-level factors, what is also required to tackle wicked problems is to take a total systems approaches to social marketing with action at all levels – micro, meso, exo, macro and chrono (Bronfenbrenner, 1979). In addition, although macro-social mar-keting identifies the importance of action at the macro level, and provides insight into some strategies for use in this domain, it does not necessarily assist us with the synthesis of complex systems and social problems and understanding the interac-tions between actors that is required to then work towards the development of effective intervention strategies. For example, the imposition of a macro-level incen-tive or penalty to encourage a particular behaviour may be subverted, or even be counterproductive, if the intended audience does not view the penalty or incentive as fair or proportionate.

As such we take the view that total systems or social ecological approaches to social marketing are desirable, but the development of effective strategies can be better fostered through engaging with critical systems thinking. As we have outlined in this chapter, this involves looking at the big picture, mapping relevant actors, considering multiple perspectives, thinking critically and facilitating reflexive practice, understanding the interactions, acknowledging the effects of time and space, thinking creatively, fostering engagement, empowerment, debate and consensus building, and identifying leverage points for the development of strategies to tackle social issues (Kogetsidis, 2012). Policy makers are increasingly recognising the importance of systems thinking to tackle health and social issues (see Hunter and Marks, 2005), and therefore further work on systems thinking and social marketing should be encouraged. To add some further insight into how systems thinking in social marketing may be encouraged, we consider one prominent framework for understanding how knowledge is created and social interactions occur – *assemblages theory* and specifically *actor-network theory*.

Social marketing assemblages

As we have suggested, there are seeds of systems thinking beginning to grow in social marketing. However, we would like to see systems thinking become a mainstay in social marketing theory and practice. Recently, social marketing scholars have begun to consider how structures and systems may be understood and may affect social issues (Cherrier and Gurrieri, 2014; Gordon and Gurrieri, 2014). One suggestion is that the *assemblages theory paradigm* and more specifically *actor-network theory* may provide a potentially useful framework for gaining an understanding of and tackling social issues.

Assemblages theory

Assemblages theory (Deleuze and Guattari, 1980; DeLanda, 2006) emerged in the philosophy and sociology disciplines as a way in which systems of social interactions may be understood from a more reflexive and critical perspective. In essence assemblages theory can help act as an aid for thinking about how systems function. Assemblages are defined by Hill et al. (2014: 2) as:

> networks of hybrid, ever-shifting and heterogeneous things in which no causal factors or outcomes are invoked beyond the relationships established within and between those networks.

Assemblages theory has some overlap with the critical systems thinking school that recognises systems are complex, often fluid and not simply coherent wholes made up of the sum of their parts. Critical scholars in systems thinking have rejected the conservative view that a system may be understood as a universally recognised and quantifiable entity (Jackson, 2001). Assemblages theory lends itself to this understanding of structures and systems, as assemblages are identified as being able to defy a common and coherent understanding, and of producing any number of interactions and effects. According to assemblages theory, 'the whole is not simply a combination of interrelated parts that signify an internal connectedness' (Gordon and Gurrieri, 2014: 268).

Assemblages theory is very relevant for understanding social marketing systems given the complexity and contested nature of social issues often involving any number of actors, each with their own interpretations. Within the assemblages paradigm, one prominent perspective to navigate the complexity of assemblages is Actor-Network Theory (ANT) (Callon, 1986; Latour, 1987).

Actor-network theory

ANT is a perspective that focuses on networks of interrelated human and non-human actors holding somewhat aligned interests that are delineated and interactively constituted in their relationships with other actors in the actor network (Law and Hassard, 2000). In some ways actor networks have synergies with the pluralist soft systems identified by Jackson (2003). According to ANT, actors coalesce to form impermanent and dynamic networks anchored by another actor. This in turn creates assemblages of interactions that are specific to an individual act or broader event, and forms a collective – also known as an *actant*. Power is distributed in actor networks as each actant has equal agency to influence any given situation. This means that people and even objects are analysed and treated in the same manner. Once networks are formed they can become unstable, with changing interactions and shifting actors and coalitions occurring that cause 'black boxes' (Callon, 1986). These networks are persistently formed and reformed.

These observations about networks of actors (e.g. individual citizens, communities, organisations and institutions in a social marketing context) help us to identify that social marketing systems are not only complex and open to multiple interpretations, but also transient and constantly produced and reproduced. Therefore, if we are to engage in systems thinking in social marketing, ANT tells us that we cannot simply map stakeholders, understand interactions and then develop strategy at one fixed and permanent point in time. Rather, social marketers would be required to acknowledge and be aware of the shifting nature of systems and the need for a continuous review and updating of strategies and plans designed to foster stakeholder and citizen engagement in strategies and programmes of action.

ANT can also assist social marketers with engaging in critical reflexivity – a concept we discuss further in Chapter 9 on research approaches and Chapter 14 on critical social marketing. ANT enables reflexivity and critical engagement for social marketing researchers by outlining how facts and truths are formed and then recognised through the mobilisation and equilibrium of actor networks (Hardy et al., 2001; Gordon and Gurrieri, 2014). As such, by facilitating engagement with the process of understanding how knowledge is constructed and how actors 'define the world in their own terms' (Latour, 2000: 20), ANT rejects positivist perspectives and acknowledges multiple perspectives and interpretations of reality. These themes are also identified in the critical systems thinking literature. Latour (2005: 144) identifies that ANT allows us to open up networks and examine the 'state of affairs at hand', that is the interactions within, the dynamics between and the actions produced by actors. Therefore, ANT permits us to shine a critical and introspective light on the 'assumed, mundane and status quo' (Doolin and Lowe, 2002: 74). Accordingly, this permits us to see and do things differently, and also acknowledges that power is not invested in a single elite, nor is it lying within social structures, but rather it is an outcome of relations in the network. This last point identifies an overlap with the *systems as a cause* approach to systems thinking described by Richmond (1997c).

According to ANT, interactions within a network are the consequence of transformation and negotiation, whereby the interests of divergent actors become aligned into commonalities. In ANT four key moments are examined in this process (Latour, 2005):

- *Problematisation* refers to how actors in a network identify and define a problem so that others recognise it as being also relevant to them. This creates an 'obligatory passage point' where convergence occurs for all actors to be able to achieve their objectives.
- *Interessement* relates to the ways in which actors negotiate, coalesce, assume roles and form allies, which serves to stabilise identities and goals.
- *Enrolment* involves how an issue or strategy (solution) becomes established and recognised as a fact through consensus, with participation and consent proffered by actors and resistance addressed.
- *Mobilisation* refers to actors' supports for agents of the various collectives with a strategic solution gaining credence and thereby creating a larger cohesive network that is stable enough to permit a particular solution to be enacted.

By tracking how social marketing systems and collectives of actors traverse these four moments, we can form an understanding of how events unfold.

Therefore, we propose that ANT provides one potentially useful framework for systems thinking in social marketing. Indeed, scholars have identified the relevance of ANT blended with systems thinking to tackle social issues such as tobacco control (Young et al., 2010; Young et al., 2012), healthcare service delivery (Wickramasinghe et al., 2007; Cresswell et al., 2010) and asthma (Prout, 1996). To illustrate how ANT can help us understand social marketing systems, we present the case study of the smoke-free Scotland social marketing assemblage based on work presented by Gordon and Gurrieri (2014).

CASE STUDY

The smoke-free Scotland social marketing assemblage

ANT has been used in the social marketing literature to help understand how systems have functioned in reaction to tobacco control (Gordon and Gurrieri, 2014). In this case we consider the smoke-free initiative to ban smoking in public places that occurred in Scotland during the 2000s. Relevant stakeholders and actors in relation to smoke-free legislation in this case included individual citizens, groups of citizens such as smokers, academic researchers, social activists, public health lobby groups, the tobacco industry, pro-tobacco lobby groups and policy makers.

Figure 7.4 presents an illustration of a social marketing actor network that could be conceived in relation to smoke-free Scotland. It shows how each actor in the network might problematise the issue – the first moment according to ANT. It follows that some actors in the network interact, reach obligatory passage points and then form collective *actants*, before traversing through *interessement*, *enrolment* and *mobilisation*.

In the case of smoke-free Scotland the issue was originally framed and *problematised* as a public health issue by tobacco control lobby groups and public health researchers (Heim et al., 2009). However, pro-smoking groups, the tobacco industry and some within the hospitality trade *problematised* the issue as impinging on the civil liberties of smokers, and having a deleterious effect on businesses and the economy. Indeed, citizens also raised such concerns (Stead et al., 2008). However, as actants formed around the issue, actors such as ASH Scotland, NHS Health Scotland, and the Scottish Tobacco Control Alliance, and importantly citizens and citizens' groups, engaged in critical reflexivity, and negotiated ways towards an obligatory passage point and a framing of the issue as not only concerned with public health, but also with the rights of workers exposed to second-hand tobacco smoke.

Politicians from all parties were also engaged as coalitions formed around support for smoke-free legislation, despite opposition from other actants supporting pro-smoking and pro-tobacco industry perspectives. The process of critical reflexivity, systems thinking, negotiation and the creation of consensus strategies for solutions facilitated actants traversing through the moments of *problematisation*, *interessment*, *enrolment* and *mobilisation*, which witnessed the introduction of smoke-free legislation in Scotland in 2006. Furthermore, citizen support for the legislation continued to increase following its introduction

(Continued)

> *(Continued)*
>
> (Hyland et al., 2009). Therefore, employing ANT to the understanding of this process can help shed light on how social marketing problems can be tackled, and how networks of actors (stakeholders) and complex systems in social marketing can function.
>
> We therefore identify that systems thinking, and assemblages theory and specifically actor-network theory, are very relevant to social marketing theory and practice.
>
> For more information see: Gordon and Gurrieri (2014).

Conclusion

In this chapter we have defined and identified the relevance and importance of systems thinking in synthesising, understanding and tackling the complex or *wicked* social problems to which social marketing is often applied. We have explored how critical systems thinking that recognises multiple perspectives and multiple methodology approaches to studying systems is relevant to social marketing theory and practice. We reviewed how we might engage with systems thinking in social marketing including considering systems thinking skills, the habits of a systems thinker, and forms of thinking that can be applied in systems thinking. We identified that embedding systems thinking and critical thinking in social marketing education, teaching and learning will be important moving into the future. We then examined the current state of play with regard to systems approaches and systems thinking in social marketing, identifying that community-based, social, ecological and macro-social marketing approaches offer some routes into systems thinking in social marketing, but that more needs to be done to realise a true total systems social marketing paradigm. Finally, we considered how assemblages theory and in particular actor-network theory can offer an aid for thinking about how social marketing problems and systems function. We illustrated this point by considering the example of the introduction of smoke-free legislation in Scotland.

We conclude this chapter by strongly encouraging social marketers to seriously consider the relevance of systems thinking to social marketing theory and practice. We argue that thinking systemically is vital to enable us to tackle the very complex and often wicked social problems that face us. It is these problems that need to be successfully tackled if social good and equitable, sustainable, happy, wellbeing fulfilled and healthy societies are to be created. In drawing together the literature in systems thinking, social marketing and assemblages theory we hope to have demonstrated the clear synergies here and to have invigorated social marketers to engage strongly in this area. We argue here that systems thinking is another important part of a socially progressive strategic social marketing perspective that is focused on value creation, mutualism, social welfare, social justice and social equality.

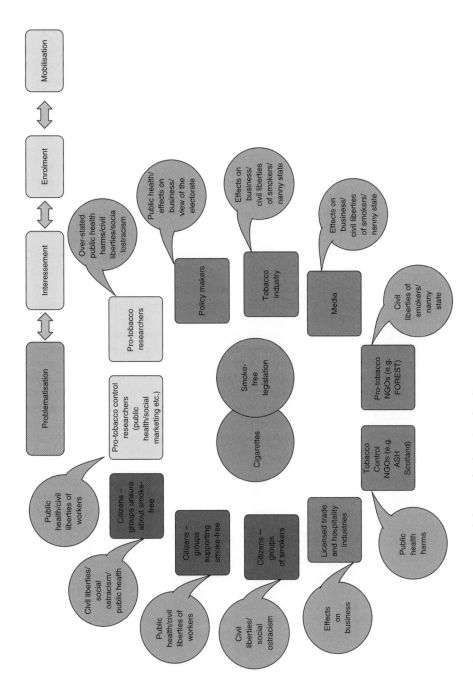

Figure 7.4 Actor network for smoke-free Scotland

Source: Gordon and Gurrieri, 2014

Reflective questions

- Think about a social issue that concerns you to which social marketing may be applied. How would you go about understanding the systems surrounding the issue?
- Do you think it is important we know and understand the perspectives of other stakeholders and actors in social marketing contexts? How can we go about engaging them and acknowledge their views on the world?
- Look at the habits of a systems thinker. Do you employ any of these habits when thinking about issues? If you do, think about why this is and how you think this has influenced your perspective on things. If you have not, think about why you haven't tried to understand things from a systems perspective – what has influenced your thinking?

Further reading

Bellinger, G. (2014) *Systems Thinking*. Available at: www.systemswiki.org/index.php?title=Systems_ Thinking (last accessed 8 August 2014).

Checkland, P. (1981) *Systems Thinking, Systems Practice*. New York: John Wiley.

DeLanda, M. (2006) *A New Philosophy of Society: Assemblage Theory and Social Complexity.* London: Continuum.

Hastings, G. (2003) 'Relational paradigms in social marketing', *Journal of Macromarketing*, 23 (1): 6–15.

Jackson, M.C. (2001) 'Critical systems thinking and practice', *European Journal of Operational Research*, 128 (2): 233–244.

Newtown, T.J. (2002) 'Creating the new ecological order? Elias and actor-network theory', *Academy of Management Review*, 27 (4): 523–540.

References

Ackoff, R. (1974) *Redesigning the Future*. New York: John Wiley.

Ashby, R.W. (1964) *Introduction to Cybernetics*. London: Routledge Kegan and Paul.

Aslanyan, G., Benoit, F., Bourgeault, I.L., Edwards, N., Hancock, T., King, A., Salamo, P. and Timmings, C. (2010) 'The inevitable health system(s) reform: an opportune time to reflect on systems thinking in public health in Canada', *Canadian Journal of Public Health*, 101 (6): 499.

Aslanyan, G., Chauvin, J., Edwards, N., King, M., Raine, K. and Taylor, G. (2013) 'Are we close to systems thinking in public health in Canada?', *Canadian Journal of Public Health*, 104 (2): e183.

Bammer, G. (2003) 'Embedding critical systems thinking in the academy', in C.H.J. Gilson, I. Grugulis and H. Willmott (eds), *International Critical Management Studies Conference (CMS-3 2003)*. Waikato: University of Waikato, pp. 1–10.

Barnett, R. (1997) *Higher Education: A Critical Business*. Buckingham: Open University Press.

Bass, F.M. (1993) 'The future of research in marketing: marketing science', *Journal of Marketing Research*, 30 (1): 1–6.

Beer, S. (1975) *Brain of the Firm*. Harmondsworth: Penguin Press.

Bellinger, G. (2014) *Systems Thinking*. Available at: www.systemswiki.org/index. php?title=Systems_Thinking (last accessed 8 August 2014).

Bertalanffy, L. von (1949) 'The concepts of systems in physics and biology', *Bulletin of the British Society for the History of Science*, 1: 44–45.

Bertalanffy, L. von (1968) *General Systems Theory*. New York: George Braziller.

Best, A. (2011) 'Systems thinking and health promotion', *American Journal of Health Promotion*, 25 (4): eix–ex.

Blanchard, K.H., Carlos, J.P. and Randolph, A. (1996) *Empowerment Takes More Than a Minute*. San Francisco: Berrett-Koehler.

Boulding, K. (1956) 'General systems theory: the skeleton of science', *Management Science*, 2 (3): 197–208.

Bourdieu, P. (1998) *Acts of Resistance: Against the Tyranny of the Market*. New York: Free Press.

Brennan, L., Voros, J. and Brady, E. (2011) 'Paradigms at play and implications for validity in social marketing research', *Journal of Social Marketing*, 1 (2): 100–119.

Bronfenbrenner, U. (1974) 'Developmental research, public policy, and the ecology of child-hood', *Child Development*, 45 (1): 1–5.

Bronfenbrenner, U. (1976) 'The experimental ecology of education', *Teachers College Record*, 78 (2): 157–204.

Bronfenbrenner, U. (1977) 'Toward an experimental ecology of human development', *American Psychologist*, 32 (7): 513–531.

Bronfenbrenner, U. (1979) *The Ecology of Human Development*. Cambridge, MA: Harvard University Press.

Bryant, C.A., Forthofer, M., McCormack Brown, K., Landis, D. and McDermott, R.J. (2000) 'Community- based prevention marketing: the next steps in disseminating behavior change', *American Journal of Health Behavior*, 24 (1): 61–68.

Butland, B., Jebbe, S., Kopelman, P., McPherson, K., Thomas, S., Mardell, J. and Parry, V. (2007) *Tackling Obesity: Future Choices – Project Report*. London: The Stationery Office.

Callon, M. (1986) 'Some elements of a sociology of translation: domestication of the scallops and the fishermen of St Brieuc Bay', in J. Law (ed.), *Power, Action and Belief: A New Sociology of Knowledge*. London: Routledge, pp. 196–233.

Checkland, P. (1981) *Systems Thinking, Systems Practice*. New York: John Wiley.

Cherrier, H. and Gurrieri, L. (2014) 'Framing social marketing as a system of interaction: a neo-institutional approach to alcohol abstinence', *Journal of Marketing Management*, 30 (7–8): 607–633.

Chomsky, N. (2002) *Media Control*. New York: Seven Stories Press.

Churchman, C.W. (1967) 'Wicked problems', *Management Science*, 14 (4): 141–142.

Cleland, D. and Wyborn, C. (2011) 'A reflective lens: applying critical systems thinking and visual methods to EcoHealth research', *EcoHealth*, 7 (4): 414–424.

Collins, K., Tapp, A. and Pressley, A. (2010) 'Social marketing and social influences: using social ecology as a theoretical framework', *Journal of Marketing Management*, 26 (13/14): 1181–1200.

Conroy, D. and Allen, W. (2010) 'Who do you think you are? An examination of how systems thinking can help social marketing support new identities and more sustainable living patterns', *Australasian Marketing Journal*, 18 (3): 195–197.

Cresswell, K.M., Worth, A. and Sheikh, A. (2010) 'Actor-network-theory and its role in understanding the implementation of information technology developments in healthcare', *BMC Medical Informatics and Decision Making*, 10: 67.

DeLanda, M. (2006) *A New Philosophy of Society: Assemblage Theory and Social Complexity.* London: Continuum.

Deleuze, G. and Guattari, F. (1980) *A Thousand Plateaus: Capitalism and Schizophrenia.* London: Continuum.

Dholakia, R.R. and Dholakia, N. (2001) 'Social marketing and development', in P. Bloom and G. Gundlach (eds), *Handbook of Marketing and Society.* Thousand Oaks, CA: SAGE, pp. 486–505.

Diez Roux, A.V. (2011) 'Complex systems thinking and current impasses in health disparities research', *American Journal of Public Health*, 101 (9): 1627–1634.

Domegan, C.T. (2008) 'Social marketing: implications for contemporary marketing practices classification scheme', *Journal of Business and Industrial Marketing*, 23 (2): 135–141.

Doolin, B. and Lowe, A. (2002) 'To reveal is to critique: actor-network theory and critical information systems research', *Journal of Information Technology*, 17 (2): 69–78.

Flood, R. and Jackson. M. (1991) *Creative Problem Solving: Total Systems Intervention.* London: Wiley.

Frauley, J. (2012) 'Post-social politics, employability, and the security effects of higher education', *Journal of Pedagogy*, 3 (2): 219–241.

Georgiou, I. (2006) *Thinking Through Systems Thinking.* New York: Routledge.

Gerst, R.M. (2013) 'Deming's systems thinking and quality of healthcare services: a case study', *Leadership in Health Services*, 26 (3): 204–219.

Giddens, A. (1984) *The Constitution of Society: Outline of the Theory of Structuration.* Cambridge: Polity Press.

Goh, Y.M., Love, P. and Dekker, S. (2014) 'Systems thinking in workplace safety and health' (Editorial for special issue), *Accident Analysis and Prevention*, 68: 1–4.

Gordon, R. (2012) 'Re-thinking and re-tooling the social marketing mix', *Australasian Marketing Journal*, 20 (2): 122–126.

Gordon, R. (2013) 'Unlocking the potential of upstream social marketing', *European Journal of Marketing*, 47 (9): 1525–1547.

Gordon, R. and Gurrieri, L. (2014) 'Towards a reflexive turn: social marketing assemblages', *Journal of Social Marketing*, 4 (3): 261–278.

Gurrieri, L., Previte, J. and Brace-Govan, J. (2013) 'Women's bodies as sites of control: inadvertent stigma and exclusion in social marketing', *Journal of Macromarketing*, 33 (2): 128–143.

Hardy, C., Phillips, N. and Clegg, S. (2001) 'Reflexivity in organization and management theory: a study of the production of the research "subject"', *Human Relations*, 54 (5): 531–560.

Hastings, G. (2003) 'Relational paradigms in social marketing', *Journal of Macromarketing*, 23 (1): 6–15.

Hastings, G. and Domegan, C. (2014) *Social Marketing: From Tunes to Symphonies* (2nd edn). London: Routledge.

Heim, D., Ross, A., Eadie, D., MacAskill, S., Davies, J.B., Hastings, G. and Haw, S. (2009) 'Public health or social impacts? A qualitative analysis of attitudes toward the smoke-free legislation in Scotland', *Nicotine and Tobacco Research*, 11 (12): 1424–1430.

Hill, T., Canniford, R. and Mol, J. (2014) 'Non-representational marketing theory', *Marketing Theory*. doi: 10.1177/1470593114533232.

Hunter, D.J. and Marks, L. (2005) *Managing for Health: What Incentives Exist for NHS Managers to Focus on Wider Health Issues?* London: King's Fund.

Hyland, A., Hassan, L.M., Higbee, C., Boudreau, C., Fong, G.T., Borland, R., Cummings, K.M., Yan, M., Thompson, M.E. and Hastings, G. (2009) 'The impact of smokefree legislation in Scotland: results from the Scottish ITC Scotland/UK longitudinal surveys', *European Journal of Public Health*, 19 (2): 198–205.

Jackson, M.C. (2001) 'Critical systems thinking and practice', *European Journal of Operational Research*, 128 (2): 233–244.

Jackson, M.C. (2003) *Systems Thinking: Creative Holism for Managers*. London: John Wiley.

Kennedy, A.-M. and Parsons, A. (2012) 'Macro-social marketing and social engineering: a systems approach', *Journal of Social Marketing*, 2 (1): 37–51.

Kløcker Larsen, R. (2011) 'Critical systems thinking for the facilitation of conservation planning in Philippine coastal management', *Systems Research and Behavioral Science*, 28 (1): 63–76.

Kogetsidis, H. (2012) 'Critical systems thinking: a creative approach to organizational change', *Journal of Translational Management*, 17 (3): 189–204.

Kretzman, J. and McKnight, J.P. (1996) 'Assets-based community development', *National Civic Review*, 85 (4): 23–29.

Latour, B. (1987) *Science in Action: How to Follow Scientists and Engineers through Society*. Milton Keynes: Open University Press.

Latour, B. (2000) 'On recalling ANT', in J. Law and J. Hassard (eds), *Actor-Network Theory and After*. Oxford: Blackwell Publishers, pp. 15–26.

Latour, B. (2005) *Reassembling the Social: An Introduction to Actor-Network Theory*. New York: Oxford University Press.

Law, J. and Hassard, J. (eds) (2000) *Actor-Network Theory and After*. Oxford: Blackwell Publishers.

Leischow, S.J., Best, A., Trochim, W.M., Clark, P.I., Gallagher, R.S., Marcus, S.E. and Matthews, E. (2008) 'Systems thinking to improve the public's health', *America Journal of Preventive Medicine*, 35 (S2): S196–203.

Levin, M. (1994) 'Action research and critical systems thinking: two icons carved out of the same log', *Systems Practice*, 7 (1): 25–41.

Levin, K., Cashore, B., Bernstein, S. and Auld, G. (2012) 'Overcoming the tragedy of super wicked problems: constraining our future selves to ameliorate global climate change', *Policy Science*, 45 (2): 123–152.

Lindridge, A., MacAskill, S., Gnich, W., Eadie, D. and Holme, I. (2013) 'Applying an ecological model to social marketing communications', *European Journal of Marketing*, 47 (9): 1399–1420.

McKenzie-Mohr, D. (2000) 'Promoting sustainable behavior: an introduction to community-based social marketing', *Journal of Social Issues*, 56 (3): 543–554.

McKenzie-Mohr, D. (2011) *Fostering Sustainable Behavior: An Introduction to Community-based Social Marketing* (3rd edn). Gabriola Island, Canada: New Society Publishers.

Naaldenberg, J., Vaandrager, L., Koelen, M., Wagemakers, A.-M., Saan, H. and de Hoog, K. (2009) 'Elaborating on systems thinking in health promotion practice', *Global Health Promotion*, 16 (1): 39–47.

O'Connor, S.C., Cohen, J.E. and Osterlund, K. (2001) *Comprehensive Tobacco Control Programs: A Review and Synthesis of Evaluation Strategies in the United States*. Toronto, Ontario: Ontario Tobacco Research Unit, Special Report.

Ouschan, R., Sweeney, J.C. and Johnson, L. (2006) 'Customer empowerment and relationship outcomes in healthcare consultations', *European Journal of Marketing*, 40 (9/10): 1068–1086.

Petticrew, M., Tugwell, P., Welch, V., Ueffing, E., Kristjansson, E., Armstrong, R., Doyle, J. and Waters, E. (2009) 'Better evidence about wicked issues in tackling health inequalities', *Journal of Public Health*, 31 (3): 453–456.

PLOS Medicine Editors (2013) 'Addressing the wicked problem of obesity through planning and policies', *PLOS Medicine*, 10 (6): e1001475.

Prout, A. (1996) 'Actor-network theory, technology and medical sociology: an illustrative analysis of the metered dose inhaler', *Sociology of Health and Illness*, 18 (2): 198–219.

Richmond, B. (1997a) 'Dynamic thinking: a behavioural context', *The Systems Thinker*, 8 (6): 6–7.

Richmond, B. (1997b) 'Forest thinking', *The Systems Thinker*, 8 (10): 6–7.

Richmond, B. (1997c) 'System-as-cause thinking', *The Systems Thinker*, 8 (8): 6–7.

Richmond, B. (1997d) 'The "thinking" in systems thinking: how we can make it easier to master', *The Systems Thinker*, 8 (2): 1–5.

Richmond, B. (1998) 'Operational thinking', *The Systems Thinker*, 9 (2): 6–7.

Scottish Parliament (2011) *Community Empowerment (Scotland) Bill 2011*. Edinburgh: Her Majesty's Stationery Office.

Senge, P.M. (1990) *The Fifth Discipline: The Art and Practice of the Learning Organization*. New York: Doubleday.

Sharpe, P.A., Greaney, M.L., Lee, P.R. and Royce, S.W. (2000) 'Assets-oriented community assessment', *Public Health Reports*, 115 (2–3): 205–211.

Simon, K.-H. (2003) 'Critical systems thinking', in F. Parra-Luna (ed.), *Encyclopaedia of Life Support Systems (EOLSS): Vol II Systems Science and Cybernetics*. Oxford: UNESCO-EOLSS. Available at: www.eolss.net/ (9 December 1014).

Sowers, W., Doner, L., Smith, W.A., Rothschild, M. and Morse, D. (2005) 'Synthesis panel presentation on stretching the limits of partnerships, upstream and downstream', *Social Marketing Quarterly*, 11 (3/4): 61–66.

Stead, M., Arnott, L. and Dempsey, E. (2013) 'Healthy heroes, magic meals, and a visiting alien: community-led assets based social marketing', *Social Marketing Quarterly*, 19 (1): 26–39.

Stead, M., Gordon, R., Holme, I., Moodie, C., Hastings, G. and Angus, K. (2008) *A Review of Initiatives that Have Resulted in Changes in Attitudes, Knowledge, and Behaviour*. Stirling: Institute for Social Marketing, University of Stirling and The Open University.

Ulrich, W. (1983) *Critical Heuristics of Social Planning: A New Approach to Practical Philosophy*. Bern: Haupt.

Ulrich, W. (2003) 'Beyond methodology choice: critical systems thinking as critically systemic discourse', *The Journal of the Operational Research Society*, 54 (4): 325–342.

Vojtko, V. (2008) *An Overview of Systems Thinking Skills: 21st Century Systems Thinking Skills*. Available at: www.vivasystems.cz (last accessed 11 August 2014).

Wanless, D. (2004) *Securing Good Health for the Whole Population*. London: The Stationery Office.

Waters Foundation (2010) *Habits of a Systems Thinker*. Available at: http://watersfoundation.org/wp-content/uploads/2012/09/habits-onepage.pdf#page=1&view=FitH (last accessed 10 July 2014).

Wickramasinghe, N., Bali, R.K. and Tatnall, A. (2007) 'Using actor network theory to understand network centric healthcare operations', *International Journal of Electronic Healthcare*, 3 (3): 317–328.

Wilkins, A. (2012) 'Pedagogy of the consumer: the politics of neo-liberal welfare reform', *Journal of Pedagogy*, 3 (2): 161–173.

Wymer, W. (2011) 'Developing more effective social marketing strategies', *Journal of Social Marketing*, 1 (1): 17–31.

Young, D., Borland, R. and Coghill, K. (2010) 'an actor-network theory analysis of policy innovation for smoke-free places: understanding change in complex systems', *American Journal of Public Health*, 100 (7): 1208–1217.

Young, D., Borland, R. and Coghill, K. (2012) 'Changing the tobacco use management system: blending systems thinking with actor-network-theory', *Review of Policy Research*, 29 (2): 251–279.

8 USING THEORY IN SOCIAL MARKETING

Introduction

Theory informed practice

Clearly human behaviour influences and is influenced by many factors including: individual personality and will power, physiology, genetics, culture, evolution, technology, social norms, upbringing, habits, economics, culture and customs. Influencing behaviour sits at the heart of any approach to most social policy objectives, be it influencing the behaviour of individuals to protect themselves and others or the behaviour of professionals to act in specific ways, for example the take-up of evidence-based guidelines.

The role that behaviour theories and methodologies can play in the planning and evaluation of social policy that seeks to influence behaviour in a broad range of issues is beginning to draw attention from policy makers and professionals (Jackson, 2005; Darnton, 2008). This interest is supported by the growing body of evidence and accumulating experience in fields as diverse as road safety, energy use, safety and health at work that evidence-based, theory-informed and well-planned and executed behaviour change interventions can make considerable contributions to tackling these key social challenges and problems.

There are large numbers of theories and models and many summary reviews of common theories already exist, therefore this chapter does not attempt to set out a comprehensive review of all theoretical models. Rather the chapter sets out briefly some of the seminal works that are most often quoted and how they can be used to inform the development and delivery of behaviour influence programmes. The chapter also includes a summary of some of the attempts to produce taxonomies and totalising models of these theories and models.

One of the big challenges facing those responsible for developing and delivering programmes designed to influence behaviour is to understand and make a reasoned selection and use of the many theories that have been articulated to inform their programme design and delivery. The broad scope of theory and models which is continuously expanding can be perceived as a barrier to its use. The literature in the field is 'enormous' (Jackson, 2005) and 'bordering on the unmanageable' (Maio et al., 2007). Time pressured policy makers and professionals, due to this complexity, may well be reluctant to engage fully with theory and behavioural modelling even though they are aware of the insights it can bring (Michie et al., 2011).

Theories and models of behaviour

The development of a more systematic approach to social behaviour change (Michie et al., 2011) and a growing body of research (The Community Guide, 2000) that goes beyond communication theory based approaches to influencing social behaviour (McQuail, 2005) has been gaining ground over recent years (NICE, 2007, 2014).

Intervention approaches such as social marketing (French et al., 2010), co-creation (Cottam and Leadbeater, 2004) and community engagement (Hills, 2004) are examples of these new forms of social policy delivery. This development along with a more general improvement in social policy implementation (Public Administration Select Committee, 2009), planning and review (Australian Public Service Commission, 2007) has resulted in a growing consensus about how to go about establishing, delivering and evaluating more successful behavioural interventions focused on social good. A large number of theories and models of behaviour have been developed and codified over the last hundred years. There is a key distinction to be made, however, between 'models' of behaviour and 'theories' of change. Behavioural models seek to explain why people behave in the way they do, and help us understand specific behaviours by identifying the underlying factors that influence them, while theories of change seek to explain how behaviours change and what might influence them. Theories of change can also help with intervention development by suggesting broad approaches to intervention design, implementation and evaluation. However, the language of theory and models tends to overlap to a large degree in the literature of this field. In addition to the distinction between theory and models, Darnton (2008) notes three further distinctions between models of behaviour:

1. models of behaviour at the individual level
2. models of behaviour at higher levels of scale
3. applied models and frameworks.

It is also necessary to add planning models to this list. These planning models, such as PRECEDE-PROCEED (Green and Kreuter, 2005), the WHO COMBI model (WHO, 2012), P-Process model (O'Sullivan et al., 2003) and STELa (French, 2010), are underpinned not only by behavioural theory but also by planning and management theories. A review of these and other planning models relevant to social marketing is included in Chapter 12.

Defining theory and its use

Theories can be defined in many ways, but essentially they are composed of a set of interrelated concepts, definitions and propositions that present how behaviour is formed or influenced in given situations. Theories are used to describe, classify and in some cases attempt to predict future behavioural responses. Theory is useful because it provides a framework for analysing and conceptualising the process of behavioural influence and change and it can also be used to guide research on specific behaviours and to assist with the planning and selection of programme interventions.

Theories and models used to guide behaviour programmes can also assist the understanding of complex sets of influences, however, due to their simplifying nature, they are not capable of providing us with a complete understanding of problems at the individual, political and environmental level (Nutbeam et al., 2010). In addition Crosby and Noar (2010) have argued that theory is often stuck within an 'academic vacuum' and is often not applied rigorously in real-world situations.

Traditionally many behavioural theories and models have been developed within the discipline of psychology. Examples of some of these models and theories, which emphasise the importance of social pressures, knowledge and beliefs in achieving change, include the health belief model (Rosenstock, 1966) and the trans-theoretical model (Prochaska and DiClemente, 1983). These models, however, are now frequently criticised for being focused on individual issues and not taking account of economic, social or environmental issues, which have a big impact on behaviour.

As well as newer ecological models and theories that do recognise the importance of environmental, social and economic factors, a new understanding and theory are also being developed by economists and brain scientists, psychologists and sociologists. This relatively new theory indicates, as we explored in Chapter 3, that as well as reasoned action and environmental influence, many decisions and behaviours are triggered by rapid cognition or mindless choosing that does not involve rational choice.

The use of theory and models of behavioural influence is not without difficulty or disputes about its helpfulness. For example, a meta-analysis by Park-Higgerson et al. (2008), which analyses interventions on violence, failed to find evidence which suggested that theory-based interventions resulted in better outcomes than those without theory. However, some studies argue that it is in fact the incorrect selection of theory which limits the potential of an intervention and not the inclusion of theory in general (Aveyard et al., 2009; Prochaska, 2009). In addition, rather than using one theory, a combination of theories is advocated, as by using more than one theory a problem can be accounted for and evaluated at all theoretical levels (Green and Tones, 2010).

In a recent systematic review to examine evidence for the effectiveness of interventions that use theories and models of behaviour change in the design and delivery of the prevention and control of communicable disease commissioned by the European Centre for Disease Control (ECDC) (see Angus et al., 2011), 61 studies passed the critical screening methodology, 21 of which were designated as being of high quality. Behaviour change theories and models were used in these studies to either inform the behavioural intervention or to design or evaluate the intervention; there was a strong preference for theories and models focused on individual behaviour. Models of interpersonal behaviour were the next most frequently used, with community and theoretical planning models used less often. Nearly one third of the studies used multiple models.

With regard to the impact of the use of theory on the impact of the programmes, results were mixed. Of the high quality studies focused on prevention, nine were successful in meeting their behavioural targets, six were not. There was no comparative evidence available to state whether using theory made the interventions effective or not. However, the researchers then looked at the characteristics of the successful and unsuccessful programmes. What emerged was that studies that use theory to inform the design and evaluation of interventions, and go beyond the use of just individual theories to encapsulate broader interpersonal and community theory, appeared to be more successful. The review also found that only one study evaluated the cost effectiveness of theory-based interventions.

So while the evidence is not categorical, it is reasonable to conclude that when theory is applied in both analysis of behavioural challenges and to guide the planning of programme responses providing a broad approach that goes beyond individual based models, it is likely to lead to or at least make a contribution to more effective and efficient programme delivery (Roe et al., 1997; Halpern et al., 2003). Using theory can also result in better planning and targeting, and the setting out of more explicit aims and objectives. Theory can also help interventions more precisely focus on influencing specific elements of a behaviour based on a theoretical conception of what has or will influence people to behave in the desired way.

Key theories and models

This section of the chapter aims to set out a selection of the most quoted and most widely used theories and models and present a set of proto tools to assist practitioners with an understanding of current studies about influencing behaviour and how to begin to use theory in the construction of social marketing programmes. This section also sets out a number of more often quoted models that have relevance to behaviour change programme development.

There are many different ways to classify and describe the wide range of behavioural theory and models that exist. For the purpose of this chapter these theories and models are set out under the following headings:

- *Individual level theories*: describing the behaviour of individuals (theories of cognition, perceptions and motivation)
- *Interpersonal level theories*: describing the relationships between individuals (theories of social norms and social influence)
- *Community/group theories*: stressing the dynamics of community structures or institutions, theories of community mobilisation, intersectorial action and organisational change.
- *Systems and ecological theory*: dealing with multiple influencing factors.
- *Health focused theories*.

The final section of the chapter looks at how to develop and apply theory in an open reflexive way.

—————— **Discussion question** ——————

When planning a social marketing intervention, do you think it is most appropriate to start by considering individual, interpersonal or wider environmental factors that influence the behaviour?

Individual level theories

There is a wide range of individually focused behaviour change theories. The individually focused theories and models set out below, based on summaries by Mulgan et al. (2004) and COI (2009), are some of the most commonly used to explain factors that impact on individual behaviour and have been used extensively in the health sector (Glanz and Rimer, 2005). Many of these models explore factors such as knowledge, attitudes, beliefs, motivation, self-concept, learning, past experience and skills and self-perception as key determinants of behaviour.

Instrumental and classical conditioning

Seminal works: Pavlov (1927), Skinner (1953)

This model based on empirical experimentation with both animals and humans emphasises the impact on learning of associations between stimuli and the subsequent impacts on behaviour. Classical conditioning occurs when an 'unconditioned stimulus', such as food, becomes associated with another stimulus, such as a bell. The establishment of such associations can be applied in many ways to set up either positive or negative associations and so influence behaviour. Classical conditioning theory can be applied in many fields associated with complex human behaviour as well as simple animal response situations. Even highly complex human behaviours can often be explained through long chains of such associations.

Relevance to social marketing

With regard to social marketing classical conditioning has relevance when rewards, incentives or punishments are being considered. Incentives and disincentives include the use of conditional cash payments to promote behaviour such as taking children to school in developing countries or the use of fines or legal sanctions for not taking children to school in developed countries. As with all social marketing tactics, incentives and penalties need to be developed based on an understanding of what the intended target audience considers to be appropriate, proportional and fair if negative reactions are to be avoided.

Cognitive consistency and dissonance theory

Seminal work: Festinger (1957)

The cognitive consistency theory proposes that people are motivated to seek consistency between their beliefs, values and perceptions. The theory postulates that where there is a clash between people's actions and values or attitudes, people often resolve the discrepancy by changing their values or attitudes rather than their behaviour. For example, if someone agrees to take on a boring task for a very limited reward, there is a 'dissonance' between their behaviour (doing the task) and their reasoning (they would only do a boring task if there's a decent reward). One way out of this dissonance is to stop doing the task – i.e. change the behaviour, another is to change their attitude – i.e. convince themselves that the task is actually quite interesting.

Relevance to social marketing

Cognitive dissonance can be used in social marketing interventions through a process of highlighting clashes of behaviour and attitudes, for example by highlighting differences in favourable attitudes to hand washing and actual poor practice as a way of triggering people to think about instigating a change in their behaviour. By highlighting implicit cognitive dissonance people can become more aware and more mindful and in so doing take more rational and considered control over their behaviour.

'Heuristics' and the consumer information processing model

Seminal works: Tversky and Kahneman (1974), Bettman (1979)

Tversky and Kahneman have documented in detail how humans use mental shortcuts or 'heuristics' to make sense of their world and decision making and the impact this has on behaviour. Under normal circumstances heuristics do not present a problem, but in certain situations the use of these mental short-cuts can make people systematically prone to misjudgement and biases. Central assumptions are that individuals are limited in how much information they can process; and in order to increase the usability of information, they combine bits of information into 'chunks', and employ decision rules to make choices faster and in a less stressful way. Major heuristics include ones relating to availability stimulation, scarcity, fear of loss, peak experience, recency and discounting over time. All of these potential biases can have large effects on behaviour.

Relevance to social marketing

There are many examples of thought processing heuristics such as fear of loss, e.g. loss of physical functioning or mental capacity, which is a powerful influence on people's behaviour. We know that loss is often a more powerful motivator in decision situations than the prospect of gain. Knowing this means that using fear of loss is often a better way to frame messages than emphasising the gains that people may get in terms of protection from the adoption of a recommended behaviour. For example, emphasising the loss of happy times with children can be a more powerful motivator to stop smoking than appeals that emphasise a longer and healthier old age. Social marketers need to understand as part of their research effort the heuristics that target audiences are using to make sense of the world and the particular behavioural responses to the behaviour that the social programme is seeking to influence. This work is part of the insight development process that underpins social marketing practice.

Stages of change or trans-theoretical model

Seminal work: Prochaska and DiClemente (1983)

This is perhaps one of the best known and most quoted models used in many public health behavioural interventions. It proposes five stages for people's readiness to change or attempt to change (see Figure 8.1). The stages are not necessarily passed through sequentially. The stages of change model treats behaviour change as a linear process with discrete ordered stages. People can enter and exit at any point, and often 'recycle' through stages of change. The model emphasises that there are distinct if not discrete stages in the change process which can be identified, and specific interventions can then be developed to encourage action and moving through the stages to a successful behavioural goal. One of the key limitations of the model is that it does not explain what the triggers to the different stages are, nevertheless insights from other psychology models and from behavioural economics and social marketing may help to address this gap.

Relevance to social marketing

This model has influenced approaches to social marketing that gradually build people's willingness to take on large-scale behaviour changes. The model is useful as it identifies that there are different elements/stages to behaviour change and also attempts to disentangle these complex processes. Therefore this model can enable practitioners to develop both segmentations of audiences dependent on the stage of change they occupy and targeted intervention mixes for people at different stages of change.

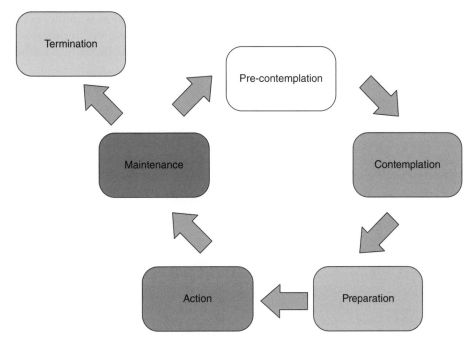

Figure 8.1 Stages of change model

Theory of reasoned action/theory of planned behaviour

Seminal works: Fishbein and Ajzen (1975), Ajzen (1985)

The theory of planned behaviour, and its precursor the theory of reasoned action, examine the relationship between behaviour and psychological issues such as beliefs, attitudes and intentions. The model was originally based on the assumption that human beings are rational and that behaviours are therefore under their control and developed for a set of reasoned decisions. However, in the 1990s, Ajzen and Driver added an element that acknowledged the importance of factors beyond the individual's control, which impact on the ability to change behaviour. This became known as the theory of planned behaviour, which has been used by many public health programmes. The theory holds that 'behavioural intention' is the key determinant of behaviour and that an individual's attitude towards performing behaviour is one of the biggest influences on behavioural intention. Subjective norms are beliefs about what others think about the behaviour under consideration, and are seen as having a key impact on behavioural intention.

The theory of planned behaviour adds 'perceived behavioural control' to the theory. This is the amount of control an individual perceives they have over a behaviour and explains when behaviour or behavioural intention is influenced by factors beyond an individual's perceived control. In highlighting the importance of subjective norms, i.e. the perceived beliefs of others as well as individual attitudes and characteristics, the theory provides a conceptual link to interpersonal and community theories of behaviour change. The theory also highlights why knowledge alone doesn't necessarily lead to a change in a person's behaviour (see Figure 8.2).

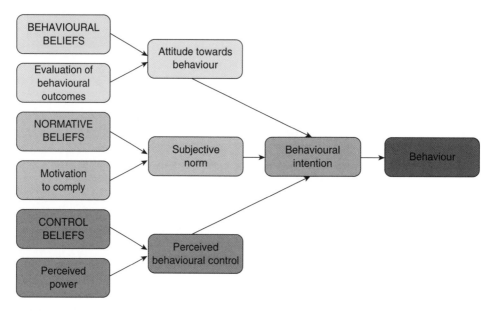

Figure 8.2   Theory of reasoned action/theory of planned behaviour

Relevance to social marketing

The theory of reasoned action/planned behaviour is a useful conceptual tool for social marketers. It can be used as a diagnostic tool when looking at a social behaviour that needs to be understood. Each of its elements can be investigated to develop an understanding of factors that are influencing behaviour. The model can also be used to identify potential intervention points. For example, if people perceive that they have little control over behaviours such as the over-consumption of energy one potential intervention approach might be to provide them with ways to exert more control, such as the provision of visible energy use meters in their homes to give feedback and so enable them to reduce their energy consumption.

CASE STUDY

Change4Life

The English cross-government obesity team's Change4Life campaign aims to help families improve their long-term health by making positive changes to their lifestyle. Obesity is caused by a wide range of factors, including environmental, economic, media, educational and technological factors, and tackling it calls for a multi-faceted, cross-societal approach. Change4Life was launched in 2009 and forms part of a wider UK cross-government strategy, Healthy Weight, Healthy Lives, which includes initiatives such as building safe places to play, promoting healthy food in schools and the development of an active transport policy. There is no single theoretical behaviour change model for obesity prevention, so the Change4Life team based its social marketing programme on a hypothetical behaviour change journey derived from a review of behaviour change theories and research with the target market.

The right conditions for change

The most relevant models included the theory of planned behaviour, social cognitive theory and social capital theory. Based on these theoretical insights the team agreed that the programme should be split into two steps: first, creating the right conditions for behaviour change; and second, supporting people on their behaviour change journey.

The marketing plan was therefore split into six phases, which map onto the following behaviour change journey:

Phase 1: engaging with workforces and partners, including local service providers and NGOs, both face-to-face and through direct marketing.

Phase 2: reframing obesity as relevant to the target audience groups with the aim of encouraging a social movement, using TV, print and outdoor advertising, PR, a helpline, a campaign website and fulfilment materials, and by building partnerships.

Phase 3: personalising the issue by making people realise that their behaviours could be putting themselves and their families at risk. The main mechanism for this was a questionnaire, asking families about a typical day in their lives. Responding to this questionnaire triggered individualised advice and guidance. Activity was targeted at postcodes with the highest risk of obesity.

(Continued)

(Continued)

Phase 4: defining the eight behaviours families should adopt and promoting them through advertising and a range of partners, using direct and relationship marketing and focusing activity on areas where target audience groups were most likely to live.

Phase 5: inspiring people to change through real-life stories in the local and national press, and locally targeted activities.

Phase 6: ongoing support and encouragement for at-risk families going through the change process, delivered by post and online.

The Change4Life programme has been continuously evaluated over its five-year life, and it has been shown to have a positive effect not only on attitudes and awareness but also on the eight specific behaviours targeted by the programme among families with young children The programme has also demonstrated changes in the buying behaviour of parents and reductions in body weight and body mass index in targeted groups. In order to create a robust evidence base 7 per cent of the total marketing budget has been spent on research, monitoring and evaluation of campaign activity. Such a complex intervention necessitates a mixed method approach to evaluation to ensure a rounded view of the programme.

Further details of the evaluation approach adopted and results can be found at: http://webarchive.nationalarchives.gov.uk/20130107105354/ and www.dh.gov.uk/en/PublicationsandstatisticsPublications/PublicationsPolicy AndGuidance/DH_112529.

Protection-motivation theory

Seminal work: Rogers (1975)

Protection-motivation theory (PMT) considers that behaviour change may be achieved by appealing to an individual's fears. It identifies three components of fear arousal: the magnitude of harm of a depicted event; the probability of that event's occurrence; and the efficacy of the proposed protective response. PMT suggests that these components combine to determine the intensity of the protection-motivation resulting in activity occurring as a result of a desire to protect oneself from danger. This theory explicitly uses the costs and benefits of existing and recommended behaviour to predict the likelihood of behaviour change (Gebhardt and Maes, 2001). The most recent version of the theory assumes that the motivation to protect oneself from danger is a positive linear function of beliefs that the threat is severe, that the individual is personally vulnerable and that the individual can perform the coping response and that the coping response is effective at reducing or eliminating risk. This theory has influenced many public health programmes that deal with risks associated with infections and to some extent chronic disease risk as well (see Figure 8.3).

Relevance to social marketing

The implication of the theory is that people need to recognise risk, their vulnerability to the risk and believe in the efficacy of the recommended action to reduce risk. Social marketing interventions can use this model to guide research into an assessment of people's perception of risk and also their understanding and attitudes towards suggested actions that they can take to reduce their risk. The model can also be used to identify potential intervention opportunities related to each of the four factors that influence behavioural intention. For example, if people do not believe that eating less sugar will reduce their chances of obesity, novel ways of convincing them that this is in fact the case may be needed before they will be willing to change their behaviour.

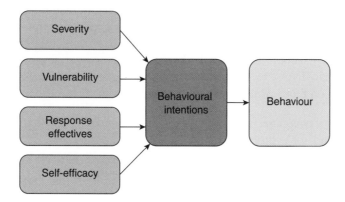

Figure 8.3   Protection-motivation theory

Interpersonal level theories

Interpersonal models and theories focus on the wider social interactions and environment and how these impact on behaviour. These models assume that people are strongly influenced by the opinions, views, beliefs and values of people that they interact with, especially close relations and significant people in their lives. These models also explore how significant others can assist with or detract from socially responsible decisions. This focus is key in terms of developing influencing strategies as it may be possible to develop interventions that target one group with the aim of influencing another. Behaviour change is often better effected by focusing not just on individuals, but also on their relationships with those around them.

These models cover not only small micro-environmental social influences such as the views of close family members but also larger social effects such as the impact of public opinions, the influence of social norms and how changes in these spread across populations. Examples include interventions that focus on the use of social networks, peer support, role models and mentors, to influence behaviour and attitudes.

Social cognitive theory

Seminal work: Bandura (1977, 1986)

This theory focuses on skill and competency, and emphasises the importance of enhancing a person's behavioural capability and self-confidence. In social cognitive theory (SCT), human behaviour is explained in terms of how personal factors, environmental influences and behaviour continually interact (see Figure 8.4). SCT postulates that behaviour can be influenced by increasing knowledge and skills and asserts that human behaviour is directly shaped by an individual's competencies and their beliefs in their own capabilities. Bandura argues that human behaviour is a result of the constant interplay of *personal factors* (cognitive, affective/emotional and biological events), *environmental* (external) *factors* and how people interpret the results of their *behaviour*. People make things happen by their own actions, drawing on a range of personal factors, including habits of thinking and self-beliefs.

SCT is based on the view that humans are instilled with certain capabilities including:

- *a capacity to symbolise*: enabling us to extract meaning from the environment around us and solve problems
- *forethought*: a capability to plan courses of action, anticipate and set goals
- *vicarious learning*: the ability to observe and learn from others
- *self-regulation*: the potential for self-directed change
- *self-reflection*: enabling us to make sense of our experiences and self-evaluation.

SCT holds that each of us has different levels of these capabilities and types of skill and competencies. Key to SCT is the concept of *self-efficacy*. Self-efficacy determines how we feel and think about ourselves and ultimately how we behave. Belief in self-efficacy can have diverse effects; it can determine the amount of effort and perseverance people put into a task and how much resilience they display in adverse or challenging situations. Importantly, what we believe we are capable of may actually differ from what we can actually do.

Bandura believes that people's self-beliefs are more likely to influence what they do than their actual skills and competencies. Self-efficacy beliefs are influenced by four main sources:

- *mastery experiences*: that is, personal experience of our own successes and failures
- *vicarious experiences*: observing the success and failure of others

- *social persuasion*: the direct influence of those around us
- *somatic and emotional states*: i.e. stress, anxiety, positive and negative moods, which can affect people's judgements of their personal efficacy as can the physical condition or state of their body, for example how tired a person is or how hungry.

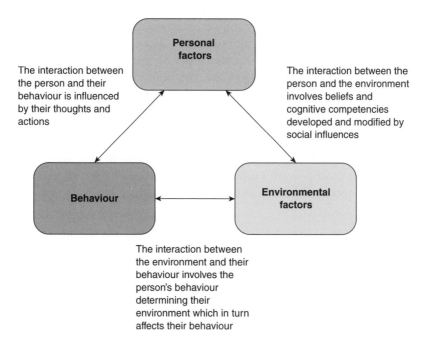

Figure 8.4 Social cognitive theory

Relevance to social marketing

SCT is a useful model because it emphasises the interplay between personal, environmental and behaviour factors. Social marketers can use this theory to help research not only the factors that exert influence on decision making and behaviour but also the interplay of the impact of these factors. As with other theories, SCT also indicates that there are at least three potential ways to seek to influence specific behaviours. These are interventions aimed at influencing self-perception and understanding, actions that seek to influence environmental triggers and prompts to behaviour and behaviours themselves. An example of influencing behaviour itself and this subsequently having an impact on personal perception and environmental factors would be the imposition of a ban on smoking in the workplace. Such an intervention directly targeting the behaviour might lead to a personal reconsideration of the need and desire to smoke. This might also lead to an impact on environmental factors such as the availability of cigarettes for sale at work, which in turn impacts on behaviour and the personal desire to smoke.

Social networks and social support theory

Seminal work: House (1981)

According to House, a social network is a web of social relationships which is characterised by a number of actions and states of mind including: reciprocity (the
behaviour of both giving and receiving or exchanging mutually beneficial goods,
services or support) and emotional closeness and social support. An effective social
network is also characterised by the extent to which members interact and get to
know each other. Additional actors in the creation and maintenance of effective
social networks that provide support relate not only to how similar members of the
network are in terms of their demographics but also intellectual, emotional and
belief systems. Other factors include ease of communication and assembly such as
geographical dispersion or compactness. Social support is characterised as a form of
aid and assistance, which is exchanged through social networks. According to this
theory some of the most powerful influences on a person's behaviour and views will
be formed and supported by the attitudes and resources within a person's social
network.

Relevance to social marketing

One of the consequences of this theory is that people will be far more influenced
by the views and actions of friends and family than by advice from government or
professionals not within their social network. When developing social marketing
strategies and tactics it is often important to consider who might be able to influence
individuals' behaviour. For example, the power of peer support or challenge can
have a big effect. Significant and trusted people from people's social networks can
often be recruited to help targeted individuals adopt positive social behaviours.
Examples include recruiting grandmothers to help promote breastfeeding, and
respected and trusted community elders or religious leaders to promote changes in
diet or increased charitable donations.

Social influence and interpersonal theory

Seminal work: Kelly and Thibaut (1978)

According to Kelly and Thibaut interpersonal communication is influenced by a number of factors associated with both the nature of the person that is seeking to exert
influence and the form or type of influencing strategy that is being applied.
Interpersonal social influence is influenced strongly by both the perceived power and
the authority that is invested in the person seeking to exert influence by the person
being influenced. According to this theory the basis of power or authority in a relationship may be categorised in six ways:

1. *Expert*: someone else is more knowledgeable.
2. *Legitimate*: someone has the 'right' to direct behaviour derived from a recognised social role that is imbued with credibility and authority.
3. *Coercive*: when another has the power to punish.
4. *Reward*: when another has the power to reward.
5. *Informational*: the person who is seeking to persuade holds important information that is of value to the receiver.
6. *Referent*: power is based on *identification* with the person trying to exert influence. This is among the most effective sources of power and is affected by factors such as 'liking' or empathy with the persuader.

Relevance to social marketing

Perceived power and authority are key factors in persuasion and may often assist with securing 'compliance' with recommended actions. When developing a social marketing programme it is important to think not only about the communication messages and strategies but also about the message giver. The organisation that is associated with any intervention or the face and voice that are selected to convey the recommended actions can have a big impact on the target audience response. The prime consideration when selecting which organisation or organisations should be seen as supporting a programme and the person or persons selected to be its face and voice is that they should be viewed favourably by the intended target audience as displaying as many as possible of the six characteristics set out in social influence and interpersonal theory.

Attribution and balance theories

Seminal work: Heider (1958)

These are theories concerning how people explain their own behaviour and the behaviour of other people. Phenomena identified by these theories include:

- *Fundamental attribution error*: this refers to the human tendency to over-emphasise dispositional (personal attributes) factors about people, and under-emphasise situational (environmental) factors.
- *False uniqueness*: this is the human tendency to hold an exaggerated view of our own positive qualities and abilities. Most people also tend to underestimate others' abilities as well as over-emphasising their own.
- *False consensus*: this is the tendency that people have to over-estimate the extent to which others agree with their own views and beliefs.
- *Inter-group bias*: this refers to similar self-serving attribution biases, but at the group level. People attribute disproportionately good qualities and virtues to groups they belong to or identify with, while seeing members of other groups as possessing fewer positive qualities.

Relevance to social marketing

An implication of these theories is that care needs to be taken to understand how these heuristics may be used to interpret efforts to create change or compliance with social marketing programme goals. When developing interventions aimed at influencing behaviour these phenomena can also be used to inform the development of strategies. For example, in relation to attribution error, a recognition of environmental barriers to change can be addressed by changing the way a social service such as access to immunisation is offered. Phenomena such as false consensus can also be the focus of social marketing programmes that aim to challenge this assumption. For example, in the field of racial tension, by making it clear to people who hold negative views about another racial group that the views are not shared by other members of their own racial group.

Theory of interpersonal behaviour (TIB)

Seminal work: Triandis (1977)

This theory takes account of individuals' less rational decision making and the impact of habit on influencing behaviour. Habit is defined as a separate and key causal factor in the model, alongside attitudes, norms, roles, self-concept, beliefs and attitudes to likely outcomes.

The model gives significant emphasis to the power of habit as well as intentions and other influencing factors in determining behaviour (see Figure 8.5). TIB indicates that our behaviour can sometimes be unplanned and unconscious and has been shown to be a good or better predictor of behaviour in situations where there is a significant habitual component. Embodied in the model is the thesis that our behaviour can follow two different paths: a deliberative path (via intentions) and an automatic path (via habits). This dual path theory has been called System One and System Two thinking (Stanovich and West, 2000). Put simply, System One cognition is fast, easy and automatic, while System Two is slow and deliberate. The two thinking systems run in parallel and much of our behaviour is automatic and directed by System One, but on occasions we perform careful deliberative decision making, and that occurs in System Two. However, System Two decision making is hard and we soon tire of it. Habits are bound up in this thinking, and the two paths or processes run in parallel, one moderating the influence of the other: we are rarely purely deliberative or purely habitual in our behaviour. See Chapter 3 for a fuller exploration of System One and System Two cognition.

Relevance to social marketing

The implications of the TIB model for social marketers is that much of our behaviour and much of our decision making is simply automatic or habitual. Therefore appeals based on rational choice may have little influence on behaviour if the behaviour in

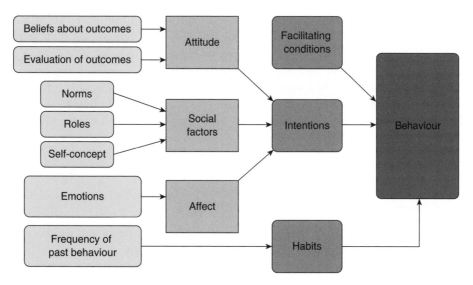

Figure 8.5 Theory of interpersonal behaviour

question is following the habitual path. One of the best predictors of people's future behaviour is how they have behaved in the past or to study their habits. When developing social marketing strategies and selecting a mix of interventions the impact of any habitual responses needs to be fully considered. Helping people to first recognise and then change a habitual response can be a powerful way to bring about a change in behaviour. For example, if people who are trying to lose weight can be helped to first recognise the times of day and under what circumstances that they are more likely to eat high calorie foods through keeping a diary, they can then begin to put in place alternative strategies to prevent such habitual responses. A practical example would be the removal of a jar of cookies from the area in a kitchen where tea or coffee is made.

——————— **Discussion question** ———————

Think of a social challenge and a specific behaviour that is associated with it such as liver disease and habitual at home drinking by older people. Select two of the individual theories and use them to analyse the causal factors of the behaviour. Try to identify, using the theories, potential intervention points and actions.

Community/group theories

Recent developments in the understanding of behaviour have focused on the importance of behaviour in a community context; there is clearly a great deal of overlap between these theories and those that relate to interpersonal influence. These theories and models explore how social systems function and change and their impact on individuals and influencers. They also aim to explain how behaviour change can be encouraged in groups and organisations. Clearly such models have utility in informing and understanding approaches to influencing communities, and in the mobilisation of intersectorial cooperation and interorganisational change, as well as a key impact on health communications and attempts to influence individuals' behaviour.

Social capital theory

Seminal works: Coleman (1988), Putnam (1995)

The 'social capital' concept or theory holds that social capital exists and can be measured in a community, and that it is made up of the quantity and quality of social networks and personal relationships and the cooperative quality of a society's social interactions. Social capital can also be discerned through observation of the consistency of application of social norms and values, and of how a community informally and formally shapes the quantity of social interactions. The core insight of this theory is that social networks and cooperative social norms have positive personal value to individuals and to wider communities.

Three types of social capital are often distinguished: *bonding* social capital (e.g. among family members or ethnic groups); *bridging* social capital (e.g. across ethnic groups); and *linking* social capital (e.g. across political classes). Variations in the strength or weakness of social capital are reflected in and may partly explain variations in key social outcomes, including crime rates, educational performance, mortality and morbidity and economic performance.

Relevance to social marketing

A key implication of this theory is that one of the prerequisites for effective social programmes may be the need to build, enhance or incentivise the development of social capital (Bourdieu, 2011 [1986]). Social marketing can help through research to determine the extent of existing and latent social capital within communities (Spotswood and Tapp, 2013). Social marketing also seeks to build relationships with target audiences and engage them individually and collectively in the development and delivery of social interventions. Scholars have for some time recognised the relevance and potential value of social capital theory for social marketing (Glenane-Antoniadis et al., 2003; Kamin and Anker, 2014). The application of what McKenzie-Mohr and Smith (1999) call community-based social marketing is an example of this approach to social marketing, which seeks not only to address specific behaviours but also to develop community capacity and links that can be used to address other social challenges.

Critical theory

Seminal works: Horkheimer (1972 [1937]), Habermas (1990)

Critical theory is a paradigm and school of thought influenced by Marxist theory, deconstructionism and several other streams of thought, which espouses a reflexive critique of society and culture by applying knowledge and ideas from the social sciences and humanities. Importantly, critical theory is not focused on critique for its own sake, but is geared towards thinking about and proposing solutions to improve the human condition. Max Horkheimer, a leading critical scholar, identified the emancipatory orientation of critical theory, describing a theory as being critical when it seeks 'to liberate human beings from the circumstances that enslave them' (1982: 244). The critical theory paradigm emerged from the Frankfurt school of social philosophers led by Horkheimer, Theodor Adorno and colleagues, and later by Jürgen Habermas. Critical theory puts a significant onus on critically reflexive practice, a concept also discussed in Chapter 7 and in Chapter 12. Critical theory has been widely engaged in a number of disciplines including sociology (Scambler, 1996), cultural studies (Gunster, 2004), politics (Dubiel, 1985), medicine (Waitzkin, 1989), marketing (Saren et al., 2007), and more recently social marketing (Gordon, 2011).

Relevance to social marketing

In social marketing critical theory can help us think reflexively about the impact that commercial forces have on society (see Gordon, 2011), as well as think critically and carefully about social marketing theory and practice and whether these are ethical, equitable and sustainable. The idea is that thinking critically about these issues can help us address problems and identify potential solutions.

Diffusion of innovations theory (DI)

Seminal work: Rogers (1995)

Diffusion of innovations theory addresses how new ideas, products and social practices spread within a society or from one society to another. Diffusion is facilitated through five key concepts: relative advantage, compatibility, complexity, observability and trialling.

- *Relative advantage*: this is the extent to which an innovation is better than what it replaces. An innovation can be a product, service idea, a behaviour programme or policy. An innovation presents a clear choice for an individual to continue with an inferior activity or embrace a superior one.
- *Compatibility*: this concept describes how well the innovation fits with the values, habits, experience and needs of the intended audience.
- *Complexity*: this acknowledges that people are more likely to make a behaviour change if the suggested innovation is easy to implement.

- *Trialability*: this refers to the concept of 'try before you buy' with innovations being more likely to succeed if individuals can try them before committing totally to a behaviour.
- *Observability*: this indicates how likely the innovation will be to produce tangible results and also how socially visible is it to other people who often want others to be able to see that they are taking up new behaviours or have bought new products.

DI theory indicates that populations can be classified by their approach to new innovations into five groups:

1. *Innovators*: this relatively small group will be the first to adopt new innovations. They place a great deal of value on being the first to get the benefits of the new innovation and being seen to be innovators by other groups. They strongly influence the next group, the early adopters.
2. *Early adopters*: this is the second fastest category of individuals to adopt an innovation. These individuals have the highest degree of opinion leadership among the other adopter categories. Early adopters are typically younger in age, have a higher social status, have more financial lucidity, advanced education, and are more socially forward than late adopters.
3. *Early majority adopters*: individuals in this category adopt an innovation after a varying degree of time. The time of adoption is significantly longer than the innovators and early adopters. Early majority adopters tend to have above average social status, contact with early adopters and show some opinion leadership.
4. *Late majority adopters*: individuals in this category will adopt an innovation after the average member of the society. The late majority adopters are typically sceptical about an innovation, have below average social status and often have less financial resources. They are in contact with others in late majority and early majority, but show very little opinion leadership.
5. *Laggards*: individuals in this category are the last to adopt an innovation. These individuals typically have an aversion to change and change-agents and tend to be older. Laggards typically tend to be focused on 'traditional solutions' and have low social status and fewer financial resources. They are in contact with family and close friends but have very little to no opinion leadership with other categories.

The rates of adoption for innovations are determined by an individual's adopter category. In general individuals who first adopt an innovation require a shorter adoption period than late adopters (see Figure 8.6). Within the rate of adoption there is a point at which an innovation reaches its critical mass or tipping point (Gladwell, 2004). This is a point in time within the adoption curve when enough individuals have adopted an innovation in order that the continued adoption of the innovation is self-sustaining. In describing how an innovation reaches its critical mass, Rogers (1995) outlines several strategies in order to help an innovation reach this stage.

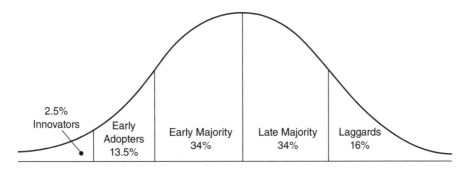

Figure 8.6 Diffusion of innovations theory

Relevance to social marketing

These strategies all have relevance to social marketing, for example the recognition that there are normally different groups in society with regard to the adoption of a new idea or behaviour enables the development of targeted strategies aimed at each different group. An example of such a segmented strategy might focus on having a social innovation such as eating less meat endorsed and adopted by highly respected individuals or groups within a social network. This can help to create demand and desire for the innovation by early adopters and early majority groups. The model also implies the need for a very different mix of interventions when seeking to influence late majority and laggard groups. These groups might need special support pro-grammes and more coercive interventions such as fines for or prohibition of certain behaviours such as smoking.

Systems and ecological theory

There is a growing consensus in many fields that social behavioural interventions should be based on what has been described as an 'ecological model' (Smedley and Syme, 2000). An ecological model (National Institutes of Health, 2005) approach views human behaviour as a form of complex ecology with multiple influences. Health behaviour in this conception is influenced by a dynamic interaction between biology, psychological factors and environmental influences. The relationship and influence of these factors are not static over time and can change depending on the life course stage of individuals.

Social ecological model

Seminal work: Bronfenbrenner (1977, 1979)

The social ecological model (SEM) is a framework that examines the multiple effects and correlations of social elements in an environment. It can provide a theoretical framework to analyse various contexts and in multiple research applications – most commonly qualitative research. The most utilised version of SEM was developed by Bronfenbrenner (1977, 1979).

He proposed four types of nested environmental systems of influence:

- *Microsystem*: immediate environments (family, school, peer group, neighbourhood).
- *Mesosystem*: a system of connections between immediate environments (such as a child's home or school).
- *Exosystem*: external environmental settings which only indirectly affect development (e.g. a parent's workplace).
- *Macrosystem*: the wider cultural context (East versus West, national economy, political culture, sub-culture).

Later a fifth system was added:

- *Chronosystem*: patterns of environmental events and transitions over the course of life.

Each system contains roles, norms and rules that shape psychological development.

Relevance to social marketing

Given the complexity of many social issues that social marketing is applied to, action at the microsystem/individual level alone is often not enough. Indeed, social marketing scholars have long been advocating for multi-level social marketing programmes involving downstream (e.g. individual), midstream (e.g. community/workplace), and upstream (policy/law/ social norms) action (Goldberg, 1995; Gordon, 2013). Therefore, social ecology offers a good framework for understanding the various levels of action that may be required in social marketing programmes. For example the Centre for Disease Control and Prevention uses a four-level system to identify SEM, to identify areas for prevention activities: societal, community, relationship and individual. Each of the levels has obvious synergies with social marketing that can act in each arena (Alcalay and Bell, 2000). The model has been used in social marketing interventions on adolescent physical activity (Elder et al., 2007), safer driving (Collins et al., 2010), and oral health (Lindridge et al., 2013).

Systems thinking and change

Seminal works: Checkland (1981), Senge (1990), Flood and Jackson (1991), Argyris and Schon (1996)

Systems thinking is a theory developed as an approach to problem solving. Many of our current social problems are conceived as consequences of wider complex social systems. The central premise of systems thinking is that systems have *emergent properties* and the components of these systems interact to create effects which the components could not have generated on their own. Systems are believed to exhibit the following characteristics:

- self-organising
- non-linear
- constantly changing
- history dependent
- tightly linked
- counter-intuitive
- governed by feedback
- resistant to change. (Sterman, 2006)

Systems thinking is focused on understanding the total system of influences and how its components interact in a holistic way rather than dissembling factors through a process of individually analysing individual elements. In this way systems thinking is the exact opposite of much public health analysis that seeks to disassemble complex problems into discrete components that can be studied. Senge (1990) makes the distinction between 'detail complexity', which traditional analysis can deal with by disassembly, and 'dynamic complexity', which involves systemic interactions over time and generates emergent properties.

In the context of influences on behaviour the feedback loop is the central construct in systems thinking. Behaviour in systems thinking develops through continuous positive and negative feedback loops or interactions, rather than through simple cause and effect relationships. Systems thinking also makes the distinction between transformational and incremental change. Transformational change requires the kind of deep insight that can expose and reshape underlying assumptions, whereas incremental change works within the existing structure. Systems thinking challenges the traditional approaches to behaviour change, which use theory to identify what works so it can be replicated elsewhere. In contrast systems thinking proposes an approach of reflective practice and continuous inquiry, rather than the implementing of set approaches or theories.

Systems thinking methods are particularly good for approaching messy problems, where diverse stakeholders are involved and cause and effects are multiple. Collective diagnosis of problems and collective development of solutions are key elements of systems thinking and organisational change models. Systems thinking is advocated by de Savigny and Taghreed (2009), who have identified a ten step approach to systems thinking in the health sector:

- Convene stakeholders.
- Determine indicators.
- Collectively brainstorm.
- Choose methods.

- Conceptualise effects.
- Select design.
- Adapt and redesign.
- Develop plan.
- Set budget.
- Source funding.

Relevance to social marketing

As strategic social marketing is a form of systems thinking, it rejects the notion that there is a single theory that can explain or describe a set of social phenomena, rather it seeks to use a range of such theories allied with a systematic and reflective process to develop bespoke strategies and mixes of interventions to influence specifically identified behaviours. The principles of systems thinking and the ten step process identified by de Savigny and Taghreed (2009) are a helpful checklist that can be used alongside the guides to developing and selecting strategy and implementing an operational social marketing plan set out in Chapter 12. Also, see Chapter 7 for a dedicated chapter on systems thinking and its implication for the strategic application of social marketing.

Assemblages and actor-network theory

Seminal works: Deleuze and Guattari (1980), Callon (1986), Latour (1987), De Landa (2006)

Assemblages theory is an approach to understanding and analysing systems as not simply a single whole. Rather this approach strongly emphasises systems as being characterised by fluidity, being ever changing, and being capable of being interpreted any number of ways and of producing any number of effects (De Landa, 2006). In some ways assemblages theory bridges the gap between operational thinking – social analysis at the level of individuals (micro-reductionism) – and systems thinking and the study of society as a whole. Assemblages theory proposes a new ontology for the study of systems by considering social entities on all levels, from sub-individual to transnational, which are best being synthesised and analysed through their components (De Landa, 2006).

Within the assemblages paradigm, one prominent approach that has emerged is *actor-network theory* (ANT) (Callon, 1986; Latour, 1987). ANT essentially maps interactions between entities that are material (between things) and semiotic (between concepts), and assumes that many interactions are material and semiotic. Actor networks are therefore networks of interrelated human and non-humans actors of associated interests that are established and characterised through their relationships with other actors in a network (Law, 2000). ANT can help us understand the interactions and associations between actors in a network, for example to understand how alcohol policies are formed, or how commercial interests may coalesce to lobby against public health interests. See the case study example of actor-network theory in social marketing contained in Chapter 7.

Relevance to social marketing

Social marketing can often involve assemblages in which materials (people, organisations, objects) and semiotics (concepts) may exist. However, given the primary focus in social marketing on the operational level, often not much thought is given to how assemblages may operate, and how actors in social marketing actor networks may interact and how issues are considered by the various actors. The relevance of understanding how such systems operate is clear for social marketing particularly at the midstream and upstream levels, as it can help us map, understand and potentially influence how things like policy and social norms may develop and change. Social marketing scholars have recently begun to consider how assemblages theory and specifically ANT are relevant to social marketing (see Gordon and Gurrieri, 2014) but further work in this area would be welcome.

Needs, opportunities and abilities model

Seminal work: Gatersleben and Vlek (1998)

The needs, opportunities and abilities (NOA) model of consumer behaviour is a good example of an ecological model that explicitly incorporates factors at the environmental level (see Figure 8.7). NOA consists of an intention-based model of individual behaviour 'nested' within a model that shows the influence of macro-level environmental factors. At the individual level, intentions are formed through both 'motivation' (which is driven by needs and opportunities) and 'behavioural control' or agency (which is driven by opportunities and abilities). At the macro level, needs, opportunities and abilities are influenced by the five environmental factors: technology, economy, demography, institutions and culture. The model shows a two-way relationship between environmental factors and consumer behaviour, with a large 'feedback loop' linking the top and bottom levels (Darnton, 2008).

Relevance to social marketing

NAO provides a valuable demonstration of how macro factors can influence behaviour and shows clearly that focusing only on personal factors may not bring about sustained and large-scale population level change.

The NOA model also shows how consumer or citizen behaviour influences societal factors, as well as being influenced by these factors; this interaction or two-way feedback loop is missing from many of the other theories covered in this chapter. One of the key implications of the model for social marketing practice is the need to develop

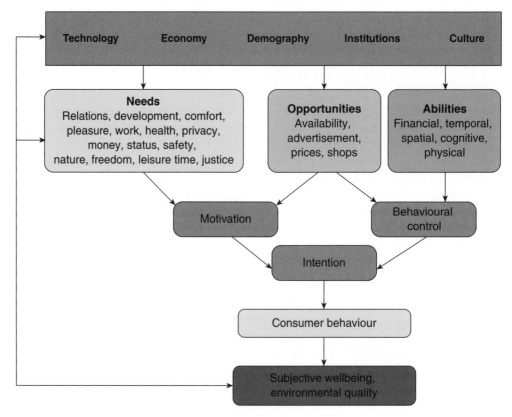

Figure 8.7 Needs, opportunities and abilities model

a strategy that includes a variety of intervention types and forms that work at multiple levels of influence to generate a change in behaviour across a social system. The model also makes it clear that there is a need to focus action on influencing people's expressed and felt needs, providing easy to access opportunities and incentives to behave in socially responsible and rewarding ways. Finally the model illustrates the need to ensure that people have the knowledge, skills, resources and ability to adopt recommended behaviours.

Motivation theory/hierarchy of needs

Seminal works: Maslow (1954), Herzberg (1966)

Motivation is a central component that causes changes in desire. A motivation is essentially a desire to behave or act in a particular way. There are a number of theories of motivation predominantly from the psychology field, some looking at general human motivation and others at more specific dimensions of human motivation.

Maslow's *hierarchy of needs* is a prominent general theory developed by psychologist Abraham Maslow (1954) to describe and understand the pattern that human motivations generally move through. His theory proposed five layers of motivation needs that humans have from the most basic and fundamental through to the most advanced: *physiological, safety, love/belonging, esteem* and *self-actualisation*. Maslow also acknowledged that humans are complex and that parallel processes and therefore different motivations from the various levels proposed in his model may operate at the one time (see Figure 8.8). To develop his model, Maslow studied humans he believed to be exemplary, such as Albert Einstein and Eleanor Roosevelt. He also usually conducted research studies with the healthiest 1 per cent of the college population.

Maslow theorised that at the basic level humans' *physiological needs* include breathing, food, water, sex, sleep, thermal comfort and excretion. Next, when the physical needs of a person are met, they focus on *safety needs* – such as security of body, of employment, of resources, of morality, of the family, of health and of property. The next level of human needs is *love/belonging* at the interpersonal level. This is especially strong in childhood, and can include friendship, family and intimacy; and when an adult sexual intimacy. *Esteem* is the next level of human needs, and focuses on self-esteem, confidence, achievement and respect of others. Finally, *self-actualisation* refers to human needs relating to morality, creativity, spontaneity, problem solving, lack of prejudice and acceptance of fact. Maslow theorised that the most basic levels of human needs must be met before a person is motivated to desire secondary or higher level needs.

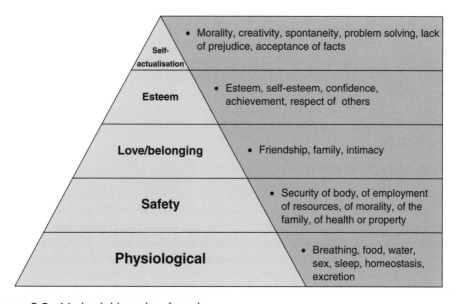

Figure 8.8 Maslow's hierarchy of needs

Context specific theories of human motivation

There are also a number of specific theories relating to certain human motivation in certain contexts. For example *cognitive dissonance theory* considers human motivation when an individual experiences discomfort emanating from an inconsistency between their views on the world around them and their own personal feelings and actions (Festinger, 1957). In the social marketing sphere understanding cognitive dissonance may be helpful, for example in gaining insight on why smokers know that society is less approving of smoking but they still experience personal motivations for doing it. Herzberg's (1966) *two-factor theory* considers human motivation in the workplace, proposing that there are certain factors in this environment that influence job satisfaction, while other factors influence job dissatisfaction. In the social marketing context ensuring that people are motivated and satisfied in their jobs such as in a health clinic may help them deliver a better service experience for users (see Chapter 6 on value for further discussions on this issue).

Relevance to social marketing

Understanding people's motivations is a key component of gaining insight and trying to influence behaviour. Understanding levels of human motivation and the interactions between different motivations can help social marketers to know how to appeal at various levels to people to change their behaviour (Lee and Kotler, 2011). However, social marketers have also recognised that it is less effective and ethically questionable to focus not only on individual motivations, but also on the motivations of communities and society around individuals (Andreasen, 2002). Furthermore, Wymer (2011) has guarded against the majority of social marketing programmes being focused on individual motivation, ignoring ignorance, pathogenic agents and privation as more fundamental drivers of social problems. Therefore, motivation theory is of relevance to social marketing, but needs to be considered within the realm of other theories and understanding at other levels.

Cultural theory

Seminal works: Douglas and Wildavsky (1982), Douglas (1992)

Cultural theory is a conceptual framework that was originally developed to explain societal conflict over risk. Cultural theory asserts that structures of a social organisation such as its rules, structures and how these rules are controlled endow individuals with perceptions that reinforce those structures in competition against alternative views.

Cultural theory sets out four types of understandings that can be found in different societies or groups: egalitarian, individualist, hierarchical and fatalist.

The particular domination of any of these types of understanding in different cultures depends on two different criteria: *grid issues* (rules and individual roles) and

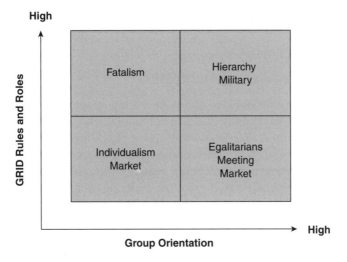

Figure 8.9 Cultural theory

group orientation (the importance of collective control and consensus within the group or society). Where there are high grid and group orientations, there will tend to be hierarchical cultures. Conversely, where there are low grid and group tendencies, there will tend to be more individualist cultures (see Figure 8.9).

Relevance to social marketing

The key practical implication of this theory is that efforts to influence behaviour and develop effective and efficient social marketing interventions, especially in countries where there are diverse sub-groups within the society, will need to be informed by and reflect all of these different cultural factors. Since every community contains some element of grid and group diversity, efforts at tackling problems are unlikely to bear fruit unless they accommodate both perspectives. The theory therefore indicates that a mixture of social rules, social norms, community values and incentives and support structures will be needed to deliver effective behaviour programmes.

——————————————— **Discussion question** ———————————————

Think about a recent big social change that you have witnessed in your community or in the global media. Thinking about the theories set out above: is it possible to use these theories to explain the change that happened or is happening?

Health focused theories

Determinants of health model

Seminal work: Dahlgren and Whitehead (1991)

The determinant of health (DoH) model is also a big systems model focused on the key factors that impact on an individual's or community's health (see Figure 8.10). The DoH model is represented diagrammatically as a rainbow-like set of tiers of social, economic and behavioural factors surrounding individuals whose biological variables (e.g. age, sex and genetics) are fixed at the centre of the model. The model illustrates four tiers, and describes intervention types for each one, as follows. The top tier is the macro-level 'structural environment'. The next tier is 'material living conditions', including housing, education and the workplace (subject to legislation/regulation and the provision of public services). Moving closer to the individual, the third tier is 'material support networks' including family and friends (subject to strengthening networks

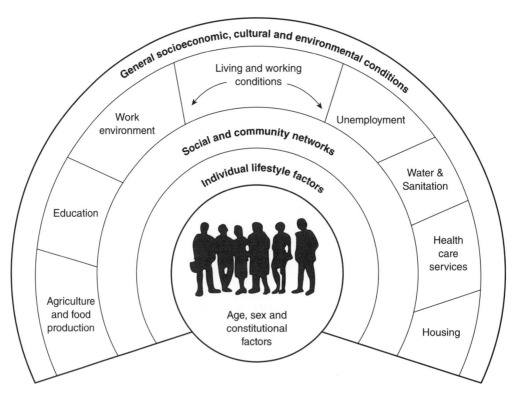

Figure 8.10   Determinants of health model

and building community capacity). The closest tier is 'lifestyle/behavioural factors' (subject to influencing interventions, including the provision of information). This model is widely quoted in many public health strategy and policy documents as a helpful summary of the influences on health.

Relevance to social marketing

The implication of the model is that social programmes should be focused on the determinants of health at every level of the model from actions directed at individual behaviour though to macro-social policy action such as the development of supportive legislative and fiscal policy. A further implication of the model is that action is needed on the detriments or causes of poor health rather than just a focus on the consequences or ultimate symptoms of poor health brought about by individual behaviour. This model, like systems theory, supports the need for a focus on upstream factors that impact on people's health and the need to develop more comprehensive responses to health challenges that have significant behavioural components.

Health belief model

Seminal work: Rosenstock (1966)

The health belief model (HBM) in Figure 8.11 was one of the first social cognition models focused on health decision making and behaviour. It was further developed by Janz and Becker (1984) and colleagues in the 1970s and 1980s. Subsequent amendments to the model were made to accommodate evolving evidence generated within the health community about the role that knowledge and perceptions play in personal responsibility. The model suggests that belief in a personal threat together with a belief in the effectiveness of the proposed behaviour will predict the likelihood of a behaviour. The four key constructs of the model are:

- *perceived susceptibility*: an individual's assessment of their risk of getting the condition
- *perceived severity*: an individual's assessment of the seriousness of the condition, and its potential consequences
- *perceived barriers*: an individual's assessment of the influences that facilitate or discourage adoption of the promoted behaviour
- *perceived benefits*: an individual's assessment of the positive consequences of adopting the behaviour.

A number of mediating factors have been added to the model, and these include demographic and socio-psychological variables. Rosenstock argues these variables on their own do not necessarily mean that an individual will be motivated to carry out the desired health behaviour. He points to the importance of 'cues to action' to prompt a change in behaviour. These cues are events that are either 'bodily' (e.g. physical symptoms of a health condition) or environmental (e.g. media publicity).

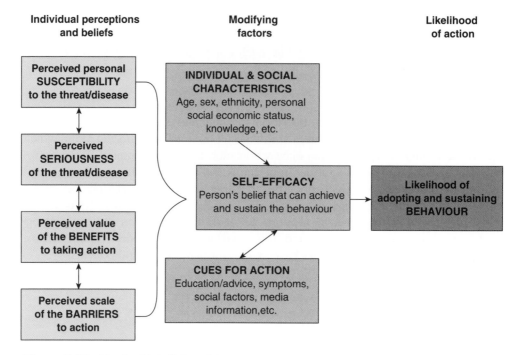

Figure 8.11   The health belief model

Relevance to social marketing

There are some general limitations to the health belief model that need to be borne in mind. The HBM does not specify how different beliefs interact and influence each other. It does not take into account environmental or economic factors that may influence health behaviours. The HBM also does not overtly consider the influence of others on people's decisions. The model, however, does indicate that a focus on threat, perceived vulnerability and the efficacy of recommended actions should form part of any approach to influencing behaviour. The model is also a useful diagnostic tool when research is being undertaken to understand potential modifying actions that may be influencing people's health behaviour.

Heath action model

Seminal work: Tones, Tilford and Robinson (1990), Tones and Tilford (1994)

The health action model (HAM) conceptually incorporates the health belief model and Fishbein and Ajzen's (1975) 'theory of reasoned action' (see Figure 8.12). The HAM takes account of beliefs, normative influences and motivating factors, including attitudes, along with other strong motivating forces, such as hunger, pain, pleasure and sex, in order to understand behaviour. Identity and self-esteem are key factors introduced by this model as important mediating factors. Self-esteem encompasses appearance, intelligence and physical skills, as well as an individual's perception of how other people view them and the ability to make choices which are different from those of the group. In this model, behaviour change depends on:

- a high level of self-esteem
- skills and strategies to resist peer group pressure
- an assessment of the pros and cons of change
- motivation to conform.

HAM is based on the idea that people with a high level of self-esteem and a positive self-concept are likely to feel confident about themselves and as a result will have the

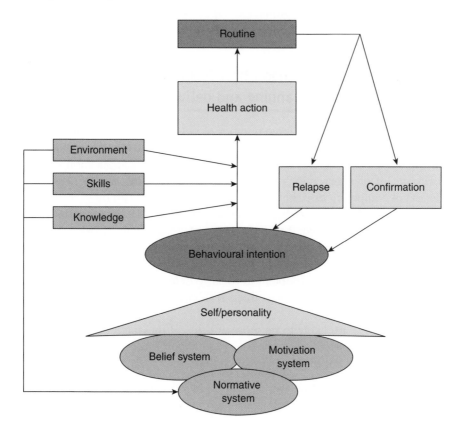

Figure 8.12 Health action model

ability to carry through a resolve to change their behaviour. Conversely, people with a low level of self-esteem are likely to believe that they have limited control over their fate and will be less likely to respond to a health promotion message, no matter how convinced they are by it at an intellectual level. The model also emphasises the need for facilitating factors, such as a supportive environment or the possession of personal skills, to support the translation of behavioural intention into action.

Relevance to social marketing

The HAM model illustrates that people's health behaviour is dependent on both personal factors such as self-esteem and norms within communities and the wider macro-social and economic conditions that impact on their lives. Many of the factors that impact on people's health behaviour can be at least partly and in some circumstances completely beyond their control. An implication of HAM is that a key part of many social marketing programmes may need to be focused on building up, through community health education programmes, self-esteem, health literacy and health skills as well as addressing wider influencing factors from the environment.

Developing an integrated theoretical framework to assist social marketing planning and delivery

As described above, there are a large number of behavioural theories and models that can be used to inform the design and evaluation of effective and social behavioural influencing strategies. There is clearly a strong case for the application of theory in the development of interventions to change behaviour (MRC, 2007). However, there may be lots of competing or partly overlapping theories that can be used and, as Noar and Zimmerman (2005) make clear, the use of many models to increase understanding is a useful approach. However, selecting the most appropriate theory and models or elements of them will require the input of expertise from the relevant disciplines (Albarracin et al., 2005; Michie et al., 2005). The review, consideration and selection of an appropriate theoretical foundation for any behavioural intervention are then a matter of some importance for a least three reasons. As Michie et al. (2008: 664) state:

> First, interventions are likely to be more effective if they target causal determinants of behaviour and behaviour change; this requires understanding these causal determinants, i.e. theoretical mechanisms of change.

> Second, theory can be tested and developed by evaluations of interventions only if those interventions and evaluations are theoretically informed.

> Third, theory-based interventions facilitate an understanding of what works and thus are a basis for developing better theory across different contexts, populations, and behaviours.

One of the first attempts made by practitioners to provide a unifying framework of various behaviour change influences is the US National Institute of Mental Health, which convened a theorists' workshop to work through the key factors influencing behaviour and behaviour change (Fishbein et al., 1992). Drawing on this, set out in Table 8.1 are the key concepts which reoccur in the models and theories reviewed.

This summary list seeks to concentrate the planner's mind on the key elements that need to be considered when developing an intervention. The question of how these key elements can and should be applied was addressed in a review commissioned by the UK government in 2008. The UK Social Research Unit commissioned a review (Darnton, 2008) to clarify the use of models of behaviour change for research analysts, with the intention of improving advice to policy makers seeking to influence behaviour related to social programmes and the evaluation of such programmes. The review was designed to provide an overview of relevant models and theories and guidance on their uses and limits.

Table 8.1 Common key behavioural concepts

ELEMENT	SUMMARY
Intention	To make a successful behaviour change an individual must form a strong positive intention or make a commitment to performing the behaviour. Therefore some measure of intention should be included in the evaluation programme.
Environmental Constraints	Barriers in an individual's environment may make behaviour change difficult, so a measure of perceived and/or actual barriers should be a key part of any evaluation programme.
Skills	An individual will need to possess the necessary skills to carry out the behaviour, so a measure of perceived skill level combined with usage and awareness of any support and education tools is an important element in any evaluation programme.
Attitudes	A positive attitude towards the behaviour change, particularly a belief that the advantages of making the change will outweigh the disadvantages, is an important step on the way to behaviour change. Evaluating attitudes and monitoring changes are therefore important measures.
Social Norms	The influences of an individual's immediate support group as well as wider social influences in promoting the behaviour change are an important indicator for evaluation. Measuring the perceived attitudes of friends, family and 'society' could act as a proxy indicator here.
Self-Image	The behaviour change needs to be consistent with an individual's self-image, so a way of capturing self-image and matching this with perception of the behaviour change will be useful.
Emotion	An individual's reaction to performing the behaviour change needs to be more positive than negative, so perceived emotion before performing the change and actual emotion once trialling it are good indicators of likelihood to continue with the behaviour change.
Self-Efficacy	An individual's capabilities to perform the behaviour change in a range of circumstances and their belief in this are important in many of the models, so a measurement of perceived and actual capability is often key in evaluation.

The Government Social Research (GSR) report recommends that policy makers should adopt an approach to intervention development which embeds behavioural models in a process shaped by theories of change. The report also makes it clear that there is no algorithm that can be applied to select models or theories and, ultimately, a theory-based approach needs to be flexible to take account of different behavioural contexts and audience groups. This should also incorporate learning from practice, having identified what works in comparable interventions.

However, the report argues for effort to be put into underpinning and developing a theoretical framework, for all social policy interventions focused on influencing behaviour, as theoretical modelling is needed to develop clear and measurable objectives and outcomes.

In the GSR review, Darnton recommends that empirical data are used to show how well they predict behaviour change and which elements of the model are most successful in predicting this. A further approach is recommended which is particularly useful when empirical data are not available. This is to revisit the audience insight for reported attitudes, barriers and drivers and use these to help identify relevant models. Reading the research in the light of several models helps ensure that the findings are not just taken at face value, and provides additional theoretical justification for their adoption. Similarly, research data help isolate the elements of the models which are most relevant for inclusion in a subsequent evaluation.

The review sets out nine principles in a logical sequence, but makes clear that they should not be regarded as discrete steps, with one being accomplished before moving on to the next. Instead the principles can be best understood as a staged but iterative process. Importantly, in terms of policy coherence, the cyclical nature of the nine principles is also in keeping with existing guidance on policy evaluation (HM Treasury, 2011) which demonstrates how research can support effective delivery throughout the policy cycle. The GSR eight principles are set out in Table 8.2.

The nine principles resemble existing theory-based guidance for planning interventions, but aim to achieve a synthesis between the different approaches. The key difference between the nine principles and other approaches such as Stern's principles (2000) is the building of an analysis of behavioural models into the heart of the developing process. The GSR nine principles can also be compared to the intervention mapping (IM) framework, which similarly centres on behavioural models, but which follows a more programmatic path to intervention development and implementation (Bartholomew et al., 1998). The GSR review principles can then be used to locate theory at the heart of the intervention planning process.

Another useful framework for considering the selection and place of behaviour change theory is work by Abraham and Michie, who have developed a taxonomy of terms used in behaviour change interventions to create a standardised terminology and a meta model they term the 'behaviour change wheel', which seeks to encapsulate sources of behavioural influence, a spectrum of intervention functions and a set of policy categories. From a review of techniques used in physical activity interventions,

Table 8.2 Government Social Research review theory-based principles for developing effective behavioural interventions

1. **Identify the audience groups and the target behaviour.** If faced with a complex behaviour, break it down into its component behaviours and/or adopt a systems thinking approach.
2. **Identify relevant behavioural models** (use both individual and societal level models). Draw up a shortlist of influencing factors.
3. **Select the key influencing factors**. Use these to design objectives in a draft strategy for the intervention.
4. **Identify effective intervention techniques** which have worked in the past on the influencing factors selected.
5. **Engage the target audience for the intervention** in order to understand the target behaviour and the factors influencing it from their perspective.
6. **Develop a prototype intervention** based on the learning from working with the actors. Cross-check this against appropriate policy frameworks and assessment tools. Pilot the intervention and monitor continuously.
7. **Evaluate** impacts and processes.
8. **Feedback** learning from the evaluation.

26 behaviour change techniques were identified, 18 of which are taken from generic behaviour change theories (Abraham and Michie, 2008).

Michie et al. (2005) undertook a consensus study to develop an integrated model of behaviour change theory that involved an analysis of 33 theories and 128 constructs generated which were subsequently simplified into 12 domains of theoretical constructs. Michie et al. have gone on to develop a framework called the 'behaviour change wheel' (Michie et al., 2011) based on previous analysis of theory and a trawl of 19 behaviour change planning and intervention frameworks (see Figure 8.13).

The 'behaviour change wheel' has at its centre what Michie et al. call the 'sources of behaviour', set out under the three COM-B headings of Motivation (sources: automatic and reflective), Opportunity (sources: social and physical) and Capability (sources: physical and psychological). The 'behaviour change wheel' makes a clear distinction between 'behavioural interventions' and 'policies' that enable or support those interventions.

The next layer of the model sets out nine types of intervention activities that can be used to influence behaviour. These are: education, persuasion, incentivisation, coercion, training, enablement, modelling, environmental restructuring and restrictions. The final element of the model is the policy enabling outer ring that consists of six possible policy approaches to enable or support each of, or combinations of, the possible nine intervention types. The policy approaches are: environmental/social planning, communications/marketing, legislation, service provision, regulation, fiscal measures and guidelines.

Michie et al. (2011) agree with Darnton (2008) that when developing effective interventions it is necessary to start with a deep analysis of the target group and

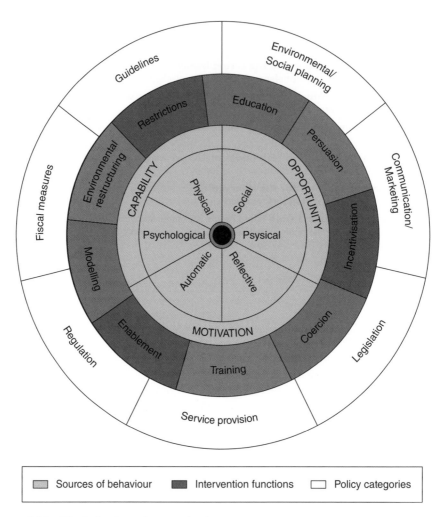

Figure 8.13 The behaviour change wheel

behaviour including a precise description of its determinants prior to model selection or development. The next step in any systematic process should be to consider the full range of possible interventions and policies before identifying specific behaviour change techniques and communication strategies to bring about change.

The 'behaviour change wheel' is one of the more comprehensive attempts to date to synthesise a great deal of previous work on theory and behaviour change intervention modelling. Like other attempts (Hendriks et al., 2013; Stephan et al., 2013) to present a totalising model, however, there are obvious critical questions regarding the exact categorisation of elements and definitions of the concepts selected. The model also has a number of fairly obvious intervention and policy omissions such as design, community development, etc. The conflation of types of decision making (automatic and reflective) with influences on behaviour is also problematic. Also the model is flawed in that it perpetuates a limited and out-of-date conception of marketing and conflates communication and marketing and categorises them as 'policy'. As explored in this book, social marketing is an integral part of every stage of policy development, research, strategy formulation delivery and evaluation. However, the model is a helpful conceptual tool, and like other models set out in this chapter, research will be needed to establish how far the 'behaviour change wheel' can lead to the more efficient selection and design of effective interventions.

Open analysis approach to selecting models and theories to inform social marketing strategy development and operational delivery

In this final section of the chapter we set out a suggested set of steps for using existing and developing bespoke theories and models to inform your social marketing programme. The following four domains of influence on behaviour should first be considered:

- bio-physical
- psychological
- social
- environmental and economic.

The first step in the process of selecting theory is to accept the influences from at least these four domains and begin a review of potential influences on behaviour from these four perspectives. Using this frame of reference potential models and theories can be sought that inform understanding about the impact of each of these four domains on behaviour. This first stage should be as unrestricted as possible.

The second set of tasks relates to the need to be pragmatic and recognise that it is impossible for single practitioners to be expected to have a detailed understanding of multiple theories or to have the time or understanding to conduct exhaustive reviews of theory prior to any strategy or action being delivered. One way to reduce the effort required and to increase the theoretical frame of reference and understanding is the tactic of bringing together multi-disciplinary teams from different backgrounds. This approach will increase the range of theoretical models that will be applied in any given situation.

As discussed above and recommended in the GSR review, if theory is to be used to inform practice it is necessary to start by first trying to get a clear understanding of what behaviour is occurring, and what different people know, think and feel about it, before going on to 'pull-down' theory to consider what might help inform or develop insight into why people are adopting a behaviour. In this way a focus on the behaviour drives the selection and development of a theoretical perspective.

The final stages of selecting or developing theoretical understanding should involve the development of 'working propositions' for how to achieve and maintain the desired change in society or how to maintain a positive situation. These propositions will be based on existing theory and bespoke models developed from existing theory and informed by the observed influences on the behaviour under consideration. Interventions can then be developed based on these propositions and tested in pilots and field trials to see if they deliver the anticipated impact on behaviour.

Conclusion

This selective review of some of the key behaviour change theories and models illustrates that there is a great deal of understanding about the many factors at individual, group and society levels that impact on health decision making and behaviour. It is also clear that there is a need to place behavioural influence, the ultimate objective of social marketing interventions, at the heart of public behaviour change planning. When planning social marketing programmes, theories and models should have a central role in assisting the design and evaluation of the effective programmes.

We also know that interventions that are based on clear theoretical models are more effective. Interventions that are systematically planned are more effective and interventions that draw on knowledge about effective interventions and apply best practice are more effective. Interventions that do all three of these things are not guaranteed to be effective and efficient but are much more likely to be so.

When constructing social behavioural interventions the use of several theories and models appears to assist with identifying the key elements that are of most use in explaining behaviour or predicting what will influence change. This understanding can be used as the foundation around which social marketing interventions can be designed, and other 'forms' and 'types' of influence developed. This is the approach Darnton (2008) recommends to policy makers. There will be occasions, however, when existing behavioural theory is not available or appropriate. In these circumstances it will be necessary to construct bespoke models and new theory to inform and guide the development of programmes.

Behavioural models and theory can help strengthen the development, delivery and evaluation of social marketing strategies and most public programme design and delivery. In most cases theories intended to modify individual level behaviours remain the most commonly applied in many social programmes. In many cases it would be appropriate if policy interventions could broaden this focus to include ecological theory and models and organisational change models and theory to guide research, intervention design and evaluation.

This chapter has demonstrated that theory and models are key tools that are vital in planning effective programmes. When planning interventions social marketing practitioners and policy makers should always start by seeking out theory and models that can help frame thinking about how to influence the specific behaviour they wish to have an impact on.

Reflective questions

- How can theory strengthen the development of social marketing planning and intervention delivery?
- What types of behavioural theory and models are there? List at least two examples of each type of theory.
- What are some of the key considerations when selecting behavioural theories to inform social marketing interventions?

Further reading

Australian Public Service Commission (2007) *Changing Behaviour: A Public Policy Perspective*. Canberra: Australian Government. Available at: www.apsc.gov.au/publications-and-media/archive/publications-archive/changing-behaviour (last accessed 18 November 2014).

Darnton, A. (2008) *Government Social Research: Behaviour Change Knowledge Review. Practical Guide: An Overview of Behaviour Change Models and Their Uses*. Centre for Sustainable Development, University of Westminster. Available at: http://resources.civilservice.gov.uk/wp-content/uploads/2011/09/Behaviour-change_practical_guide_tcm6-9696.pdf (last accessed 19 November 2014).

Michie, S., Johnston, M., Francis, J., Hardeman, W. and Eccles, M. (2008) 'From theory to intervention: mapping theoretically derived behavioural determinants to behaviour change techniques', *UK Applied Psychology: An International Review*, 57 (4): 660–680, doi: 10.1111/j.1464-0597.2008.00341.x.

References

Abraham, C. and Michie, S. (2008) 'A taxonomy of behavior change techniques used in interventions', *Health Psychology*, 27 (3): 379–387.

Ajzen, I. (1985) 'From intentions to actions: a theory of planned behaviour', in J. Kuhl and J. Beckman (eds), *Action-control: From Cognition to Behaviour*. Heidelberg: Springer, pp. 11–39.

Albarracin, D., Gillette, J., Earl, A., Durantini, M. and Moon-Ho, H. (2005) 'A test of major assumptions about behaviour change: a comprehensive look at the effects of passive and active HIV-prevention interventions since the beginning of the epidemic', *Psychological Bulletin*, 131 (6): 856–97.

Alcalay, R. and Bell, R.A. (2000) *Promoting Nutrition and Physical Activity through Social Marketing: Current Practices and Recommendations*. Prepared for the Cancer Prevention and Nutrition Section, California Department of Health Services, Sacramento, California. Davis, CA: Center for Advanced Studies in Nutrition and Social Marketing, University of California.

Andreasen, A.R. (2002) 'Marketing social marketing in the social change marketplace', *Journal of Public Policy and Marketing*, 21 (1): 3–13.

Angus, K., Cairns, G., Purves, R., Bryce, S., MacDonald, L. and Gordon, R. (2011) *Systematic Literature Review to Examine the Evidence for the Effectiveness of Interventions that Use Theories and Models of Behaviour Change: Towards the Prevention and Control of Communicable Diseases*. Institute for Social Marketing, University of Stirling and the Open University. Commissioned by ECDC.

Argyris, C. and Schon, D. (1996) *Organizational Learning II*. Reading, MA: Addison Wesley.

Australian Public Service Commission (2007) *Changing Behaviour: A Public Policy Perspective*. Canberra: Australian Government. Available at: www.apsc.gov.au/publications-and-media/archive/publications-archive/changing-behaviour (last accessed 18 November 2014)

Aveyard, P., Massey, L., Parsons, A., Manaseki, S. and Griffin, C. (2009) 'The effect of transtheoretical model based interventions on smoking cessation', *Social Science and Medicine*, 68 (3): 397–403.

Bandura, A. (1977) 'Self-efficacy: toward a unifying theory of behavioral change', *Psychological Review*, 84: 191–215.

Bandura, A. (1986) *Social Foundations of Thought and Action: A Social Cognitive Theory*. Englewood Cliffs, NJ: Prentice Hall.

Bartholomew, K., Parcel, G. and Kok, G. (1998) 'Intervention mapping: a process for developing theory and evidence-based health education programs', *Health Education and Behavior*, 25: 545–563.

Bettman, J. (1979) *An Information Processing Theory of Consumer Choice*. Reading, MA: Addison-Wesley

Bourdieu, P. (2011 [1986]) 'The forms of capital', in I. Szeman and T. Kaposy (eds), *Cultural Theory: An Anthology*. Oxford: Wiley Blackwell, pp. 72–80.

Bronfenbrenner, U. (1977) 'Toward an experimental ecology of human development', *American Psychologist*, 32 (7): 513–531.

Bronfenbrenner, U. (1979) *The Ecology of Human Development*. Cambridge, MA: Harvard University Press.

Callon, M. (1986) 'Some elements of a sociology of translation: domestication of the scallops and the fishermen of St Brieuc Bay', in J. Law (ed.), *Power, Action and Belief: A New Sociology of Knowledge*. London: Routledge, pp. 196–223.

Checkland, P. (1981) *Systems Thinking, Systems Practice*. New York: John Wiley.

COI (Central Office of Information) (2009) *Communications and Behavior Change*. London: COI/GCN.

Coleman, J. (1988) 'Social capital in the creation of human capital', *American Journal of Sociology*, 94: S95–S120.

Collins, K., Tapp, A. and Pressley, A. (2010) 'Social marketing and social influences: Using social ecology as a theoretical framework', *Journal of Marketing Management*, 26 (13/14): 1181–1200.

The Community Guide (2000) *What Works to Promote Health?* Centres for Disease Control and Prevention (CDC). Available at: www.thecommunityguide.org/worksite/supportingmaterials/IES-AHRFAlone.html (last accessed 19 November 2014).

Cottam, H. and Leadbeater, C. (2004) *Red Paper No. 1 Health: Co-creating Services*. London: The Design Council.

Crosby, R, and Noar, S. (2010) 'Theory development in health promotion: are we there yet?', *Journal of Behavioural Medicine*, 33 (4): 259–263.

Dahlgren, G. and Whitehead, M. (1991) *Policies and Strategies to Promote Social Equity in Health*. Stockholm: Institute of Futures Studies.

Darnton, A. (2008) *Government Social Research: Behaviour Change Knowledge Review. Practical Guide: An Overview of Behaviour Change Models and Their Uses*. Centre for Sustainable Development, University of Westminster. Available at: http://resources.civilservice.gov.uk/wp-content/uploads/2011/09/Behaviour-change_practical_guide_tcm6-9696.pdf (last accessed 19 November 2014).

De Landa, M. (2006) *A New Philosophy of Society: Assemblage Theory and Social Complexity*. London: Continuum.

Deleuze, G. and Guattari, F. (1980) *A Thousand Plateaus: Capitalism and Schizophrenia*. London: Continuum.

De Savigny, D. and Taghreed, A. (eds) (2009) *Systems Thinking for Health Systems Strengthening*. Geneva, Switzerland: Alliance for Health Policy and Systems Research, WHO.

Douglas, M. (1992) *Risk and Blame: Essays in Cultural Theory*. London: New York: Routledge.

Douglas, M. and Wildavsky, A.B. (1982) *Risk and Culture: An Essay on the Selection of Technical and Environmental Dangers*. Berkeley: University of California Press.

Dubiel, H. (1985) *Theory and Politics: Studies in the Development of Critical Theory* (trans. Benjamin Gregg). Cambridge, MA: MIT Press.

Elder, J.P., Lytle, L., Sallis, J.F., Young, D.R., Steckler, A., Simons-Morton, D., Stone, E., Jobe, J.B., Stevens, J., Lohman, T., Webber, L., Pate, R., Saksvig, B.I. and Ribisl, K. (2007) 'A description of the social–ecological framework used in the trial of activity for adolescent girls (TAAG)', *Health Education Research*, 22 (2): 155–165.

Festinger, L. (1957) *A Theory of Cognitive Dissonance*. Stanford, CA: Stanford University Press.

Fishbein, M. and Azjen, I. (1975) *Belief, Attitude, Intention and Behaviour. An Introduction to Theory and Research*. Reading, MA: Addison-Wesley Publishing.

Fishbein, M., Bandura, A. and Triandis, H. (1992) *Factors Influencing Behaviour and Behaviour Change: Final Report – Theorist's Workshop*. Rockville, MD: National Institute of Mental Health.

Flood, R.L. and Jackson, M.C. (1991) *Critical Systems Thinking: Directed Readings*. New York: Wiley.

French, J., Blair-Stevens, C., Merritt, R. and McVey, D. (eds) (2010) *Social Marketing and Public Health: Theory and Practice*. Oxford: Oxford University Press.

French, J. (2010) *STELa Social Marketing Planning Model*. Available at: http://stelamodel.com/ (last accessed 19 November 2014).

Gatersleben, B. and Vlek, C. (1998) 'Household consumption: quality of life and environmental impacts', in K.J. Noorman and A.J.M. Schoot-Uiterkamp (eds), *Green Households? Domestic Consumers, Environment and Sustainability*. London: Earthscan, pp. 141–183.

Gebhardt, W. and Maes, S. (2001) 'Integrating social-psychological frameworks for health behaviour research', *American Journal of Health Behavior*, 25: 528–536.

Gladwell, M. (2004) *The Tipping Point*. New York: Back Bay Books.

Glanz, K. and Rimer, B.K. (2005) *Theory at a Glance: A Guide for Health Promotion Practice* (2nd edn). Washington: National Cancer Institute, National Institutes of Health, US Department of Health and Human Services.

Glenane-Antoniadis, A., Whitwell, G., Bell, S. and Menguc, B. (2003) 'Extending the vision of social marketing through social capital theory in the context of intricate exchange and market failure', *Marketing Theory*, 3 (3): 323–343.

Goldberg, M.E. (1995) 'Social marketing: are we fiddling while Rome burns?', *Journal of Consumer Psychology*, 4 (4): 347–370.

Gordon, R. (2011) 'Critical social marketing: definition, application and domain', *Journal of Marketing Management*, 1 (2): 82–99.

Gordon, R. (2013) 'Unlocking the potential of upstream social marketing', *European Journal of Marketing*, 47 (9): 1525–1547.

Gordon, R. and Gurrieri, L. (2014) 'Towards a reflexive turn: social marketing assemblages', *Journal of Social Marketing*, 4 (3): 261–278.

Green, L. and Kreuter, M. (2005) *Health Promotion Planning: An Educational and Ecological Approach* (4th edn). Mountain View, CA: Mayfield Publishers.

Green, J. and Tones, K. (2010) *Health Promotion: Planning and Strategies*. London: SAGE.

Gunster, S. (2004) *Capitalizing on Culture: Critical Theory for Cultural Studies*. Toronto: University of Toronto Press.

Habermas, J. (1990) *Moral Consciousness and Communicative Action*. Cambridge, MA: MIT Press.

Halpern, D., Bates, C. and Beales, G. (2003) *Personal Responsibility and Behaviour Change*. London: Prime Minister's Strategy Unit, Cabinet Office.

Heider, F. (1958) *The Psychology of Inter-Personal Relations*. New York: Wiley.

Hendriks, A.M., Jansen, M., Gubbels, J., De Vries, N., Paulussen, T. and Kremers, S. (2013) 'Proposing a conceptual framework for integrated local public health policy, applied to childhood obesity – the behavior change ball', *Implementation Science*, 8 (46). doi: 10.1186/1748-5908-8-46.

Herzberg, F. (1966) *Work and the Nature of Man*. Cleveland: World Publishing.

Hills, D. (2004) *Evaluation of Community-level Interventions for Health Improvement: A Review of Experience in the UK*. London: HDA.

HM Treasury (2011) *The Green Book: Appraisal and Evaluation in Central Government*. London: The Stationery Office.

Horkheimer, M. (1972 [1937]) 'Critical theory and traditional theory', in M.J. O'Connell (ed.), *Critical Theory: Selected Essays*. New York: The Seabury Press, pp. 188–243.

Horkheimer, M. (1982) *Critical Theory*. New York: Seabury Press.

House J. (1981) *Work, Stress and Social Support*. Reading, MA: Addison-Wesley.

Jackson T. (2005) *Motivating Sustainable Consumption: A Review of Evidence on Consumer Behaviour and Behavioural Change. A Framework for Pro-Environmental Behaviours*. London: Sustainable Development Research Network (SDRN) and Defra.

Janz, N. and Becker, M. (1984) 'The health belief model: a decade later', *Health Education and Behavior*, 11 (1): 1–47.

Kamin, T. and Anker, T. (2014) 'Cultural capital and strategic social marketing orientations', *Journal of Social Marketing*, 4 (2): 94–110.

Kelly, H. and Thibaut, J. (1978) *Interpersonal Relations: A Theory of Interdependence*. New York: Wiley.

Latour, B. (1987) *Science in Action: How to Follow Scientists and Engineers through Society*. Milton Keynes: Open University Press.

Law, J. (2000) 'Transitivities', *Society and Space*, 18 (2): 133–148.

Lee, N. and Kotler, P. (2011) *Social Marketing: Influencing Behaviors for Good*. New York: SAGE.

Lindridge, A., MacAskill, S., Gnich, W., Eadie, D. and Holme, I. (2013) 'Applying an ecological model to social marketing communications', *European Journal of Marketing*, 47 (9): 1399–1420.

McKenzie-Mohr, D. and Smith, W. (1999) *Fostering Sustainable Behavior: An Introduction to Community-based Social Marketing*. Gabriola Island, Canada: New Society Publishers.

McQuail, D. (2005) *Mass Communication Theory* (5th edn). Thousand Oaks, CA: SAGE.

Maio, G., Verplanken, B., Manstead, A., Stroebe, W., Abraham, C., Sheeran, P. and Conner, M. (2007) 'Social psychological factors in lifestyle change and their relevance to policy', *Journal of Social Issues and Policy Review*, 1 (1): 99–137.

Maslow, A. (1954) *Motivation and Personality*. New York: Harper.

Michie, S., Johnston, M., Abraham, C., Lawton, R., Parker, D. and Walker, A. (2005) 'Making psychological theory useful for implementing evidence based practice: a consensus approach', *Quality and Safety in Healthcare*, 14: 26–33.

Michie, S., Johnston, M., Francis, J., Hardeman, W. and Eccles, M. (2008) 'From theory to intervention: mapping theoretically derived behavioural determinants to behaviour change techniques', *UK Applied Psychology: An International Review*, 57 (4), 660–680. doi: 10.1111/j.1464-0597.2008.00341.x.

Michie, S., van Stralen, M.M. and West, R. (2011) 'The behaviour change wheel: a new method for characterising and designing behaviour change interventions', *Implementation Science*, 6 (42). doi: 10.1186/1748-5908-6-42.

MRC (Medical Research Council) (2007) *Developing and Evaluating Complex Interventions: New Guidance*. Prepared by P. Craig, P. Dieppe, S. Macintyre, S. Michie, I Nazareth and M. Petticrew. Available at: www.mrc.ac.uk/complexinterventionsguidance (last accessed 19 November 2014).

Mulgan, G., Aldridge, S., Beales, G., Heathfield, A., Halpen, D. and Bates, C. (2004) *Personal Responsibility and Changing Behaviour: The State of Knowledge and Its Implications for Public Policy*. London: Prime Minister's Strategy Unit.

National Institutes of Health (2005) *Theory at a Glance: A Guide for Health Promotion Practice* (2nd edn). National Cancer Institute and US Department of Health and Human Services.

NICE (National Institute for Health and Clinical Excellence) (2007) *Behaviour Change at Population, Community and Individual Levels: Reference Guide*. London: NICE.

NICE (National Institute for Health and Care Excellence) (2014) *Behaviour Change Individual Approaches: NICE Public Health Guidance No. 49*. London: NICE.

Noar, S. and Zimmerman, R. (2005) 'Health behaviour theory and cumulative knowledge regarding health behaviours: are we moving in the right direction?', *Health Education Research*, 20 (3): 275–290.

Nutbeam, D., Harris, E. and Wise, M. (2010) *Theory in a Nutshell* (3rd edn). Sydney: McGraw-Hill.

O'Sullivan, G.A., Yonkler, J.A., Morgan, W. and Merritt, A.P. (2003) *A Field Guide to Designing a Health Communication Strategy*. Baltimore, MD: Johns Hopkins Bloomberg School of Public Health/Centre for Communication Programs.

Park-Higgerson, H., Perumean-Chaney, S., Bartolucci, A., Grimley, D. and Singh, K. (2008) 'The evaluation of school-based violence prevention programs: a-meta-analysis', *Journal of School Health*, 78 (9): 465–79.

Pavlov, I.P. (1927) *Conditioned Reflexes*. London: Oxford University Press.

Prochaska, J. (2009) 'Flaws in the theory or flaws in the study: a commentary on the effect of transtheoretical model based interventions on smoking cessation', *Social Science and Medicine*, 68 (3):404–406.

Prochaska, J. and DiClemente C. (1983) 'Stages and processes of self-change of smoking: toward an integrative model of change', *Journal of Consulting and Clinical Psychology*, 51: 390–395.

Public Administration Select Committee (2009) *Good Government. House of Commons*. London: The Stationery Office.

Putnam, R. (1995) 'Bowling alone: America's declining social capital', *Journal of Democracy*, 6 (1): 65–78.

Roe, L., Hunt, P., Bradshaw, H. and Rayner, M. (1997) *Health Promotion Effectiveness Reviews 6: Health Promotion Interventions to Promote Healthy Eating in the General Population: A Review*. London: Health Education Authority.

Rogers, E.M. (1995) *Diffusion of Innovations* (4th edn). New York: The Free Press.

Rogers, R. (1975) 'A protection motivation theory of fear appeals and attitude change', *Journal of Psychology*, 91: 93–114.

Rosenstock, I.M. (1966) 'Why people use health services', *Milbank Memorial Fund Quarterly*, 44 (3): 94–124.

Saren, M., MacLaran, P., Goulding, C., Elliott, R., Shankar, A. and Catterall, M. (eds) (2007) *Critical Marketing: Defining the Field*. London: Elsevier.

Scambler, G. (1996) 'The "project of modernity" and the parameters for a critical sociology: an argument with illustrations from medical sociology', *Sociology*, 30 (3): 567–581.

Senge, P. (1990) *The Fifth Discipline*. London: Random House.

Skinner, B. (1953) *Science and Human Behavior*. New York: Macmillan.

Smedley, B.D. and Syme, L.S. (eds) (2000) *Promoting Health: Strategies from Social and Behavioral Research*. Washington, DC: National Academies Press

Spotswood, F. and Tapp, A. (2013) 'Beyond persuasion: a cultural perspective of behaviour', *Journal of Social Marketing*, 3 (3): 275–294.

Stanovich, K. and West, R. (2000) 'Individual differences in reasoning: implications for the rationality debate?', *Behavioural and Brain Sciences*, 23: 645–726.

Stephan, U., Patterson, M. and Kelly, C. (2013) *Business Driven Social Change: A Systematic Review of the Evidence*. Ontario: Network for Business Sustainability.

Sterman, J. (2006) 'Learning from evidence in a complex world', *American Journal Public Health*, 96 (3): 505–514

Stern, P. (2000) 'Towards a coherent theory of environmentally significant behaviour', *Journal of Social Issues*, 56 (3): 407–424.

Tones, K. and Tilford, S. (1994) *Health Education: Effectiveness, Efficiency and Equity* (2nd edn). London: Chapman and Hall.

Tones, K., Tilford, S. and Robinson, Y. (1990) *Health Education .Effectiveness .and Efficiency*. London: Chapman and Hall.

Triandis, H. (1977) *Inter-personal Behaviour*. Monterey, CA: Brooks/Cole.

Tversky, A. and Kahneman, D. (1974) 'Judgment under uncertainty: heuristics and biases', *Science*, 185: 1124–1131.

Waitzkin, H. (1989) 'A critical theory of medical discourse: ideology, social control, and the processing of social context in medical encounters', *Journal of Health and Social Behaviour*, 30 (2): 220–39.

WHO (World Health Organization) (2012) *Communication for Behavioural Impact (COMBI): A Toolkit for Behavioural and Social Communication in Outbreak Response*. Geneva: WHO. Available at: www.who.int/ihr/publications/combi_toolkit_fieldwkbk_outbreaks/en/ (last accessed 9 December 2014)._

Wymer, W. (2011) 'Developing more effective social marketing strategies', *Journal of Social Marketing*, 1 (1): 17–31.

9 RESEARCH APPROACHES IN SOCIAL MARKETING

Learning objectives

By the end of this chapter, readers should be able to:

- understand the importance and contribution of research to social marketing
- identify and understand different research paradigms that may inform social marketing research
- understand the basics of research design, and consider research ethics and reflexivity in research.

Introduction

This chapter and the following chapter outline the integral role that research plays in social marketing – identifying that without rigorous, ethical, representative and informative research for scoping, gaining insight, planning, monitoring and evaluating, strategic social marketing is not possible. It is important to state that Chapters 9 and 10 are not designed to replace the wide range of high quality specialised textbooks on research methods that readers are encouraged to consult for more detail on social research. Examples of good research methods textbooks include *Social Research Methods* by Alan Bryman (2012), *Research Design: Qualitative, Quantitative, and Mixed Methods Approaches* by John Creswell (2014), *The SAGE Handbook of Qualitative Research* by Norman Denzin and Yvonna Lincoln (2011), *The Interpretation of Cultures* by Clifford Geertz (1973), *Discovering Statistics Using IBM SPSS Statistics* by Andy Field (2013), and *Structural Equation Modeling with AMOS: Basic Concepts, Applications, and Programming* by Barbara Byrne (2009). This chapter and the next aim to supplement such texts, and assist readers in identifying the role of research in strategic social marketing. This chapter is also not a detailed 'how to' guide to research and evaluation. Readers can access further assistance regarding how to undertake research and develop an evaluation plan via the online material that supplements the book (study.sagepub.com/frenchandgordon).

The chapter starts by discussing the importance of research in social marketing and its central role at each stage of the social marketing process. We then consider research paradigms – varying views about what research is and how this relates to the kind of knowledge being developed. Research paradigms guide how we make decisions and conduct research and it is important to understand how different paradigms can inform and influence social marketing research. We then examine the importance of research ethics before discussing the topic of reflexivity in research and its relevance to producing representations of meaning from research inquiry. Following this discussion, we consider important things to think about in relation to selecting a research design. Finally, we consider the key topic of sampling in qualitative and quantitative research, considering topics such as what size of sample should be selected.

Research: its importance in social marketing

Good research lies at the very heart of social marketing and is used at almost all stages of the social marketing process, from defining a social issue, to scoping what is known and what needs to be known about a subject, to developing insight and understanding from participants, groups, stakeholders and institutions, to testing social marketing programme components, to monitoring implementation, all the way through to programme evaluation.

Research acts as the eyes and the ears of social marketing, and helps guide what we do. It also helps us develop insight, understand the issues, establish objectives and goals, identify benchmarks, check on our progress, make adjustments, and determine when we have been able to make a difference. In many ways, research in social marketing is action research – a process of inquiry conducted by and for those taking action (Lewin, 1946). In social marketing our ultimate goal is to increase wellbeing, not just learn more about a topic. Social marketing research and evaluation should have a direct feed into decisions about the focus of social programmes, budget allocations, and the development of plans of action that define immediate and long-term goals and objectives, all of which can be adapted and are flexible to changing needs and situations as a social marketing programme is implemented. This flexibility is important, as in strategic social marketing we are dealing with attitudes, behaviours, and practices, whether of individuals, groups, stakeholders, institutions or systems that will be subject to change over time. Most social challenges and phenomena are complex and changeable; therefore we need to avoid committing to rigid strategies. Rather, a strategic approach should be adopted, which builds in reflexive thinking, continuous adjustment and refinement so that a continuous process of improving and refining policy and programme delivery takes place.

Indeed, given the attitudinal, behavioural, and practice focus of social marketing, anything we do has to be guided by our understanding of the people or actors we seek to influence. To gain this understanding, social marketers need to get underneath people's skin, to understand what moves and motivates them and gain insight on what makes them tick. The way we do this is by using research. Importantly, as social marketing is participant-oriented, any research conducted should be done ethically – adhering to the highest standards of ethical conduct, minimising any inconvenience on participants, being cognisant of their needs and any risks or implications from taking part in research, and being representative of their views, thoughts and experiences. Furthermore, research is also important for conducting evaluation. Evaluation also sits at the heart of the social marketing approach. Continuous tracking of programme efficiency, effectiveness, quality and adherence to ethical standards together with summative evaluation focused on behaviour, social impact and improvement are also essential tasks that enable the refinement of both the overall strategy and the tactical delivery of programmes. Before discussing what types of research approaches are available to us, it is worth examining the concept of research paradigms.

Research paradigms

A core issue for social research relates to the range of approaches and methods available and the main cleavages along which they are divided (della Porta and Keating, 2008). Thomas Kuhn (1962) suggested that mature scientific disciplines rely upon a paradigm that defines *what* to study, *why* to study and *how* to study.

The presence of a research paradigm therefore allows for the accumulation of knowledge. In the social sciences, which social marketing aligns with, there is considerable debate about valid research paradigms. Some scholars believe that social science is pre-paradigmatic, and is still in search of unifying principles and standards. Others argue that it is post-paradigmatic, and has shed scientific assumptions that are tied to particular conceptions of modernity. Another position is that social science is non-paradigmatic, and there can never be one dominant approach and set of standards, or that it is multi-paradigmatic, with different paradigms competing against each other (della Porta and Keating, 2008). Indeed, the nature of social research, and the social world that researchers seek to investigate and explain, can be understood in multiple ways. The suggestion that social marketing research is multi-paradigmatic seems a reasonable and pragmatic position to take, given the complexity of the social world we seek to understand and explain, and the comparative utility and weaknesses of the various paradigmatic approaches available to us. Strictly adhering to one particular paradigmatic approach may be limiting, and restrict the ability to comprehensively research and explain social marketing phenomena. Whatever position one takes, it is important to recognise that there are various ways in which to see and understand the world of research. This is important for social marketing, as research is often used to understand, explain, predict, evaluate and influence human behaviour – therefore the way in which such knowledge is developed is a very important consideration.

Research paradigms reflect the view of the world used to inform the framework for a research project. They define the nature of the world, the researcher's place within it, and the diverse relationships to the world and its constituent parts (Guba and Lincoln, 1994). Essentially research paradigms define for the researcher what it is they are about, and what falls within and outside the limits of legitimate research. Given how much research paradigms shape things, it is important for social marketers to consider these issues. Guba and Lincoln (1994) state that the basic beliefs that define a research paradigm can be summarised by the responses given to three fundamental questions:

1. The *ontological* question, i.e. what is the form and nature of reality?
2. The *epistemological* question, i.e. what is the basic belief about knowledge (that is, what can be known)?
3. The *methodological* question, i.e. how can the researcher go about finding out what they believe can be known?

Normally, competing approaches in the social sciences are contrasted on their ontological, epistemological and methodological base (Corbetta, 2003). Researchers are encouraged to consider their research paradigm, and its potential effect on the research, early on in the process (Easterby-Smith et al., 2004). The following section briefly examines issues relating to ontology, epistemology and methodology, and the relevance to social marketing.

Ontology

Ontology is the philosophical study of the nature of being, existence or reality, in addition to basic categories of being and their relations. It is traditionally regarded as part of the major branch of philosophy known as metaphysics, which is concerned with explaining the fundamental nature of being and the world (Gale, 2002).

Ontology concerns questions over what entities exist, or can be said to exist, and how such entities can be classified, related hierarchically, and subdivided according to similarities and differences. Ontology is an important consideration when conducting any research, as it encourages reflection upon philosophical questions. In research, ontology refers to the logic of enquiry utilised by the researcher when looking at the nature of the world, how it operates, what the researcher can study, and what claims they can make in relation to knowledge. Therefore, for social marketers it is important to be aware of one's values and worldview, in terms of their influence on the research approach utilised to observe, measure or understand social realities. Although some may argue that there is only one reality, there are many potential alternative perceptions of it. Therefore, the ontological question is about what we study, that is, the object of investigation: for example, in social marketing a study might seek to explain the lived experiences and socialisation processes of people who smoke.

Heraclitus, a philosopher who lived in ancient Greece (c. 535–c. 475 BC), placed an emphasis on a changing and emergent world (Le Poidevin et al., 2009). This is often described as the Heraclitean ontology of becoming, and is associated with a more fundamental and elementary ontic plurality (Gray, 2009). Parmenides, another philosopher in Ancient Greece (c. 515–c. 445 BC), placed a different emphasis on a permanent and unchanging reality. He proposed an ontological characterisation of the fundamental nature of existence, stating that existence is eternal, and is what can be conceived of by thought, created or possessed. As such, the entirety of creation is eternal, uniform and immutable, and everything that can be apprehended is one part of a single entity (Le Poidevin et al., 2009). Traditionally, this approach is known as the Permenidean ontology of being. Most of Western philosophy and science has emerged from this view (Gray, 2009). Only relatively recently has postmodern epistemology challenged the being ontology with the idea of a becoming orientation, and describing the limitations of truth seeking (Chia, 2002). The ontological position subsequently affects research epistemology and methodology.

Epistemology

Following ontology, the second consideration in terms of research paradigm concerns epistemology. The etymology of epistemology comes from the Greek words *episteme* – meaning knowledge – and *logos* – meaning explanation. The term relates to the nature of knowledge and justification, and concerns how we know what we know (Miller and Brewer, 2003). Identifying a suitable epistemological research paradigm when conducting social marketing research, which is often complex, interdisciplinary, multi-faceted and involves using multiple research methods, can be problematic (Bryman, 2007). This is partly explained by the dominance and divergence of thought between the two traditional types of research paradigms involving quantitative research or qualitative research (Johnson and Onwuegbuzie, 2004). The extant research methods literature displays two dominant research paradigms, that present 'ways of knowing' – namely positivism and interpretivism (Crotty, 1998) – but there are others including critical theory and pragmatism. These different epistemologies are all relevant to social marketing, given the crucial role that research plays in the field. Here we consider four of the main epistemological approaches to research: *positivism*, *interpretivism*, *critical theory* and *pragmatism*.

Positivism

Positivism is a collection of perspectives and philosophies, which presume that scientific methods offer the best approach to understanding the processes by which physical and human events occur. A positivist ideology therefore proposes that all true knowledge is scientific and that all things are measurable. Positivist research takes a scientific approach that is argued to be objective, and follows set rules and laws to limit error. For social marketing, positivist approaches can offer quantifiable information that can help draw conclusions on attitudes and behaviours, and the efficacy of programmes. However, it has been criticised for its universalist nature, by contending that all processes, and practices are reducible to physiological, physical and chemical elements. Critical theorists such as Max Horkheimer (1972 [1937]) argue that positivism does not accurately represent human social action, ignoring the role of the observer and failing to consider the historical and social conditions affecting the constitution of social reality. Furthermore, critical theorists hold that the representation of social reality produced by positivism is inherently conservative, dogmatic and focused on maintaining the status quo. Positivism remains a dominant approach to both research and theory construction. This is especially the case concerning the mainstream marketing discipline (Bartels, 1983). Social marketing survey research to evaluate the effect of interventions on knowledge, attitudes and behaviour of participants is an example of research usually identified as within the positivist paradigm.

Interpretivism

Interpretivism rejects the notion of an absolute reality, believing that knowledge or meaningful reality is contingent upon human practices, is constructed through interaction between humans and the world around them, and is developed and disseminated within a social context (Crotty, 1998). The interpretivist research paradigm displays a preference for research methodologies that are interpretive and qualitative, assessing multiple contextual and situational realities (Denzin and Lincoln, 2011). Interpretivism offers multiple perspectives in research, and access to different aspects of reality. For example, ethnographic studies in social marketing may seek to explore how participants identify social capital in engaging in practices relating to physical activity (Spotswood and Tapp, 2013). However, it can sometimes be difficult to reach conclusions from interpretivist research, and arguably anything can be claimed without validation of the data or a scientific approach.

Critical theory

Critical theory is a third research paradigm that has emerged and has received increasing attention within the research literature. Critical theory is an approach led by scholars such as Max Horkheimer, and later Jürgen Habermas (1970) from the Frankfurt School of social philosophers. Critical theory has attempted to develop an approach to inquiry and action in the social sciences, which could describe the historical forces that restrict human freedom and expose an ideological justification of these forces. Therefore, critical theory proposes to provide emancipation by offering solutions to these limitations on human endeavour. Critical theorists have been critical of other research paradigms, as they were not designed to question or transform the status quo. Habermas (1970) postulated three types of interest, which generate three types of knowledge:

1. A technical interest concerned with controlling the physical environment, generating empirical and analytical knowledge.
2. A practical interest focused on understanding the meaning of a situation, generating hermeneutic and historical knowledge.
3. An emancipating interest concerned with providing growth and advancement, generating critical knowledge and an exposition of constraints and domination.

Critical theorists have suggested two different types of research methodology: critique and action research. Critical theory has influenced much of the *critical social marketing* research discussed in Chapter 14 that has critically examined the impact of commercial marketing on society (Gordon, 2011a).

Pragmatism

Pragmatism is a further epistemology that guides research, and one that appears particularly relevant to social marketing research. Given the nature of social marketing research, it is often not wise to identify solely with one of the dominant epistemologies. The need to properly understand, gain insight from, engage with and empower participants in social marketing programmes often necessitates a recognition that the world is socially constructed, created and perceived by individuals, groups, institutions and systems, and is bound by both interactions with others and environmental constraints. However, social marketing research may also align with a critical realist ontology, i.e. knowing that things exist out there but recognising that as humans our own presence as researchers and actors influences what we are trying to measure. Acknowledging these complex relations, pragmatic ontology and epistemology have enjoyed renewed attention since the 1960s thanks to the work of philosophers such as W.V.O. Quine, who critiqued the logical positivism dominant in the UK and US (Quine, 1960). Under this approach, theory is extracted from practice, and then applied back to practice. This de-limiting approach arguably seems to fit well with social marketing – as it lends focus when selecting a research design and method that fit the needs of the issue at hand, rather than adhering dogmatically to a particular ontological or epistemological position. For instance, a social marketing study exploring and assessing the cumulative impact of alcohol marketing on youth drinking used multiple research methods such as content analysis, depth interviews, focus groups and survey research that could each be identifiable with different research paradigms (Gordon, 2011b). The study in fact took a pragmatic approach, and avoided the limitations of identifying with one single paradigmatic approach.

Methodology: the link between research paradigms and research methods

Traditionally, research paradigms, ontological and epistemological approaches have clustered around one (quantitative) or the other (qualitative) research approaches. Howe (1988) has discussed the incompatibility thesis, which has been supported by purists from either side positing that the qualitative and quantitative research paradigms cannot and should not be mixed. Yet mixed methods research, which is often used in social marketing, has become increasingly prominent. Tarrow (1995) set out some ideas on how mixed methods can be combined. He stated that qualitative methods could aid quantitative work, through process tracing or the identification of variables. In recent years, mixed methods scholars have begun to set out how philosophical questions regarding ontology and epistemology can be addressed (Creswell, 2014).

In social marketing research, quantitative research may be used to identify the baseline knowledge, attitudes and behaviours of participants; qualitative formative research may then be used to gain insight and understanding on the issues that influence whether individuals, groups, institutions or systems can change. Quantitative research may then be used to evaluate the effect of social marketing programme delivery, while qualitative research may be used to gain insight on the process of programme delivery and gain comment and feedback from people involved in the programme. The nature of the social phenomenon often under consideration in social marketing requires a sophisticated research approach, which utilises different methods of inquiry, cutting across the recognised epistemologies. Furthermore, using multiple methods in research facilitates the collection of data from several sources, which can then be triangulated to give 'a more detailed and balanced picture of the situation' (Altrichter et al., 2008: 147).

Discussion questions

- Does it matter which research paradigm informs a piece of social marketing research?
- How do you think adherence to each of the four paradigms discussed in this chapter – *positivism, constructivism, critical theory* and *pragmatism* – may affect a piece of social marketing research undertaken to help inform an intervention designed to increase energy efficiency among householders? Write in some notes for how each paradigm may influence and guide the research:

Positivism

_____

Constructivism

_____

Critical theory

_____

Pragmatism

_____

Research ethics

Ethics are an important consideration in social marketing research and should be considered well before any research is actually done. Research bodies such as the Economic and Social Research Council have developed research ethics frameworks to inform researchers about ethical issues (ESRC, 2010). Furthermore, many organisations such as universities, funding bodies and public sector organisations have developed their own codes of research ethics, and often have ethical approval procedures that must be understood and followed. Diener and Crandall (1978) identify four main areas for ethical principles in research:

1. Whether there is harm to participants.
2. Whether there is a lack of informed consent.
3. Whether there is an invasion of privacy.
4. Whether deception is involved.

To ensure high ethical standards are maintained research should be carried out with integrity and quality, with researchers and participants fully informed about the purpose, methods and intended possible uses of the findings, what participation in the study entails, and what risks, if any, are involved. Furthermore, the confidentiality of information provided, and anonymity of participants, must be respected. Participants should only participate in research freely and voluntarily. Harm to participants must be avoided, and the research should be independent, with any conflicts of interest declared.

It is vitally important for social marketers to understand the importance of research ethics, and to maintain the highest ethical standards when conducting research. Often the topics that are the focus for social marketing research are sensitive, private, embarrassing, taboo or even illegal. Furthermore, participation in research is often fairly intensive, particularly in qualitative research. In addition, participation in research may cause worry, increase fears, generate alarm or create embarrassment. For instance, focus group research on sexual health among young people in NSW identified that people were often afraid to tell the truth about their experiences in front of other people (Gilchrist et al., 2012). Research can also prompt risky behaviours, often in opposition to the behaviour change we are trying to achieve – for example by creating an impression that teenage drinking is more common than is actually the case. However, there is also an argument that doing no research is unethical, as without gaining real insight and understanding of participants, it is difficult to develop strategic programmes to facilitate social good.

CASE STUDY

Energy efficiency in the third age and the issue of research ethics

There are a number of good reasons why social marketers should consider and engage with the topic of research ethics. Doing research ethically can protect participants, protect organisations and help ensure that social marketing is viewed as an honest, fair and ethical approach to social change.

The topic of research ethics was central to a project currently underway in the Illawarra region of Australia. The project, funded by the Australian government, is focused on encouraging low-income older residents to use energy efficiently, and also to live in thermal comfort (i.e. keep warm enough in winter and cool enough in summer). The project is interdisciplinary, and multi-component and involves various phases of research and programme activities.

For example, a three-wave face-to-face questionnaire survey aims to track participant knowledge, attitudes and behaviours in relation to energy use.

Qualitative formative research with low-income older residents is being used to explore current knowledge, attitudes, behaviours, and energy use practices, and identify barriers and potential incentives and strategies to facilitate energy efficiency and thermal comfort. An ethnographic study with select households is being undertaken to track their lived experiences before and after receiving a package of retrofits in their homes (such as hot water systems and insulation). Approximately 200 participants in the study will receive retrofit packages. Finally, post-programme process evaluation research workshops will aim to identify learning about the project from stakeholders and participants.

Given the complexity of the project, and the amount of research carried out, consideration of ethical issues has been a central theme.

- Firstly, the ethical principal of protecting participants has been paramount. Given the potentially vulnerable participant group, researchers have been trained on what to do if they encounter participants who are unwell and distressed. For example, providing leaflets or contact details for health and social support services.
- Extra care has been taken to properly explain each element of the project to participants as relevant, and time taken to answer any questions, whether face-to-face, by email or over the phone. This helps to ensure participants are fully informed and can provide informed consent.
- All information on research participation is issued verbally and in written form. All participants must indicate verbal and written signed consent before any research activity can proceed.
- Participants have been given clear guidance that they can leave any aspect of the project at any time of their own volition without any adverse implications. This is particularly important given some people in the project will receive retrofits in their homes.
- Project staff have been trained on how to identify potential risks to themselves or other project staff and in such cases to take remedial action or to leave the vicinity.
- People taking part in the programme are encouraged to be active participants and are permitted a full say and final choice in what occurs. For example, if people receive a retrofit, they get to choose and have the final say on which package they will get.
- A number of planning tools, and health and safety frameworks have been developed for the project to deal with any number of eventualities and contingencies that may occur in the course of the programme. For example, if equipment fails or there is an accident in a participant's home there is a process to deal with such events.

(Continued)

(Continued)

- Detailed and continuing engagement with the relevant research ethics committees has facilitated informative discussions about ensuring all ethical issues have been identified and addressed in the project plan.

The amount of work involved in ensuring that such as project as this one is carried out ethically is considerable. Yet, the importance of doing research ethically means that investing the time and effort on properly considering and planning for doing so is a small price to pay. Furthermore, doing research ethically not only requires careful planning and resources, but also an element of trust and good judgement on the part of project staff. Researchers need to ensure that they not only have planned to do research ethically on paper, but that they also bring this into practice. Walking the talk is a very important concern in relation to research ethics, as no amount of planning can replace staff that know and act upon ethical standards in practice.

　　For more information see: http://globalchallenges.uow.edu.au/news/UOW156636.html

　　Source: http://www.ee3a.com.au/

Bryman (2012) provides a useful checklist for issues to consider in relation to research ethics that can act as a guide when doing social marketing research (see Table 9.1). For more details on research ethics see Chapter 6 of *Social Research Methods* by Alan Bryman (2012), or various other research methods and research ethics textbooks that provide more detail on this important topic.

Table 9.1　Research ethics checklist

✓　Have you read and incorporated into your research the principles published by at least one of the major professional research associations such as the Economic and Social Research Council/Market Research Society or equivalent?

✓　Have you read and incorporated ethical guidelines from your own institution?

✓　Have you identified whether the proposed research needs to be submitted to an ethics approval committee?

✓　If only certain types of research need to be submitted, have you checked whether and what type of clearance is required?

✓　Does your research conform to the principle of informed consent so that participants understand:

- What the research is about?
- The purpose of the research?
- Who is sponsoring it?

- • The nature of their involvement?
- • How long their participation will take?
- • That their participation is voluntary?
- • That they can withdraw from participation at any time without any negative implications to them?
- • What is going to happen with the data and how it will be stored?
- ✓ Are you confident that the privacy of participants will not be violated?
- ✓ Do you appreciate that you should not divulge information that participants have given you to other participants?
- ✓ Have you taken steps to ensure that participants will not be deceived about the research and its purposes?
- ✓ Have you taken steps to ensure that the confidentiality of data relating to participants will be maintained?
- ✓ Once data are collected have you taken steps to ensure that personal information of participants is not identifiable?
- ✓ Does your strategy for keeping data comply with data protection legislation?
- ✓ Once the research is completed, have you met obligations that were a requirement of doing the research (such as producing a report to an organisation that facilitated the research)?

Source: adapted from Bryman, 2012

Reflexivity

Another important consideration prior to doing any research, and to engage with while undertaking research, is reflexivity. Reflexivity refers to a researcher's reflection on their contribution to the construction of meanings throughout the research process, and the way that this may have affected the outcomes (Nightingale and Cromby, 1999). Reflexivity involves the researcher being aware of their effect on the process and outcomes of research by acknowledging that knowledge cannot be separated from the knower (Steedman, 1991). Indeed, Denzin (1994) argues that nothing speaks for itself, and there is only interpretation. Reflexive research takes into account the role of the researcher as an actor in the research process, and in the representation and interpretation of meanings. Doing reflexive research involves being aware of your contribution to the construction of meaning in the research process, and that it is impossible to remove your influence over its outcomes and interpretations. Reflexivity is often recognised as a central feature uniting critical studies (Fournier and Grey, 2000), and in many ways has synergies with critical theory discussed in Chapter 8, and the critical theory research paradigm discussed earlier in this chapter, as these espouse critique and reflection upon power relations and dominant institutions. Reflexivity is another way in which we can think critically. This is important, as the more we think about and reflect upon the decisions we make, the more likely we can make good strategic decisions. Jarvis (1995) outlines seven different levels of reflection:

1. *Reflectivity*: awareness of specific perception, meaning, behaviour.
2. *Affective reflectivity*: awareness of how the individual feels about what is being perceived, thought or acted upon.
3. *Discriminant reflectivity*: assessing the efficacy of perception and so on.
4. *Judgemental reflectivity*: making and becoming aware of the value of judgements made.
5. *Conceptual reflectivity*: assessing the extent to which the concepts employed are adequate for the judgement.
6. *Psychic reflectivity*: recognition of the habit of making percipient judgements on the basis of limited information.
7. *Theoretical reflectivity*: awareness of why one set of perspectives is more or less adequate to explain personal experience.

Given the complexity of social marketing research, and the importance of developing as informed and representative an understanding of issues, people, groups and systems as possible, reflexivity is an important consideration. Understanding how the biases, backgrounds, personalities and power relations of actors in the social marketing process influence meaning and outcomes generated from research can help create more engaging and effective social marketing programmes. Furthermore, engaging in reflexivity as a researcher is a key part of critical thinking, something that we identify as crucial in social marketing and is discussed in more detail later in Chapter 14.

A good way to facilitate engagement in reflexivity is to take down notes at each stage of the research process with your reflections on how you as a researcher have influenced each step. Some important issues to reflect upon when conducting research are set out in Table 9.2.

Table 9.2 Important issues to reflect upon when conducting research

- The wider relevance of the setting and the topic for research, and the grounds on which any empirical generalisations may be made. In social marketing this often involves considering what the social and policy environment is, what existing research is already out there, and what the current research evidence base says and how your research will relate to it.

- The features of the topic or setting left un-researched, discussing why these choices have been made and what implications follow from these decisions for the research findings. For example, a social marketing programme tackling binge drinking may seek to engage adolescents – but why not older adults? What are the reasons for working with adolescents, and what are the implications from not conducting research with older adult participants?

- The theoretical framework that you as the researcher are operating within, and the broader values and commitments (political, religious, theoretical and so on) that you bring to your work. For example, if you are very religious you may have a different view on a sexual health intervention than an atheist.

- Critically assess your integrity as a researcher. This can involve considering the grounds on which knowledge claims are being justified (length of fieldwork, the special access negotiated, discussing the extent of the trust and rapport developed with the participants and so on). Also, you should consider your background and experiences in the setting and topic: Are you new to this area? What effect will your inexperience have? Are you very experienced and perceive yourself to have lots of knowledge in this area? Might this affect what meanings you interpret and could it introduce bias? Consider your experiences during all stages of the research and acknowledge any issues and constraints. Recognise and discuss the strengths and weaknesses of the research design and strategy.

- Critically assess your data, by discussing any problems that arise during all stages of the research; outlining the rationale for the way in which data have been organised, coded, analysed and interpreted; and identifying whether this is a rationale understood and proffered by research participants or is a researcher constructed one. Explore rival explanations and other ways of organising your data. Provide enough extracts of data in your text to allow readers to make their own evaluations and generate their own inferences and interpretations. Discuss power relations in the research process between researcher(s), participants and other relevant actors. Consider whether class, gender, race and religion have affected these practices.

- Show the complexity of your data, and avoid suggesting that there is perfect fit of your data to the social world you seek to understand. Discuss data that fit outside the general patterns and categories identified, and stress the contextual nature of participants' accounts and descriptions.

Source: adapted from Brewer, 2000

By acknowledging, reflecting and, importantly, writing about these considerations, social marketing researchers can strive towards more representative and objectivist meanings. Given the core focus on participant orientation in social marketing, it is vital that social marketers recognise the importance of reflexive research and practice, otherwise there is a danger that social marketing research is riddled with misrepresentation and bias.

Research design

The selection of an appropriate research strategy should be influenced by the particular needs of the research problem (Kumar et al., 1999). The research design is also strongly influenced by other factors including cost, time, resources and access to an appropriate sampling frame (Hakim, 1987). In choosing a research design for conducting social marketing research, it is important to consider what type of research is being conducted, which type of data are required, and what data collection methods are available and appropriate. Furthermore, resources are also a major issue to consider when selecting a research design and method: what staff, equipment, finances and expertise are available to conduct the research?

Generally, there are two main types of social research: *exploratory research* or *conclusive research* (Chisnall, 1992). Exploratory research is appropriate when a problem has not been clearly defined or when little previous research has been conducted. It provides insight into, and comprehension of, an issue or situation. Exploratory research can help to determine the best research design, data collection method and sample selection procedure. Therefore this type of research is appropriate for the initial stage of a broader research project and can be used to develop research hypotheses that are later tested (Kinnear and Taylor, 1996). It is normally qualitative in nature and will not lead to findings that are generalisable.

Conclusive research draws conclusions and is used to verify insights or hypotheses with results often generalised to the whole population. It is usually quantitative in nature. Conclusive research is often designated as either descriptive or causal (Parasuraman, 1991). Descriptive studies collect data that describe the characteristics of a particular group of respondents, for example, the UK Office for National Statistics (ONS) omnibus survey of adult drinking behaviour and knowledge describes the socio-demographic characteristics of adult drinkers. Such studies can be carried out as a survey at one point in time to obtain a 'snapshot' of data (a cross-section), or at repeated intervals over time (a cohort). Cohort studies are longitudinal studies that can be used to determine the impact of certain variables on the characteristics of a sample. Conclusive research can also investigate causality, and this might involve survey research or experiments. Randomised control trials (RCTs) are often held up as the gold standard of experimental research design and involve the random allocation of different interventions, treatments or conditions to subjects (Stead and Gordon, 2010). Survey research can also be used to determine causality and is often preferred in marketing research due to lower cost. Conclusive research is often appropriate for informing policy, making decisions and testing hypothesis (May, 2001).

However, researchers are increasingly recognising the importance of mixed methods research. Mixed methods research has been identified as 'the type of research in which a researcher or team of researchers combines elements of qualitative and quantitative research approaches (e.g. use of qualitative and quantitative viewpoints, data collection, analysis, inference techniques) for the broad purpose of breadth and depth of understanding and corroboration' (Johnson et al., 2007: 123). Scholars have argued that mixed methods research, with its pragmatic approach, is not aligned with a single system or philosophy (Creswell et al., 2003). Rather a mixed methods approach tends to be driven by the research question rather than being restricted by paradigmatic assumptions (Johnson and Onwuegbuzie, 2004). This is important for social marketing, as the main purpose of social marketing programmes is outcomes like social change, social wellbeing, social equality and social justice, rather than purely academic or theoretical purposes. Following a pragmatic approach and using a mixed methods research design offers the flexibility that is often required when designing, delivering and evaluating social marketing programmes. Therefore, mixed methods research design uses pragmatism as a system of philosophy. Pragmatic inquiry includes use of induction or the discovery of patterns; deduction, which involves testing theories and hypotheses; and abduction, which involves uncovering and relying on the best set of explanations for understanding the results of research (Morgan, 2007).

Sampling

Sampling is the process of selecting a sub-group of units (e.g. people, organisations) from a population of interest. By studying the sample we may identify insights and understanding; and in the case of quantitative research generalise our results back to the general population. The first thing to consider in relation to sampling is the population we are interested in conducting research with. We then need to consider the unit of analysis. Most often in social marketing research we are interested in people, though this may not always be individuals but could include pairs, groups or organisations. It is then appropriate to consider what the sampling frame is – the list of sampling units from which the sample is selected. For example, this may be a list of all pupils on a school roll, or even a selection of your acquaintances you suspect might have something to say about a topic. We then need to consider what the sampling design is and whether we are using *probability* or *non-probability sampling*. The type of research we are doing and what we hope to achieve from it will affect this decision.

Sampling in qualitative research

In qualitative research the focus is on exploring concepts and ideas, rather than testing them. Therefore, the focus is on generating depth of understanding among a particular group of people – not generalising to a larger population. Generally, sample sizes in qualitative research are normally smaller than in quantitative research. They should be adequate enough so that enough data are collected to reach data saturation (the point at which no new prominent themes are identified from data analysis), but they should not be so large that it is difficult to undertake a deep and insightful analysis of the research questions. Two forms of sampling are commonly used in qualitative research.

Purposive sampling

This is a non-probability form of sampling. That is, the researcher does not seek to sample participants on a random basis. The focus in purposive sampling is to sample participants in a strategic way so that they are relevant to the research questions that are being asked. For example, if you wish to do some qualitative research to understand the attitudes of adolescent smokers, you would seek to sample adolescents who are smokers.

Snowball sampling

This is a technique in which the researcher initially samples a small group of people through networks or contacts who are relevant to the research questions, and then these participants that are sampled propose other participants who are relevant to the research. For example, you may sample a group of middle-aged drinkers to discuss the topic of drinking cultures, and they recommend other groups of middle-aged drinkers that they know or have socialised with.

Sampling in quantitative research

Sampling in quantitative research involves different considerations from those for qualitative research. Sample sizes in quantitative research are larger than qualitative samples, and are often designed so that general inferences can be made about a topic or a population – whether that is a specific group of people, or the population of an entire country. However, the sampling approach chosen affects the *representativeness* of your sample, and your ability to *generalise* your findings to a larger population. Calculating the required sample size depends on whether you need the sample to be representative, findings to be generalisable, the number of issues/topics/variables to be tested, and the expected effect sizes or level of influence you wish to identify in your analysis. Researchers sometimes use power calculations to help calculate required sample sizes, especially for representative samples – see software such as G-Power for more information. Two main approaches to quantitative sampling are discussed here.

Probability sampling

This is a sample that has been selected using a random selection method, so that each participant in the population has a known per centage chance of being selected for inclusion in the study. It is usually assumed that a representative sample is more likely to emerge when using this approach. Probability sampling keeps *sampling error* (errors in the findings due to the difference between a sample and the population from which it is selected) to a minimum. There are several forms of probability sampling:

- *Simple random sample*: when each participant in a population has an equal chance of being included in a sample normally done through using random tables of numbers to select participants from the overall sample frame (the list of potential participants).
- *Systematic sample*: when we systematically select participants from the same sample frame as with a simple random sample – for example, we may select one person every 20 names as a participant.
- *Stratified random sampling*: stratifying the sample population according to categories – and then randomly or systematically sampling from within each category. For example, if we want to ensure that an equal number of participants from each of five organisations is included in the sample, we would stratify according to organisation, and then select cases within each category.
- *Multi-stage cluster sampling*: when the primary sampling unit is not the units of population to be sampled but the groupings of those units – known as *clusters*. For example, if we generated a sample of adolescents across a country we might get a wide geographic spread making the study difficult to administer. Instead we could sample cities and towns, and then participants within each city and town selected. A probability sampling method is employed at each stage – that is we might say select ten towns randomly from the entire list of towns in a country, and then randomly select 100 participants from each town to be included in the study. (Adapted from Bryman, 2012.)

Non-probability sampling

This is an umbrella term covering all forms of sampling that are carried out not using probability sampling techniques. These include:

- *Convenience sampling*: when a sample of participants is generated based on convenience and accessibility by the researcher – for example, if we have a large group of friends we may sample all of those we are able to speak to.
- *Purposive sampling*: involves sampling participants in a strategic way so that they are relevant to the research questions that are being asked. For example, if we wish to understand the practices of young adult gamblers, you would seek to sample young adults who identify as gamblers.
- *Snowball sampling*: a technique in which the researcher initially samples a small group of people through networks or contacts who are relevant to the research questions, and then these participants propose other participants who are relevant to the research.
- *Quota sampling*: when we generate a sample that is proportionally reflective of a population according to different categories such as gender, ethnicity, age groups, socio-economic groups and so on. For example, if we know 50 per cent of a population is female a quota would be set to sample 50 per cent of participants who are female. However, selection of participants in these categories is left up to the researcher rather than done randomly. (Adapted from Bryman, 2012.)

Conclusion

Research is an integral part of social marketing, and acts as the eyes and ears of a social change programme. Research is used at every stage of the social marketing process. Given the importance of research it is vital that social marketers consider some of the important philosophical, moral, ethical and technical issues that should be considered when using research. This chapter has considered research paradigms, and how ontology influences how we see and understand the world around us. We then identified four dominant research epistemologies – *positivism*, *interpretivism*, *critical theory* and *pragmatism* – and how they frame and can influence how we think about, conduct, interpret and represent the findings from research. We discussed how research epistemology often influences what research methods we may use for inquiry. We then identified the importance of research ethics, and how crucial it is that social marketing studies are conducted to the highest ethical standards, particularly when sensitive topics or potentially vulnerable participants are involved. We explored the topic of reflexivity, discussing how reflexive practice as a social marketing researcher can help us identify how we, and research participants, influence the research process, and can also encourage us to think about power relations, biases and how we represent meanings derived from research data. We then examined considerations when selecting a research design for inquiry. Finally, we addressed the topic of sampling, outlining key things to think about when deciding on the sampling approach and sample size in qualitative and quantitative social marketing research. This chapter identifies the 'what' and the 'why' of doing research, and in Chapter 10, we examine how we do research in social marketing.

Reflective questions

- What research paradigm would an ethnographic study on low-income people's attitudes towards physical activity belong to? Explain your selection.
- How would you ensure that research on the topic of alcohol consumption among adolescents was carried out ethically? What specific actions would you take to ensure this?
- If you wanted to conduct research to understand whether fast food marketing influences consumption patterns of young females what kind of research design would you use? Provide three key reasons supporting your answer.

Further reading

Bryman, A. (2012) *Social Research Methods*. Oxford: Oxford University Press.

della Porta, D. and Keating, M. (eds) (2008) *Approaches and Methodologies in the Social Sciences: A Pluralist Perspective*. Cambridge: Cambridge University Press.

ESRC (Economic and Social Research Council) (2010) *ESRC Framework for Research Ethics 2010*. Swindon: ESRC.

Jarvis, P. (1995) *Adult and Continuing Education: Theory and Practice*. London: Routledge.

Johnson, R.B., Onwuegbuzie, A.J. and Turner, L.A. (2007) 'Toward a definition of mixed methods research', *Journal of Mixed Methods Research*, 1 (2): 112–133.

Quine, W.V.O. (1960) *Word and Object*. Cambridge, MA: The MIT Press.

References

Altrichter, H., Feldman, A., Posch, P. and Somekh, B. (2008) *Teachers Investigate Their Work: An Introduction to Action Research Across the Professions*. London: Routledge.

Bartels, R. (1983) 'Is marketing defaulting its responsibilities?', *Journal of Marketing*, 47 (4): 32–35.

Brewer, J.D. (2000) *Ethnography*. Buckingham: Open University Press.

Bryman, A. (2007) 'Barriers to integrating quantitative and qualitative research', *Journal of Mixed Methods Research*, 1 (1): 8–22.

Bryman, A. (2012) *Social Research Methods*. Oxford: Oxford University Press.

Byrne, B. (2009) *Structural Equation Modeling with AMOS: Basic Concepts, Applications, and Programming*. New York: Routledge.

Chia, R. (2002) 'The production of management knowledge: philosophical underpinnings of research design', in D. Partington (ed.), *Essential Skills for Management Research*. London: SAGE, pp. 1–19.

Chisnall, P.M. (1992) *Marketing Research*. New York: McGraw-Hill.

Corbetta, P. (2003) *Social Research: Theory, Methods and Techniques*. London: SAGE.

Creswell, J.W. (2014) *Research Design: Qualitative, Quantitative, and Mixed Methods Approaches*. Thousand Oaks, CA: SAGE.

Creswell, J.W., Plano Clark, V.L., Gutmann, M.L. and Hanson, W.E. (2003) 'Advanced mixed methods research designs', in A. Tashakkori and C.B. Teddlie (eds), *Handbook of Mixed Methods in Social and Behavioral Research*. Thousand Oaks, CA: SAGE, pp. 209–240.

Crotty, M. (1998) *The Foundations of Social Research: Meaning and Perspective in the Research Process*. London: SAGE.

della Porta, D. and Keating, M. (eds) (2008) *Approaches and Methodologies in the Social Sciences: A Pluralist Perspective*. Cambridge: Cambridge University Press.

Denzin, E. (1994) 'The art of politics of interpretation', in N.K. Denzin and Y.S. Lincoln, *Handbook of Qualitative Research*. Thousand Oaks, CA: SAGE, pp. 500–515.

Denzin, N.K. and Lincoln, Y.S. (2011) *The SAGE Handbook of Qualitative Research*. Thousand Oaks, CA: SAGE.

Diener, E. and Crandall, R. (1978) *Ethics in Social and Behavioral Research*. Chicago: University of Chicago Press.

Easterby-Smith, M., Thorpe, R. and Lowe, A. (2004) *Management Research: An Introduction*. London: SAGE.

ESRC (Economic and Social Research Council) (2010) *ESRC Framework for Research Ethics 2010*. Swindon: ESRC.

Field, A. (2013) *Discovering Statistics Using IBM SPSS Statistics*. London: SAGE.

Fournier, V. and Grey, C. (2000) 'At the critical moment: conditions and prospects for critical management studies', *Human Relations*, 53 (1): 7–32.

Gale, R.M. (2002) *The Blackwell Guide to Metaphysics*. Oxford: Blackwell.

Geertz, C. (1973) *The Interpretation of Cultures: Selected Essays*. New York: Basic Books.

Gilchrist, H., Smith, K., Magee, C.A. and Jones, S. (2012) 'A hangover and a one-night stand: alcohol and risky sexual behaviour among female students at an Australian university', *Youth Studies Australia*, 31 (2): 35–43.

Gordon, R. (2011a) 'Critical social marketing: definition, application and domain', *Journal of Social Marketing*, 1 (2): 82–99.

Gordon, R. (2011b) 'Critical social marketing: assessing the cumulative impact of alcohol marketing on youth drinking', PhD thesis, Stirling: University of Stirling.

Gray, D.E. (2009) *Doing Research in the Real World*. London: SAGE.

Guba, E.G. and Lincoln, Y.S. (1994) 'Competing paradigms in qualitative research', in N.K. Denzin and Y.S. Lincoln (eds), *Handbook of Qualitative Research*. Thousand Oaks, CA: SAGE, pp. 105–117.

Habermas, J. (1970) *Knowledge and Human Interests*. London: Heinemann.

Hakim, C. (1987) *Research Design: Strategies and Choices in the Design of Social Research*. London: Allen and Unwin.

Horkheimer, M. (1972 [1937]) 'Critical theory and traditional theory', in M.J. O'Connell (ed.), *Critical Theory: Selected Essays*. New York: The Seabury Press, pp. 188–243.

Howe, K.R. (1988) 'Against the quantitative-qualitative incompatibility thesis, or, dogmas die hard', *Educational Researcher*, 17: 10–16.

Jarvis, P. (1995) *Adult and Continuing Education: Theory and Practice*. London: Routledge.

Johnson, R.B. and Onwuegbuzie, A.J. (2004) 'Mixed methods research: a research paradigm whose time has come', *Educational Researcher*, 33 (7): 14–26.

Johnson, R.B., Onwuegbuzie, A.J. and Turner, L.A. (2007) 'Toward a definition of mixed methods research', *Journal of Mixed Methods Research*, 1 (2): 112–133.

Kinnear, T.C. and Taylor, J.R. (1996) *Marketing Research: An Applied Approach*. New York: McGraw-Hill.

Kuhn, T.S. (1962) *The Structure of Scientific Revolutions*. Chicago: University of Chicago Press.

Kumar, V., Aaker, D.A. and Day, G.S. (1999) *Essentials of Marketing Research*. New York: John Wiley.

Le Poidevin, R., Peter, S., McGonigal, A. and Cameron, R.P. (2009) *The Routledge Companion to Metaphysics*. London: Routledge.

Lewin, K. (1946) 'Action research and minority problems', *Journal of Social Issues*, 2 (4): 34–46.

May, T. (2001) *Social Research: Issues, Methods and Process*. Maidenhead: Open University Press.

Miller, R.L. and Brewer, J.D. (eds) (2003) *The A–Z of Social Research*. London: SAGE.

Morgan, D.L. (2007) 'Paradigms lost and pragmatism regained: methodological implications of combining qualitative and quantitative methods', *Journal of Mixed Methods Research*, 1 (1): 48–76.

Nightingale, D. and Cromby, J. (eds) (1999) *Social Constructionist Psychology*. Buckingham: Open University Press.

Parasuraman, A. (1991) *Marketing Research*. Reading MA: Addison-Wesley.

Quine, W.V.O. (1960) *Word and Object*. Cambridge, MA: The MIT Press.

Spotswood, F. and Tapp, A. (2013) 'Beyond persuasion: a cultural perspective of behaviour', *Journal of Social Marketing*, 3 (3): 275–294.

Stead, M. and Gordon, R. (2010) 'Providing evidence for social marketing's effectiveness', in J. French, C. Blair-Stevens, D. McVey and R. Merritt (eds), *Social Marketing and Public Health: Theory and Practice*. Oxford: Oxford University Press, pp. 81–96.

Steedman, P.H. (1991) 'On the relations between seeing, interpreting and knowing', in F. Steier (ed.), *Research and Reflexivity*. London: SAGE, pp. 53–62.

Tarrow, S. (1995) 'Bridging the quantitative-qualitative divide in political science', *American Political Science Review*, 89 (2): 471–474.

10 RESEARCH METHODS IN SOCIAL MARKETING

Learning objectives

By the end of this chapter, readers should be able to:

- identify the differences between, strengths and weaknesses of, and applications of qualitative and quantitative research
- identify and understand a range of different research methodologies that can be used to design, implement and evaluate social marketing programmes
- understand the factors that influence what types of research methodologies can be used during different parts of the process of designing, implementing and evaluating social marketing programmes.

Introduction

Chapter 9 introduced why research is integral to social marketing as it acts as a navigational aid and offers us insight on why social issues may occur, how citizens may be thinking and acting, and what potential intervention strategies might work. Research acts as the eyes and ears of social marketers, keeping us close to people we hope to work with to facilitate social good. In Chapter 9 we considered some of the important philosophical, moral, ethical and technical issues that should be considered before we do any research. In this chapter we consider how we do research and what research methods and strategies are available to us. We begin by considering the topic of methodology and identify the strengths and weaknesses of and applications for the two main methodological approaches: qualitative research and quantitative research. We then examine qualitative research as an overall approach to doing research. Following this we examine some key qualitative research methods including depth interviews, focus groups, participant observation research, ethnography (presenting a case study by Fiona Spotswood on ethno-graphic social marketing research), netnography and document analysis. We then examine ways of analysing and disseminating qualitative research data. The next part of this chapter discusses quantitative research as a research approach. Subse-quently we consider some key quantitative research methods including survey research, quantitative content analysis, literature reviews and systematic reviews, and experiments. We then discuss ways of analysing and disseminating quantitative research data. We finish the chapter by discussing when and how we might use research in social marketing, before concluding with a recap of the chapter and what we have learned.

Methodology

Generally two types of methodological approach have been developed: qualitative and quantitative (Neuman, 2003). Each approach makes different assumptions about scientific enquiry, and involves different relationships with data and uses different research methods (Brannan, 1992).

Qualitative research

Qualitative research refers to a range of methodological approaches, normally based upon diverse theoretical principles such as grounded theory, phenomenology and social interactionism, which involve the collection and interpretation of non-numerical data. Qualitative research is able to explore flexible and changeable concepts, rather than testing hypotheses and measuring relationships between variables (Parasuraman, 1991). This type of research aims to gather an in-depth understanding of human behaviour and the reasons influencing this behaviour. It investigates the why and how of behaviour and not just the what, where and when (Denzin and Lincoln, 2011). In social marketing, topics such as checking reactions to media materials used in an intervention, understanding of language, or more complex issues such as likes and dislikes and emotional responses, can be investigated using qualitative techniques. For example, research on the use of fear appeals in road safety social advertising in Australia identified that participants often disassociated themselves from the crash, bang, wallop depictions in the adverts. Participants commented that they were not like those depicted in the adverts, and believed they were more skilled drivers who were unlikely to get into an accident (Stead et al., 2009). Such insights can normally only be gained from qualitative research.

Normally smaller, more focused samples are used in qualitative research. As a research strategy, qualitative research is inductivist, constructionist and interpretivist (Strauss and Corbin, 1998). From these perspectives it is assumed that reality is a social construct and individuals act according to meanings derived from their socially constructed reality (Cunningham-Burley and Kerr, 1999). Therefore, rather than seeking to establish objective facts, qualitative researchers aim to understand how participants make sense of their world and what moves and motivates their behaviour.

Good qualitative research can also offer a way in which researchers can approach a subject in a more open-minded manner, and engage and represent the perspectives of participants, using their language and concepts to develop a discussion and utilise their experiences to illustrate meanings. For example, the qualitative research from the alcohol marketing study discussed earlier included showing adolescents alcohol products and asking them to map their feelings towards the various brands, such as whether they were popular and cool or drinks for experienced drinkers. These types of approaches are known as projective techniques (see Table 10.1).

Using these types of approaches in qualitative research can unlock insight on the underlying motivations and reasons for participants' views and emotional responses towards things. Qualitative research also permits us to monitor *how* things are said. Tone of voice, context and non-verbal cues such as body language can all be important here. It is important when conducting qualitative research to recognise and record such phenomena. Qualitative research also permits us to examine delicate, embarrassing and even illegal topics and behaviours. It is often difficult to delve into such sensitive topics without establishing trust and a rapport with participants that qualitative research can generate.

Qualitative research uses a number of techniques, and we consider some of the main ones here. This list is not exhaustive, and dedicated textbooks on social research offer greater coverage than here.

Table 10.1 Common projective techniques

Word association tests: this technique involves presenting participants with a topic, an object, an image or a list of words one at a time, and asking them to respond with the first word that comes to mind.

Sentence completion: participants are asked to complete a number of partial sentences with the first word or phrase that comes to mind e.g.:

People who drink beer are ...

Third person/role play: participants are asked why a third person may behave in a certain manner or think in a certain way. They may also be asked to act out someone else's behaviour in a particular setting.

Thematic apperception test: participants are presented with a series of images and then asked to provide a story about or description of the image. Themes are then elicited on the basis of the perceptual-interpretive (apperception) use of the images. The image that is used as a stimulus needs to be interesting enough to stimulate discussion, but ambiguous enough not to disclose an answer. Versions of this test may also use a cartoon image with participants asked to suggest dialogue for the characters depicted.

Personification: participants are asked, if the product/image/slogan/entity were a person how would you describe them/what kind of life would they lead/how would others perceive them?

Perceptual mapping: participants are asked to position each product/image/entity on a two- or three-dimensional grid to indicate their feelings or perceptions towards them – such as how much they like it or how popular it is.

Depth interviews

Depth interviews are defined as 'an unstructured personal interview, which uses extensive probing to get a single respondent to talk freely and express detailed beliefs and feelings on a topic' (Kinnear and Taylor, 1996: 315). In these types of interviews, there is a big emphasis on formulating ideas, and gaining insight on the interviewees' own perspectives. Depth interviews offer participants the opportunity to go off on tangents, and talk about what they think is important. In contrast to questionnaire survey interviews, qualitative depth interviews do not necessarily follow a strict protocol in terms of the order, type and number of questions asked. For example, there is greater flexibility for certain topics to be discussed in greater detail if this is deemed appropriate, or for new topics to be explored as they emerge. Interviewers can therefore depart from any schedule or guide that may be used. They can ask new questions, follow up on interviewee's replies and vary the order and even the wording of questions.

Generally there are two types of approach to conducting qualitative depth interviews: the *unstructured interview* and the *semi-structured interview*. In many ways unstructured interviews are similar to a natural conversation or eliciting a story from a participant.

In a semi-structured interview, the researcher has a list of questions or reasonably specific topics to be covered – often referred to as a discussion guide. Depth interviews can permit interviewees to offer their own views, attitudes and impressions on topics. However, depth interviews can be time consuming (usually lasting from 30 to 90 minutes each), and can also be resource intensive. In social marketing research, which often involves sensitive topics and different and potentially vulnerable participant groups, depth interviews are often used to generate insight from experts, for example the NPRI alcohol marketing study in Scotland used semi-structured depth interviews with marketing managers working on alcohol accounts to get their insights on contemporary alcohol marketing (see Gordon et al., 2010). This type of approach worked well with busy experts, and when participants were talking about potentially sensitive commercial information, or talking about topics they might not necessarily want to share in a group environment.

Focus groups

A focus group is a semi-structured group interview (Bryman, 2012) in which the focus is on a particular topic, behaviour or practice. It is one of the most widely used qualitative research methods in marketing research (Hornig Priest, 1996; Bryman, 2012). Focus groups are well placed to explore people's feelings, motivations and concerns and allow respondents to frame themes and concepts in view of their own experiences and relatively free of the bias of the researcher. Furthermore, they are useful for examining the social nature of people's views, which is often of interest in social marketing (Barbour and Kitzinger, 1999). However, focus groups can be difficult to control compared to individual interviews and depend on the ability and role of the moderator to ensure the participation of all members of the group and that the discussion is led in a non-directive way (Morgan, 1995; McDougall, 1999). Group effects such as the dominance of particular speakers or reticence of some participants to contribute require careful management by the moderator (Krueger, 1998). Focus groups can also be difficult to organise in terms of ensuring participant attendance, especially with young people (Tinson, 2009). In addition, focus group data can be difficult to analyse given that a huge amount of data can be created very quickly (Bryman, 2012). Nevertheless, focus group research has gained increasing academic respectability (Krueger, 1995).

The aim in a focus group is to promote informal discussion and interaction and probe covert attitudes and beliefs that respondents would otherwise find difficult to articulate (Chisnall, 1992). Focus groups can help generate information, insight and ideas on social issues and social behaviours and practices that are often the focus of social marketing research – for example, adolescents' views towards alcohol consumption, or the perceived benefits of smoking tobacco for long-term smokers (May, 2001). Employing a focus group methodology also allows for the interaction between participants to be observed, thus offering the researchers insight into the environment and context in which the respondents are socialised (Sarantakos, 1998). This is useful when aiming to understand group dynamics, for instance if we wished to gain insight on how members of a particular community views energy efficiency.

Focus group samples are small and not intended to be statistically significant, as their purpose is to generate rather than test hypotheses (Miles and Huberman, 1994).

Therefore, non-probability sampling techniques are normally used, for example convenience sampling or snowball sampling. Sample sizes for focus groups normally range from four to twenty-four groups, with three to twelve participants, although the exact numbers will depend on the topic, feasibility and practicalities. What is important is that focus group interviews are continued until the point of data saturation is reached and no knew or relevant information is identified. Sometimes this may only require running a small number of focus groups, while in others when complex topics and themes are being explored a larger number of focus groups may be required.

Participant observation research

Participant observation is a method that aims to gain a close and intimate familiarity with individuals or groups, and their attitudes, behaviours, and practices, through extensive observation in their own environment, usually over an extended period of time. Participant observation can be overt – in which the researcher makes their presence known – or covert, when participants do not know they are being observed. Use of covert observation usually requires good reasons why that approach is used (for example, to observe behaviours naturalistically or to gain insight on hidden behaviours) as it can be deemed unethical to not inform people they are being observed. Participant observation often involves using multiple methods at the same time such as depth interviews, direct observation, participation in the life and practices of the group, collective discussions, oral histories and self-analysis. Doing such research over an extended period of time permits the researcher to obtain more detailed and accurate information about the individuals, communities and populations under study. Observable details such as how people spend their time, and hidden details such as taboo behaviours, can be more readily observed and interpreted over time. A major strength of this approach is that discrepancies between what people say they believe should happen, and what actually does happen, can be identified. To enable researchers to engage in overt participant observation, it is usually necessary to establish a rapport and gain the trust of the participants under study; immerse themselves in the field by fitting in with participants, and moderating their language and behaviour accordingly; studiously recording observations and data through field notes, interviews and reflexive journals; and analysing data thematically by organising the data collected according to recurrent themes and constructing a coherent story from the data (Howell, 1972).

This type of research is often very useful in gaining an in-depth insight and representation of participants' lives, and the benefits from doing so for social marketing are quite apparent. Given the key focus on participant orientation in social marketing, and the aim to really understand what moves and motivates people, participant observation research is very relevant. For example, participant observation research was conducted in Scotland to gain insight and understanding on how people in pubs responded to a ban on smoking in public places (Eadie et al., 2008). However, given the time, resources and, on occasions, difficulties in gaining access to participant groups, it may not always be possible to carry out such in-depth research. Social marketers need to make informed and strategic decisions about what resources and limitations they face, and decide accordingly on what research methods they can and should use. Participant observation research has many synergies, and often overlaps with what is known as ethnographic research.

Ethnography

Ethnography is research that is designed to explore cultures and cultural phenomena (Brewer, 2000). Doing ethnography essentially means going beyond observing, to represent visually or in writing the culture of a group. Traditionally used in anthropology, ethnography is increasingly used across the social sciences, including in marketing and consumer research, and in social marketing (see Spotswood and Tapp, 2013). In keeping with the orientation of this textbook, ethnography uses a holistic approach to generating knowledge, and usually involves developing a brief history, and an analysis of the environment and the habitat in which groups exist. Although many of the methods and approaches used in participant observation research are also present in ethnography, this approach goes further in its approach to representing meaning derived from the research. Ethnographic research should observe and present the world through the eyes of the participants under investigation.

Data collection in ethnography can involve participant observation, field notes, interviews, recording images, sound or footage, and surveys. Secondary research and documentary analysis can also feature. The research is oriented towards capturing social meanings, ordinary activities and the everyday occurrences of participants in naturally occurring settings. Ideally, the researcher should minimise the amount of their own bias that is imposed on the data. This approach often differs from more structured and formal depth interviews, focus groups or questionnaire surveys in which participants are put in an artificial environment and asked about phenomenon. Similar to participant observation, establishing trust and rapport, fitting into the group and social life, recording a wealth of data, and reflecting upon their role and influence as a researcher, and upon the interpretations and representation of meanings emerging from the data, are important considerations in doing ethnographic research (Brewer, 2000). Ethnographic research aims to present a 'thick description' – a detailed and in-depth account of the culture and cultural mores that participants are engaged with (Geertz, 1973). Fiona Spotswood's case study below, which applied Bourdieu's habitus theoretical framework to ethnographic research, generated useful insight on participants' challenges in eating well and being physically active (see also Spotswood and Tapp, 2013). Spotswood's research also identified how social theory, such as Bordieu's habitus (see Chapter 8), can help make sense of such ethnographic findings. More recently, there has been increasing attention given to *visual ethnography*, which is research concerned with the study and production of ethnographic photography, film, and new media (Rose, 2001). Some forms of visual ethnography even encourage participants to record things themselves, through issuing them with cameras or recording devices. This provides a novel and engaging way for participants to take part in the research and show the world through their own eyes – a perspective that seems advantageous to social marketing research. For example, research in Ireland used visual ethnography by getting young people to take images of alcohol marketing they were exposed to – offering valuable insights on contemporary alcohol promotion (National Youth Council of Ireland, 2009).

CASE STUDY

Learning from Bourdieu: lessons in behaviour change theory from an ethnographic study of 'working-class' British adults

Strategic and policy context

The starting point for this study was that obesity in the UK, as elsewhere in the West, is socio-economically patterned. This is thought to be due to the low rates of physical activity within lower socio-economic groups and the social-patterning of other behaviours, such as a working-class propensity to favour unhealthy, energy dense food (NOO, 2010). However, a large-scale piece of qualitative research into the barriers of British adults from lower socio-economic groups to participate in voluntary exercise left me perplexed. Despite 46 face-to-face interviews and six focus groups with people at the extreme ends of the socio-economic spectrum, I felt that I had still failed to get to the bottom of the 'reasons' for the social class gulf in leisure time physical activity participation. One interviewee's comment perfectly explained the problem. She was a mother of eight, living in a deprived estate in the north west of England. Her life was chaotic, and managing her finances, her children and her own mental health and emotional problems was a daily struggle. She was overweight, smoked and ate a poorly nutritious diet. She would have liked to be slimmer and occasionally went to the community leisure centre with the intention of exercising regularly. She told me that 'I wish I wanted to exercise. I wish there was a way someone could force me to do it. I *want to want* to exercise. I just don't'. For this woman, physical activity was simply culturally alien (Bourdieu, 1978).

Traditional approaches to behaviour change, which are so often based on psychological theory and rely on the target audience's direct engagement and ultimately self-regulation of behaviour for success, failed to make any impact on this research participant, and the many others like her who I met. I realised that an alternative approach to understanding the social patterning of physical activity was required. I therefore took a cultural perspective and my research set out to understand the mechanisms at play in the 'background'; behind people's cognitive understanding of reasons 'why' they don't participate. I wanted to understand the cultural structures in which people live, that shape their every thought and act, of which they are unaware. This approach, which saw me using Bourdieu's habitus as a theoretical framework (Bourdieu, 1984) – but could just as easily have been done using social practice theory (Bourdieu, 1990) – led to a completely alternative set of conclusions about the best way of designing behaviour change interventions to target the social patterning of leisure time physical activity.

Methodology

As I discovered during my preliminary research project, when trying to explore a behaviour that has its roots in unthinking, non-cognitive processes, asking people direct questions about 'why' they behave in a certain way has serious limitations. Bourdieu wrote that people do not know the significance of their own actions. This is because we are all 'subject' to the cultural frameworks in which we live. A cultural framework is not a rigid structure in which we have no agency or choice. Rather, our everyday activity is a negotiation between the structures and our agency (Bourdieu, 1980). Through the performance of our daily routines we subtly change those structures but also, through the repetition of culturally acceptable behaviours, we reinforce them (Bourdieu, 1984).

For Bourdieu, the 'habitus', which was his model of cultural structures, is the best way of explaining social class (Bourdieu, 1987). People who have similar habituses tend to live together. Their worldview is framed by the portfolio of cultural, social and economic capital they own, and as a result they feel most comfortable with other people with a similar portfolio. 'Birds of a feather flock together'. Certain behaviours (and indeed tastes for certain things) tend to be acceptable within the socio-cultural structures of social class, and others less so (Bourdieu, 1984; 1987). I chose to do my research in the north west, in a very deprived housing estate somewhat cut off from the main town of which it was a part. Here, physical activity was considered abnormal, whereas smoking was absolutely acceptable. The estate had a 52 per cent smoking rate at the time.

To gain insight into the automaticity of leisure time physical inactivity, an observation methodology was required. I therefore conducted ethnography, living on the estate for five months and basing my observation around intensive episodes of observation with five families. The families were not aware until after the research that I was interested primarily in their physical activity

(Continued)

(Continued)

participation, but knew that their 'lifestyles' were being researched. Extensive field notes were taken as well as formal, recorded and transcribed depth interviews with various community workers and leaders. Three weeks after the end of the project, all the key research participants were interviewed formally in an 'exit' interview, where the purpose of the research was divulged.

Findings

The families I studied had chaotic lives due to their daily struggle to cope with the stresses leading from low cultural and economic capital and their uniquely bonded social capital. This latter type of capital refers to social networks that are tightly bonded between people with similar capital portfolios, rather than between larger networks of people who are varied, and bonded more loosely. As a result, perspective and objectivity about a potentially healthier, more balanced life-course were out of reach. Rather, the residents of the estate were preoccupied with presenting an image of themselves as tough and aggressive; with seeking opportunities to 'escape' the real world in their leisure time (through alcohol, drugs, screen-based entertainment and social-media avatars); and predominantly with coping with the daily survival of their families.

In addition, their worldview was firmly bounded not only by these personal capital-based constraints but also by the physical environment in which they lived. The estate was insular, blocked by a river on one side, an industrial zone on the other and cut off from the main town centre by a motorway. Within the estate there were a few shops, dominated by a large cut-price alcohol retailer. There was a pharmacy, a couple of community centres, two fast food outlets and two corner shops as well as a run-down leisure centre. There were no supermarkets and nowhere to buy fresh goods. The streets were dirty, bus stops graffitied and green spaces overgrown and littered. The environment seemed to encourage an avoidance of community life. The overall tone of many discussions on the estate was defensive. People were wary of 'outsiders' and untrusting of health initiatives, including those aimed at encouraging participation in physical activity. Despite the local leisure centre's efforts, participation was low and new classes tended to fail. Physical activity simply was not the 'norm'; was not accepted and those who did participate were considered culturally alien.

Detailed analysis using thematic analysis procedures of the 85,000 words of field notes and additional interview data concluded that there are fundamental elements of leisure time physical activity which do not 'fit' with the cultural frameworks that were observed. Participation in physical activity requires some organisation, for example, rarely possible in the chaotic, stressful lives on the estate. Physical activity can be unpleasant and uncomfortable; not welcomed in a culture which values the presentation of a 'tough' and aggressive image and one where 'escaping' real life was often the aim of leisure activities. Physical activity was not perceived to contribute to the daily responsibilities of managing a family. Physical activity often does not provide instant gratification, like the screen-based leisure activities that were favoured. In short, physical activity had no place in the cultural structures of the people I observed.

As a result of this research, the traditional focus of social marketing and other individualist behaviour change approaches are brought into question. It is my conclusion that approaches based on psychological theory, as social marketing tends to be, can be severely limited when strong cultural structures are in place. When such an embedded, unthinking worldview is the foundation

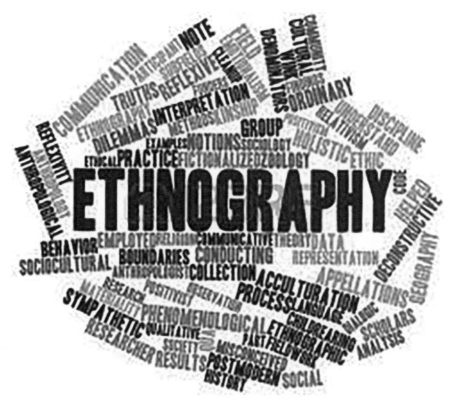

Source: www.123rf.com/photo_16571929_abstract-word-cloud-for-ethnography-with-related-tags-and-terms.html

(Continued)

(Continued)

of a behavioural problem like the lack of physical activity participation, it is my contention that behaviour change activity must consider the factors underpinning the cultural worldview rather than seek change at the point of 'decision making'. According to Bourdieu's habitus, 'decisions' are simply a manifestation of the cultural worldview (Bourdieu, 1984).

Using the framework of the habitus, structural factors can be organised around the theory's four components: social capital, financial capital, cultural capital and physical environment (Bourdieu, 1993). Although not without limitations (in terms of ethics, planning, monitoring, evaluation and resources), targeting change interventions based around these large-scale components will likely have far more long-term effectiveness at 'behaviour change' than downstream individualist targeting of individuals' decisions. This approach naturally requires interdisciplinary thinking, engagement with policy makers and the application of approaches far broader than those traditionally used by social marketers.

Acknowledgements to Dr Fiona Spotswood, Lecturer, Bristol Social Marketing Centre, University of the West of England, for this case study.

Discussion questions

- Thinking about Fiona Spotswood's case study – do you think an ethnographic approach was the best research method to use for this study? List some reasons to back up your argument.
- Do you think another approach would have been better? What research methods would you use, and how and why you would use them?

Netnography

Netnography is a branch of ethnography that analyses the behaviour of participants on the Internet – usually on platforms such as discussion forums, bulletin boards, listservs, chat rooms, web pages and social media sites like Facebook and Twitter. The concept was coined by consumer researcher Dr Robert Kozinets, and as a method it can be faster, simpler and less expensive than conducting traditional ethnographic research, yet is more naturalistic and unobtrusive than conducting focus groups or depth interviews (Kozinets, 2010). However, the amount of data and depth of insight that can be generated may be less than traditional ethnography as participants may not explicate all of their attitudes and behaviours in online forums.

Yet given the seemingly ever-increasing importance and prominence of social media, netnography has emerged in recent years as a useful research method. Netnography is similar to ethnography in that it is naturalistic, immersive, descriptive, multi-method and adaptable. Researchers who undertake netnography research may do so covertly by merely observing, or overtly and participate in the culture. The latter usually requires researchers to establish trust and rapport with members of online platforms, fit in with the group, record data diligently but also ethically, and reflect upon their role in the research and how they interpret meanings and representations. The aim of netnography is to provide insight on the symbolism, meaning and behaviours of participants who engage in online platforms.

While netnography originally emerged as a method for understanding consumers in the commercial field, social marketing research is beginning to make use of the technique. For example, a critical social marketing study at the University of Wollongong that was recently funded by the Australian Research Council, proposes to use a netnography of online betting platforms to generate insight on participants' engagement with and responses to the marketing of online sports betting (see http://social-sciences.uow.edu.au/has/research/projects/index.html). Given the importance of online platforms for people to communicate, interact and even socialise, understanding what is going on in these platforms holds the potential to inform our understanding of phenomena – such as people's responses to commercial marketing, or how people feel about behaviours such as exercising or dieting.

Document analysis

Document analysis is a qualitative research method that involves a systematic procedure for reviewing or evaluating documents, printed or electronic, from a variety of sources. These may include:

- personal documents in written form such as diaries, letters, and books; or visual form like photographs and photo albums
- official public documents such as parliamentary/Hansard records; or policy documents, background papers, minutes of meetings, manuals, agendas, maps and charts
- documents from the private sector such as organisational/annual reports
- mass media outputs such as newspapers and magazines, advertisements, press releases, programme scripts
- online/virtual outputs such as blogs, online articles and so on.

These types of documents can be found in libraries, newspaper archives, offices of public records, organisational and institutional depositories, and increasingly in online depositories such as digital libraries (Bowen, 2009). What links the written or image-based content contained in any such sources is that this has been recorded without the researcher's intervention. The analytical process in document analysis involves finding, selecting, making sense of and synthesising data contained in the documents under consideration. Document analysis is often used in combination with other qualitative research techniques as a method of providing a 'triangulation' of data – data from multiple sources that are combined to form a more complete and representative understanding of phenomena.

Key considerations when selecting documents for analysing include whether the documents can be accessed and read/understood, and making sure that they have not been produced specifically for the purposes of research but for other genuine purposes, and that they are relevant to the focus of the research. The quality of documents under consideration is also important. Scott (1990) suggests four important criteria to consider when selecting documents:

1. *Authenticity* – are the documents genuine and of unquestionable origin?
2. *Credibility* – are the documents largely free of errors, distortion and bias?
3. *Representativeness* – are the documents typical of their kind, and do they offer a reasonable representation of the phenomenon under investigation?
4. *Meaning* – are the documents clear and comprehensible?

Bryman (2012) identifies three main ways in which document analysis can be undertaken. They are *qualitative content analysis, semiotics* and *hermeneutics*.

> *Qualitative content analysis* involves searching for underlying themes in the documents being analysed. Although the exact processes through which themes are extracted in document analysis are often not specified in detail, the approach often follows established ideas for organising, coding and interpreting qualitative data (see the following section).
>
> *Semiotics* involves analysing the 'symbols' of everyday life and offering interpretations of their meaning. A range of terminologies in semiotics is used to explain how it works. *Signs* in semiotics refers to something that stands for something else – with the sign being made up of the *signifier* and the *signified*. The *signifier* is the entity that points to an underlying meaning. The *signified* is the meaning to which the *signifier* refers. A *denotative meaning* is the overt meaning of a *signifier* and indicates its function or role. A *sign-function* is an entity that denotes a certain function. A *connotative meaning* is a meaning associated with a certain social context that exists in addition to its *denotative meaning*. *Polysemy* refers to a quality of signs – especially that they are always capable of being interpreted in many ways. The *code* is the generalised meaning that parties may seek to instil in a sign – this is also sometimes called a *sign system*. While this sounds complex, Bryman (2012: 559) offers a simple way to think about semiotics. Take the example of a person's curriculum vitae document. A typical CV might include personal details, education,

employment, responsibilities and information on key skills, training and qualities. We can treat the CV document as a system of interrelated signifiers, that signify at the level of denotative meaning a summary of the person's experience (its sign function); and at the connotative level an indication of the person's value – especially in relation to their prospective employability. Every person's CV is capable of being interpreted in different ways, and this is often the case if you have ever sat on an interview panel. Therefore, this means CVs are polysemic, but that in general there is a code according to which certain attributes contained in a CV are viewed as particularly desirable. Therefore, applicants for jobs often aim to write their CVs to amplify these desired attributes, and present a symbol and representation of themselves that will hopefully be interpreted in a particular (and positive) way by the prospective employer.

Hermeneutics refers to an approach to document analysis that seeks to bring out the meanings of a text from the perspective of its author. This often requires paying attention to the social, political, cultural and historical context within which the text was produced. Phillips and Brown (1993) outline an approach in which hermeneutic analysis can be undertaken. The *social-historical moment* involves examining the producer of the document, its intended recipients, its place in the world and the context in which it was produced and received. The *formal moment* involves 'a formal analysis of the structural and conventional aspects of the text' (Phillips and Brown, 1993: 1563). The *interpretation-reinterpretation moment* involves creating a synopsis from the first two moments to provide an interpretation of the documents under investigation.

Document analysis is a method that is relevant to social marketing, particularly as it can provide the context around how attitudes, behaviours and phenomena occur. Document analysis research has been used to understand the context of media and public attitudes and perceptions towards tobacco advertising, and tobacco industry advertising strategy through an audit of the printed press (Moodie and Hastings, 2011), and was similarly used in the NPRI alcohol marketing study in Scotland to understand contemporary marketing and media portrayals of alcohol and alcohol brands (Gordon and Hastings, 2007). Thinking towards a strategic social marketing approach, the utility of document analysis becomes even more apparent, as consulting documents from a range of stakeholders, actors and influencers on social phenomena can help social marketers form a more complete understanding of the context in which they are working, and also help to identify issues and potential strategies for dealing with these when designing and delivering programmes.

Analysing and disseminating qualitative data

Analysis of qualitative research data can be subjective, and lacks structure. Often, there are no clearly defined rules on how to analyse such qualitative data, but guiding principles.

Research methods textbooks are more appropriate for offering details on how qualitative data can and should be analysed. However, some general principles are discussed briefly here. For the most part, qualitative data analysis is largely unstructured, and depends on the researcher making sense of the data, and identifying themes and forming codes in which to organise data, and then forming a story, identifying meanings and presenting representations.

What links most forms of qualitative data analysis is the requirement to code data. While dedicated research methods texts provide much greater and important detail on coding data, McCracken (1988) offers a useful five-step process, an adaptation of which is presented here:

1. Transcribe interviews/process data, and then organise/upload them. Read transcripts/view data carefully, making notations in the margin (or using software such as QSR NVivo).
2. Organise observations into preliminary descriptive and interpretive categories based on the content of the transcripts/data sources, and information obtained from a literature review and understanding of the theoretical framework(s) guiding the research. This is often referred to as coding – whereby certain themes are named and data are coded and categorised according to these themes.
3. Conduct a thorough examination of preliminary codes to identify patterns and connections between codes.
4. Determine basic themes by examining clusters of comments made by participants and memos made by the researcher.
5. Examine all interviews across groupings to identify the predominant themes contained in the data.

Another approach to analysing and presenting qualitative data is narrative analysis, which emphasises the stories that people transmit in the course of the research. An advantage of narrative analysis is that it is arguably more naturalist, and unlike coding, it does not potentially fragment and decontextualise data.

When it comes to the dissemination of qualitative research, or indeed any research or ideas in social marketing, it is important that insights, understanding and learning are transmitted to all stakeholders involved in a social marketing programme, but also just as importantly, as far and as wide as possible. This is something that social marketing has been poor at in the past. Often great research is carried out, and insight and learning generated, but this knowledge is never made available in the public domain and shared with other actors who may be working in the same space. A big implication from this is that it creates wastage, and can lead to actors repeating research that may have already been done, or making mistakes that could have been avoided if they knew about existing research. Therefore, it is important in social marketing programmes to try to build in as much capacity for writing up and dissemination as possible. Dissemination comes in many forms, and can consist of academic journal articles and conference papers, news articles, websites, public relations and advocacy activities, email communications, newsletters, blogs and so on. What is important is to get information out there, so that it can make a difference, however small that may be. By sharing all of our learning in the social marketing domain, it can help us think and act more strategically and be more effective at achieving social change or socially beneficial outcomes.

Quantitative research

Quantitative research refers to systematic and numerical empirical investigation of quantitative properties, phenomena and variables, and their relationships, in a measureable or quantifiable way. It aims to develop, test and employ models, theories and hypotheses relating to the subject area. It normally employs quantitative measurement and the use of statistical analysis. Quantitative research is based upon the methodological principles of positivism and neo-positivism and adheres to a strict research design developed prior to the research being conducted (Filmer et al., 1972; Sarantakos, 1998). Normally the research is conducted with a statistically representative sample of the population using larger sample sizes than in qualitative research. Data collection methods used in quantitative research include experimentation, analysis of secondary data sources, questionnaire based surveys and structured observation (Bryman, 2012).

Survey research

Survey research is used to quantitatively measure, assess and/or evaluate thoughts, opinions, feelings, attitudes and behaviours. Survey research is useful for reducing error to the variation in the asking and answering of questions, and offers greater accuracy in and ease of processing participants' answers. A survey consists of a predetermined and structured set of questions that is given to a sample of participants – sometimes called structured interviewing. If the sample of participants is a representative sample, then it is possible to describe the attitudes of the population from which the sample is drawn. This is known as generalisability – from such survey research with a representative sample, we are able to ascribe the findings from our research more generally to the population at large. This type of survey research approach is common in national population surveys, such as census research, household surveys or national health surveys. Survey research is important to social marketing as it can help assess the current attitudes and behaviours of participants, track changes in these over time, and help evaluate social marketing programmes. Surveys may also be used to test a theory or concepts among a group of participants, or to measure and assess the views of a particular group of people.

Survey research can either be administered by an interviewer or self-completion surveys can be administered in which participants answer independently without an interviewer present. Survey questions are normally administered using a questionnaire survey, an instrument containing a list of questions on the topics of interest for the research.

Questionnaire surveys can come in a physical form (paper-based surveys), and be administered face-to-face or be sent by mail for self-completion; can be administered over the telephone (e.g. CATI surveys); or can be administered online (web-based surveys). There are important issues to consider and advantages and disadvantages to each approach: see Bryman (2012) for greater details on this. Ideally the approach should aim to utilise available resources, and ensure that the topics of interest are measured comprehensively, that issues with bias are limited (when results are affected in a way that they are different from the population parameter of interest), and that the research is done ethically.

To offer some examples of issues to consider, paper-based face-to-face surveys offer control and easy quality assurance to the researchers as they can address issues and deduce whether people are answering questions honestly but they are expensive and resource intensive. Web-based surveys are low cost and easy to administer but there is little control over how people answer the survey and using online samples of participants means that generating a random probability sample is almost impossible. Deciding which approach to use requires weighing up the pros and cons of the various methods, and assessing what resources are available. These are common challenges in social marketing, as a desire to act strategically and conduct comprehensive research is often limited by resources – as social marketing is usually funded by the public or not-for-profit sectors these resources can be thin on the ground.

As opposed to qualitative interviews in which questions are open-ended and can be answered in a variety of ways, questions in survey research are usually though not always closed (i.e. participants are given a series of selected responses). Some questions in survey research are open-ended (for example: What is the first thing you think about when you see the word 'smoking'?), but these are usually kept to a minimum and are normally used to get a participant to start thinking about a topic or to collect some limited qualitative information about a topic. Other questions may require a participant to input free text but within stated boundaries – such as inputting their age or job title.

Questionnaire survey development is an important topic, and one that warrants considerable attention. A lot of effort is required to make sure that a survey questionnaire asks questions (or *items*) that make sense, measure what they purport to measure, and are comparable with existing measures on the same topic. Indeed, when developing a survey, researchers are often encouraged to check whether existing sets of questions (known as *scales*) are available. The reason for using existing scales is that they have usually been developed using a proper scale development procedure. This means that the questions have been developed and tested over a period of time to check their *validity* (the degree to which the tool measures what it claims to measure) and *reliability* (the consistency of the measure – it should produce similar results under consistent conditions). If existing scale items are not available, then scale development may be undertaken following appropriate procedures (see Churchill, 1979). Surveys should also be pre-tested prior to being used in the field – to ensure the acceptability, appropriateness and comprehension of questionnaire survey content, and that participants can accurately reflect their views and experiences without constraining responses (May, 2001).

The administration of survey research can utilise a number of research designs, or what is also known as temporal classifications (Zikmund et al., 2011). Cross-sectional studies are survey research with the measurement of issues at one fixed point in time. Cross-sectional designs offer a quick way to gain information on topics, and they cost less than other designs. However, given that measurement is only made at one fixed point, the predictability and meaning of the results can be questionable. An example is a study in Queensland, Australia that surveyed people about their perceptions towards social marketing brands – while the study offered some useful insights on what might be important when developing social marketing brands and the impact they may have on behaviours, this does not offer definitive proof of these relationships.

Longitudinal studies are when participants are questioned at two or more different times. These can consist of cohort studies or panel studies in which the same individuals are surveyed repeatedly permitting analysis of changes in individuals over time. The NPRI alcohol marketing study in Scotland is an example of a longitudinal cohort study in which young people were surveyed about their exposure to alcohol marketing, and their drinking behaviours at age 13; and then were asked the same questions again at age 15. This allowed for analysis to identify whether exposure to alcohol marketing at age 13 was associated with changes in drinking behaviour between the ages of 13 and 15. Tracking studies are when largely the same questions on the same topics are asked repeatedly at different points in time, but the participants who answer the questions do not always stay the same. An example is a study in the UK that has monitored young people's awareness of and involvement with tobacco marketing along with their smoking attitudes, knowledge and behaviours, since the introduction of an advertising ban in 1999 (see www.stir.ac.uk/management/research/centre-for-tobacco-control-research/tobacco-control/).

Randomised control trials (RCTs) (mentioned earlier on in this chapter) can also involve survey research and this is viewed as the gold standard of research. In an RCT, participants in an intervention group are surveyed at baseline (i.e. before any intervention is delivered), along with a sample of participants in a control group. An intervention of some sort is then delivered to the participants in the intervention group, but not to participants in the control group. Both participant groups are then surveyed again to assess for changes over time, and between the participant groups to assess whether the intervention had an effect. However, while RCTs are of a high standard they are expensive, and often assigning people to a control group is not possible. For example, with the NPRI alcohol marketing study (see Gordon, 2011) it was not possible to generate a sample of adolescents who had never been exposed to alcohol marketing. Therefore, use of RCTs is less common in social marketing research.

Quantitative content analysis

Content analysis is defined as 'a research technique for the objective, systematic and quantitative description of the manifest content of communication' (Berelson, 1952: 18).

Content analysis in quantitative research is different from the equivalent content analysis of documents in qualitative research, as numerical data are recorded rather than textual data. Often content analysis involves the recording of both qualitative textual data, and quantitative numerical-based data. The aim of content analysis is to describe and make inferences about the characteristics and consequences of information and/or communications contained in a document (Holsti, 1969). The two most important qualities that should be applied to content analysis research are objectivity and being systematic. In terms of objectivity, in content analysis rules need to be and are clearly specified in advance for the allocation of raw materials (e.g. newspaper articles) to categories. Having clear and transparent rules for how the data are categorised aids objectivity and limits the possibility of a researcher's personal bias influencing the research process (Krippendorff, 2012). Being systematic means that the application of the rules is consistent, rigorous and cross-checked – often by conducting *inter-coder reliability* checks in which researchers will check how each other researcher has categorised and coded content analysis data to check for consistency. Normally when disagreements occur a third or more researcher will make a majority decision. The idea with content analysis is that anybody could apply the rules used and replicate the study. Content analysis has been used in social marketing research fairly regularly, for example to assess and interpret adolescent responses to alcohol advertising (Gordon et al., 2011).

Literature reviews and systematic reviews

Literature reviews involve synopsising the critical points of current published knowledge including summarising substantive findings, theoretical and methodological contributions to a particular topic. Systematic reviews involve doing the same but systematically to identify, appraise, select and synthesise all published research literature relevant to the topic.

Literature reviews

Literature reviews should form an integral part of the scoping phase of a strategic social marketing programme, as this allows us to understand the context of an issue, and identify what is already known, and what concepts and theories are relevant to this area. Literature reviews also allow us to identify what research methods and intervention strategies may already have been employed in a given area. Furthermore, the extant literature can tell us if there are any controversies in the knowledge base, and if there are inconsistencies in research findings, as well as help identify what the gaps in knowledge may be.

Most literature reviews are in the form of narrative reviews, meaning that they aim to offer an overview of a field of study or a topic through a reasonably comprehensive assessment and critical reading of the literature. Electronic databases such as Scopus and Web of Science, which are available from university digital library websites, offer a good vehicle for searching through published journals and reports that may contain relevant literature. Google searches can also be conducted – and both approaches often use a series of search terms that a researcher generates which are known to be relevant to the topic. Hard copy books may also contain relevant literature, and be consulted. This approach to a literature review is largely qualitative and descriptive. Furthermore, what is reviewed in a literature review can often be down to the interests and biases of the researcher, or can be left to chance.

Systematic reviews

A systematic review is defined as a:

> replicable, scientific and transparent process ... that aims to minimise bias through exhaustive literature searches of published and unpublished studies and by providing an audit trail of the reviewer's decisions, procedures and conclusions. (Tranfield et al., 2003: 209)

A systematic review that includes only quantitative studies, and then offers a calculating of the effect size – or size of influence that one variable may have on another – is known as a *meta-analysis*. Brief reviews that use some systematic review processes but are not deemed to be absolutely comprehensive are known as *rapid reviews*.

Systematic reviews are increasingly utilised by policy makers to inform evidence-based approaches to decision making as they are viewed as being robust and comprehensive enough. Bryman (2012) identifies four key steps to conducting systematic reviews:

1. Define the purpose and scope of the review.
2. Seek out studies/research literature relevant to the scope and purposes of the review.
3. Appraise the studies/literature identified during step 2.
4. Analyse each study and then synthesise the overall results of the review.

Systematic reviews are increasingly used in social marketing. For example, the UK National Social Marketing Centre commissioned the Institute for Social Marketing at the University of Stirling to conduct three systematic reviews on evidence of the effectiveness of social marketing for health improvement – which demonstrated that it can be an effective approach (Gordon et al., 2006; Stead et al., 2007). This work helped inform the strategic development and activities of the NSMC. Systematic reviews of the influence of alcohol marketing on youth drinking (Anderson et al., 2009) have been used by policy makers to inform regulation and policy in relation to alcohol, as well as informing social marketing programmes on alcohol (Gordon, 2011). Similarly, a rapid review of lung cancer signs and symptoms campaigns commissioned by the Sax Institute and Cancer Institute NSW in Australia (see Gordon et al., 2012) was used to help inform a campaign using social marketing principles to alert Australians to lung cancer signs and symptoms (see www.youtube.com/watch?v=3TprzRL6gzs).

Experiments

Experimental research is a systematic and scientific procedure in which the researcher manipulates one or more variables, and controls and measures any change in other variables (Bryman, 2012). Experimental research is often conceived as a research design, but it also encompasses a research methodology. RCTs, discussed previously, are a form of experimental research. A *true experiment* is where the researcher manipulates one variable and controls and/or randomises other variables. This approach features a control group, in which participants have been randomly assigned between different groups, and the researcher only tests one effect at a time. True experiments are more common in the physical sciences such as physics, chemistry and geology. Quasi-experiments are when the researcher actively influences something to observe the consequences but does not necessarily include a control group, or randomise participants to different groups. This approach is more common in social sciences such as sociology, psychology and consumer research. The use of experimental research in these latter disciplines identifies the relevance of these methods to social marketing. For example, experiments can be a useful approach to testing participants' physical, emotional or psychological responses to social marketing stimulus – such as advertising, branding or messaging. Such research approaches may also utilise newer technologies such as galvanic skin response sensors (to measure participants' electrodermal responses to stimulus), or even magnetoencephalography (MEG) machines that can map brain activity in response to stimulus. For example, experimental research at Monash University in Melbourne has used eye-tracking devices to gauge participants' responses to gambling advertising (www.buseco.monash.edu.au/behavioural-lab/research/current/).

   Such experimental research in social marketing is fairly novel, but potentially offers useful approaches for pre-testing social marketing programme activities, or as a component of formative research to understand issues – for example, experimental research could test participant responses to cigarette packaging.

Analysing and disseminating quantitative data

Quantitative data analysis is varied and can range from simple descriptive analysis to sophisticated modelling. In quantitative research it is key to consider how you are planning to analyse the data prior to collecting it. This helps ensure that your survey questionnaire, observation schedule or coding frame is appropriate and will allow you to test the relationships you are interested in. It is important to recognise that you cannot just apply any technique to any variable; techniques have to be matched appropriately to the types of variables you have created in your research. There are various rules and procedures for guiding how quantitative data analysis should be conducted. While this section does not cover how to conduct quantitative data analysis in detail, we do consider some of the main ways of analysing data. Detailed information on how to conduct particular forms of quantitative analysis should be sourced from dedicated textbooks such as *Discovering Statistics Using IBM SPSS Statistics* by Andy Field (2013), or *Structural Equation Modeling with AMOS* by Barbara Byrne (2009).

Before analysis, quantitative data need to be coded and cleaned. Coding involves assigning each question, and the various possible responses, a numerical code. Data then need to be prepared and cleaned, which involves deciding how to deal with missing data, and dealing with or removing questionable data.

The different types of data collected then need to be identified. For example, a *dichotomous variable* is one that has two possible responses, usually yes and no. An *ordinal variable* is data containing a numerical score (normally a code e.g. 1, 2, 3, etc.) that exists on an ordinal scale – that is it is an arbitrary numerical scale in which the numerical value has no particular value of significance beyond giving it a ranking (Field, 2013). Metric data include *interval data* (which allows for a degree of difference between items but not the scale – for example, temperature in °C is interval data as 20°C is not twice as hot as 10°C) and *ratio data* (where the measurement is the estimation of a ratio between values and has an absolute zero – e.g. mass, length, duration, etc.). It is important to consider and identify which type of data you are dealing with prior to analysis, as this can affect the types of analysis that can be conducted. (See Table 10.2 for a guide on types of data and a selection of quantitative analyses that can be carried out accordingly.)

Descriptive statistics

Descriptive statistics is the discipline of quantitatively describing the main characteristics of a sample, for example: gender, age, employment or even how many people answered a question in a particular way. This is the simplest and usually the first type of quantitative analysis that is conducted. Running this type of analysis provides basic summaries about your sample and observations about them. In software programs such as SPSS, this is done by:

- running frequencies – a command used to obtain counts on a single variable's values
- cross-tabulations – a command used to obtain counts on more than one variable's values, for example males who are smokers and females who are non-smokers
- graphs and charts – visual records of descriptive data from the study sample.

Univariate analysis

Univariate analysis is the simplest form of statistical analysis, and describes a single variable. However, moving beyond basic descriptive statistics, this often involves creating

Table 10.2 Types of data and quantitative analysis techniques applicable to them

Purpose	Variables	variables	Statistic	While controlling for another variable
Determine level of relationship (correlations)	Dichotomous	Metric	Point-biserial	Partial Correlation
	Metric	Metric	Pearson's	
	Ordinal	Metric	Spearman's Rho	
	Ordinal	Ordinal	Spearman's Rho	
	Dichotomous	Ordinal	Spearman's Rho	
	Dichotomous	Dichotomous	Phi Coefficient	
	Independent Variable	**Dependent V**		
Predict or determine the amount of explained variance	1 Metric	1 Metric	Simple Regression	
	Multi Metric	1 Metric	Multiple Regression	
	1 or more Metric	Dichotomous	Discriminant Analysis	
	1 or more Metric	Categorical>2	Multiple Discm Analysis	
	1 or more Metric	Multi Metric	Canonical Correlation	
	Ordinal	Ord or Metric	Logit Loglinear	
Test to see if there is a significant difference	1 Nominal testing frequencies	1 Nom or Ord	Chi Square Goodness of fit	Note: Comparing Frequencies
	1 or > Nominal testing frequencies	1 Nom or Ord	Chi Sq Test of Association	
	Dichotomous (independent)	1 Ordinal	Mann Whitney	Note: Comparing Ranks
	Dichotomous (repeated)	1 Ordinal	Willcoxon	
	Non Dichotomous (independent)	1 Ordinal	Kruskal Wallis	
	Non Dichotomous (repeated)	1 Ordinal	Freidman's ANOVA	
	Dichotomous (independent)	1 Metric	Independent T-test	Note: Comparing Means
	Dichotomous (repeated)	1 Metric	Dependent T-test	
	1 with 2 or more levels	1 Metric	ANOVA	A confounding variable may be controlled with a covariate
	2 with 2 or more levels	1 Metric	Factoral ANOVA	
	1 with 2 or more levels	>1 Metric	MANOVA	
	2 with 2 or more levels	>1 /Ratio	Factoral MANOVA	

Source: Emmerson, 2013

frequency distributions and reporting measures of central tendency such as mean, median or mode. For example, we may run a frequency that tells us the mean age from the survey sample in the NPRI alcohol marketing study was 13.2, but also that 20 people in the sample were aged exactly 12 years old. Furthermore, statistical dispersion tests may also be run – looking at how values are distributed around the central tendency. Such tests include range, interquartile range, standard deviation, skewness and kurtosis (Field, 2013).

Bivariate analysis

As the name suggests, bivariate analysis involves the analysis of two variables to assess whether there is a significant relationship between them. The most common type of bivariate analysis is a correlation (or test for significance), which goes beyond merely describing data and identifies whether there is a significant relationship between two variables. Other tests include *ANOVA* – which assesses the difference between groups, e.g. males and females – or *simple linear regression* – which fits a line through measures in such a way that the sum squared of residuals of the model (the vertical distance between points of the data set and the fitted line) is as small as is possible (Field, 2013).

Multivariate analysis

Multivariate analysis involves observing and analysing more than one outcome/dependent variable. This can involve tests such as *MANOVA* – the difference between groups on more than one variable – *factor analysis* (discussed earlier) and *multivariate regression analysis*. Multivariate analysis is important in social marketing, as it allows us to consider the relationships between various sets of variables; and to check these relationships while controlling for other factors that may have an influence. For example, if we want to assess what effect alcohol marketing has on adolescents' drinking, we also need to understand how other factors such as peer drinking and perceived social norms of drinking may affect the relationships.

Factor analysis

Factor analysis is a method for describing validity among observed, correlated variables known as factors. This is important as it can help us identify and then use in analysis groups of questions that together can measure certain knowledge/attitudinal/social/behavioural constructs. For example if we take attitudes – these can be cognitive (relating to what you think) and affective (what you feel). Therefore, to measure attitudes we may use several questions to properly measure and record cognitive and affective attitudes. Factor analysis then allows us to combine a number of single questions/items into factors or latent variables so these constructs can then be used in subsequent analysis – e.g. what effect does cognitive and affective attitudes have on a behavioural outcome.

Mediation and moderation

Mediation analysis involves testing the indirect relationships between two or more variables through another variable known as a mediator. For example, we may suppose that there is a relationship between smoking and drinking, but this may be mediated by social norms. To test if this was the case, we would run a mediation model using the *bootstrap method* or a similar analytical test. Moderation is where the relationship between two variables depends on a third variable and can be tested using a moderation model test (Field, 2013).

Statistical modelling

Statistical modelling goes beyond uni-, bi-and multi-variate analysis, by modelling the relationships between several sets of variables. This type of analysis is particularly useful when analysing or predicting human behaviour, which is complex and influenced by numerous factors. For example, in the energy efficiency project mentioned earlier, sophisticated statistical modelling not only will assess whether the social marketing programme influences participants' energy efficiency knowledge, attitudes and behaviours; but also will identify how other factors influence these over time, and whether there are different groups within the sample with respect to outcomes.

Path analysis

Path analysis is a form of statistical modelling that is focused on causal associations between single indicators, i.e. does one single item significantly affect another within a structural model? Indeed, path analysis can be conceived of not only as a type of multiple regression, but also as a special case of structural equation modelling focused on only single indicators rather than groups of indicators that form constructs. Models may consist of several paths between different indicators, and offer a more robust way of understanding the relationships between indicators.

Structural equation modelling

Structural equation modelling (SEM) can be simply described as a combination of doing factor analysis (involving constructs formed from several indicators), and then regression analysis (identifying significant causal relationships between those constructs). SEM allows both confirmatory and exploratory modelling, meaning it is suited to theory testing and theory development (Byrne, 2009). One of the key strengths of SEM is the ability to create and test the effect of what are known as *latent variables* – i.e. things that are not measured directly, but are estimated in the model from several measured variables. For example, *personality* is an example of a latent variable in that it is normally assessed using several measures rather than one measure. Another key strength of SEM is it allows the researcher to calculate and constrain errors and unreliability in the model, meaning a more accurate picture of the relationships between variables and latent variables can usually be formed (Byrne, 2009). Therefore, SEM permits a more complete and informed understanding of the relationships between phenomena. The relevance of this is clear for social marketing as it means that we can form a more complete understanding of how people form their knowledge, attitudes, perceptions and behaviours; and how they may change or be influenced by social marketing programmes.

Multi-level models are a form of SEM in which data for participants are organised at more than one level (i.e. nested data) – for example, pupil, class, school and district. The lowest level of data is usually an individual, although repeated measures of individuals may also be examined – i.e. survey data collected on more than one occasion. This is particularly relevant to strategic social marketing research in which we want to understand what is happening not only with individuals, but also with higher units of analysis such as the community, workplaces and so on. Other forms of sophisticated SEM include *latent class analysis*, which identifies classes of participants within data sets according to select parameters – for example, people who are binge drinkers, regular drinkers and non-drinkers. *Growth mixture modelling* is a form of latent class analysis that can also identify people who do not fall into particular classes (known as unobserved populations), but also can assess longitudinal data (repeated measures). Again, the relevance and utility of such techniques for social marketing are clear – the ability to identify classes of participants when measuring knowledge, attitudes, perceptions and behaviours can assist with understanding, and with the segmenting, targeting and positioning of social marketing programmes, as well as offering robust approaches for programme evaluation.

Using research in social marketing

Problem definition and scoping

Problem definition and scoping in social marketing involve examining the issue or challenge; building an understanding of existing knowledge regarding an issue and participants' attitudes and behaviours; and identifying and mobilising the resources available to deliver a programme (French et al., 2010). Scoping also facilitates an assessment and the selection of options that are to be utilised in the programme – for example, what are the key goals and objectives, what primary research will be done, and what are the potential components of the programme?

Therefore, research methods such as secondary data analysis, literature reviews and systematic reviews offer good ways for identifying, summarising and interpreting existing knowledge regarding an issue. In the event that information is required on particular groups of participants (for example, demographics or existing knowledge, attitudes and behaviours) performing a baseline survey study can offer useful insight for the development of social marketing programmes.

Formative research and pre-testing

Formative research in social marketing involves using research to gain insight and understanding on what moves and motivates participants, and to understand their needs and wants. This process permits the collection of useful information from the right people – the participants; making decisions with a participant focused mindset; and refining the social marketing programme to ensure it is more engaging, representative and ultimately successful. Pre-testing involves testing components of a social marketing programme with participants prior to it being fully implemented – this can involve testing new services, products, programmes, communication messages, materials and brands.

Due to the focus on generating deep insights and representations and interpreting meanings from participants during the formative research phase of social marketing programmes, qualitative research methods such as depth interviews and focus groups are normally employed. Participant observation and ethnographic research go further and can offer insight on what people actually do. Qualitative techniques are also used when developing and pre-testing social marketing programme elements, for example advertising or messaging.

Pre-testing of social marketing programme components can be facilitated through focus group testing in which participants are shown and asked to comment on materials. Experimental research can also be used to test non-verbal or physiological responses to a social marketing stimulus such as an advert or a brand.

Implementation research

Implementation research in social marketing provides feedback systems that enable problems with delivery to be identified and dealt with, and offer indicators of the progress of the programme. Implementation research in social marketing can involve monitoring the delivery of programme components through basic quantitative statistical analysis of media coverage, the placement of advertisements, responses to calls to action among participant groups (for example, calls or visits to a service), and the evaluation of programme activities using qualitative techniques such as interviews and focus groups.

Evaluation research

Evaluation research in social marketing involves using research methods to generate evidence of the effectiveness or otherwise of a social marketing programme. However, good evaluative research should also involve what is termed *process evaluation*, which provides insight on the process of delivering a social marketing programme and how front-line staff and participants experienced and perceived it. For more information and guidance on evaluation in social marketing please see the online resources included with the textbook located at: study.sagepub.com/frenchandgordon.

Survey research normally has a prominent role in the evaluation of social marketing programmes as data collected from participants on their knowledge, attitudes, values, perceptions, behaviours, and practices can be mapped against baseline survey data to identify any changes that may be attributed to the programme. However, we cannot say this definitively from this type of research as other factors removed from the social marketing programme may have caused these changes. Ideally, such survey research will also involve a control group of people who are surveyed on their knowledge, attitudes and behaviours but are not exposed to the social marketing programme. This type of control study research design permits an evaluation of whether the social marketing programme actually had an effect on changing knowledge, attitudes and behaviours rather than may have had an effect.

Process evaluation can involve different activities such as the survey research of front-line staff to get their views on the delivery of a social marketing programme. Qualitative research techniques such as depth interviews, focus groups, and discussion workshops with front-line staff and participants are often useful for process evaluation, as they can add depth and meaning to some of the problems and issues encountered during delivery, and for assessing why an intervention may not have had the desired effect on knowledge, attitudes and behaviours. This sort of process evaluation research can generate useful insight and learning to inform future activities – indeed the sharing of such learning among organisations involved in designing, delivering and evaluating social programmes should be strongly encouraged.

Conclusion

Research is an integral part of social marketing, and acts as the eyes and ears of a social change programme. As discussed in this chapter, research is used at every stage of the social marketing process. This chapter has discussed and reviewed the main qualitative and quantitative research methodologies available to social marketers, and examples of their application to social issues have been presented. As highlighted in this chapter, there is an expansive toolbox of research methods available to us, each with their own strengths and weaknesses. Furthermore, challenges with available time, resources, and skills and experiences available to organisations involved in social marketing programmes mean that it can seem challenging to decide how to use research in social marketing. In reality, there is no perfect plan for using research, but what is important is that the most appropriate methods are used for the context to offer insight and understanding. This chapter concludes by offering some guidance on how research may be used at different points during the process of social marketing programme delivery. Research plays a central and often critical role in social marketing. Good research helps our understanding of problems, existing knowledge, marketing tools and techniques, and participant and stakeholder groups and their knowledge, attitudes, behaviours, and practices. It also helps us evaluate whether social marketing programmes are effective and well received. However, we need to remember that research should be used to guide us, and not replace informed decision making – good social marketing requires action as much as robust research.

Reflective questions

- How would you use research to identify knowledge, attitudes and behaviours among low income older residents on the topic of using energy efficiency? Jot down some notes on how you would do this.
- Imagine that you have a limited budget for research, and you want to evaluate the impact of a social marketing programme. How would you use research to do this?
- In multi-cultural societies how would you conduct research that overcomes issues concerning cultural differences and gaining access and insight to participants, to form a representative understanding of citizens' views on smoke-free legislation?

Further reading

Bourdieu, P. (1984) *Distinction*. London: Routledge.
Bryman, A. (2012) *Social Research Methods*. Oxford: Oxford University Press.
Byrne, B. (2009) *Structural Equation Modeling with AMOS: Basic Concepts, Applications, and Programming*. New York: Routledge.
Field, A. (2013) *Discovering Statistics Using IBM SPSS Statistics*. London: SAGE
Krippendorff, K.H. (2012) *Content Analysis: An Introduction to Its Methodology*. Thousand Oaks, CA: SAGE.
Stead, M., Gordon, R., Angus, K. and McDermott, L. (2007) 'A systematic review of social marketing effectiveness', *Health Education*, 107 (2): 126–140.
Tinson, J. (2009) *Conducting Research with Children and Adolescents: Design, Methods and Empirical Cases*. Oxford: Goodfellow.

References

Anderson, P., De Bruijn, A., Angus, K., Gordon, R. and Hastings, G. (2009) 'Impact of alcohol advertising and media exposure on adolescent alcohol use: a systematic review of longitudinal studies', *Alcohol and Alcoholism*, 44 (3): 229–243.
Barbour, R. and Kitzinger, J. (1999) *Developing Focus Group Research: Politics, Theory and Practice*. London: SAGE.
Berelson, B. (1952) *Content Analysis in Communication Research*. New York: The Free Press.
Bourdieu, P. (1978) 'Sport and social class', *Social Science Information*, 17 (6): 819–840.
Bourdieu, P. (1984) *Distinction*. London: Routledge.
Bourdieu, P. (1987) 'What makes a social class?', *Berkeley Journal of Sociology*, 22 (1): 1–18.
Bourdieu, P. (1990) *The Logic of Practice*. Cambridge: Polity Press.
Bourdieu, P. (1993) *Sociology in Question*. London: SAGE.
Bowen, G.A. (2009) 'Document analysis as a qualitative research method', *Qualitative Research Journal*, 9 (2): 27–40.
Brannan, J. (ed.) (1992) *Mixing Methods: Qualitative and Quantitative Research*. Aldershot: Avebury.
Brewer, J.D. (2000) *Ethnography*. Buckingham: Open University Press.

Bryman, A. (2012) *Social Research Methods*. Oxford: Oxford University Press.

Byrne, B. (2009) *Structural Equation Modeling with AMOS: Basic Concepts, Applications, and Programming*. New York: Routledge.

Chisnall, P.M. (1992) *Marketing Research*. New York: McGraw-Hill.

Churchill, G.A. (1979) 'A paradigm for developing better measures of marketing constructs', *Journal of Marketing Research*, 16 (1): 64–73.

Cunningham-Burley, S. and Kerr, A. (1999) 'Defining the "social": towards an understanding of scientific and medical discourses on the social aspects of the new human genetics', *Social Science of Health and Illness*, 21 (5): 647–668.

Denzin, N.K. and Lincoln, Y.S. (2011) *The SAGE Handbook of Qualitative Research*. Thousand Oaks, CA: SAGE.

Eadie, D., Heim, D., MacAskill, S., Ross, A., Hastings, G. and Davies, J. (2008) 'A qualitative analysis of compliance with smoke-free legislation in community bars in Scotland: implications for public health', *Addiction*, 103 (6): 1019–1026.

Emmerson, G. (2013) *Applied Statistical Procedures: Slides and Labs*. Brisbane: ACSPRI.

Field, A. (2013) *Discovering Statistics Using IBM SPSS Statistics*. London: SAGE.

Filmer, P., Phillipson, M., Silverman, D. and Walsh, D. (1972) *New Directions in Sociological Theory*. London: Macmillan.

French, J., Blair-Stevens, C., McVey, D. and Merritt, R. (eds) (2010) *Social Marketing and Public Health: Theory and Practice*. Oxford: Oxford University Press.

Geertz, C. (1973) *The Interpretation of Cultures: Selected Essays*. New York: Basic Books.

Gordon, R. (2011) 'Critical social marketing: assessing the cumulative impact of alcohol marketing on youth drinking', PhD thesis, Stirling: University of Stirling.

Gordon, R., Barrie, L. and Jones, S. (2011) *Alcohol Sponsorship of the National Rugby League: What Is Its Impact on Young Males?* Prepared for NSW Health. Wollongong: Centre for Health Initiatives, University of Wollongong.

Gordon, R. and Hastings, G. (2007) 'Critical marketing from theory into practice: the role of social marketing'. Paper presented at the European Academy of Marketing Conference, Reykjavik, May.

Gordon, R., Hastings, G., Moodie, C. and Eadie, D. (2010) 'Critical social marketing – the impact of alcohol marketing on youth drinking: qualitative findings', *International Journal of Nonprofit and Voluntary Sector Marketing*, 15 (3): 265–275.

Gordon, R., McDermott, L., Stead, M. and Angus, K. (2006) 'The effectiveness of social marketing interventions for health improvement: what's the evidence?', *Public Health*, 120 (12): 1133–1139.

Gordon, R., Magee C., Jones, S.C., Phillipson, L. and Barrie, L. (2012) *Effectiveness of 'Signs and Symptoms' Campaigns for Lung Cancer: A Rapid Review*. Report prepared for the Sax Institute. Wollongong: Centre for health Initiatives, University of Wollongong.

Holsti, O.R. (1969) *Content Analysis for the Social Sciences and Humanities*. Reading, MA: Addison-Wesley.

Hornig Priest, S. (1996) *Doing Media Research: An Introduction*. London: SAGE.

Howell, J.T. (1972) *Hard Living on Clay Streets: Portraits of Blue Collar Families*. Garden City, NY: Anchor Press.

Kinnear, T.C. and Taylor, J.R. (1996) *Marketing Research: An Applied Approach*. New York: McGraw-Hill.

Kozinets, R.V. (2010) *Netnography: Doing Ethnographic Research Online*. London: SAGE.

Krippendorff, K.H. (2012) *Content Analysis: An Introduction to Its Methodology*. Thousand Oaks, CA: SAGE.

Krueger, R.A. (1995) 'The future of focus groups', *Qualitative Health Research*, 5 (4): 524–530.

Krueger, R.A (1998) 'Moderating focus groups – volume 4', in D. Morgan and R.A. Krueger (eds), *The Focus Group Kit*. Newbury Park, CA: SAGE, pp. 1–136.

McCracken, G. (1988) *The Long Interview*. Newbury Park, CA: SAGE.

McDougall, P. (1999) 'Focus groups: an overview of their use as a research method', *Community Practitioner*, 72 (3): 48–49.

May, T. (2001) *Social Research: Issues, Methods and Process*. Maidenhead: Open University Press.

Miles, M.B. and Huberman, A.M. (1994) *Qualitative Data Analysis: An Expanded Sourcebook*. Thousand Oaks, CA: SAGE.

Moodie, C. and Hastings, G.B. (2011) 'Making the pack the hero, tobacco industry response to marketing restrictions in the UK: findings from a long-term audit', *International Journal of Mental Health and Addiction*, 9 (1): 24–38.

Morgan, D.L. (1995) 'Why things (sometimes) go wrong in focus groups', *Qualitative Health Research*, 5 (4): 516–523.

National Youth Council of Ireland (2009) *Get 'Em Young: Mapping Young People's Exposure to Alcohol Marketing in Ireland*. Dublin: National Youth Council of Ireland.

Neuman, W.L. (2003) *Social Research Methods: Qualitative and Quantitative Approaches*. Boston, MA: Allyn and Bacon.

NOO (National Obesity Observatory) (2010) *Adult Obesity and Socioeconomic Status*. London: National Obesity Observatory.

Parasuraman, A. (1991) *Marketing Research*. Reading, MA: Addison-Wesley.

Phillips, N. and Brown, J.B. (1993) 'Analyzing communication in and around organizations: a critical hermeneutic approach', *Academy of Management Journal*, 36 (6): 1547–1576.

Rose, G. (2001) *Visual Methodologies: An Introduction to the Interpretation of Visual Materials*. London: SAGE.

Sarantakos, S. (1998) *Social Research*. London: MacMillan.

Scott, J. (1990) *A Matter of Record: Documentary Sources in Social Research*. Cambridge: Polity Press.

Spotswood, F. and Tapp, A. (2013) 'Beyond persuasion: a cultural perspective of behaviour', *Journal of Social Marketing*, 3 (3): 275–294.

Stead, M., Gordon, R., Angus, K. and McDermott, L. (2007) 'A systematic review of social marketing effectiveness', *Health Education*, 107 (2): 126–140.

Stead, M., Gordon, R., Holme, I., Moodie, C., Hastings, G. and Angus, K. (2009) *Changing Attitudes, Knowledge and Behaviour: A Review of Successful Initiatives*. York: Joseph Rowntree Foundation.

Strauss, A. and Corbin, J. (1998) *Basics of Qualitative Research: Techniques and Procedures for Developing Grounded Theory* (2nd edn). Thousand Oaks, CA: SAGE.

Tapp, A. and Spotswood, F. (2013) 'From the 4Ps to COM-SM: reconfiguring the social marketing mix', *Journal of Social Marketing*, 3 (3): 206–222.

Tinson, J. (2009) *Conducting Research with Children and Adolescents: Design, Methods and Empirical Cases*. Oxford: Goodfellow.

Tranfield, D., Denyer, D. and Smart, P. (2003) 'Towards a methodology for developing evidence-informed management knowledge by means of systematic review', *British Journal of Management*, 14 (3): 207–222.

Zikmund, W.G., Ward, S., Lowe, B., Winzar, H. and Babin, B.B. (2011) *Marketing Research: Second Asia-Pacific Edition*. Melbourne: Cengage.

11 SOCIAL MARKETING AND SOCIAL PROGRAMME DESIGN

Learning objectives

By the end of this chapter, readers should be able to:

- understand the scope and nature of strategic social marketing strategy development
- understand the components, tools and sequencing of strategy development in social marketing
- describe how social marketing adds value to the social policy and strategy development and selection process
- analyse and contribute to the development of policy and strategy development that aims to influence positive social behaviour.

Introduction

In this chapter we will explore how to develop social policy that is informed by social marketing principles, concepts and techniques. As discussed in the first three chapters of the book, social marketing has a clear role to play in the development of more citizen focused and citizen responsive social programme selection, design and delivery and that applying marketing principles can add value to social policy development, strategy development and tactical delivery. As we explored in Chapters 3, 5 and 8, influencing behaviour is significant in many areas of social policy. One of the key lessons from Chapter 12 is that it is important to distinguish between strategic programme goals and specific social behavioural goals. For example, governments might be interested in increasing employment but to achieve this strategic goal it will be necessary to define specific behaviours that need to be encouraged, for example more people actively applying for jobs or registering on training programmes. We know that most social challenges are compounded by sets of multiple interrelated causal factors that impact on behaviours. We also know that increased knowledge alone about social issues does not automatically lead to increased positive social behaviour.

In addition to this understanding we know that governments and other organisations that are seeking to influence social behaviour need to be mindful of the fact that a more holistic view of how all policies might impact on behaviours is necessary. It also needs to be recognised that some policy might result in unintended negative behavioural responses. For example, a policy intended to encourage a reduction in smoking by increasing taxation may lead to the increase in smuggled cigarettes across boarders that are not only cheaper but also contain more carcinogenic material.

In this chapter we will explore what is known about how to develop effective and efficient social policy and strategies designed to influence the behaviour of citizens.

Marketing's contribution to social policy development and selection

As discussed in Chapters 1 and 2 the authors make the case for repositioning social marketing away from a situation in which it is currently seen as a discreet activity that sits alongside other approaches to policy development and implementation. Rather, adopting a 'strategic social marketing' stance is concerned with making a marketing informed contribution to all social policy and strategy development regardless of any direct marketing activity that may be associated with the operational delivery of social programmes. As set out in Chapter 5, strategic social marketing can be defined as:

> The systemic, critical and reflexive application of social marketing principals to enhance social policy selection, objective setting, planning and operational delivery.

Adopting a strategic social marketing approach implies that marketing concepts and principles are being used to inform policy selection and strategic development as well as goal setting, selecting interventions, assisting with the process of determining how success will be measured and ensuring that the most effective and efficient mix of interventions is deployed, managed and coordinated.

Strategic social marketing also has a critical role to play in ensuring that understanding and insights about the beliefs, values and needs of target groups for any social intervention such as citizens, community leaders, politicians and professionals are captured, analysed and fed into the policy selection and development process. The added value of applying a social marketing approach to social policy selection and strategy development is directly related to its focus on creating social value for communities and individuals. This added value is based on an approach that emphasises respect for citizens' views as well as their expressed and felt needs and a willingness to engage in a process of co-creation and solution generation and delivery with citizens. Applying a strategic social marketing approach is also distinguished by its focus on mutuality, exchange and reciprocity as positive social goods in their own right and as key enablers of social development and the delivery of more effective, efficient and publicly supported social programmes. Social marketing also brings to the policy selection and strategy development arena concepts and techniques that can promote a better understanding and engagement with these processes.

Rothschild's (1999) article entitled 'Sticks and promises' made the case for governments to go beyond just using the law and information as the default options to bring about desired changes in behaviour for social good. Rothschild advocated the use of marketing thinking to assist the development of more value focused propositions to citizens, in order to persuade them to adopt positive social behaviours. However, as we have explored in this book, one of the biggest hurdles to the application of marketing principles in social policy selection and programme implementation is the misinterpretation and major under-utilisation of key marketing principles.

Social marketing is often viewed as a second or third order task in many public-sector policy and strategy development situations. Even when social marketing is applied, it is most often seen as a set of techniques that can be used to improve the delivery of communication aspects of social programmes, but not as an essential component of policy and strategy analysis and development. There is a challenge that is explored in Chapter 13 to promote and embed marketing principles within the public and not-for-profit sector if they are to be applied in the way set out in this chapter.

In this chapter we will focus on the development of social policy and strategy and how marketing concepts and techniques can add value to this process. However, it needs to be recognised that social policy is not developed in a vacuum.

Figure 11.1 illustrates the three contexts that all have a substantial impact on the policy development and selection process. Organisational capacity and capability, constraints and accepted practices can obviously impact on policy selection as can the degree of political support or opposition to a possible new policy initiative. Ultimately

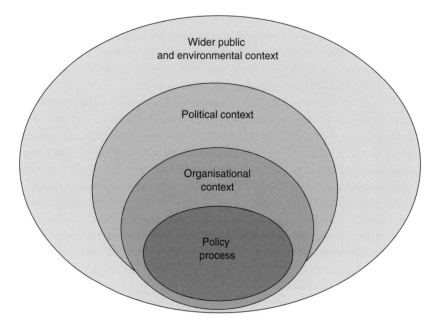

Figure 11.1 The policy development context

in democratic societies public opinion, support, opposition and apathy can also all have an impact on what social policy is selected and how it is selected.

An important driver that is encouraging the use of marketing to enhance the policy making and the strategy development process is the increasing dominance of a more citizen centric approach to social policy development (Berglund and Matti, 2006; Clarke et al., 2007). This development is based on greater insight and understanding about what citizens feel, say, do and value, and the increasing conviction by more and more governments and agencies that they need to understand citizens' views about acceptability and about what they think will and will not work. If social policy and programmes are not supported and valued by citizens they will ultimately, and sometimes very rapidly, fail to deliver the desired social improvement and may even cause an unintended social backlash. For example, the riots witnessed in Turkey during June 2013 in response to the demolition of a civic park to be replaced by retail outlets.

The policy development process

We know that in any area of policy where there is a strong knowledge base, and broad consensus about what to do, a high degree of central policy specification can work, so long as it focuses on a few key priorities. Where there is less knowledge about what works a better strategic approach is to set out broad policy objectives, and leave more freedom for managers and staff to develop and test new approaches (Mulgan et al., 2004). We also know that involving practitioners in policy making and ensuring that their knowledge is used early in the policy process improve effectiveness (Dawnay and Shah, 2005). Both of these findings illustrate the potential of social marketing to the policy and strategy development process.

Marketing can help with the development of policy goals that are agreed and valued by all relevant stakeholders. Marketing can be used to ensure that stakeholders and service delivery workers and target groups are engaged in the development of programmes of action and in so doing add value to the policy making process by ensuring the early pre-testing of potential policy initiatives (Brennan and Douglas, 1999; Curtain, 2003).

We also know that effective policy making results when horizontal networks are developed to assist in the capture and sharing of learning (Public Health Agency of Canada, 2007). Social marketing can assist with this process through the development of marketing and engagement strategies that ensure early and consistent engagement with the policy development and refinement process (Lefebvre, 2012).

In essence effective policy making should involve:

1. Designing policies around outcomes. Marketing adds value by ensuring that outcomes are set out in the form of measurable objectives.
2. Policy should be informed by end user wants and needs. Marketing adds value by ensuring that what citizens value informs policy selection.
3. Policies should be, and be seen to be, inclusive and fair. Marketing adds value by testing perceived fairness with stakeholders and citizens.
4. Policy should be evidence-based. Marketing adds value by being a field of study that draws together a wide range of theory and evidence to inform policy development.
5. Policy should avoid unnecessary burdens on delivery agencies or other sectors. Marketing adds value through citizen focused services planning and the development of lean systems.
6. All relevant stakeholders should be involved in policy making. Marketing adds value through stakeholder analysis and stakeholder management planning.
7. Policy making should be forward- and outward-looking. Marketing adds value by applying analytic tools to assess current and future strengths, weaknesses, opportunities and threats.
8. Policy should have systems in place to learn from experience. Marketing adds value through systematic planning and evaluation related to specific behavioural objectives. (Adapted from Bullock et al., 2001 and Baldock et al., 2007.)

Social marketing concepts and principles may be used strategically to ensure that a strong customer focus directly informs the identification and selection of appropriate interventions. All of these eight features of policy making can be enhanced by the application of marketing concepts. To this list of policy best practice two other features that can also be supported by social marketing can be added: the communication and the coordination of policy (Economic Policy Unit, 2013).

The core policy making process is essentially about understanding social problems, understanding the context and causal factors, understanding the people and stakeholders who are affected by the issue and who might be part of the solution, and understanding what is known about the social problem and how to tackle it. Next follows the selection of strategies and agreeing challenging but achievable aims and how they can measured. Finally selected interventions are put in place, monitored and evaluated and adjusted as necessary to ensure that they deliver in an ethical, effective and efficient way the selected policy goals and strategic aims.

The establishment of consistent and sustained policy in the social arena is important as many big, complex social challenges will require sustained intergenerational action to solve them. There are many challenges associated with developing and sustaining a consistent and coherent policy supported by congruent strategies, programmes and projects. A consistent policy stance requires the development of a long-term vision and the tenacity to stick with it often over time-frames that span more than one elected administration. This implies the necessity for building as much cross-party consensus as possible about what represents the most effective, efficient and ethical policy approach in any given situation.

Given the nature of politics in democratic countries it is inevitable that governments will change and the policy focus will shift. However, it is possible for politicians and policy makers to build cross-party consensus on key issues: for example, in areas such as food security, defence, energy supply, transportation and health protection. Typically interventions that require a consistent consensus still allow for the development of different approaches to be developed and enacted at the level of implementation. For example, the World Health Organization has done much to build a consensus about the key importance of investment in health promotion and primary healthcare while still leaving individual countries to develop their own interpretations of this broad policy objective (WHO, 1986). Social marketing can assist this process of sustaining a broad policy consensus. It can do this by ensuring that insight data are used alongside situational, competition and exchange analysis from the perspective of target audiences, the general public, professionals and experts to inform the co-production and cross-party buy-in to a sustained policy response to tackling complex social challenges.

Policy that does not have the broad support of the public and strategy that does not meet the needs of the target audiences at which it is directed is unlikely to be successful. There is a need to engender a sense of public ownership or at least acceptance for any policy intended to improve social conditions among recipients or affected communities and by those who are developing, delivering and monitoring the progress of the policy.

Policy that can't or won't be implemented is counterproductive as it serves only to distract resources and attention from interventions that will help solve social challenges.

The selection of public policy in democracies is ultimately the responsibility of elected officials supported by professional who are able to give advice on the state of evidence and situational issues that will inform the policy and subsequent strategy and operational delivery (Lindblom and Woodhouse, 1993). Public policy should set out clear goals to be achieved, supported by an equally clear needs assessment and evidence base for the approach to delivering the policy. The wider political and ideological rationale for the policy and its accompanying strategy should also be set out. Social marketing can help with the positioning, dissemination and engagement strategies that will be required to achieve public and professional support for policy and processes that are developed.

Social marketing interventions can be developed to ensure that all relevant stakeholders, partners and target groups understand the policy, and how to support and engage with it. Social marketing can be used to ensure that stakeholders' partners and target groups also understand the imperatives that necessitate the policy and the rationale for the strategic and operational response selected to deliver it. Social marketing can also help politicians and public officials to test policy ideas and refine them through a process of target audience engagement and review. The use of focus groups, surveys, citizens' juries, deliberative events, interviews, observational studies and other methods of gathering citizens' views can be a powerful tool for ensuring that policy and strategy are developed in such a way that they will be supported and taken up by those whom they are designed to help. The application of this kind of citizen focused approach to the development and testing of policy and strategy is being increasingly used by governments and political parties to help them develop manifestoes that carry popular support (Newman et al., 2004; Nicholson, 2005).

CASE STUDY

The California Project LEAN

School Board Member social marketing programme, California (USA)

The prevalence of overweight youth in the United States has increased remarkably over recent decades. Overweight and obese children are at elevated risk of chronic diseases and other adverse health conditions. The foods and beverages that young people have access to at school canteens, from vending machines and from school shops, if they are high in sugar, fat and carbohydrates, can contribute to overweight and obesity prevalence. Enacting policy to

(Continued)

(Continued)

ban or restrict such unhealthy foods and beverages in schools can play a role in managing the epidemic of obesity. School board members who control policy about what can be sold or made available in schools are, therefore, a priority audience for introducing healthier food and beverage alternatives through the articulation of specific policy initiatives.

This policy focused programme used a social marketing approach to move local school board members to establish and enforce school nutrition policies. Working with the California School Board Association, California Project LEAN embarked on a programme to motivate policy makers to address and enact local school district policies that support healthy eating. This programme undertook research among school board members and parents about attitudes to and understanding of food provision and obesity. As a result of this research it developed material that provided school board members with guides on policy options about nutrition, and the role that schools can play, as well as training and professional workshops, and factsheets about the issue for board members and parents of students.

In less than two years after implementing the programme, a significant increase in nutrition-related issues on school board meeting agendas occurred. As a result more positive nutrition-related policies were put in place, and school board members reported a greater readiness to support school nutrition-related issues. Specifically there were significant changes in school board members' support for: banning fast food sales in elementary schools (2001 – 53 per cent, 2004 – 64 per cent), banning fast food and soda advertising in schools (2001 – 52 per cent, 2004 – 57 per cent), banning fast food sales (2001 – 21.8 per cent, 2004 – 37 per cent), and banning à la carte food sales (2001 –10.3 per cent, 2004 – 22 per cent).

Approximately 10 per cent of school districts had at least one high school that had developed or was developing a healthier nutrition policy. The programme helped create nutrition policies to increase the availability of healthy foods to 1 million of California's 6.3 million students. Policies were also introduced to set standards for fundraising activities, classroom celebrations and the banning of soft drinks.

This policy intervention based on social marketing principles shows that a social marketing strategy that is informed by formative research and the careful development of strategies that are pre-tested before being brought to scale, and are supported by monitoring, can be effective in modifying school board members' preparedness to initiate and support policy change.

Source: McDermott et al. (2005)

Generating and selecting social policy

Usually social policy is developed in the shadow of past experience and policy focused on the same issue that a newly elected political party judges to be insufficient or inappropriate. Social policy can be generated from a variety of sources. Typically political parties set out the policies they will seek to deliver in their party manifestos. However, these commitments are often triggered by pressure for change from community groups and professionals, and from research evidence, public opinion and lobbying from the private, voluntary and community sectors. Policy can also be generated by new data, significant changes in the environment or in the field of technology or from the planned review of existing policies. New policy may also be generated by the reported experience of other similar countries, for example if a similar country develops a policy such as the introduction of minimum pricing for alcohol that is seen to have a significant positive impact on alcohol related harm, politicians may consider the implementation of such a policy domestically.

New policy can also be triggered by the need to respond to new policies instigated by other organisations or governments. For example, if neighbouring countries change their immigration policy this may well lead to a need to change domestic policy to reflect this. Changes in economic circumstances, either positive or negative, can also trigger the need for a new policy response. Often, the pressure for new policy or policy change will come from several of these sources at once.

Social marketing can assist in the development of potential new policy through a process of gathering research data about public, specific target group, professional and expert opinion about the need for new policy responses. Public opinion surveys and other forms of data collection can also be used to assess the acceptability of existing or potential new policy and to indicate how policy can be adjusted to ensure more support for it (French, 2011).

Determining social policy aims, strategic goals, tactical and operational objectives

Figure 11.2 sets out a scheme of how policy aims, strategic goals, operational and tactical objectives relate to each other. The terms 'aim', 'goal' and 'objective' are often used interchangeably and with little precision. As illustrated in Figure 11.2, for the purposes of this book and chapter these terms are used more specifically. Bringing clarity to this aspect of social policy development is a key added value of social marketing, as often confusion about what is to be achieved and how different layers of organisational delivery will be assessed is not made explicit in social policy, strategy, tactics and operational delivery.

Social policy aims are general position statements that set out what social challenge is to be tackled and how the intended policy will help solve the issue and generate increased social value – for example, 'We will bring an end to world hunger'.

Strategic goals are more specific commitments about what social challenge will be tackled and the focus of the social actions that will be put in place – for example, 'We will ensure that every child has access to sufficient food and clean water'.

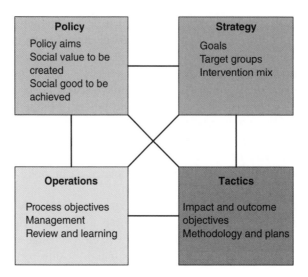

Figure 11.2   Policy, strategy, tactical and operational aims, goals and objectives

Tactical objectives are sets of specific SMART objectives; these will be focused on specific behaviours. Objectives will indicate specifically what behaviours will be targeted and how progress will be measured in achieving them – for example, '80 per cent of farmers in X Land will by the spring of 2016 be using the provided new maize strain as a part of their crop rotation scheme'.

Operation objectives set out how the efficiency and quality of programmes will be measured – for example, 'The programme will have delivered 200 village-based empowerment sessions for a per person cost that does not exceed $4 that achieve over 80 per cent satisfaction rating by participants'.

The mission statement of the social programme should encapsulate the policy aims of the programme, the values that underpin it, and the scope of the programme. For example, the first element of the 'Purposes statement' of the United Nations (1945) is a good example of such a mission statement:

The Purposes of the United Nations are:

- to save succeeding generations from the scourge of war, which twice in our life-time has brought untold sorrow to mankind, and
- to reaffirm faith in fundamental human rights, in the dignity and worth of the human person, in the equal rights of men and women and of nations large and small, and
- to establish conditions under which justice and respect for the obligations arising from treaties and other sources of international law can be maintained, and
- to promote social progress and better standards of life in larger freedom.

United Nations (1945)

This statement is underpinned by 110 articles that set out in detail the rights, responsibilities and guiding principles that underpin all the actions of the UN.

Strategic goals are intended to set out in more detail the focus of the strategy. Strategic goals can normally be divided into three types: goals that set out what is to be achieved and how this will be measured; goals that describe what service, product or experience that will be offered; goals focused on creating value for money, efficiency and return on investment. A good example of social programme goals is the existing UN Millennium Development Goals (MDGs). The eight MDGs are goals that were agreed after the Millennium Summit of the United Nations held in 2000. All United Nations member states and over 23 international organisations committed to take action to reach the MDGs (see www.un.org/millenniumgoals/).

When developing social policy aims and strategic goals it should be borne in mind that these should be:

1. *As focused as possible in terms of what is to be achieved.* For example, MDG one: Eradicate extreme poverty and hunger.
2. *Means of verification of both progress and success should be possible.* For example, MDG two: Achieve universal primary education.
3. *They should be clear and unambiguous and have a single focus.* For example, MDG three: Promote gender equality and empower women.
4. *They should be challenging but feasible.* For example, MDG four: Reduce child mortality.

When developing a mission statement and a set of strategic goals for a social programme, social marketing can help by engaging target groups' partners, stakeholders and the general public in reviewing the acceptability and feasibility of proposals. Social marketing can also assist though a process of validating the value and benefits that are associated with the strategy in relation to the perceived costs of the strategy by all relevant stakeholder partners and target groups. The relevance of the suggested mission statement and goals that underpin it can also be assessed and amended through this kind of consultative and collaborative activity that is an example of relationship marketing and management. McKenzie-Mohr and Smith (2011) advocate this kind of co-creation process in what they call 'community-based social marketing'. The value of such a collaborative process is also advocated by others as a way of creating social value in its own right (OECD, 2001).

A good way to test the potential robustness of social mission statements and sets of social programme goals is to use the checklist of characteristics of effective strategic decision making set out in Table 11.1, adapted from work by Jones and Scholes (2010).

Table 11.1 Checklist of characteristics of effective strategic decision making

Strategic decisions are likely to be concerned with the scope of an organisation's activities and the weight of action focused on particular aspects of its interventions. For example, when seeking to develop a strategy to reduce teenage pregnancy, decisions about how much effort is put into education as opposed to incentives, such as conditional cash payments to encourage at risk girls to stay on at school and not become pregnant.

Strategy is to do with matching the activities of an organisation to the environment in which it operates. For example, in developing countries a changing economic and technological environment might open up opportunities to more effectively promote the uptake of solar powered lighting as a viable alternative to health damaging alternatives such as kerosene lamps.

Strategy is to do with matching the an organisation's activities to its resource capacity. For example, if an organisation has established good community networks but a very small disposable budget it would make sound strategic sense if it was seeking to influence the community it serves to adopt a strategy that focused on interpersonal face-to-face briefing rather than use a mass media approach to engage communities.

Strategic decisions often have major resource implications. For example, if an NGO focused on promoting the dangers of landmines established a policy goal of eradicating mines from a country the significant costs associated with the detection, removal and disposal of land mines would have to be factored into the feasibility of such a strategy.

Strategic decisions are likely to impact on operational decisions. For example, a strategic decision to promote the drinking of more water by young children as part of a programme to reduce health problems associated with being overweight might result in the need to develop and target operational interventions that seek to educate teachers and parents about the scheme and how they can support it.

Strategic decisions are likely to have a significant impact on the long-term policy of an organisation. For example, a strategic decision to encourage riders to always wear a safety helmet when riding their motorcycle or moped might result in a situation of fewer serious head traumas and deaths as a positive strategic goal but also a reduction in the number of donor organs that are available from people who would have otherwise died in such accidents.

The strategy of an organisation will be influenced not only by environmental forces and resource availability but also by the values and expectations of those who have the power to influence the decisions made. For example, politicians in many countries or powerful businesses or NGOs can lobby for social marketing interventions to address issues that are of less importance in terms of overall social wellbeing than others. An example would be the propensity of positive health campaign spending to be directed at younger people rather than older people.

Policy appraisal

When it comes to apprising and selecting new social policy or updating existing policy, some form of option appraisal will need to be carried out. Option appraisal is a tool that needs to be tailored to the specific policy under review. Appraisal should be undertaken early in the policy development process. It may be appropriate to conduct an initial appraisal and then develop it or re-visit it at various stages, e.g. following consultation with key stakeholders and partners as well as the intended target beneficiaries of the policy. A useful set of questions that can be used to both develop and test potential policy initiatives is set out in Table 11.2.

Table 11.2 Policy and programme start-up questions

1. Why do we need to act?
2. What is our vision?
3. Who are the stakeholders and potential partners?
4. Who are the most important stakeholders and what outcomes do they want?
5. What mechanisms, systems, processes and changes does the vision suggest?
6. What's the scope of this initiative? What are we prepared to do and not do?
7. What are the success criteria?
8. What are the pre-conditions of success?
9. Who will oppose the policy and how do we deal with the opposition?
10. What evidence is there that we can act successfully?
11. What are we going to have to produce, deliver or change?
12. What will it cost?
13. Who needs to participate in the project?
14. What do we need from others?
15. What sequence do they need to be done in?
16. What resources do we have available?
17. What assumptions are we making?
18. What are the constraints?
19. What are the barriers to success?
20. What assets do we have that will help deliver the policy?
21. What are the likely consequences and side-effects of our success?
22. Who/what is likely to be disadvantaged by our success?
23. What risks are there and what are the likely probability and impact of each risk?
24. What should we do to reduce the probability and/or impact?
25. What contingency arrangements do we need?
26. How will this policy fit with existing or planned policy?

Source: adapted from Economic Policy Unit, 2013

Social marketing can assist with policy appraisal by testing with all relevant stakeholders, partners, citizens and target populations the perceived need for such a policy and if the expected costs and benefits are deemed to be acceptable. Social marketing can also be used to test other aspects of the policy such as the target audience response to potential alternative intervention approaches regarding their acceptability and perceived risks. Social marketing can also assist with engaging stakeholders and potential partners through the development of interventions aimed at influencing their behaviour with regard to supporting and collaborating with the development and delivery of the policy.

The role of social marketing in social programme strategy development and delivery

Strategy as discussed in Chapter 5 is the coordinated application of all the organisation's resources to achieve stated policy goals. Strategy, as well as being focused on setting out clear aims to be achieved, is also focused on how an organisation, service or department is structured and operates and how it develops and applies specific plans and resources to achieve the overall aims of the policy.

Strategic social marketing is not the same as operational social marketing as it involves making a contribution to strategic analysis, strategic choice and strategic implementation and coordination. Operational social marketing is focused on the development, implementation and evaluation of a mix of tactical interventions to influence specific behaviours. As described in Chapter 5, strategy development typically consists of three main clusters of actions and decisions. First is the process of strategic analysis to understand the operating environment and internal capabilities and policy goals of the organisation. Next comes a set of choice processes to select the most appropriate strategic approach. Finally strategy involves the development of plans to ensure the effective execution, coordination and review of the strategy. All three of these tasks are iterative in nature rather than being undertaken in a simple mechanistic linear fashion.

As set out in Chapter 5 marketing strategy consists of the seven sets of actions depicted in Table 11.3. These activities are set out in an idealised logical sequence but in reality most strategic planning is an ongoing iterative process. Strategy is ideally a cyclical process involving feedback and reflection focused on ensuring that the right aims and objectives are being pursued by the right mix of interventions and tactics using the optimum level of resources to deliver the aims that have been agreed.

How to determine the mission aims and objectives of the social programme

The first of the seven processes set out in Table 11.3 is the most vital. As we have explored in this chapter it is crucial that there is clarity of policy aim, strategic

Table 11.3 Seven strategic processes

1. Determine the mission, aims and objectives of the social programme.
2. Analyse the current intervention strategy and assess its strengths and weaknesses.
3. Assess current and future external and internal threats and opportunities.
4. Generate new options, and analyse each against conclusions from internal and external analysis and mission goals and objectives.
5. Agree the criteria and apply criteria for selecting any new strategy.
6. Summarise the results of analysis and conclusions and articulate a new strategy.
7. Plan and deliver the new strategy through selected operational and tactical approaches.

goals and objectives when developing social policy and strategy. Without such clarity subsequent strategy development processes will flounder. The remaining six common strategic processes are now explained and the potential role of social marketing within each process is explored. The setting-out of clear strategic goals similar to those used by WHO is a precursor for the development of a deliverable social strategy.

How to analyse the current intervention strategy and assess its strengths and weaknesses

Existing approaches to influencing social behaviour need to be continually assessed and also subject to formal review on a regular basis. A key feature of social marketing is that it is an iterative and reflective process that seeks to continuously improve the performance of social programme delivery. One of the strengths of social marketing is this focus on testing the appropriateness and utility of existing interventions to see if and how they can be improved (Andreasen, 2002).

A tool that is commonly used to analyse current intervention strategies is SWOT analysis. SWOT analysis is a management and marketing tool that is used to assess internal strengths and weaknesses and external threats and opportunities to an organisation or programme. SWOT stands for: strengths, weaknesses, opportunities and threats (Humphrey, 2005: see Figure 11.3).

SWOT analysis can be carried out on policies, services, interventions, products, industries or even individual people. It involves specifying the aims and goals of the organisation or policy and identifying the internal and external factors that are supportive or oppositional to the achievement of those aims and goals. The opportunities and threats element of SWOT analysis is often undertaken simultaneously with an analysis of strengths and weaknesses but can also be done separately as part of the next strategic process focused on external factors that might impact on social policy. The process consists of listing all the factors that are perceived to be strengths and weaknesses of the current approach to the social challenge and then giving them weightings based on data and evidence if possible. The strengths and weaknesses are then prioritised. The third stage of the process is to further differentiate the strengths and weaknesses based on the likely impact on performance. For example, the strength of a road traffic safety programme might be that there is strong legislation in place to encourage the wearing of safety helmets by riders of mopeds, as is the case in India. However, as any observer will confirm most people in India who ride motorcycles do not wear safety helmets. So in this case while legislation is a strength it would not be ranked as one of the primary strengths in an assessment of the current Indian road safety programme aimed at moped rider safety.

SWOT analysis is important as it should be used to inform later stages of the strategic planning process by informing which existing interventions should be continued and which may need to be modified.

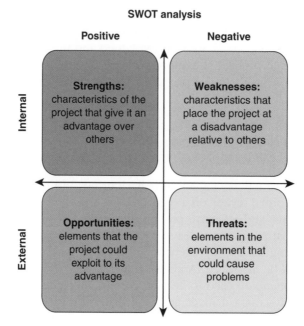

Figure 11.3 SWOT analysis

SWOT analysis can also be used through the process of matching and converting to generate potential intervention tactics. Matching is identifying potential new ways to influence social behaviours by matching the strengths of an existing strategy to opportunities within the environment. For example, matching a strength such as expertise in digital communication with the opportunity afforded by the increased ownership of smart phones. Converting is a process of converting weaknesses into strengths. Converting can be used to convert a weakness into strength by focusing on finding a new target market for a service, product or programme that is not being taken up by an existing target market. For example, refocusing a promotion to use safety helmets that is not having an impact on male drivers of mopeds at an alternative audience of female passengers who may be more likely to adopt the recommended protective behaviour. SWOT also indicates areas of social policy weakness that if they cannot be converted should be reduced or stopped. SWOT typically proceeds through these five steps:

1. List existing programme strengths and weaknesses.
2. Prioritise in terms of importance and feasibility in achieving programme aims and objectives.
3. Seek to match strengths with opportunities.
4. Seek to convert weaknesses into strengths.
5. Identify existing elements of the programme to reduce or cut.

SWOT is a very adaptable strategic analysis tool that can also be used to assess individual social marketing interventions and the strengths and weakness of competitive forces that might be pushing against the aims and objectives of a social marketing programme. For example, SWOT can be used as part of competition analysis to assess the strengths and weakness of the pro-tobacco lobby. It can also be used as a horizon scanning mechanism to identify opportunities that competitors could exploit. For example, the development of the e cigarette market as an opportunity for the traditional tobacco industry to buy into in order to continue their strategy of normalising cigarette smoking.

Used in this way SWOT and PESTLE analysis can help social marketers understand the total operating environment. They can also help the identification of potential intervention strategies. For example, knowing that tobacco companies are seeking to dominate the e cigarette market as a way of circumventing increasing bans and restrictions on cigarette use, social policy can be directed to widening such bans and restrictions to cover e cigarette use and promotions. (Also see Chapter 12 for further coverage of how SWOT and PESTLE analysis can be applied in social marketing.)

How to assess current and future external and internal threats and opportunities

As stated above SWOT analysis can be used to identify opportunities and threats in both the internal organisational and policy environment and threats and opportunities from the external environment. A complementary analytical tool is PESTLE or, as it is also know, STEEPL, SLEPT, PEST or STEP analysis. PESTLE is an acronym for factors that include:

- political factors
- economic factors
- social factors
- technological factors
- legal factors
- environmental factors.

All of the PESTLE factors in the present and future can have significant impacts on social policy and social strategy selection and delivery. When developing social strategies all these factors need to be considered. PESTLE analysis is intended to help future-proof interventions by analysing potential future scenarios and how factors such as a downturn in economic circumstances or the development of new technologies will necessitate a change in policy, strategy or tactics.

The process for undertaking PESTLE analysis starts with a listing of all possible factors in the external environment that may impact on the social policy, strategy or its tactical delivery. In addition to the main PESTLE factors it is also possible to add other factors that may be specific to the social issues or target population group under consideration. These factors are then prioritised and ranked in terms of their potential impact and their likelihood of coming to fruition. This analysis can then be used to inform the development of future policy strategy and tactics to maximise opportunities and reduce the impact of potential threats. Figure 11.4 illustrates how PESTLE factors can be clustered using a probability and level of threat/opportunity matrix.

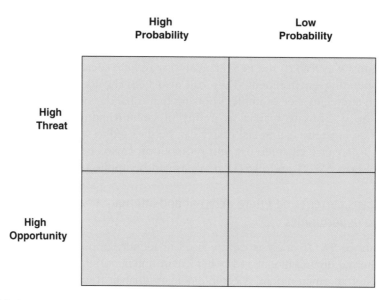

Figure 11.4   PESTLE probability/opportunity/threat matrix

CASE STUDY

The Kiama Health Plan: creating environments for health and sustainable living (Australia)

The Kiama Local Government area is located on the South Coast of New South Wales (NSW), Australia, and is approximately 120 kilometres south of Sydney. It has an area of 256 square kilometres and is essentially a rural community surrounded by beaches, rainforest and farmland.

The role and subsequent boundaries of responsibility within local government are increasingly expanding and include a focus upon providing services for the health and wellbeing of not only the individual within a municipality, but also community and environmental wellbeing. Kiama Municipal Council has embraced the World Health Organization's (WHO) definition of health in recognition of the interaction between the health of the community and the wider environment. This socio-ecological definition of health is promoted by the development of local government initiatives, which offer a holistic and collaborative approach to solving local issues.

Kiama Council was one of the first councils in NSW to develop and implement a municipal health plan. The plan came about by a chance opportunity when the Kiama District Health Watch was required to undertake community consultation using vision processes to identify priority health needs at the same time as Healthy Cities Illawarra and Kiama Council were examining a proposal to develop a health plan. The development and implementation of the plan relied on the establishment of strong partnerships particularly between Healthy Cities Illawarra, Kiama Council and the Local Health District and with the support of the community and local organisations.

The Kiama Municipal Health Plan documents this holistic planning approach and outlines strategies to address the interaction between human and environmental health. It includes health, environment, social, strategic and land-use planning, and economic development issues. It is a 'whole of community' collaborative approach, and links international, commonwealth, state, regional and local issues, goals and programmes. Ultimately, it attempts to encourage and provide every citizen with the opportunities to become responsible for improving their own health and to preserve, protect and improve the local environment.

The aims of the plan

- To improve the health, wellbeing and quality of life for all residents and visitors to the Kiama Municipality.
- To improve, protect and enhance the environment for the benefit of present and future generations.
- To promote an ecological sustainable development that minimises hazards and maintains the local environment to a degree that human health and safety are not impaired and yet encourages the development to proceed.

The process

The first Kiama Municipal Health Plan 2001–2004 had a strong focus on vision workshops to identify health issues within the areas of environment, community and economy. To do this, participants were asked what their vision was for an ideal healthy municipality in the future (20–25 years). A diversity of people participated including farmers, business, youth and tourists. Their visions

(Continued)

(Continued)

included clean air and no pollution, maintaining viable land for food production, open spaces and a village atmosphere, and fostering a feeling of 'belonging' and sense of community. The data collected were analysed to identify priorities in 12 theme areas. These were health, safety and injury, tourism, employment, transport, social and cultural, food and nutrition, leisure and recreation, pollution control, education and training, built and physical environment. Strategy workshops were then conducted with residents, community groups and government and non-government organisations.

Achievements of the Municipal Health Plan

- Safe Communities Project.
- Kiamasphere – a sustainable living programme. The objective of Kiamasphere projects is: 'To manage, improve and protect the total environment to attain a sustainable and high quality lifestyle for present and future generations'. The logo incorporates council colours and represents the holistic approach required to achieve sustainable living.
- Sustainable Living Expo, conducted annually to showcase the activities of the council, community groups and commercial products which promote sustainable living environment.
- Sustainable Living Grants, which provide funding to community groups and schools to implement health and environmental strategies to create a more sustainable community. Grants have included the funding of tree planting, the establishment of indigenous gardens, sun protection activities, the building of a school chicken coup, and the development of community information resources.
- The development of a comprehensive physical activity programme including the provision of marked walking paths (the Heart Care Walks) to encourage regular physical activity and the development of a 12 kilometre coastal walking track between Kiama Heights and Werri Beach.
- The establishment of the Kiama Produce Market, which came about through two significant activities – the lack of access to fruit and vegetables except through one large chain grocery store which was very expensive and the need for local farmers to look at potential uses for their land other than dairy farming due to the deregulation of the dairy industry.
- The establishment of a community garden at Blue Haven Retirement Village, which is maintained by a wide range of community groups.

The successful outcomes of the first plan demonstrate how local government can lead and partner the community and local organisations to build a strong, healthy and safe community.

The Second Municipal Health Plan

Development of the second Kiama Municipal Health Plan 2005–2008 involved widespread community participation using focus groups, interviews and surveying. Research and a review of literature including local, state and national goals were conducted to identify key priorities for council. The priorities identified through these processes are:

- Strengthening community through building partnerships and networks and community connections: the council undertook many public infrastructure projects involving community participation in the planning and construction, ensuring ongoing use of facilities and improved health outcomes. The projects included: The Pavilion (a town hall, community meeting place and home of the agricultural show); the redevelopment of the library to include an adult education college; a bridge club constructed on the AFL field (senior citizens and young footballers sharing and socialising in a common public space).
- Supporting social environments for health particularly through healthy lifestyles strategies, safety and injury prevention, and quality health services.

Kiama Healthy and Sustainable Cities Plan (2011–2017)

In the evaluation and review of the plan Kiama Council engaged with community focus groups to provide vital feedback and recommendations. Overall there was broad consensus on the council's established priorities and in turn the community delivered rich discussion and opinions which were valued by the council. An emerging theme was 'Building Partnerships, Networks and Community Connections', acknowledging that positive relationships, social contact and a strong sense of 'belonging' and connection to the community in which one lives can greatly enhance an individual's health status.

The priorities identified are:

- Building stronger partnerships with government and non-government organisations and community groups.
- Addressing social isolation, particularly for new residents, young families and the ageing population.
- Researching how residents in Kiama interact and how individuals connect and relate with each other, creating a generous society.
- Sustainability and healthy equity.
- Bringing the community together with the celebration of food as a cultural experience.

(Continued)

(Continued)

- Development of a new Residents Kit to welcome new residents to the municipality. The aim is to empower residents to form social connections and actively participate in the community.

Social marketing principles applied

1. Citizen orientation: the plan has been community driven from the start, with strong leadership and commitment from a former mayor, Sandra McCarthy, encouraging community members to be involved in all the activities, and essentially planning for they own good health and the health of the community. The mayor used her political role to promote the good heath of Kiama through an interactive media campaign, e.g. 'personal stories', mayoral columns, health kiosks at community events. Community members were valued by being supported by the council to attend meetings, forums and conferences. The governance structure has transitioned over time from the intersecting oral collaboration of the council and initial health groups to community advisory management committees for the Health Plan and Kiama community garden

2. Behaviour: the strong participation and community support initiated behavioural and organisational change within the council. Elected councillors recognised a growing commitment for the health plan by residents and that 'Good health = Good politics'. The community participation process was being valued as an equity approach and the community were being more and more encouraged to have their say on all local issues beyond health. The council developed a new vision statement –'A municipality working together for a healthy, sustainable and caring community' – and improved health outcomes became a performance measure for every strategic action of the council.

3. A demonstrated social ecological model, which has achieved long-term government and community sustainability: factors that contributed to this were that the health plan was embedded in the local government structure (critical). The championing of the project by the long-serving mayor (12 years) fostered intersectoral relationships across health, social and welfare groups and developed strong international partnerships with South Korea, Taiwan, China, Malaysia, Vietnam and other Australian healthy cities. In 2008 the WHO formally recognised the Kiama Municipality as a healthy, sustainable community. I believe it was the sustainability factors that ensured the health plan transformed from a project to a policy approach, i.e. inspiring the way of life for Kiama citizens, and thus has also inspired the current council to continue to engage with the community.

4. The principles of equity, access, participation and rights (social justice) are at the heart of the process and I believe strongly influenced the willingness of the community to be involved and take ownership with responsibility.

Conclusion

The health plan is an evolving, interactive policy which needs to be constantly reviewed, evaluated, changed and socially marketed to ensure it remains relevant and responsive to the changing needs of a growing community. It is essential to continue to encourage the public to participate in the development, implementation and evaluation of the health plan. The future in Kiama is positive, as it is through collaboration and engagement that the community can look forward to better health, wellbeing, and a safe, sustainable environment. Simply, a greater quality of life achieved within the council's operating budget for basic community services.

Acknowledgements to Sandra McCarthy, Chair of the Australian Chapter of Healthy Cities, Emeritus Mayor of Kiama and Honorary Senior Fellow (CHI) of Centre of Health Initiatives, University of Wollongong (UOW) for this case study.

For more information see: www.kiama.nsw.gov.au/Your-Community/Healthy-Communities/Kiama-Health-Plan/Kiama-Health-Plan.

Competition analysis

A noted in Chapter 2 competitive analysis is the assessment of the strengths and weaknesses of existing and potential competitors. In commercial marketing this provides insight on opportunities and threats for a company, and forms an essential part of corporate strategy development (Fleisher and Bensoussan, 2003). In social marketing competition analysis is both a form of situational analysis and a way of generating potential intervention strategies and tactics.

In addition to PESTLE analysis and SWOT analysis, competition analysis is a powerful tool for assessing current and future threats to social programme delivery. As noted earlier in this chapter SWOT analysis and PESTLE analysis can be used to review not only social policy strengths and the strengths of social marketing strategies but also the strength of competitive forces and opportunities to reduce them.

Social marketing competition analysis can be thought of in two main ways. First as depicted in Figure 11.5 there are often opposing forces that seek to resist the application of social marketing as an integral part of social policy and strategy. As well as these five forces other forms of competition are explored in more detail in Chapters 2 and 14. Status quo bias as discussed in Chapters 3 and 8 is also a form of passive competition that is rooted in a preference for sticking with existing ways of developing

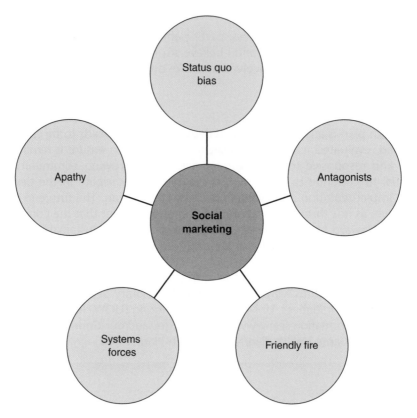

Figure 11.5 Competitors to the application of social marketing within social policy strategy and delivery

and delivering social programmes rather than an outright antagonistic stance towards social marketing. Apathy is another form of competition which is related to but distinct from status quo bias. Some organisations are simply not ready to adopt any form of systematic review and development process to improve the impact and efficiency of social programme implementation. In addition to status quo bias and apathy there will be some politicians, policy makers, and other professionals who will object to the application of social marketing on both ethical grounds and perceived efficacy grounds (Witkowski, 2005). This issue is further explored in Chapter 13.

Competition in social marketing also comes in the form of friendly fire. By this we mean the potential crowding out of social marketing interventions in one area of policy by interventions in another that are competing for the attention of a particular target group. For example, attempts to influence young people not to misuse alcohol may be crowded out by bigger and more intensive campaigns aimed at getting them not to smoke. Finally social marketing will face competition and barriers from existing systems and ways of working. These will include systems that do not value or use insight about target audience needs and wants and also systems that are not geared towards under-taking systematic review, the setting of clear behavioural objectives and the use of evaluation and appraisal to influence the development of social programme delivery.

A second form of competition in social marketing comes from internal and exter-nal factors that oppose behaviours being promoted by social marketing strategies and programmes. These factors will be specific to the behaviours that are being influenced. For example, if a social marketing strategy is seeking to influence the behaviour of older men to come forward early if they detect potential skin cancer, competition may come in the form of internal completion related to a belief that any potentially cancerous lesions are not serious or in the form of competition derived from the reality that contacting the cancer screening service is complicated and involves a prohibitive cost. This form of completion analysis is straightforward to carry out but is rarely done well in many social programmes.

The process for undertaking this form of competition analysis is depicted in Table 11.4 with regard to a simplified version of competition analysis in relation to competitive forces from two sources, fast food and high sugar content drinks that have an impact on weight and obesity. In a full analysis there would be many more factors than these two.

The process consists of identifying key factors from each of these competitors. In this example four such factors are identified – in reality there may be many more than this. These factors are then given a weighting to indicate the relative strength of this factor: the weighting of the factors should always total 1.0. This weighting should be based on data and evidence if these exist.

Next the two forms of completion are assigned a rating of their strength of influence regarding each of the behavioural influencing factors. In the example given, fast food is given a rating of 7 in relation to low price being a causal factor and soft drinks are given a rating of 4. Next the rating is multiplied by the weighting factor and totalled to

Table 11.4 Example of comparative competition analysis in the field of obesity

Key Behaviour Influencing Factors	Weighting	Fast Food rating	Fast Food weighted	Soft Drinks rating	Soft Drinks weighted
1 – Extensive distribution	.2	6	2.4	3	1.2
2 – Customer focus	.3	4	1.2	5	1.5
3 – Promotions and marketing	.4	3	.6	3	.6
4 – Price	.1	7	.7	4	.4
Totals	1.0	20	4.9	15	3.7

produce an overall competitor score. Using this type of comparative competition analysis it is possible to determine which forms of competition are most important and also how best to reduce their impact. For example, using the example depicted in Table 11.4, fast food comes out as a more important competitor than soft drinks. Therefore it might merit more attention in terms of strategies to encourage a move away from this kind of food. In addition in the area of customer focus, soft drinks score highly, so there may be a case for developing policy or programmes to reduce the strength of this threat, for example by restricting promotions of soft drinks in certain locations such as schools and hospitals.

In addition to the comparative ranking approach to competitor analysis another useful approach is competitor profiling. Competitor profiling is a process that involves analysis of specific organisations or social factors that oppose the overall social strategy and specific tactical social marketing intervention. When organisations or sectors are identified as competitors the list of attributes of the competitor set out in Table 11.5 can be used to develop a comprehensive profile of the competitor. This profiling also identifies potential weaknesses that can be exploited. For example, if a competitor organisation in the private sector has a very low profit margin on the sale of environmentally damaging products a small increase in tax and restrictions on promotion of that product may be enough to discourage the company from its manufacture and promotion.

Table 11.5 Competitor profile checklist

Background
- location of offices, plants and online presence
- history – key personalities, dates, events and trends
- ownership, corporate governance and organisational structure

Financials
- profit and loss ratios, dividend policy and profitability
- various financial ratios, liquidity and cash flow
- profit growth profile, method of growth (organic or acquisitive)

Products/services
- products offered, depth and breadth of product line, and portfolio balance
- new products developed, new product success rate and R&D strengths
- brands, strength of brand portfolio, brand loyalty and brand awareness
- patents and licenses
- quality control conformance
- reverse engineering

Marketing strategy
- objectives and targets
- segments served, market shares, customer base, growth rate and customer loyalty
- promotional mix, promotional budgets, advertising themes, ad agency used, sales force success rate, online promotional strategy

- distribution channels used (direct and indirect), exclusivity agreements, alliances and geographical coverage
- pricing strategy

Facilities

- plant capacity, capacity utilisation rate, age of plant, plant efficiency, capital investment
- location, distribution, logistics and product mix by plant

Personnel and other organisational assets

- number of employees, key employees and skill sets
- strength of management and management style
- compensation, benefits and employee morale and retention rates
- shareholder profile and issues

Corporate strategy

- vision, mission statement
- growth plans, acquisitions and divestitures

In the case of competitive factors such as cultural beliefs, economic influences, fashion or technological innovations that may have a negative impact on the social strategy or social marketing interventions, these factors can also be profiled and potential management strategies developed using a similar process and the factors set out in Table 11.6.

Table 11.6 Competitive forces profile factors

Scale and scope of influence

- how many people are engaged or being influenced
- geographical focus of influence
- organisations being influenced
- systems being influenced

Sources of influence

- types of influence
- form and type of influence
- channels of influence
- media influence
- digital influence

Key players

- key leaders or individuals
- key conduits
- key organisations
- key networks

Temporal issues

- trends
- seasonal or cyclical influences
- likely life cycle
- sustainability factors

How to generate new options

Based on environmental analysis, data about the problem that is being targeted, evidence about what works and what does not, target audience insight and acceptability, stakeholder and partner acceptability and competition analysis, and potential intervention approaches can be developed.

The generation of options for interventions can come from a variety of sources and these include:

- ideas from meta reviews
- ideas from national or international guidance documents
- ideas from other countries or areas
- ideas from case study or programme write-ups or presentations
- ideas from related fields (e.g. examples from the health sector being used to trigger interventions in the environment sector)
- ideas from analysis of existing intervention programmes
- ideas from suggestions by target audience members
- ideas from stakeholder and partner organisations.

When generating new ideas and reviewing existing programmes of action it is a good idea to hold some form of deliberative event or meetings to generate, review and then assess all potential options. This is especially the case when there is less consensus and weight of evidence. In situations where there is strong consensus and considerable evidence it is more likely that intervention programmes will be based on best practice protocols and proven intervention mixes (NICE, 2014). For example, in the field of smoking cessation there is a strong evidence base about who should run and promote the uptake of group support programmes to assist people to stop smoking (West et al., 2000). When evidence is weak consideration should be given to investment in a robust trial of the planned approach by the use of control trials if possible (Haynes et al., 2013).

How to agree and apply the criteria for selecting a strategy

When it comes to choosing the strategic mix of interventions an agreed set of criteria will need to be selected to screen potential interventions that might be included in the strategy. These criteria need to be selected to reflect the focus and nature of the behaviours that are being targeted and also the policy and values held by those developing the strategy and those responsible for delivering it. Common criteria will involve those set out in Figure 11.6.

In addition to these criteria other criteria can be used to further filter potential intervention elements. These criteria can include but are not limited to:

- Is there insight data that indicate targeted citizens will respond positively?
- How many people are at risk or will be if no action is taken?
- Is there a strong evidence base that indicates a plausible intervention?

Figure 11.6 Criteria for evaluating strategic options

- Do the potential negative side-effects have public support?
- Are there any ethical issues that need to be addressed?
- What is the most cost effective mix that can deliver sub-optimal ROI and VFM?

Reaching agreement about which criteria will be used to screen potential strategic mix elements and how much weight each criterion will carry is something that needs be decided by the key stakeholders and partners responsible for developing the strategy and those with the responsibility for delivering it. Typically key stakeholders will include politicians, who are responsible, and senior managers, technical experts, key partner delivery staff and agencies, and ideally members of the target audience as well as representatives of the general public.

The selection criteria used to make such decisions should also ideally be placed in the public domain so that the process used for selection is transparent and open to public scrutiny. Figure 11.7 summarises the analysis and selection process associated with strategy development and selection.

How to summarise the results of analysis and conclusions and articulate the new strategy

The penultimate step in developing a social strategy that has been influenced by social marketing concepts and techniques is the summarising and setting out of the rationale, data and evidence that underpin the selection of the intervention mix selected, together with a clear description of all the interventions that will be delivered, who will deliver them, what resources will be used and over what time-frame. The strategy will also set

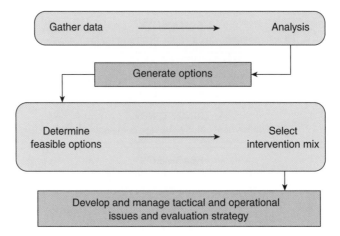

Figure 11.7 Summary of strategic review analysis and intervention mix development

out how this will be monitored, coordinated and evaluated against its stated goals, aims and objectives and how it will be refined over time.

The strategy will include details of what mix of forms of intervention and types of intervention make up the strategy and the evidence, citizen insight, environmental analysis and rationale that underpin their inclusion in the strategy. Figure 4.2 in Chapter 4 is a useful tool for summarising the elements that might make up the strategy. In most instances not all cells of such a matrix will be occupied by an intervention or interventions.

In addition to the 'types' and 'forms' of intervention that will make up the strategy the strategy will also set out the level and approach that will be adopted to influence social behaviour. Figure 11.8 is a matrix that can be used to summarise the societal level that a strategy will aim to influence, ranging from actions aimed at influencing individuals through to action at an international level. It also indicates on the Y axis the approaches that will be used, ranging from policy initiatives through to how the operational delivery of all the elements of the strategy will be delivered.

The following 12 elements set out in Table 11.7 will typically be included in a marketing informed social strategy. These elements can be used as both a checklist to assess strategy and also as a guide to constructing a strategic plan.

A final element and task associated with the summarising and setting out of the overall strategy is the need to communicate this effectively with all relevant stakeholders, target groups, partners and the public. The delivery of many social programmes is hindered by the fact that key players are not aware of the strategy or the part that they need to play in ensuring that it is delivered effectively and efficiently. Social marketing can help with this aspect of strategy engagement and dissemination by developing marketing and communication plans. It can also ensure the development of stakeholder engagement and management plans. Investment in a planned approach to promoting understanding about the need for a strategy, why the approaches that have been selected have been chosen, and how all relevant stakeholders can assist in the delivery of the strategy, is an important component in the successful implementation of any new social strategy.

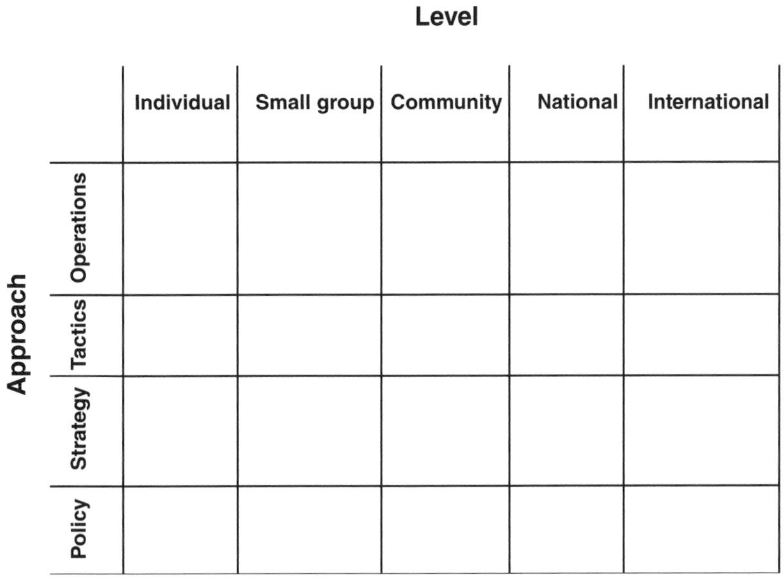

Level

Figure 11.8 Social programme level and approach matrix

Table 11.7 Components of marketing informed social strategy

1. Overall policy aims
2. Strategic goals
3. Summary of threat, opportunity, situation and competition analysis
4. Understanding about the citizens, evidence and theory that underpin the rationale for the selected approach
5. Key responsibility of stakeholders and partners
6. Intervention types and forms that will be used
7. How the strategy will be managed and coordinated
8. How the strategy will be operationalised and who will be responsible for each sub-element of delivery
9. Resources, assets and budget that are being allocated to each element of the strategy
10. How the strategy will be monitored and progress reported
11. How the success of the strategy will be measured and over what time-frame
12. How lessons learnt will be used to inform future strategy

How to plan and deliver new strategy via selected operational and tactical approaches

The development of intervention tactics and the implementation of each specific strategic intervention that constitutes a component of the strategy and their operational management and evaluation are the final elements in the strategic development process. The process of developing operational social marketing interventions is explored in Chapter 12. When developing and delivering tactical interventions it will be important from a strategic perspective to ensure that learning that is gained about the success and failure of specific interventions is rapidly fed back to those responsible for the overall evaluation of a programme so that any necessary adjustments to the strategy can be made. It is also vital from a strategic perspective that intelligence gathered about how target audiences, secondary audiences, partners and stakeholders are engaging with intervention is also fed rapidly back to those in charge of overall strategy. These forms of intelligence often result in opportunities being spotted and exploited to positive effect or potential delivery problems being identified early and addressed before they become major problems or impediments to the delivery of the strategy.

Conclusion

We have explored in this chapter the advantages of applying a marketing approach to the development of social policy and strategy. Additionally we have explored the need when developing new social policy and strategy to review the current policy response and its strengths and weaknesses. We have also looked at the need to understand potential opportunities and threats related to the wider environment in which a particular strategy is being developed. Analytical tools such as PESTLE and completion analysis have been introduced as useful ways to promote understanding and develop social strategies from a marketing perspective. The chapter then examined the processes for developing and selecting potential elements and approaches that might be included in social strategies and how to select those with the most potential to result in positive outcomes. This chapter has illustrated how introducing a marketing perspective to social strategy development can enhance the process and better reflect the needs of citizens. There is now a great deal of understanding about how to select, plan, deliver and evaluate social programmes based on a deep understanding of citizens' needs, wants, beliefs and behaviours. There is also a great deal of understanding about how to systematically select, develop, implement and evaluate such strategies. The challenge now is to apply this understanding in a systematic and consistent way.

Reflective questions

- List the added value of social marketing to the generation of policy making and selection.
- How and why should citizens be engaged in the policy selection and social intervention programme design, delivery and evaluation?
- What are the main steps associated with developing evidence, data and research informed social policy that seeks to influence behaviour?

SOCIAL MARKETING AND SOCIAL PROGRAMME DESIGN   343

- What are some of the main conceptual tools set out in this chapter that can be used to develop effective and efficient social policy intervention programmes?
- What forms of competition analysis can be performed to help develop more effective social policy?

Further reading

Australian Public Service Commission (2007) *Changing Behaviour: A Public Policy Perspective.* Canberra: Australian Government. Available at: www.apsc.gov.au/publications-and-media/archive/publications-archive/changing-behaviour (last accessed 18 November 2014).

Economic Policy Unit (2013) *A Practical Guide to Policy Making in Northern Ireland.* Office of the First Minster and Deputy First Minister, Belfast. Available at: www.ofmdfmni.gov.uk/index/making-government-work/improving-public-services/policylink/policylink-a-practical-guide-to-policy-making.htm (last accessed 20 November 2014).

French, J. (2011) 'Business as unusual: the contribution of social marketing to government policy making and strategy development', in G. Hastings, K. Angus and C. Bryant (eds), *The SAGE Handbook of Social Marketing.* London: SAGE, pp. 359–374.

HM Government (2013) *Twelve Actions to Professionalise Policy Making: A Report by the Policy Profession Board.* Available at: http://resources.civilservice.gov.uk/wp-content/uploads/2011/09/Twelve-Actions-Report-Web-Accessible.pdf (last accessed 20 November 1014)

UK Cabinet Office policy and strategy publications. Available at: www.gov.uk/government/publications (last accessed 20 November 2014).

References

Andreasen, A.R. (2002) 'Marketing social marketing in the social change marketplace', *Journal of Public Policy Marketing*, 21 (1): 3–13

Baldock, J., Manning, N. and Vickerstaff, S. (2007) *Social Policy.* Oxford: Oxford University Press.

Berglund, C. and Matti, S. (2006) 'Citizen and consumer: the dual role of individuals in environmental policy', *Environmental Politics*, 15 (4): 550–571.

Brennan, C. and Douglas, A. (1999) 'Best value: improving services by talking to people', *Consumer Policy Review*, 9: 4.

Bullock, H., Mountford, J. and Stanley, R. (2001) *Better Policy Making.* London: Centre for Management and Policy Studies.

Clarke, J., Newman, J., Smith, N., Vidler, E. and Westmarland, L. (2007) *Creating Citizen Consumers: Changing Publics & Changing Public Service.* London: SAGE.

Curtain, R. (2003) *How Citizens Can Take Part in Developing and Implementing Public Policy.* Melbourne: Australian Public Policy Research Network.

Dawnay, E. and Shah, H. (2005) *Behavioural Economics: 7 Principles for Policymakers.* London: New Economics Foundation.

Economic Policy Unit (2013) *A Practical Guide to Policy Making in Northern Ireland.* Office of the First Minster and Deputy First Minister. Belfast. Available at: www.ofmdfmni.gov.uk/index/making-government-work/improving-public-services/policylink/policylink-a-practical-guide-to-policy-making.htm (last accessed 20 November 2014).

Fleisher, C. and Bensoussan, B. (2003) *Strategic and Competitive Analysis: Methods and Techniques for Analyzing Business Competition.* London: Prentice Hall.

French, J. (2011) 'Business as unusual: the contribution of social marketing to government policy making and strategy development', in G. Hastings, K. Angus and C. Bryant (eds), *The SAGE Handbook of Social Marketing.* London: SAGE, pp. 359–374.

Haynes, L., Service, O., Goldacre, B. and Torgerson, D. (2013) *Test, Learn Adapt: The Development of Public Policy with Randomised Control Trials.* London: Cabinet Office.

Humphrey, A. (2005) 'SWOT analysis for management consulting', SRI Alumni Newsletter (SRI International), December.

Jones, G. and Scholes, K. (2010) *Exploring Corporate Strategy.* London: Prentice Hall.

Lefebvre, R.C. (2012) 'Transformative social marketing: co-creation and the social marketing brand', *Journal of Social Marketing*, 2 (2): 118–129.

Lindblom, C. and Woodhouse, E.J. (1993) *The Policy-making Process* (3rd edn). Englewood Cliffs, NJ: Prentice Hall.

McDermott, R.J., Berends, V., McCormack Brown, K., Agron, P., Black, K. and Pitt Barnes, S. (2005) 'Impact of the California Project LEAN school board member social marketing campaign', *Social Marketing Quarterly*, 9 (2).

McKenzie-Mohr, D. and Smith, W. (2011) *Fostering Sustainable Behavior. An Introduction to Community-based Social Marketing* (3rd edn). Gabriola Island, Canada: New Society Publishers.

Mulgan, G., Aldridge, S., Beales, G., Heathfield, A., Halpen, D. and Bates, C. (2004) *Personal Responsibility and Changing Behaviour: The State of Knowledge and Its Implications for Public Policy.* London: Prime Minister's Strategy Unit.

Newman, J., Barnes, M., Sullivan, H. and Knops, A. (2004) 'Public participation and collaborative governance', *Journal of Social Policy*, 33 (2): 203–223.

NICE (National Institute for Health and Care Excellence) (2014) *Behaviour Change Individual Approaches. NICE Public Health Guidance No 49.* London: NICE.

Nicholson, L. (2005) *Civic Participation in Public Policy-making: A Literature Review.* Edinburgh: Scottish Executive.

OECD (2001) *Citizens as Partners: Information, Consultation and Public Participation in Policy-making.* Paris: OECD.

Public Health Agency of Canada (2007) *Crossing Sectors – Experiences in Intersectoral Action, Public Policy and Health.* Available at: www.phac-aspc.gc.ca/publicat/2007/cro-sec/pdf/cro-sec_e.pdf (last accessed 19 November 2014).

Rothschild, M. (1999) 'Carrots, stick and promises: a conceptual framework for the management of public health and social behaviours', *Journal of Marketing*, 63: 24–37

United Nations (1945) *Charter of the United Nations.* Available at: www.un.org/en/documents/charter/index.shtml (last accessed 19 November 1014).

West, R., McNeill, A. and Raw, M. (2000) 'Smoking cessation guidelines for health professionals: an update', *Thorax*, 55: 987–999, doi:10.1136/thorax.55.12.987.

WHO (World Health Organization) (1986) *The Ottawa Charter for Health Promotion.* Available at: www.who.int/healthpromotion/conferences/previous/ottawa/en/index.html (last accessed 19 November 2014).

Witkowski, T. (2005) 'Anti-global challenges to marketing in developing countries: exploring the ideological divide', *Journal of Public Policy and Marketing*, 24 (1): 7–23.

12 PLANNING SOCIAL MARKETING INTERVENTIONS

Learning objectives

By the end of this chapter, readers should be able to:

- describe the rationale and reasons for the application of systematic planning in the delivery of operational social marketing interventions
- identify the basic components necessary for developing an efficient and effective social marketing intervention, their subcomponents and their optimal sequence of application
- comprehend the range of available operational social marketing planning tools and their key components
- critically assess the strengths and weaknesses of a social marketing interventions planning system.

Introduction

This chapter is focused on setting out the key elements and sequence of the application of operational social marketing planning tasks and stages. As stated in Chapter 2, one of the defining features of social marketing is the application of systematic and transparent planning to achieve defined and measurable social objectives. However, a common weakness of many social interventions is that there is often a lack of systematic planning that matches best practice. This chapter emphasises the need to invest resources and time in planning social marketing interventions if optimum results are to be achieved.

This lack of systematic planning in many public programmes exists despite a number of well-designed systematic planning models that have been developed over many years. One of the clear challenges that face those who wish to adopt a more strategic approach to the application of social marketing is to encourage practitioners to use these models and for sponsors to insist that some form of recognised and auditable systematic planning is utilised to structure programme delivery and evaluation. Rather alarmingly, one study by Godin et al. (2007) found that of 123 projects assessed only 15 per cent properly completed an objective setting stage and only 25 per cent completed any form of theory–practice assessment.

As discussed in Chapter 8, when planning social marketing interventions aimed at influencing behaviour, behavioural theories and models should have a central role in assisting the intervention design and evaluation of the programme (Donovan and Henley, 2003; Green and Tones, 2010), However, an equally important factor in the delivery of an intervention is the application of a logical and documented planning approach that is capable of interrogation and able to produce learning about what worked well and what did not. A well-planned and delivered programme can also be evaluated and provide lessons for the future about which aspects of a programme were efficient in terms of demonstrating a good return on investment and value for money, measure the quality of the programme delivered in terms of compliance with any agreed standards of practice, and obviously measure its actual impact on behaviour, beliefs, attitudes and knowledge. In short, systematic planning processes are key to understanding not only which elements of a social marketing programme are most successful but also which are the most efficient.

At the moment many social projects and campaigns, including those labelled as social marketing, demonstrate a number of characteristics of weak planning as set out in Table 12.1. The consequence of this is that they are difficult to evaluate and fail to add to our understanding about how to develop and deliver successful and efficient programmes.

The application of systematic and transparent planning is an integral part of social marketing. This focus on systematic planning is a key way to ensure that the weaknesses

Table 12.1 Seven common weaknesses in many social programme intervention plans

1. Many behaviour change programmes use top down approaches, and are constructed by experts and policy planners who attempt to drive the changes they desire down through populations. This approach, which is influenced by political as well as professional assessments of risk and solutions, does not always include citizen insight research into the behaviours and beliefs of the target group. The result is that often the interventions can be misunderstood or viewed as irrelevant by the people they are targeted at. This approach results in recipients filtering out or rejecting the programme.

2. Many programmes are short lived and open to constant revision. Timescales are often short-term with little baseline evidence for action and evaluation of the impact. These short-term programmes are often focused on and evaluated through an assessment of impact on agenda management rather than population behaviour.

3. Activity is often focused around developing messages and targeted media buying or developing new products, environmental design solutions, or new media interventions. This focus on activity and tactical solution generation often results in suboptimal delivery as interventions fail to meet the needs of target audiences or address causal agents of the problem in the environment.

4. Interventions are often poorly managed and lack co-ordination and integration between policy directives and interventions aimed at the same problem or target group. This can result in social programmes and campaigns that provide contradictory advice which in turn can confuse the target groups leading to inefficient and ineffective interventions.

5. Many public programmes often set either unrealistically ambitious goals that are not achievable in the short term, or fail to set clear measurable objectives.

6. There are few programmes that utilise and coordinate a full intervention mix of education, design, support services and control measures.

7. Programmes are often insufficiently funded to achieve their stated goals and objectives and budgets are set based on historical allocations or fixed allocations rather than being constructed from an analysis of the task to be achieved and what it will cost.

identified in Table 12.1 are addressed and mitigated. It should also be noted that as explored in Chapters 5 and 7 there is clearly a need to think through the total strategy associated with a social change programme aimed at influencing people's behaviour before developing and implementing specific social marketing interventions.

> The laziest thing people do is go right to tactics. You have to start with what you are trying to get done, who can get it done for you, what you have to tell them, and who has to tell them to persuade them. (Fenton Communications, 2001)

Discussion question

Why do planners and practitioners not apply systematic planning processes to many social interventions?

The characteristics of successful behavioural intervention planning

There is clearly a case, as Haglind et al. (1998) suggest, for more user friendly planning instruments for practitioners, quality assessment instruments that reflect the reality of practice, and more professional training for those responsible for developing and delivering plans. The rest of this chapter attempts to make a small contribution to tackling these three issues.

There are a number of universal underlying social intervention planning principles that have been shown to increase the likelihood of success irrespective of the social issue, target group, targeted behaviour or country context (Schorr, 2003; Klassen, 2010). These characteristics include:

- developing a long-term strategic approach based on a deep understanding of the causes of problems and how people affected by them view the issue and their recommendations about who to tackle it
- developing SMART programme objectives
- the application of a logical planning system, targeting interventions to particular audience needs
- developing strategies that address causal factors as well as reactions to them
- developing systems to evaluate and track programme success and failure.

These characteristics of effective social planning in many ways set out a counterpoint to those weaknesses of many social programmes outlined in Table 12.1.

Although specific programmes themselves cannot often be exactly replicated, evidence derived from academic and policy literature, field trials and programme evaluations demonstrates that there are a number of common characteristics that most successful programmes exhibit. Clearly programmes aimed at influencing human beliefs, attitudes and behaviour are complex in nature. While it is not possible to develop an exact formula that can be universally applied for delivering population focused behaviour programmes that will result in success every time in every situation, there is an emerging set of principles that can aid us in the development and application of interventions.

The sources of evidence about good social programme intervention planning are considerable. Many social marketing texts set out key planning elements (Kotler et al., 2002; French et al., 2010; McKenzie-Mohr and Smith, 2011; Weinreich, 2011; Lefebvre, 2013). Other sources come from reviews of good social intervention design such as Halpen (2004) and generic social programme implementation such as the Australian Public Service Commission (2007) through to specific guidance in areas such as health improvement (French and Mayo, 2006), environmental interventions (Darnton et al., 2006; McKenzie-Mohr et al., 2012) and behavioural design (New Economics Foundation, 2005; Dolan et al., 2010).

There are also a number of specific planning guides and checklists that have been developed for planning specific aspects of social marketing, such as how and when to use new media (Mays et al., 2011), engaging with corporate partners and stakeholders (Kotler and Lee, 2005), enabling community empowerment (Bracht et al., 1999), using advocacy programmes (Maylock et al., 2001), cultural change (Cabinet Office, 2008) and the use of mass media (Hornik, 2002).

A good summary of much of this planning and other social programme design considerations is encapsulated in the Medical Research Council's (2010) guidance on developing and evaluating complex interventions. This guidance sets out a number of helpful questions that planners and researchers should address when seeking to set up such programmes. In the planning and early development stages of a programme these questions include:

1. Are you clear about what you are trying to do, what outcome you are aiming for, and how you will bring about change?
2. Does your intervention have a coherent theoretical basis?
3. Have you used this theory systematically to develop the intervention?
4. Can you describe the intervention fully, so that it can be implemented properly for the purposes of your evaluation, and replicated by others?
5. Does the existing evidence, ideally collated in a systematic review, suggest that it is likely to be effective or cost effective?
6. Can it be implemented in a research setting, and is it likely to be widely implementable if the results are favourable?

The MRC paper recommends that if any of these questions cannot be fully answered there is further development work needed before projects are initiated. With regard to piloting and feasibility studies the guidance sets out six additional questions that need to be considered:

1. Have you done enough piloting and feasibility work to be confident that the intervention can be delivered as intended?
2. Can you make safe assumptions about effect sizes and variability and rates of recruitment and retention in the main evaluation study?
3. What design are you going to use, and why?
4. Is an experimental design preferable and, if so, is it feasible?
5. If a conventional parallel group randomised controlled trial is not possible, have you considered alternatives such as cluster randomisation or a stepped wedge design?
6. Have you set up procedures for monitoring delivery of the intervention and overseeing the conduct of the evaluation?

The paper also recommends that a focus on process evaluation is a good investment to explain discrepancies between expected and observed outcomes. Such evaluation will also help build understanding about how the intervention context influenced outcomes. Including an economic evaluation will likewise make the results of the evaluation much more useful for decision makers.

The National Institute of Health and Clinical Excellence (NICE, 2007) has also developed a planning guidance framework for behavioural interventions, making recommendations that cover much of the same ground as the MRC guidance. Specifically NICE sets out three core actions related to generic planning and intervention design principles:

1. Plan carefully interventions and programmes aimed at changing behaviour, taking into account the local and national context and working in partnership with recipients. Interventions and programmes should be based on a sound knowledge of community needs and should build upon the existing skills and resources within a community.
2. Equip practitioners with the necessary competencies and skills to support behaviour change, using evidence-based tools. (Education providers should ensure courses for practitioners are based on theoretically informed, evidence-based best practice.)
3. Evaluate all behaviour change interventions and programmes, either locally or as part of a larger project. Wherever possible, evaluation should include an economic component.

It is possible to add to this list of core recommendations a further common characteristic associated with effective social programme planning: the need for clarity of purpose. Programmes that seek to influence behaviour for social good require a set of clear measurable behavioural objectives that are achievable within the timescales and resource of the programme. However, as already discussed, often programmes have unrealistic or, at the opposite extreme, no clear measurable objectives identified. Objectives need to be based on thorough research about what is achievable, realistic and ethically and socially acceptable.

> A successful programme, no matter how we define it, has got to begin with very clear, realistic, measurable goals. (Fenton Communications, 2001)

Having no clear goal or picking the wrong goal is a common mistake that organisations often make. For example, an environmental programme that is seeking to influence behaviour to reduce carbon emissions by households should set specific measurable behaviours related to things such as reductions in fossil fuel used for heating and car miles driven, rather than just measure people's perception of their energy use or their general attitudes towards reducing carbon emissions. As can be seen by the Dying Matters case study below a fundamental principle for social marketing planning is that organisations need to focus on developing a set of unambiguous behavioural goals and the means of measuring outcomes as well as focusing on process activity and tracking. Clear outcome targets that accurately measure behaviour and its social impacts are an essential element of any social marketing intervention. The setting of realistic goals and SMART objectives is considered in depth later in this chapter.

CASE STUDY

Dying Matters

Dying Matters is a fully evaluated programme that was designed using a systematic social marketing plan from its inception. It is a good example of a social marketing programme that has demonstrated, via independent review, statistically significant changes in reported social behaviour and attitudes at a population level.

The Dying Matters Programme

The End of Life Care Strategy, published by the Department of Health in 2008, identified a number of significant issues affecting dying and death in England. As part of the new strategy the formation of a new national programme was agreed to promote a more open dialogue and better planning for the end of life. The Dying Matters Coalition's mission is: 'To support changing knowledge, attitudes and behaviours towards death, dying and bereavement, and through this to make "living and dying well" the norm'.

Dying Matters from the outset was designed as a social marketing initiative applying international best practice planning and evaluation criteria to both its overall strategy and subsequent campaigns. The aim was to develop a social marketing strategy on a small budget that could have a measurable impact on attitudes and behaviours in society towards dying, death and bereavement. To this end a lot of planning went into the scoping phase of the programme, to identify and quantify why people believe and act in the way that they do, which usually means putting off or simply not having conversations about what they want to happen at the end of their life. During the scoping phase reviews of the evidence literature were also conducted to ascertain if any previous interventions had been shown to have an impact in this area. Baseline data were also gathered about people's attitudes and behaviour regarding expressing their wishes about the end of life. Next as part of the development phase a segmented behavioural change strategy was developed using insight and baseline data about knowledge, attitudes, beliefs, behaviours and what

(Continued)

(Continued)

influences them. During the scoping and testing stages of the programme a set of SMART measurable key performance indicators were agreed to measure attitudinal and behaviour change among the general public and community Doctors who were identified as the primary professional audience to help. The development of a set of SMART behavioural objectives also enabled work to be undertaken at the start of the programme to develop an evaluation strategy and means of collecting robust data that could be used in the learning and action phase of the programme.

When considering the enact stage of the programme, given the small budget available for the programme – approximately £1 million over five years – it was decided based on reviews of similar social norm focused programmes that the most effective strategy to enable population level impact was to develop a large coalition of individuals and organisations from the public, NGOs and private sectors to act as champions for change. A process target was set of recruiting 15,000 members to help deliver the aims of the programme. By 2014 over 30,000 members had been recruited to promote the programme aims and objectives. The central team also developed an extensive range of teaching, learning and informational material based on field trials that help members of the public and professionals to start and continue conversations about end of life planning. This material is now being used internationally as well as across the UK. Specialist interventions have also been developed for hospitals, care homes, GPs and young people.

Table 12.2 Dying Matters behavioural impact on having a conversation about end of life wishes by age 2009–2012

	2009	2012
Dicussed...	%	%
18–34	26	23
35–44	25	28
45–54	27	33
55–64	32	39
65–74	36	35
75+	39	45
All	29	31
Weighted base	*1323*	*2149*
Unweighted base	*1350*	*2145*

Source: British Social Attitudes Survey, 2013: 9

For more information about Dying Matters Programme see: www.dyingmatters.org/.

Reflective questions

- If you were developing an intervention to encourage people to talk about what they wanted at the end of their life, what understanding would you want to develop about attitudes and beliefs?
- When setting behavioural objectives for programmes what kinds of proxy behaviours, such as more people writing wills, do you think could be developed to evaluate success?
- What challenges do you think are associated with delivering a programme via a broad coalition of multiple partner agencies?

Social marketing planning models

For many social marketers the 4Ps of marketing (product, price, place promotion) are still the bedrock of social marketing planning (Kotler and Lee, 2009; Weinreich, 2011), The 4Ps framework has some real strengths in that it presents a clear set of principles that a marketer needs to address when developing and implementing a programme. However, many leading social marketers (Peattie and Peattie, 2011; Gordon, 2012; Tapp and Spotswood, 2013) continue to question the utility and theoretical basis of this model. For a fuller discussion of the 4P model see Chapter 4.

There are a number of specifically developed social marketing operational planning frameworks and models that practitioners can either use or adapt to their own situation. One of the best know planning models is the five-stage total process planning (TPP) model (French and Blair-Stevens, 2008; French et al., 2010), which consists of five stages of planning (see Figure 12.1): scoping the problem issue, developing potential interventions and testing them, implementing the programme, evaluating it and the following up, which includes feeding learning back into subsequent rounds of delivery. This model follows a simple logical approach to planning that is commonly found in most planning approaches.

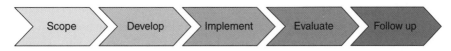

Figure 12.1   The total process planning model (TPPM)

Source: French and Blair-Stevens, 2008

The six-stage CDCynergy social marketing planning tool (2005) (see Figure 12.2) is similar in approach and stages. This model sets out six stages of planning and is accompanied by a large section of tools and reference material. In 2012 CDC produced a lite version for smaller-scale projects.

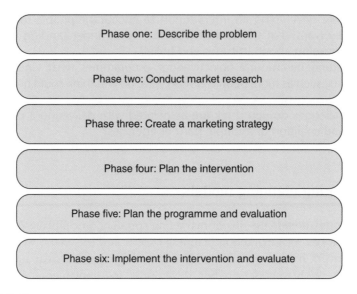

Figure 12.2   CDCynergy social marketing planning model

Source: CDC, 2005

The WHO COMBI planning model (2012) (see Figure 12.3) is another well-known and widely used planning model that is focused specifically on health issues and has been developed for application in developing world settings. Another useful eight step model called BEHAVE-based marketing plan is set out by Smith and Strand (2008).

There are numerous other models from very simple plans contained in texts such as Hastings (2007) to the ten step approach advocated by Lee and Kotler (2011). In addition to these models many specialist social marketing companies and institutions have developed their own planning models and frameworks.

Each of these planning models sets out a number of steps that proceed from analysis through development and into implementation and then evaluation. Each of these planning models also has advantages and disadvantages. Some are very simple and easy to apply, others are more comprehensive and require more effort. Key issues to consider when selecting a social marketing planning model are the scale and complexity of the behaviour you are seeking to influence. Social marketing can be applied to small-scale local projects with little or no budgets or to large-scale sustained international programmes. When a large-scale investment is being made in a social marketing programme it will require a more thorough planning approach and reporting process.

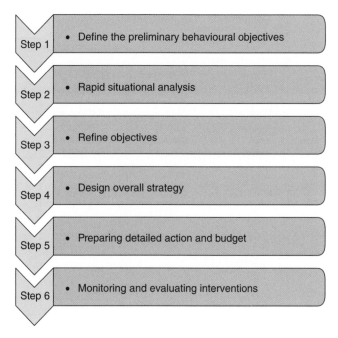

Figure 12.3 COMBI planning model steps

Source: WHO, 2012

Many of these planning models have been influenced by a planning process known as 'logical frameworks'. Log frames, as they are also often known, have their roots in military planning (Nanacholas, 1998). According to Hills (2010) the log frame approach is popular because it uses a simple visual framework with key headings to describe a logical and staged process and a set of key tasks. Log frames require practitioners to identify and describe a number of key elements of their intended intervention. These include:

- the issues being addressed and the context within which the intervention takes place
- the inputs – resources and activities – required in order to achieve intervention objectives
- outputs (e.g. in terms of target groups to be engaged, roads built, products developed)
- outcomes (i.e. short- and medium-term results, such as changes in traffic flow levels and model shifts)
- impacts (i.e. long-term results such as better quality of life, improved health, environmental benefits, etc.).

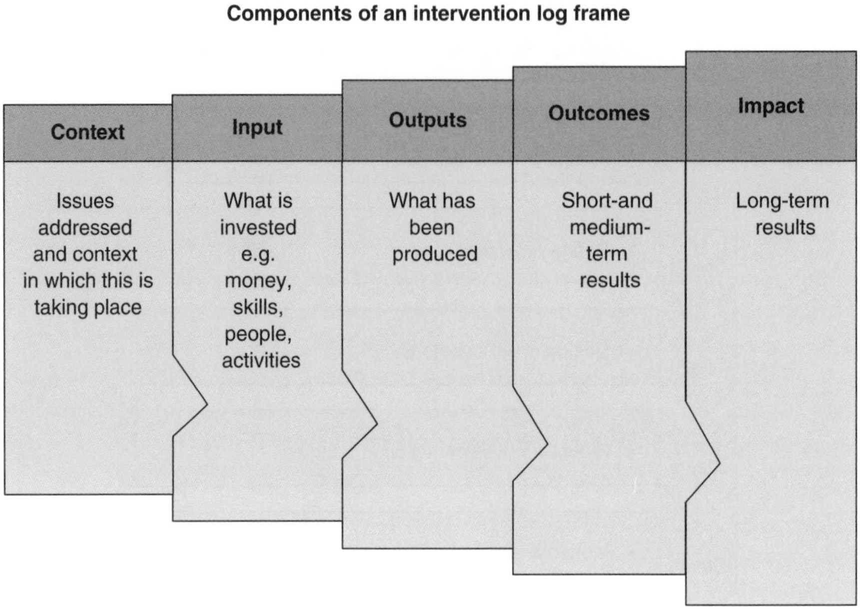

Components of an intervention log frame

Context	Input	Outputs	Outcomes	Impact
Issues addressed and context in which this is taking place	What is invested e.g. money, skills, people, activities	What has been produced	Short-and medium-term results	Long-term results

Figure 12.4 Components of an intervention log frame

Source: Rosenberg et al., 1970

As depicted in Figure 12.4 the log frame process also involves developing consensus among stakeholders about interventions, outcomes and impacts. Log frames emphasise the identification of objective verifiable indicators (OVIs) and means of verification (MOV) to ensure that what is expected to happen is tracked and reported on. As with other planning models log frames can have the danger that they are sometimes rather rigidly applied and so stifle the opportunity to react to changes in circumstances outside the programme plan.

―――――――――――――――――――― **Discussion question** ――――――――――――――

What are the main reasons that commissioners or funders of services should insist that comprehensive and transparent planning is established for social marketing interventions?

A guide to planning your own social marketing intervention

The STELa social marketing planning framework (French, 2010b), presented in Figure 12.5, will be used to illustrate the key steps and tasks that are normally required when planning a social marketing intervention. STELa is an interactive web-based planning tool that includes 129 planning tools aligned to each of its four stages and 12 tasks that can be accessed online at: www.stelamodel.com.

The principle that guided the design of the STELa planning framework was the need for a simple but robust planning framework based on best evidence about what planning tasks lead to improved programme performance. STELa was also developed as a response to the need for a planning model that can be applied by practitioners and those not trained in formal planning systems and procedures. It was also clear that practitioners needed easy access to specific planning tools to help them complete each stage and task in the planning process, so STELa was designed with a set of in-built planning tools that can be simply pulled down and used when completing each task. The online tool prompts users to use these tools. STELa was also developed following an extensive analysis of all previous social marketing planning tools and other generic planning approaches such as log frame planning. STELa also reflects the characteristics of effective planning described in meta reviews discussed earlier in this chapter.

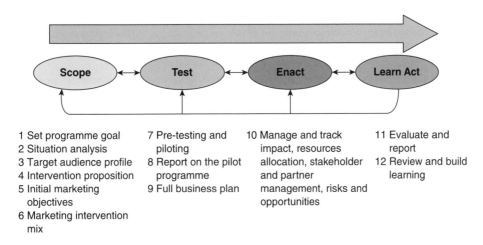

Figure 12.5 The STELa social marketing planning model

Source: French, 2010b

The 12 task areas within each of the four stages do not have to be necessarily undertaken in the sequence set out: some can be undertaken in parallel and in many cases there is a need to revise early findings in one task area in the light of subsequent learning. Some tasks can be completed by simply reviewing existing evidence or analysis that an organisation has access to. The STELa planning framework makes specific reference to a number of planning processes such as PESTLE (Political, Environmental, Social, Technological, Legal, Economic), SWOT (Strengths, Weaknesses,

Opportunities and Threats) and force field analysis (a process of applying weightings to factors that are enabling or resisting the desired social behaviour) that can help the development of social marketing interventions. Chapter 11 covers in more detail how these analytical processes can enhance both strategic and operational planning in social marketing.

Though all stages of social marketing planning are important, investing time in the *scoping* stage is particularly critical. This helps to avoid a tendency to start generating and crafting solutions before a deep understanding and insight into the citizen is achieved. It also ensures that a clear behavioural focus is identified from the start, and that relevant theory and ethical issues are considered early in the process. The understanding and insights gained during scoping are used to inform the development of working propositions about what will help bring about the desired behaviour and the selection of appropriate methods that can be taken into the testing and development stage. Table 12.3 sets out some of the key advantages that accrue if time and resources are invested in scoping.

Table 12.3   Advantages of investing in the scoping stage

- Full scoping will help ensure that subsequent resources and time invested in addressing the challenge(s) can be used to greatest potential effect.
- Scoping provides a valuable way to begin to engage and mobilise key partners and stakeholders, who (whatever interventions are selected) will be crucial to on-going work.
- Scoping provides important baseline understanding and insights on which all subsequent work can be based.
- Scoping helps to grow the evidence base by setting out a clear hypothesis and objectives that can subsequently be tested, evaluated and reported on.

The four key stages and 12 key tasks of the STELa social marketing planning framework

Stage 1: Scoping

Task 1   Set out the programme rationale and goal

- Set out why action is needed on the identified social issue, the target audience and why they have been selected. Set out the need for action, the relevant policy and organisational context and the overall strategic objectives of the intervention.

Task 2   Situation analysis

- SWOT (strengths, weaknesses, opportunities and threats) and PESTLE (Political, Environmental, Social, Technological, Legal, Economic) analysis.

- Competition analysis and force field analysis: list and assign the relevant weighting to factors influencing adoption of the behaviour including positive enabling factors and barriers to change; analyse what or who may be influencing the target audience to act in a way that is detrimental or positive and assess the relevant weight of the influence.
- Evidence and data reviews: gather information about what is known about the causes of and how to tackle the issue from published and unpublished sources, i.e. professional journals, case study reports, interviews with others who have undertaken work in the field.
- Asset mapping: the recording of all assets including social networks, community assets, environmental assets, stakeholder assets that could be used to tackle the problem.

Task 3 Target audience profile and segmentation

- Describe the primary audience, i.e. the people you are seeking to influence. Also, set out the secondary and tertiary audiences, i.e. the people who are influencing or could influence the primary audience; these can often be intermediaries such as parents.
- Data analysis, including the gathering and analysis of service uptake data, demographics, geographic data, relevant behavioural data including risk taking and protective behaviours.
- Target audience insight and understanding, developed from qualitative and quantitative target audience research such as surveys, focus groups and observational studies.
- Set out an audience segmentation model. Cluster people based on factors including understanding, attitudes, beliefs, and behaviours and risk.

Task 4 Intervention proposition

- Describe the social marketing exchange. Based on target audience insight and understanding set out how the proposed behaviour will be positioned with the target audience. In the case of a positive behaviour change, e.g. recycling, how the benefits will be maximised and costs reduced for the target audience. In the case of a problematic behaviour, e.g. driving too fast, how the costs will be maximised and the benefits reduced. In the case of non-rational choice situations, set out how the choice environment will be structured, or what policy or service transformation will be introduced.
- List the 'forms' and 'types' of intervention that will be applied and the rationale for their selection.
- Set out the level of funding that will be required to deliver the proposed intervention objectives and over what time-frame.

Task 5 Initial social marketing objectives

- Set out:
  - o cognitive objectives: measuring knowledge
  - o affective objectives: measuring beliefs and attitudes
  - o psychomotor: measuring behaviour

- Note: all objectives should be SMART: specific, measurable, achievable, relevant, time bound.

Task 6 Marketing intervention mix strategy

- Set out which combination of the five intervention 'forms' will be used – 1 Inform, 2 Educate, 3 Support, 4 Control, 5 Design – and how they will be applied. Also consider how the desired behaviour will be positioned with the target audience so that they perceive it to be of value, plausible and sustainable.
- Design and deliver the product, system, environment or services offered to assist adoption of the desired behaviour. Consider the price or cost that will be associated with adopting the behaviour and how this will be reduced. Also consider the use of incentives and disincentives. Ensure easy and convenient access is possible. Finally consider how to promote the desired behaviour in relation to the language to 'frame' the offer, the channels of communication and the 'voice' and 'face' of the promotion.

Stage 2: Testing and development of the intervention

Task 7 Pre-testing and piloting

- Agree which potential interventions to test and how to test them.
- Set aside a budget and agree a timetable and plan for the pilot phase.

Task 8 Report on the impact of the pilot programme

- Report on the immediate effect of the intervention on issues such as knowledge gain, attitude and beliefs.
- Measure the impact on short-term behaviours and systems efficiency such as the cost of generating interest in the programme and the costs of different methods of generating contact with the intervention or short-term behavioural action.

Task 9 Full social marketing implementation plan

- Set out the intended audience segmentation and SMART behavioural objectives for the programme and how these will be measured.

- Detail the anticipated impact and outcomes for the selected target audiences over a designated time-frame.
- Set out the intervention mix that will be used and how it will be coordinated and managed to achieve the agreed objectives of the programme.
- Set out the resources required from main sponsors, partners and stakeholders and how they will be deployed against the intervention and social marketing mix you have proposed.
- Set out how the budget will be allocated to achieve the agreed objectives of the intervention, tracked and reviewed.
- Set out a plan for stakeholder and partner engagement management and review.
- Detail how the programme will be managed and its governance arrangements. Set out project process milestones, e.g. when will the launch take place and when will the first review take place?

Stage 3: Enact

Task 10 Manage the implementation

- Manage and track the impact of the staff support and development plan.
- Manage and track the impact of the stakeholder and partner management plan.
- Review and manage risks associated with the project.
- Track and manage the intervention budget ensuring that there are no significant cost overruns or underspends and that the intervention is being delivered in the most cost effective way possible.
- Undertake opportunity spotting, horizon scanning and programme adjustment.
- Gather process, impact and outcome data. Record progress and setbacks, analyse and report.
- Regularly review progress against objectives using agreed data sets.
- Report to sponsors and stakeholders

Stage 4: Learn and act

Task 11 Evaluate and report

- Record learning and share findings.
- Report to sponsors, stakeholders and partners.
- Report back to target audiences.
- Report to professional audiences.

Task 12 Review and build learning into the next wave of implementation

- Feed learning and evaluation into the next wave of scoping, development, testing and implementation.

This planning checklist should assist those wishing to develop a systematically planned and delivered social marketing intervention. A fuller set of explanations, guidance notes and tools can be found in the online version of STELa or in many of the other guides referenced in this chapter.

The need for sustained and outcome focused budgeting

When investing in behaviour change programmes there is a threshold point that must be reached in terms of population awareness, attitude and action before any return on investment can be measured. In an increasingly competitive environment for attention and engagement, public programmes that aim to bring about positive social behaviour are often not funded to a sufficient level that they are able to bring about a measurable impact on their intended target audiences. Also, as discussed at the start of this chapter, insufficient levels of investment are often compounded by stop-start approaches to investment.

The amount to be invested to achieve measurable impact on behaviour in target segments is a key factor to be determined in the development phase of any planned programme. A second key consideration is the time-frame over which an investment will need to be maintained to achieve the targets of the programme. If funders are not able to commit sufficient funds over the required period they must be made aware that the impact of their more limited investment may be reduced further by a lack of perseverance. Impact over time is a key issue to be addressed when putting together a full business case for investing in behavioural change. A move towards outcome based budgeting can be aided by the adoption of what has been called the 'three step process' (French, 2010a) for budget allocation to behavioural programmes.

This model recommends that rather than allocating a fixed amount of financial resources to scope, develop, implement and evaluate a programme it is more effective if budgets are allocated in three steps:

1. First a budget should be allocated to scope an issue, to understand the problem audiences and the assets that exist or could be brought into play and the obstacles to success. The key output from this scoping phase is a report that sets out a clear statement of the problem and desired improvement, initial intervention propositions based on a review of evidence, data and market research and a costed plan for a development phase to refine the proposed interventions.
2. The second step begins on completion of a scoping stage. Based on the findings and recommendations of the scoping report commissioners should allocate a second budget for development. This phase will work up the proposals, undertake field testing and refinement, or if necessary redesign the proposed interventions so that they meet the requirements of the programmes and are acceptable to the target market and stakeholders.

3. The third stage commences after the development phase. A full business plan should be developed that will form the basis of a full and sustained funding allocation to scale up and fully implement the recommended interventions and evaluate their impact.

If this three-step approach to funding is applied by practitioners in the public sector, setting out the evidence for their recommendations, estimates of projected savings and value for money analysis, the chances of well-executed behavioural intervention can increase. Such an approach would also result in the development of a growing costed evidence base for social behavioural interventions that would inform future planning and budgetary decision making. However, the need to develop a greater focus on the design of efficient as well as cost effective programmes is not without complexity as a number of economic factors will need to be taken into account when assessing the overall economic and return on investment impact of a programme. For example, in the health field:

> There are also wider economic benefits to individuals and society, arising from reductions in the effects of passive smoking in non-smokers and savings to the health service and the employer. These wider benefits are often omitted from economic evaluations of cessation interventions, which consequently tend to underestimate the true value for money afforded by such programmes. (Parrott and Godfrey, 2004: 947)

The development of comprehensive econometric measures of social marketing programme impacts is not simple but detailed guidance has been developed (Central Office of Information, 2009) about how such evaluations can be undertaken. The issue of research, evaluation and learning are explored further in Chapters 9 and 10.

Conclusions

In summary the literature concerned with social behaviour change planning and management provides a reasonably tight consensus on the importance of the application of planning principles. The setting out of clear aims and objectives, a development phase that includes reviewing and applying relevant theory, and interrogating data about the problem, clear identification and the understanding of target audiences, piloting, pre-testing and programme refinement, and the robust management, monitoring and evaluation of programme implementation are all key elements in planning any social intervention. However, the existence of planning templates or checklists is not sufficient to ensure the delivery of effective and efficient programmes.

Other factors such as the need for appropriate leadership, well-trained and supported staff, and systems for learning and review are also important. Taken together with the planning stages and steps set out in this chapter these principles can be used to create a planning and performance culture which can lead to a more efficient and effective social marketing programme performance and ultimately better social outcomes.

It is also clear that despite there being a number of logical well-constructed planning models within the social marketing field there is a need to encourage a more comprehensive application of these models in practice. This is necessary not only for reasons of better delivery but also because it will help to improve the capture and dissemination of what does and does not work and which intervention approaches are most efficient. There also appears to be a need for more training in the use of these planning models and to develop simpler, more user friendly starter models such as STELa and CDCynergy Lite to encourage the adoption of systematic planning.

As stated at the beginning of this chapter it is not possible to develop an exact formula that can be universally applied for delivering social marketing programmes that will result in success every time. However, the following checklist has been developed to assist both funders and planners of social marketing interventions to assess the robustness of their planning efforts. The features within the list are drawn from the multiple references cited in this chapter. These features are summarised in the following planning quality assurance checklist, which can be used to test the utility and strength of social marketing planning.

Social marketing planning review checklist

1. Clear aims and measurable behavioural objectives should be set out in the programme plan together with the target audience(s) and segments that will be the focus of the intervention.
2. Programmes should set out and justify how funding and other resources will be applied and over what time period. A clear expected return on investment case should be set out to justify the level of planned investment.
3. The programme should be endorsed by policy makers, commissioners and managers and deliverers of the programme. The programme plan should set out the political, policy, managerial and institutional commitment to the programme.
4. The programme team should capture what evidence exists about effective practice from reviews, case studies and observational data. Target audience demographic, behavioural, risk and psychographic data should be gathered and analysed to formulate insights and interventions.
5. The programme plan should set out a clear rationale for the types of intervention selected for the programme and why the particular mix of interventions has been selected. The programme plan should also indicate the theoretical perspectives and models that have been used to inform planning which are congruent with the form, focus and context of the intervention.
6. The programme plan should demonstrate that the target group(s) will be involved in needs assessment, target setting and strategy development.

The plan should also demonstrate how target groups will be engaged in the delivery and evaluation of the programme.

7. The programme plan should set out how prototype interventions or pilots will be tested and used to develop full-scale programmes.

8. The plan should set out how the programme will be funded to the level required to achieve agreed levels of impact and how it will be sustained over the recommended timescale for delivery. Plans should also set out key process checking mechanisms that should include an assessment of the short-term impact, quality measures and ethical practice.

9. Programme plans should set out how coalitions, stakeholders, partners and interest groups will be engaged over the lifetime of the intervention. The plan should also set out the mechanism for coordinated action between international, national, regional and local delivery, and how decision making, governance and coordination of the programme will operate.

10. Key barriers and enabling factors and other risks should be identified in the programme plan together with what actions will be taken to address these factors.

11. Evaluation, performance management, learning and feedback mechanisms should be clear in the programme plan. Evaluation should encompass short-term impact measures, process measures of efficiency and quality and outcome evaluation related to the specific behavioural and social outcome objectives of the programme.

12. All programme plans should be recorded and published, and the plan should be based on an established and logical planning template.

The focus of this chapter has been on setting out the rationale and key features of operational social marketing planning. There is no one correct way to plan a social marketing intervention, therefore practitioners will need to consider which model or approach to adopt. There is now thankfully a variety of social marketing planning models for the practitioner to select from. Regardless of the model adopted there should always be a written plan that is capable of being interrogated by those who are the recipients of an intervention, those delivering the intervention and those sponsoring it. Readers have been introduced to a number of possible planning models and some of the key reasons why planning is an essential element of social marketing.

We have introduced the simple four step STELa approach to social marketing planning and set out a number of recommended sub-steps under each of these four main stages that practitioners can use to guide their planning. We have suggested a three step process for allocating budgets to social marketing programmes. We have also set out a 12-point checklist of features of effective programme planning that can be used by both practitioners and sponsors of programmes to assess the quality of the planning process being used. The more these features are included in the development and execution of a social marketing programme, the more likely it will be that the intervention is both efficient and effective.

Reflective questions

- Make a list of at least six features that should be included in any behaviour change programme plan.
- List at least three reasons why scoping is a key stage in social marketing planning.
- Describe some of the key tasks associated with managing a social marketing project.
- Using the 12-point checklist set out in this chapter make an assessment about how many of the characteristics of effective planning are evident in a social marketing project you are familiar with.

Further reading

Andreasen, A.R. (1991) *Marketing Social Change: Changing Behaviour to Promote Health, Social Development, and the Environment*. San Francisco: Jossey-Bass.
Central Office of Information (2009) *Communications and Behavior Change*. London: COI/ Government Communication Network.

References

Australian Public Service Commission (2007) *Changing Behaviour: A Public Policy Perspective*. Canberra: Australian Government. Available at: www.apsc.gov.au/publications-and-media/ archive/publications-archive/changing-behaviour (last accessed 18 November 2014).
Bracht, N., Kingsbury, L. and Rissel, C. (1999) 'A five stage community organisation model for health promotion', in N. Bracht (ed.), *Health Promotion at the Community Level: New Advances*. Thousand Oaks, CA: SAGE, pp. 83–118.
Cabinet Office (2008) *Cultural Change: A Policy Framework*. London: Cabinet Office.
CDC (Centers for Disease Control) (2005) *CDCynegy planning tool for social marketing*. Atlanta, GA: Centres for Disease Control.
Central Office of Information (2009) *Payback and Return on Marketing Investment (ROMI) in the Public Sector*. London: GNC.
Darnton, A., Elster-Jones, K., Lucas, B. and Brooks, M. (2006) *Promoting Pro-environmental Behaviour: Existing Evidence to Inform Better Policy Making*, Chapter 1: Theory. London: Defra.
Dolan, P., Hallsworth, M., Halpern, D., Kind, D. and Vlaev, I. (2010) *Mindspace: Influencing Behaviour through Public Policy*. Full Report Cabinet Office. London: Institute for Government.
Donovan, R. and Henley, N. (2003) *Social Marketing: Principles and Practice*. Melbourne: IP Communications.

Fenton Communications (2001) *Now Hear This*. Washington, DC: Fenton Communications. Sponsored by the David and Lucile Packard Foundation.

French, J. (2010a) 'Commissioning social marketing', in J. French, C. Blair-Stevens, D. McVey and R. Merritt (eds), *Social Marketing and Public Health: Theory and Practice*. Oxford: Oxford University Press, pp. 123–138.

French, J. (2010b) *STELa Social Marketing Planning Model*. Available at: http://stelamodel.com/ (last accessed 20 November 2014).

French, J. and Blair-Stevens, C. (2008) *The Total Process Planning Framework for Social Marketing*. London: National Social Marketing Centre.

French, J., Blair-Stevens, C., McVey, D. and Merritt, R. (eds) (2010) *Social Marketing and Public Health: Theory and Practice*. Oxford: Oxford University Press.

French, J. and Mayo, E. (2006) *It's Our Health! National Review of Social Marketing Strategy*. London: National Consumer Council.

Godin, G., Gagnon, H., Alary, M., Levy, J. and Otis, J. (2007) 'The degree of planning: an indicator of the potential success of health education programmes', *Programmes and Education*, 14 (3): 138.

Gordon, R. (2012) 'Re-thinking and re-tooling the social marketing mix', *Australasian Marketing Journal*, 20 (2): 122–126.

Green, J. and Tones, K. (2010) *Health Promotion: Planning and Strategies*. London: SAGE.

Haglind, B., Jansson, B., Petterson, B. and Tillgren, P. (1998) 'A quality assurance instrument for practitioners', in J. Davis and G. MacDonald (eds), *Quality, Evidence and Effectiveness in Health Promotion: Striving for Certainties*. Thousand Oaks, CA: SAGE, pp. 93–116.

Halpen D. (2004) *Personal Responsibility and Changing Behaviour: The State of Knowledge and its Implications for Public Policy*. London: Prime Minister's Strategy Unit.

Hastings, G. (2007) *Social Marketing: Why Should the Devil Have All the Best Tunes?* London: Butterworth-Heinemann.

Hills, D. (2010) *Logic Planning Hints and Tips*. London: Tavistock Institute.

Hornik, R. (2002) *Public Health Communication: Evidence for Behaviour Change*. Mahwah, NJ: Lawrence Erlbaum Associates.

Klassen A. (2010) 'Performance measurement and improvement framework in health, education and social services: a systematic review', *International Journal for Quality of Health Care*, 22 (1): 44–69.

Kotler, P. and Lee, N. (2005) *Corporate Social Responsibility: Doing the Most Good for Your Company and Your Cause*. Hoboken, NJ: John Wiley.

Kotler, P. and Lee, N. (2009) *Up and Out of Poverty: The Social Marketing Solution*. Upper Saddle River, NJ: Prentice Hall.

Kotler, P., Roberto, W. and Lee, N. (2002) *Social Marketing: Improving the Quality of Life* (2nd edn). New York: SAGE.

Lee, N. and Kotler P. (2011) *Social Marketing: Influencing Behaviours for Good*. New York: SAGE.

Lefebvre, R.C. (2013) *Social Marketing and Social Change*. San Francisco, CA: Jossey-Bass.

Maylock, B., Howat, P. and Slevin, T. (2001) 'A decision making model for health promotion advocacy', *Promotion and Education*, 8 (2): 59–64.

Mays, D., Weaver, J.B. and Rernhart, J.M. (2011) 'New media in social marketing', in G. Hastings, K. Angus and C. Bryant (eds), *The SAGE Handbook of Social Marketing*. London: SAGE, pp. 178–190.

McKenzie-Mohr, D., Lee, N., Wesley Schultz, P. and Kotler, P. (2012) *Social Marketing to Protect the Environment: What Works*. Thousand Oaks, CA: SAGE.

McKenzie-Mohr, D. and Smith, W. (2011) *Fostering Sustainable Behavior: An Introduction to Community-based Social Marketing* (3rd edn). Gabriola Island, Canada: New Society Publishers.

Medical Research Council (2010) *Developing and Evaluating Complex Interventions: New Guidance*. Available at: www.mrc.ac.uk/complexinterventionsguidance (last accessed 20 November 2014).

Nanacholas, S. (1998) 'How to do (or not do) a logic framework', *Health Policy and Planning*, 12 (2): 189–193.

New Economics Foundation (2005) *Behavioural Economics: Seven Principles for Policy-makers*. London: New Economics Foundation.

NICE (National Institute for Health and Clinical Excellence) (2007) *Behaviour Change at Population, Community and Individual Levels: Reference Guide*. London: NICE.

Parrott, S. and Godfrey, C. (2004) 'Economics of smoking cessation', *British Medical Journal*, 328 (7445): 947–949.

Peattie, K. and Peattie, S. (2011) 'The social marketing mix: a critical review', in G. Hastings, K. Angus and C. Bryant (eds), *The SAGE Handbook of Social Marketing*. London: SAGE, pp. 152–166.

Rosenberg, L., Posner, L. and Hanley, J. (1970) *Final Report. Project Evaluation and the Project Appraisal Reporting System. Vol. One Summary*. Agency for International Development by Fry Consultants Incorporated.

Schorr, L.B. (2003) *Determining 'What Works' in Social Programs and Social Policies: Towards a More Inclusive Knowledge Base*. Harvard: The Brookings Institution.

Smith, W. and Strand, J. (2009) *Social Marketing and Behaviour*. Washington, DC: AED.

Tapp, A. and Spotswood, F. (2013) 'From the 4Ps to COM-SM: reconfiguring the social marketing mix', *Journal of Social Marketing*, 3 (3): 206–222.

Weinreich, N. (2011) *Hands-on Social Marketing. A Step-by-Step Guide to Designing Change for Good* (2nd edn). Thousand Oaks, CA: SAGE.

WHO (2012) *Communication for Behavioural Impact (COMBI): A Toolkit for Behavioural and Social Communication in Outbreak Response*. Geneva: WHO. Available at: www.who.int/ihr/publications/combi_toolkit_fieldwkbk_outbreaks/en/ (last accessed 9 December 2014).

13 EMBEDDING SOCIAL MARKETING WITHIN SOCIAL PROGRAMMES

Learning objectives

By the end of this chapter, readers should be able to:

- understand the key motivations of policy makers and senior strategists and how this understanding can be used to develop a compelling case to embed marketing into social programme design
- understand the importance of undertaking organisational analysis prior to developing plans to embed social marketing into a social programme strategy
- set out the four key stages of embedding marketing into an organisational strategy and list tactics that will facilitate this
- explain the strengths and weaknesses of differing organisational options for positioning marketing expertise within social programmes.

Introduction

In the Foreword to this book and in Chapter 1 the case was made that marketing in the form of social marketing has a strong and currently under-utilised capacity to increase the efficiency and effectiveness of most social programmes. In Chapter 2 we explored the fundamental nature of marketing's contribution to both commercial and social programmes and in Chapter 5 we described how strategic marketing can enhance the selection, development and implementation of all social programmes.

In this chapter we will explore how we can ensure that marketing is incorporated into organisations that plan and deliver interventions that seek to deliver social good. We will also explore which processes and tactics can be used to convince policy and decision makers that social marketing should be seen as an essential function within their organisations. In this chapter we make a distinction between policy makers (i.e. those who formulate policy) and decision makers (i.e. those who decide whether formulated policies should be implemented). In some contexts these may be the same person, but in most government contexts the policy maker may be a civil servant or local government officer, while the decision maker may be a minister or elected member (or a group of ministers or elected members – e.g. cabinet, parliament or local council). We will also explore in this chapter how to position marketing as a function of social policy development and implementation. Finally we will examine how the influence of marketing insights and principles can be sustained in organisations over time.

The need to promote the strategic use of social marketing in all social programmes

We know that many social programmes are developed without the benefit of the insights and rigour that a social marketing approach can contribute. This suggests that many policy makers and decision makers are not aware of, or do not understand, how marketing can help them; or that they reject its application.

A key challenge for social marketers is ensuring that the benefits and costs of adopting a social marketing approach are fully understood by politicians and public officials. This is not just a matter of selling the empirical evidence of the effectiveness of social marketing because, as we explored in Chapter 11, policy and strategy are not formed purely on the basis of evidence.

The real challenge is understanding what policy makers and strategists need in terms of both political acceptability and policy success. The next challenge is to then develop a narrative that helps policy makers see the value to them and the value for target audiences in applying social marketing. The start of this process can involve a challenge to the status quo. In Table 13.1 five key benefits of applying social marketing are set out that, if brought to the attention of policy and decision makers, may help them consider applying social marketing in the development and implementation of social programmes.

Table 13.1 Key added value associated with applying social marketing principles in social policy selection and development and programme planning

1. Better reflect the needs and wants of citizens in policy selection and intervention delivery.
2. Establish clear and measurable behavioural objectives.
3. Reduce sub-optimal ROI and VFM of existing policy and interventions.
4. Increase investment on interventions that demonstrate good ROI and VFM.
5. Increase learning about what works, and which interventions are efficient and are supported by publics.

These five ways of adding value by applying social marketing can all be used to make the case for social marketing's contribution to both policy making and strategy development. Most politicians operating in liberal free market economies with developed democratic structures and institutions are especially interested in the last of these benefits. Technical professional advisors to politicians such as scientists, educators, medics and subject specialist will be interested in tackling the first three challenges, as many of them will wish to be operating in an evidence informed way and are constantly pressed by politicians to develop policy and interventions that not only work but are also good value for money. How each of these challenges is framed and presented will vary depending on the organisational culture and individual preferences in specific situations. The key value of using social marketing to inform social interventions that address the economic, environmental and social drivers of behaviour, as well as influencing individual behaviour, also sits at the heart of what we call 'strategic social marketing'. These issues are explored more fully in Chapters 3 and 5.

CASE STUDY

Developing a national strategy for social marketing in England

The first country in the world to develop a national social marketing strategy was England in 2008. The strategy was developed and published following a commitment to undertake a national review of social marketing set out in the UK government's health strategy called 'Choosing health' published in 2004. A review team under the leadership of Professor Jeff French was established at the National Consumer Council by the UK government to undertake the review and bring forward recommendations. The National Consumer Council was a government funded NGO responsible for providing advice on making public

(Continued)

(Continued)

service and private sector firms more responsive to public needs. The reason for establishing an independent review by a body outside of government was to prevent vested interests from standing in the way of the production of the guidance.

The review team undertook extensive research involving seven separate research projects looking at best practice in the UK and internationally. Reviews of the effectiveness of social marketing were also commissioned and extensive assessments of current approaches to influencing health behaviour were completed as part of these.

The review recommendations were published in a 2005 report called *It's Our Health!* (French and Mayo, 2005). The report's main conclusion was that there was ample evidence and experience to demonstrate the added value of embedding social marketing principles into the design and implementation of all future efforts to influence social good, not just in the health sector but also across all government policy. In total, the report contained 38 main recommendations about how to reconfigure services and embed social marketing. Two of the key recommendations of the report were to develop a national government strategy for social marketing to guide all future practice and investment and to establish a national social marketing centre to capture and promote good practice.

The National Social Marketing Centre was opened by the Public Health Minister Caroline Flint in June 2006. The first full national social marketing strategy was called 'Ambitions for Health' and was published in 2008, setting out why and how social marketing should be an integral part of all government strategy. In 2009 a national set of occupational standards for social marketing was agreed by the government and a national archive of social marketing case studies was launched. A second updated and expanded version of the social marketing strategy was published by the new coalition government in 2011 called 'Changing Behaviour Improving Outcomes'. This was a significant act as often when a new government takes office old policy is ended.

From 2005 onwards there has been a significant expansion in the academic base of social marketing in the UK to respond to the demand for education and training as a result of the national strategy. There has also been a growth in private companies offering specialist social marketing services, a mass government funded training programme for public workers in the basics of social marketing, the establishment of a Chartered Institute of Marketing special interest group for social marketing with over a 1000 members, and a series of regular conferences and seminars. More importantly, however, is the acceptance across all government departments and agencies that social marketing is a valuable addition to their toolbox for both policy formulation and delivery.

Building a compelling case for social marketing with policy and decision makers

The value associated with adopting social marketing as a standard approach for policy making needs to be considered when seeking to persuade politicians and senior public officials to adopt social marketing. It is well known (Lindblom and Woodhouse, 1993) that politicians develop policy in response to a number of factors. Some of these factors are rational and others include ideological beliefs, and emotional and moral reactions to social threats or change. To persuade politicians and those that advise on policy development it is necessary to recognise and seek to influence both rational and non-rational influences on decision making just as is the case when seeking to influence any target group.

Rational factors include an analysis of both the costs and benefits associated with the adoption of social marketing. The costs for policy makers are focused on the probable need to invest more time and resources in planning, pilot testing, research and gathering users' views. There are also time costs associated with the need to synthesise different forms of evidence and influence, and develop and test plausible interventions. One of the real political costs is a resulting possible delay in being able to deliver high-profile visible action, often in the form of a social advertising programme, if this is not supported by the evidence about what will work. The clarity or intention and a thorough review of the evidence also mean that social marketing informed and structured programmes are explicit about what they aim to achieve. While this is a benefit to programmes it also has potentially significant political and institutional costs. If a social marketing approach is applied it will be possible to judge if a policy and its associated interventions have worked or not and how efficient they have been in achieving their objectives. If programmes are evaluated and they fail or are very inefficient this can be politically damaging for the people who instigated the intervention; for politicians negative results may have a price in terms of the potential to be elected, or for officials in government the chance to be promoted.

On the benefits side of the 'exchange', politicians and policy officials get a more defendable programme of action because it is based on sound evidence and in addition support from the intended audience. The benefit of developing a programme of action more likely to be effective and one that, due to its explicit measurable objectives, can be used to inform the development of future interventions (notwithstanding the potential costs outlined above) is an attractive proposition to many politicians. Politicians and planners also get a programme of action that is fit for purpose and that can be tested for its utility because it has clear aims and measurable behavioural objectives, as well as known input costs and outcome measures. Through a process of rigorous evaluation and cost–benefit analysis, even if programmes are not 100 per cent effective or efficient, they will have still been valuable because they can add to our knowledge about what works and what it costs. The accumulation of this kind of knowledge through the development of a performance culture in the not-for-profit sector is highly praised by many commentators (Cabinet Office, 2009; Central Office of Information, 2009; Haynes et al., 2013).

―――――――――――― **Discussion question** ――――――――――――

Who in your organisation needs to be persuaded about the merits of adopting social marketing at both a policy level and as part of a strategy?

There are at least five key benefits that can be used to frame the four propositions set out in Figure 13.1, and these benefits are presented side by side with costs that need to be accepted by policy makers and strategists.

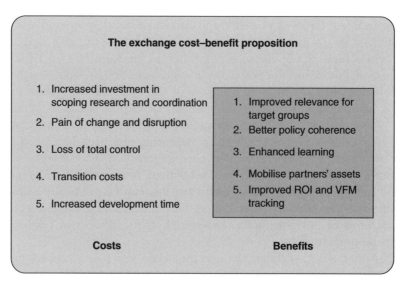

The exchange cost–benefit proposition

1. Increased investment in scoping research and coordination

2. Pain of change and disruption

3. Loss of total control

4. Transition costs

5. Increased development time

Costs

1. Improved relevance for target groups
2. Better policy coherence
3. Enhanced learning
4. Mobilise partners' assets
5. Improved ROI and VFM tracking

Benefits

Figure 13.1   The exchange cost–benefit proposition

Politicians and public officials are interested not only in efficiency and effectiveness but also in generating popular support for their programmes. Many governments, NGOs and other organisations are attempting to bring about a fundamental shift in the business model of not-for-profit service providers. We need to move beyond an approach where solutions are derived principally by policy analysts working with subject experts utilising limited forms of evidence and data. We need a model that is also influenced by a deep contextual understanding about what target audiences know, believe, value and say will help them. Such a model has political benefits that many politicians can relate to as most politicians seek to serve the public and improve society and want to be responsive to the expressed needs of citizens.

The benefits of setting out clear aims and objectives from a political perspective are related to politicians' ability to demonstrate that the policies they instigate are coordinated, have clear aims and objectives and are being evaluated to determine if they are good value for money, and the size of the impact they are having in relation to the aspect of social wellbeing they are directed at.

Governments and other not-for-profit agencies also want to ensure that there is optimum use of resources invested in social improvement programmes. Governments are increasingly incorporating evaluation metrics that focus on efficiency, effectiveness and value for money. The costs of additional planning time and the need for investment in data gathering, competition analysis and programme planning can be positioned as worthwhile as they will lead to more transparent evaluations and assessments of impact (Moor, 1995).

This increased focus on the measurable return on investment is a feature that many governments and other organisations trying to bring about change will value. Social marketing can also be attractive to governments because of its emphasis on developing deep customer insight, and population segmentation enabling governments to develop interventions that can respond to a broad diversity of needs and target specific subgroups, often those with the most need (Prime Minister's Strategy Unit, 2006). Ultimately social marketing is focused on delivering improved wellbeing, happiness and equity by assisting in the selection and delivery of interventions that are valued by citizens, and are deliverable and sustainable given the social resources and competencies that are available.

At a time when civic institutions face a host of complex 'wicked' problems (Australian Public Service Commission, 2007), many of which have considerable behavioural components, social marketing can also be positioned as a systematic and proven approach for tackling the key behavioural challenges faced by many governments. Social marketing also offers a methodology that embraces the reality of markets, choice and mutual responsibility. It offers a way to select, plan and deliver interventions that reflect the rights and responsibilities of individuals and the rights and responsibilities of wider society through the exercise of choice, and the development of meaningful appeals, incentives and penalties to behave in a way that maximises personal advantage and the wellbeing of others. Social marketing also emphasises the mobilisation of cross-sector cooperation and partnership delivery, which is also attractive to politicians and social planners. Partnership and stakeholder analysis and management together with competition analysis and strategy are features of social marketing that will be welcomed by policy makers and strategy development staff, especially in times of financial restraint.

--------------------------------- **Discussion question** ---------------------------------

If you were seeking to persuade the senior staff in the organisation where you work, or that you know of, about the reasons why they should apply social marketing, what arguments would you use?

There are now some good examples from around the world of how to get social marketing taken seriously by policy makers and decision makers based on a process of demonstrating how social marketing principles can add value to social programme development, implementation and evaluation. The experience pioneered by Mintz (2005) in Canada to embed social marketing principles into Health Canada, the development of a national social marketing strategy in the UK (French and Mayo, 2005), the inclusion of social marketing standards within the American Healthy People 2020 strategy (US Department of Health and Human Services, 2010), the inclusion of social marketing as a core principle in the French EPODE programme (Borys et al., 2011) and the Netherlands JOGG programme (Leenaars et al., 2013), and the inclusion of social marketing in the new WHO Europe Health 2020 programme (WHO, 2012) are all good examples of social marketing being successfully embedded in the strategy of social programmes.

French (2014) has described three key lessons that can be identified and applied when seeking to embed social marketing as an integral part of all social programmes:

1. *Understand what matters to your policy and strategist customer*: in this case, the customers are those who control the policy and strategy making procedure, and those who will be responsible for programme delivery. There is a need to be precise about what these customers care about. Politicians in most countries want to do a good job and be recognised for it so that they, or their party, will be re-elected. Most senior policy makers and planners are focused on these two issues but are also often driven by performance management systems and care about efficacy and effectiveness, as well as public perception (Gordon, 2013). The needs of delivery-level staff also need to be considered as they often influence policy makers and decision makers about new interventions or approaches. These staff are often concerned about the fit of any new intervention with existing practice and their capacity and capability to deliver. They also often want to be engaged in the intervention development process. Andreasen's (2006) benefits, costs, others and self-assurance (BCOS) model can also be a useful starting point for a fuller analysis of these kinds of potential motivating forces.

2. *Build compelling stories and keep promoting them*: this involves creating a narrative that policy makers, decision makers and professionals understand and value. They should also be able to use the narrative to persuade peers and others. For example, one of the most effective ways that was discovered in the UK to get a government minister to become a champion for social marketing was to get a local social marketing project to invite them to come and see the project at work in a community.

This was incredibly effective in getting ministers to appreciate the principles and impact of social marketing and increased their desire to promote its uptake. This experience also gave ministers a story that they could tell others. It is important to keep refreshing and repeating the positive narrative with new examples, until it becomes part of the everyday language of the key advocates.

3. *Build a set of required standardised processes*: one of the best ways to ensure the continued application of social marketing is to develop a set of systems that require its principles to be applied. These systems can range from budgetary systems that require applicants to show that they are applying the principles before budgets are allocated, through to national training programmes, sets of auditable professional standards and guidance on issues such as segmentation, planning and evaluation. Examples of such systems are the National Occupational Standards for social marketing in the UK (National Occupational Standards, 2014) and the Healthy People 2020 social marketing competency programme targets in the USA (US Department of Health and Human Services, 2010). The uptake and use of quality standards are something that policy makers, decision makers and professional associations can be asked to champion. For example, the International Social Marketing Association is currently developing a set of global standards for social marketing practice.

The only way to persuade policy makers, decision makers and professionals is to convince them that social marketing can help them solve the challenges they face. Social marketing should not be presented as a magical new and additional set of solutions that policy makers and practitioners need to accept if they are to create more effective and efficient social programmes. Rather, social marketing needs to be positioned as an enabler that senior managers, politicians and practitioners can use to help them solve their problems. This means it is often not necessary or even helpful to be dogmatic about use of the phrase 'social marketing'. Use language that resonates with the target audience. If the terms behavioural science, behavioural change, behavioural influence or something similar work better, use them rather than being fixated on gaining acceptance of the language of social marketing.

Segmenting policy and decision makers

A sound approach to take when developing a plan to market social marketing to policy and decision makers is to segment those to be influenced in relation to both their power of influence and their level of support or opposition to the use of social marketing to inform the policy and strategy.

Experience in the UK in the development of a National Social Marketing Strategy (Department of Health, 2008; 2011) showed that there were four basic sub-groups or segments of public officials and politicians in terms of their attitudes and beliefs with regard to social marketing (French, 2013). These four groups are illustrated in Figure 13.2.

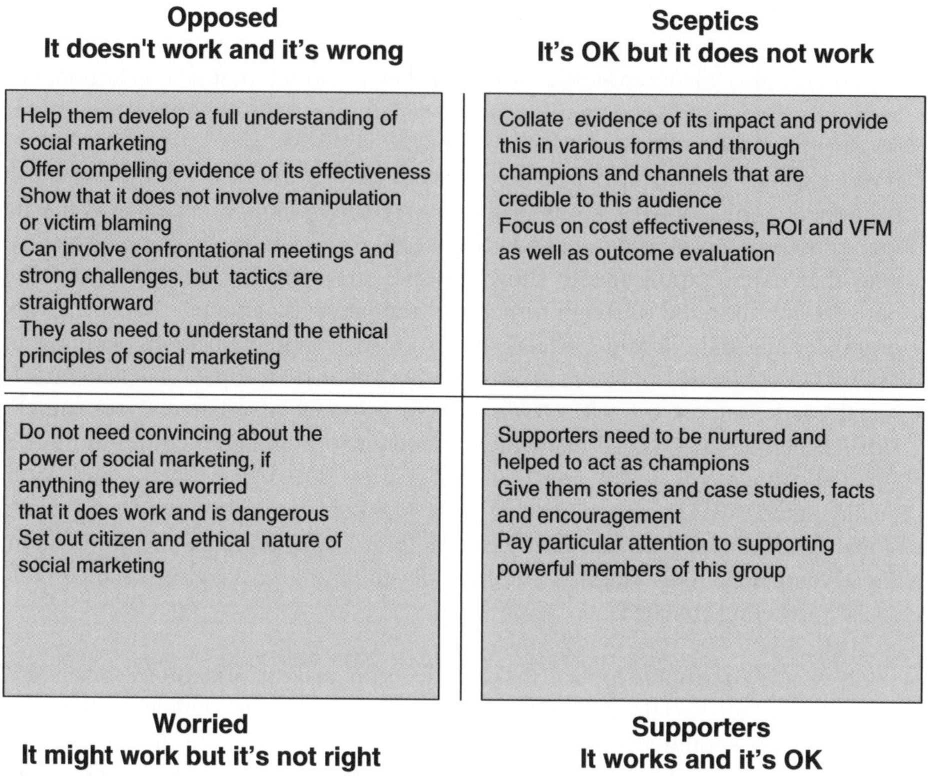

Opposed
It doesn't work and it's wrong

Help them develop a full understanding of
social marketing
Offer compelling evidence of its effectiveness
Show that it does not involve manipulation
or victim blaming
Can involve confrontational meetings and
strong challenges, but tactics are
straightforward
They also need to understand the ethical
principles of social marketing

Sceptics
It's OK but it does not work

Collate evidence of its impact and provide
this in various forms and through
champions and channels that are
credible to this audience
Focus on cost effectiveness, ROI and VFM
as well as outcome evaluation

Do not need convincing about the
power of social marketing, if
anything they are worried
that it does work and is dangerous
Set out citizen and ethical nature of
social marketing

Supporters need to be nurtured and
helped to act as champions
Give them stories and case studies, facts
and encouragement
Pay particular attention to supporting
powerful members of this group

Worried
It might work but it's not right

Supporters
It works and it's OK

Figure 13.2 Different strategies and tactics required to influence policy and decision makers

The *opposed* group needs compelling evidence that social marketing can help tackle social issues and convincing that it does not involve the manipulation of people or placing undue responsibility on individuals for what some of this group perceive to be political economic drivers to social problems. Convincing this group of the merits of social marketing can also involve confrontational meetings and strong challenges to existing ways of working if they are not supported by evidence, insight data and evaluation results that demonstrate existing practice is working. This group needs to be helped to understand that social marketing's principles are based on a deeply respectful relationship with the target audience and ethical principles that are opposed to manipulation. This group also needs to understand that social marketing is not just slick media advertising and emotional appeals that work on people's vulnerabilities.

This set of tactics is also the principle means of convincing the *sceptics* group; however, this group will also need to be convinced of the practical utility of social marketing. The sceptics group should be provided with evidence to convince them that social marketing is a good investment in terms of both its effectiveness and efficiency. This means collating and synthesising evidence about the short and longer term impact of social marketing on measurable behavioural change and providing it in forms and through channels that are credible to this audience such as professional peer reviewed journals, presentations at conferences, and having independent academic institutions review and synthesise evidence reviews. This group will also be concerned with programme efficiency, therefore studies focused on proving the relative ROI and VFM associated with applying a social marketing approach should also be used to develop their support or at least lower their resistance.

The *worried* group does not need convincing about the power of social marketing, if anything they are worried that it does work and therefore is dangerous. This danger comes in two forms. The first form of concern is focused on the potential negative connotations of manipulating citizens to behave in ways that bypass their critical cognitive decision making. Here the worry is that social marketing, like propaganda and other forms of manipulation, results in people doing things that, if they rationally considered them, they would not want to do. A more negative form of worry is that social marketing might actually empower citizens and communities and increase their voice and ability to inform social policy, thus challenging the existing elite-dominated social policy selection and development process.

For the worried group there is a need to convince them about the ethical basis of social marketing practice and that, while it does seek to influence behaviour, it does so with reference to a rigorous set of ethical principles and is informed by insights from professional and target audiences about what are considered to be reasonable 'forms' and 'types' of interventions and trade-offs between social value creation and potential costs such as the curtailment of some freedoms – for example the enforcement of car speed restrictions in urban areas. One practical solution to addressing the concerns of the worried group is to develop and publish sets of national and local ethical guidance and codes of conduct for social marketing (Eagle, 2009). This is a good way to convince this group that safeguards against questionable forms of intervention are in place.

The *supporters* group is in many ways the most important group and needs particular effort rather than just leaving them because they are already on your side. This group of politicians and public officials can be supported to promote the uptake of social marketing with others. This group needs to be nurtured and connected together to form a self-supporting group of advocates. Putting this group in touch with each other through seminars, conferences and briefings can help to build a sense of momentum and a community of interest that can have powerful effects on the policy making machine. This group can also help to normalise the language of social marketing and get it considered as a possible element in new policy making and strategy development. This group can also be influenced by other more subtle channels such as local party caucuses, attending and feeding in ideas to policy writing groups and working parties, attending committees, developing briefings for professional organisations and attending network events.

All of these four groups can be further subdivided by the amount of influence they have and how easy or difficult it might be to influence them. Just like in any social marketing plan, a detailed segmentation should be constructed and tailored interventions should be developed and implemented to influence each group's beliefs and behaviours. It is also a good idea to set out some specific objectives to be achieved with each of these groups and key individuals within them. Some clear measurable metrics such as how often the principles of social marketing are used in speeches and policy documents can help track progress.

Table 13.2 Influencing governments about the power of social marketing: a checklist of possible actions

1. Scan for and respond to policy proposals and strategies that are put out for consultation and could benefit from the application of social marketing.
2. Inform politicians and public officials about the positive effects of social marketing by running seminars, conferences, debates and workshops and producing briefing packs.
3. Arrange for social marketing experts and people who have led successful social marketing programmes to speak at events for politicians and senior public officials.
4. Provide summaries of evidence for the impact of social marketing.
5. Encourage social marketing practitioners at a local and regional level to communicate with their elected officials and senior public servants about social marketing.
6. Work with special interest groups, such as charities who are interested in social marketing or are already applying it, to influence politicians and public officials.
7. Work with public policy research institutions, academic institutions and policy think tanks on joint papers or joint events to promote the benefits of applying social marketing in the policy arena.
8. Brief and offer training to public officials and professional associations in the application of social marketing.
9. Approach the business community and trade federations and coalitions, and seek areas of potential collaboration.

There are many ways to lobby and influence politicians and public officials. For example, interventions such as writing to elected officials about how policies might be improved by the application of social marketing, or making personal contact with the editors of relevant TV, radio, newspapers and magazines. Or appearing at hearings and committees and other public functions where policy is debated and making points about the relevance of and need for the application of social marketing to the issue being considered. The proactive development of policy papers and discussion papers about how social marketing can help tackle behavioural challenges or public service reform is also a useful tactic. French (2013) has set out a number of additional tactic for influencing policy and decision makers to embrace social marketing (see Table 13.2).

A four stage process to embedding social marketing in social policy and strategy

Those who lead social policy development and strategy formulation and the social marketers who assist them will need to undertake an organisational diagnostic on how marketing orientated the current organisation is before seeking to develop a plan to embed social marketing. Figure 13.3 sets out four stages of this assessment and development process.

The first stage is focused on developing a clear picture of just how user-centric (or not) the organisation or team is, and, if necessary, creating a new vision of what needs to be done. This stage needs to involve a great deal of dialogue with all stakeholders and the gathering of information about existing systems to understand end users' needs, wants and motivations and how services currently respond and track the target audience response to interventions.

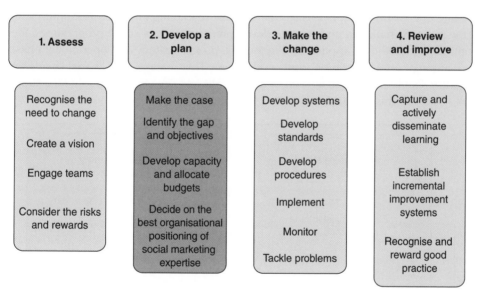

Figure 13.3 Four-step model for embedding social marketing

The second stage of the embedding process is focused on developing a clear plan about how to move the organisation to a more citizen centric marketing culture and develop a set of systems to ensure that marketing principles are factored into policy development and strategy formulation. This stage needs to be characterised by the engagement and involvement of all stakeholders in developing the new approach if the rejection and sabotage of efforts are to be avoided.

One of the key structural issues to consider in stage two is where social marketing expertise is positioned within organisational, managerial and reporting structures. There are several options, including:

1. The establishment of a discrete social marketing function to advise on policy strategy and operational delivery teams.
2. The integration of specialist social marketing expertise within policy, strategy and operational teams.
3. The development of the social marketing expertise of staff who work in policy, strategy and operational teams.
4. The commissioning and buying-in of specialist social marketing expertise for policy, strategy and operational teams as and when needed.
5. Hybrid variations of 1–4.

Each of these options clearly has strengths and weaknesses. The selection of which option best suits a particular organisation should flow from the analysis undertaken in stage one. However, it is crucial that if social marketing is to add maximum value to the policy formulation and strategy development phases of social programmes, then its principles should be applied throughout the policy, strategy and operational phases of planning, implementation and evaluation. This means that social marketing expertise should be applied at each of these levels and organisational solutions should seek to enable this to happen.

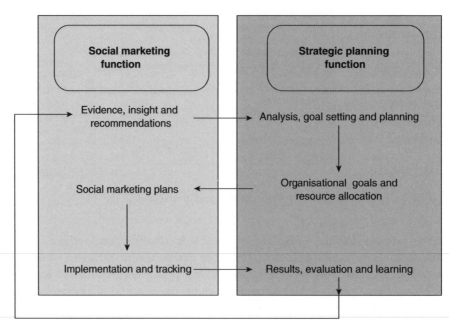

Figure 13.4 How social marketing should be positioned to support the strategic planning function within organisations

Figure 13.4 sets out a schematic illustrating how social marketing can be positioned to support the strategic planning function within organisations. The key issue here is that social marketing is integrated with strategic planning and not distinct from it. Social marketing influences strategic planning through the input of evidence, target audience insight, behavioural understanding and evaluations of interventions in terms of their effectiveness, efficiency and acceptability. Social marketing interventions are influenced by strategic goals and resource allocations. A symbiotic relationship should exist between social policy development, delivery and evaluation and social marketing. Such a relationship can help to create virtuous cycles of continuous improvement in the social programme selection, design and implementation, based on a deep understanding of citizens' needs and wants together with a forensic examination and review of the intervention performance.

The third stage of an integration process consists of actions that will be required to deliver the change and embed social marketing principles in the organisation. The key actions include setting out a clear set of operational standards of good practice that can be audited, and systems that enable the standards, and the development of a detailed implementation plan with clear sets of metrics that can be used to measure the success of the process of embedding social marketing in the organisation.

The final stage is about a commitment to a continuous cycle of review and improvement. Key elements of this stage are the recognition and rewarding of good practice and the establishment of processes that facilitate the sharing of learning and systems to ensure that what is learnt is fed into subsequent rounds of policy and strategy development and implementation.

CASE STUDY

The Water campaign: one example of a city wide application of social marketing (Rotterdam)

In 2010 after a period of investigation about how to improve the impact and efficiency of its health promotion, Rotterdam Municipal Health Service in the Netherlands decided to apply social marketing in a systematic way to a wide range of its programmes across the city. To do this it realised that it needed to develop the capacity of all relevant staff responsible for leading public health projects but also ensure that service managers and elected officials supported the new approach. During 2010 the municipality commissioned training for its staff and also ran sessions for elected officials and senior managers on the nature and added value of using social marketing to augment health promotion programmes.

(Continued)

(Continued)

During the following years a wide range of social marketing programmes has been developed and delivered across Rotterdam. As an example one such programme was the 'Water Campaign'.

The campaign was the main product of the 'Family Approach Project', aimed at getting parents involved in their children's lifestyles to prevent obesity and inactivity. The 'Family Approach Project' is just one component of the Rotterdam Lekker Fit! (Enjoy Being Fit in Rotterdam) Programme. The programme's objective is to prevent overweight and increase physical activity among children aged 0–14 living in multi-ethnic, socially deprived neighbourhoods.

The Lekker Fit! Programme (RLF!) is commissioned by the elected alderman for sports and culture on the Rotterdam City Council. As well as preventing childhood overweight a further important aim of the programme is to mobilise citizens to be more self-sufficient. The programme was set up against a background of major budget cuts and changing attitudes about the role of government and citizens.

Figure 13.5

The aim of the 'Family Approach Programme' was to change a single type of behaviour that is known to contribute to overweight/BMI increase in children, using parents as one of the key agents of change. The behaviour selected was to reduce the intake of sugar-sweetened beverages (SSB), often provided by parents. The strategy involved promoting an alternative behaviour for water consumption by positioning the behaviour as attractive, desirable and achievable. Activities included providing support, encouragement, education and access to free water, the provision of attractive water bottles and community engagement. Information about the disadvantages of SSB was also a key part of the intervention approach.

The Water Campaign was developed and implemented using the total process planning framework for social marketing (French et al., 2010). The total project lasted for three years and the budget was €50,000. The scoping stage included desk research, individual interviews with professionals, and focus group interviews within the target segment. The target segment was selected using the TARPARE model (Donovan et al., 1999) and the target behaviour on the basis of knowledge gained during interviews and desk research.

During the development stage, to ensure client orientation a marketing mix analysis (identifying the main underlying benefits, a tailored exchange proposition, price, place, promotion) was used. Also health promotion tools such as the EnRG framework (Kremers et al., 2006) and intervention mapping (Bartholomew et al., 2006) were applied to ensure a strong theoretical basis. A Water Campaign brand was then developed, along with interventions for both mothers and children.

The implementation stage began with the launch of the Water Campaign, followed by activities to promote water drinking during the summer holidays and interventions aimed at habitual behaviour within school policies and practices. From the start, key partners were mobilised through knowledge sharing and were actively involved in co-creation and implementation. The campaign applied social marketing principles from its inception as part of the city wide systematic application of social marketing concepts. For example:

- *Citizen orientation*: social marketing interventions are built from a citizen centric orientation based on research planning, delivery and evaluation. For example, desk research, interviews with professionals/semi-professionals, focus groups with mothers, pre-testing of interventions within the target audience.
- *Behaviour focused*: a specific focus on behaviour, based on analysis and synthesis. The key behaviour was that mothers would offer water to their child/children at least twice a day and ensure the child drank the water.

(Continued)

(Continued)

- *Theory*: behavioural theory was used to assist the development, implementation and evaluation of this programme and all other programmes. The 'Water Campaign' used the EnRG or **En**vironmental **R**esearch framework for weight **G**ain prevention model (Kremers et al., 2006), which combines the theory of planned behaviour with a socio-ecological model, as well as studies (3–5) on how parenting styles are related to the eating behaviour of children.
- *Insight*: the key insight derived from research with the target audience was that 'Giving food/SSB was a gesture of love and care', and that the weight of their children was of little concern to mothers. A third key insight was that mothers needed confirmation that they were a good parent and a loving and caring mother.
- *Exchange/value*: an exchange that was developed was based on the proposition that 'With water, you give your child the best'. It was supplemented by propositions that it was achievable through support provided by the city council and other stakeholders that included: we can help you to be a good mother; we can help you to make drinking water fun and easy (you are kind, loving mother); we can help you to say 'no' to SSB drinks (you are a good caregiver/educator). The programme also emphasised the power of social norms and community action with its stress on talking about water together with other mothers in a friendly atmosphere, and getting practical tips and skills to effectively serve your children water.

Figure 13.6

- *Competition*: competition analysis consisted of identifying all the practical environmental, social, behavioural and economic barriers that prevented water promotion and encouraged SSB selection. Key insights that were developed were summarised as: 'My child must drink something but does not like water'; 'My child performs better with sugary drinks, they give him energy'; 'My child keeps whining for fizzy drinks'. Strategies were developed to tackle all of these perceived barriers.
- *Segmentation*: the main target group for the intervention was Turkish and Moroccan mothers who were more likely to provide SSB drinks. This group was subdivided into traditional and modern mothers with a Turkish or Moroccan cultural background (traditional mothers are defined as those came to the Netherlands after the age of twelve; modern mothers are defined as those who came to the Netherlands before the age of twelve or were born in the Netherlands). Specific programmes were developed for each sub-segment of the target group.
- *Methods mix*: a wide range of interventions was put in place including: a 1.5-hour workshop for mothers, including interactive informal discussions about children drinking water, and decoration of a water jug to take home; a humorous sketch about water drinking and SSB; a specifically designed magazine. Children were enabled and encouraged to drink water during physical education in primary schools. Water facilities were made available in schools and children were given reusable water bottles which were 'Pimped Up', i.e. designed as an educational activity with attractive logos. Stakeholders and community groups including religious groups were engaged from the start of the programme and helped promote the new social norm that was at the heart of the programme. A wide range of promotional tactics was also used including posters and informal recruitment through home–school liaison officers.

Findings

A controlled trial (2011–2012) conducted among children aged six to twelve showed significant positive effects of the Water Campaign regarding SSB: based on observations (n=959) and parent reports (n=356) children in the intervention group, compared with children in the control group, brought less SSB to school, reduced their average number of SSB servings per day, and reduced their average SSB consumption by 150ml SSB per day (Lekker Fit, 2013).

A follow-up study (at the end of 2013, approximately one year after the first effect study described above) showed a stabilisation in the decline of SSB brought to school by the children in the intervention group, suggesting a lasting effect (Rapport Rotterdam Lekker Fit!, 2014).

(Continued)

(Continued)

Wider impact

The findings of the Water Campaign led to an ongoing commitment to water drinking in the pilot schools and in many other organisations in the Rotterdam area, both public and private. The results also initiated the implementation of the Water Campaign in all of the Rotterdam Lekker Fit! primary schools (90 schools, 20,000 children). The water theme was also picked up by the national JOGG initiative (the Dutch version of the EPODE movement), resulting in the spread of the Water Campaign to several other cities. The success of the campaign also boosted the use of social marketing in Rotterdam. Staff reported that 'We came to realise how little we know about the people we work for. We also learned how social marketing provides a strong but subtle tool to capture the hearts and minds of target audiences. Professionals with a background similar to that of the target audience often commented: this is the first project we've seen that is really about us'.

The Water Campaign also increased the involvement of parents, which is an important issue for the city of Rotterdam in many different fields of policy. The knowledge and insights gained from the social marketing analysis were used not only by other programmes and departments within the city, but also on a national scale.

For more details about the approach to applying social marketing in Rotterdam see: Municipal Health Service Rotterdam, www.ggdrotterdamrijnmond.nl/language/en.html.

Acknowledgements to the staff of the Rotterdam Lekker Fit! Programme (city of Rotterdam). For more details about the approach to applying social marketing in Rotterdam see: www.rotterdam.nl

Sustaining social marketing within public sector organisations

A key challenge associated with embedding social marketing within organisational systems and culture is to buttress it from the disruption associated with policy and managerial change. One of the facts of life within any organisation is that people, policy and strategy can change. This shift can be down to factors such as new evidence, increased experience about better ways to do things, new imperatives such as the need to save money, or because of ideological or political reasons.

One of the key protective actions is to use ongoing proactive briefing of policy and decision makers and practitioners regarding the rationale and evidence for the continued application of social marketing. The case needs to be set out for the efficiency and effectiveness gains associated with applying social marketing. As evaluation evidence emerges together with programme tracking data this should be communicated with policy and decision makers and practitioners to ensure they are aware of the impact that applying social marketing is delivering. This line of argument, however, also needs to be supplemented by a more emotional appeal that focuses on the ideological positioning of social marketing as a reflection of a citizen-centric and a population empowering approach to social programme delivery. As Wood (2012) argues, advocates should emphasise that social marketing is a practical approach to delivering mutually developed and delivered programmes of action with the consequential benefits of social cohesion, and as a marker of responsive, listening public services.

As discussed above, rather than promoting social marketing, advocates should be in the business of helping politicians, policy makers, strategists and practitioners to devise more effective, efficient, relevant and citizen empowering approaches to social improvement. Social marketing needs to be positioned as a key part of the solution to many social policy challenges. The strategic mission of advocates of social marketing is to get social marketing principles embedded into the total policy selection, development, delivery and evaluation process. To date marketing is hardly mentioned in most policy making texts (Baldock et al., 2007) and if it is, it is considered to be principally with the communication of ideas or facts. What is needed is the development of a more citizen driven and responsive approach to social policy, one based on marketing principles and reflecting an obsession with understanding citizens, engaging them in the policy making process to deliver valued social progress.

Conclusion

Social marketing adds value for both politicians and citizens in the process of policy development and strategy formulation. The vast majority of politicians and public officials in liberal democratic states are interested in both the efficiency and effectiveness of social policy delivery but also want to ensure that interventions meet the needs of citizens and are delivered in ways that assist them to lead healthy, happy and productive lives. The benefits of setting out clear behavioural aims and objectives from a political perspective are related to politicians' ability to demonstrate that they are having a positive effect of the wellbeing of society and that they are developing programmes that are well planned and can be evaluated. In so doing politicians and officials also add to the sum total of what is known about how best to improve the delivery of social policy in order to bring about social advancement. Many governments are also attempting to bring about a fundamental shift in the business model of public and not-for-profit sector service providers and institutions. Moving governments from an approach where solutions are derived principally by policy analysts working with subject experts and utilising limited forms of evidence and data towards a model that is also influenced by a deep contextual understanding target audiences. Understanding what people know, believe, value and say will help this process. This understanding together with an appreciation of how people can be influenced to act in socially and individually constructive ways should be the cornerstone of modern social policy. Social policy constructed without an input from social marketing will continue to deliver sub-optimal results and also continue to exclude the multiple assets that engaged and empowered citizens can bring to developing new, effective and efficient solutions to many of the big challenges faced by communities around the world.

This chapter has emphasised the need when advocating the uptake of social marketing to stress the value that it can bring to the policy making process, to the individuals responsible for developing social policy and implementing it, and its contribution to enhancing the democratic process itself. Social marketing is not about telling people what to do or coercing them into doing it, but rather encompasses the science of understanding what will help people make choices and take action that will enable them to have better lives. In short, politicians and public officials who seek to serve the public and make the world a better place have to learn how to make positive life choices become the easy and natural choices for people. This means that they will need to embrace social marketing principles as a core approach to policy and strategy development as well as a powerful tool for developing specific interventions. Social marketing is focused on developing social value defined by what people say they need and want, what they respond to and what they reject. Social marketing is a process that seeks to understand and engage citizens in the selection, development, implementation and evaluation of social policy. This citizen centric approach to developing social policy is a manifestation of a mature relationship between the state and its citizens based on respect and listening and a desire to reflect citizens' views and aspirations. Such an approach is also a reflection of the new and more responsive relationship that is emerging all over the world between governments and the people they are elected to serve (Clarke et al., 2007). This relationship is one where governments have a more facilitatory role rather than a role characterised by authoritarian leadership and coercion. If social policy is to become more reflective of public opinion and better serve the needs of citizens, then politicians, public servants and professional practitioners will need to invest time and effort in developing their understanding of social marketing's principles so that they can become stronger champions for the communities they serve; it is the role of social marketers to help them do this.

Reflective questions

- Make a list of the key individuals that you would need to persuade to adopt a more strategic approach to social marketing in the organisation in which you work or an organisation that you would like to work in. Segment these individuals into different sub-sets depending on their level of support and power. Set out how you would position social marketing with each of these groups and the tactics you could adopt to influence them.

- Make a list of the costs and benefits of incorporating social marketing within the policy and strategy development process from the perspective of both politicians and those responsible for developing intervention strategies.
- Describe how social marketing can contribute to the policy and strategy making process.

Further reading

Boyce, T., Robertson, R. and Dixon, A. (2008) *Commissioning and Behaviour Change: Kicking Bad Habits Final Report*. London: The King's Fund.

Mulgan, G. and Lee, A. (2001) *Better Policy Delivery and Design: A Discussion Paper*. London: Performance and Innovation Unit, Cabinet Office.

References

Andreasen, A.R. (2006) *Social Marketing in the 21st Century*. Thousand Oaks, CA: SAGE.

Australian Public Service Commission (2007) *Tackling Wicked Problems: A Public Policy Perspective*. Canberra: Australian Government. Available at: www.apsc.gov.au/publications-and-media/archive/publications-archive/tackling-wicked-problems (last accessed 18 November 2014)

Baldock, J., Manning, N. and Vickerstaff, S. (2007) *Social Policy*. Oxford: Oxford University Press.

Bartholomew, K., Parcel, G., Kok, G. and Gottlieb, N. (2006) *Planning Health Promotion Programs: An Intervention Mapping Approach*. San Francisco, CA: Jossey-Bass.

Borys, J., Le Bodo, Y., Jebb, S., Seidell, J.C., Summerbell, C., Richard, D., De Henauw, S., Moreno, L., Romon, M., Visscher, T., Raffin, S. and Swinburn, B. (2011) 'EPODE approach for childhood obesity prevention: methods, progress and international development', *Obesity Reviews*, 13 (4): 299–315.

Cabinet Office (2009) *A Guide to Social Return on Investment*. London: Cabinet Office.

Central Office of Information (2009) *Payback and Return on Marketing Investment (ROMI) in the Public Sector*. London: GNC.

Clarke, J., Newman, J., Smith, N., Vidler, E. and Westmarland, L. (2007) *Creating Citizen Consumers: Changing Publics & Changing Public Service*. London: SAGE.

Department of Health (2008) *Ambitions for Health: A Strategic Framework for Maximising the Potential of Social Marketing and Health-related Behaviour*. London: Department of Health.

Department of Health (2011) *Changing Behaviour, Improving Outcomes: A New Social Marketing Strategy for Public Health*. London: The Stationery Office.

Donovan, R.J., Egger, G. and Francas, M. (1999) 'TARPARE: a method for selecting target audiences for public health interventions', *Australian and New Zealand Journal of Public Health*, 23 (3): 280–284.

Eagle, L. (2009) *Social Marketing Ethics: Report Prepared for the National Social Marketing Centre*. London: NSMC. Available at: http://eprints.uwe.ac.uk/54/1/NSMC_Ethics_Report.pdf (last accessed 9 December 2014).

French, J. (2013) 'Business as unusual: the contribution of social marketing to government policymaking and strategy development', in G. Hastings, K. Angus and C. Bryant (eds), *The SAGE Handbook of Social Marketing*. London: SAGE, pp. 359–374.

French, J. (2014) 'From the periphery to the core: embedding social marketing in the strategic DNA of all social programmes', in K. Kubacki and S. Rundel-Theile (eds), *Contemporary Issues in Social Marketing*. Cambridge: Scholars Publishers, pp. 6–20.

French, J., Blair-Stevens, C., McVey, D. and Merritt, R. (eds) (2010) *Social Marketing and Public Health: Theory and Practice*. Oxford: Oxford University Press.

French, J. and Mayo, E. (2005) *It's Our Health! National Review of Social Marketing Strategy*. London: National Consumer Council

Gordon, R. (2013) 'Unlocking the potential of upstream social marketing', *European Journal of Marketing*, 47 (9): 1525–1547.

Haynes, L., Service, O., Goldacre, B. and Torgerson, D. (2013) *Test, Learn, Adapt: The Development of Public Policy with Randomised Control Trials*. London: Cabinet Office.

Kremers, S.P.J., De Bruijn, G.J., Visscher, T.L.S., Van Mechelen, W., De Vries, N.K. and Brug, J. (2006) 'Environmental influences on energy balance-related behaviors: a dual-process view', *International Journal of Behavioral Nutrition and Physical Activity*, 3: 9. doi: 10.1186/1479-5868-3-9.

Leenaars, K., Jacobs-van der Bruggen, M. and Renders, C. (2013) 'Determinants of successful public–private partnerships in the context of overweight prevention in Dutch youth', *Preventing Chronic Disease*, 10, Doi: http://dx.doi.org/10.5888/pcd10.120317.

Lekker Fit (2013) Factsheet JOGG aanpak, Rotterdam. Available at: www.jogg.nl/ (last accessed 9 December 2014).

Lindblom, C. and Woodhouse, E. (1993) *The Policy-making Process* (3rd edn). Englewood Cliffs, NJ: Prentice Hall.

Mintz, J. (2005) 'Social marketing in health promotion: the Canadian experience'. Available at: www.pollutionprobe.org/old_files/Happening/pdfs/complementarymeasJune28/mintz.pdf (last accessed 9 December 2014).

Moor, M. (1995) *Creating Public Value: Strategic Management in Government*. Cambridge, MA: Harvard University Press.

National Occupational Standards (2014) Available at: http://nos.ukces.org.uk/Pages/results.aspx?u=http%3A%2F%2Fnos%2Eukces%2Eorg%2Euk&k=social%20marketing (last accessed 24 November 2014).

Prime Minister's Strategy Unit (2006) *The UK Government's Approach to Public Service Reform*. London: Cabinet Office.

Rapport Rotterdam Lekker Fit! (2014) Derde nameting Watercampagne pilotscholen, Onderzoek en Business Intelligence (OBI) Rotterdam.

US Department of Health and Human Services (2010) *Healthy People 2020*. Washington, DC: Office of Disease Prevention and Health Promotion. Available at: http://healthypeople. gov/2020/topicsobjectives2020/objectiveslist.aspx?topicId=18 (last accessed 24 November 2014).

WHO (World Health Organization) (2012) *Health 2020: The Europe Policy for Health and Wellbeing*. Geneva: WHO. Available at: www.euro.who.int/en/what-we-do/health-topics/health-policy/health-2020 (last accessed 17 December 2013).

Wood, M. (2012) 'Marketing social marketing', *Journal of Social Marketing*, 2 (2): 94–102.

14 CRITICAL SOCIAL MARKETING

Learning objectives

By the end of this chapter, readers should be able to:

- understand the importance and contribution of critical social marketing to competitive analysis, and of critical debate to strategic social marketing
- understand and evaluate the potentially harmful impact of commercial marketing and institutions on individuals and society, and how this understanding can be used to inform the development and evaluation of strategic social marketing programmes
- consider the role and importance of critical debate in social marketing to the development of the field
- engage with and understand the relevance of critical reflexivity in social marketing with respect to researchers, participants and stakeholders involved in social change programmes.

Introduction

This chapter considers the important role that critical thinking and the *critical social marketing* paradigm play in strategic social marketing. Critical social marketing can be defined as critical reflection on competitive forces, dominant concepts and ideas, and the role and influence of actors in the social marketing process.

As outlined in the foreword of this book, social marketing was defined by Lazer and Kelley (1973: ix, emphasis added) as:

> Concerned with the application of marketing knowledge, concepts, and techniques to enhance social as well as economic ends. *It is also concerned with the analysis of the social consequences of marketing policies, decisions and activities.*

The first sentence in Lazer and Kelley's definition concerns the use of marketing concepts and techniques to effect social change. This is where the bulk of work in social marketing has concentrated to date. However, the second part of their definition identifies that social marketing is also concerned with critically analysing the effect of commercial marketing on individuals and society as part of a wider analysis of competitive forces. It is this second area of focus that has led to the development of the emerging critical social marketing paradigm. Work in this area has emanated from the considerable work done on understanding the effect of tobacco marketing on smoking. This work was important not only to understand how commercial tobacco marketing influenced knowledge, attitudes and behaviours, but also provided insight into the strategies and tactics of the tobacco industry – insight that was valuable in developing informed intervention strategies. The knowledge generated was used to help develop individual level social marketing programmes tackling smoking, as well as inform upstream action in the form of regulation, policy and law. However, as discussed in this chapter, work in critical social marketing has begun to expand beyond consideration of the potentially deleterious effects of commercial marketing, to consider the role of commercial and corporate systems, institutions and forces; to critically debate about social marketing theories, concepts and ideas; and to debate about the role of critical reflexivity in social marketing. This chapter reviews some of the important ideas and discussions in this area, and relates them to the need to think critically when developing strategic social marketing programmes to promote social good.

The chapter starts by discussing the importance of critical thinking in social marketing, and reviews the work considering the potentially harmful effects of commercial marketing on individuals and society. We outline how this knowledge and understanding act as a form of competitive analysis for social marketing by offering insight on not only the competing interests, behaviours, and practices available to participants (for example, eating a cheap, tasty and satisfying burger rather than spending the time and effort to create a nutritionally balanced meal), but also the competition offered by commercial forces – such as the tobacco, alcohol and fast food industries. We consider how this insight can be used to help develop social marketing strategies – at the individual, community and structural/policy level. We then examine the importance of critical debate in social marketing – identifying that it is often crucial and indeed healthy to critique and re-examine dominant concepts and ideas to advance knowledge. Finally, we consider the role of critical reflexivity in social marketing at the researcher, participant and stakeholder levels, identifying that engaging in reflexivity can help us make more informed and balanced decisions.

Competitive analysis

As we previously discussed in Chapter 2, *competitive analysis* is the assessment of the strengths and weaknesses of existing and potential competitors. Performing competitive analysis requires engagement with critical thinking to assess market conditions and our own organisation. In commercial marketing this provides insight about opportunities and threats for a company, and forms an essential part of corporate strategy (Fleisher and Bensoussan, 2003). Competition is a clear and powerful force in business – Coca Cola and Pepsi, Airbus and Boeing, Apple and Samsung are major rivals consistently seeking to outdo one another to gain competitive advantages (plural or singular) in the marketplace. Indeed, Albert W. Emery, an American advertising executive, argues that 'Marketing is merely a civilized form of warfare in which most battles are won with words, ideas and disciplined thinking'. Such corporations use competitive analysis to ensure they can stay one step ahead of their rivals – or at least react effectively to what they do.

   Through competitive analysis firms can identify who their key competitors are, and develop an understanding of each competitor. They can identify competitors' objectives, strategies, strengths and weaknesses, and assess the threat that they pose. Also, they can use competitive analysis to anticipate their reaction to competitive actions, to refocus and to identify opportunities, and to improve their strategic direction.

Discussion question

- Consider what customer needs Budweiser beer satisfies for a group of adolescents.

An obvious way to answer this question would be to conduct market research asking adolescents why they choose to purchase Budweiser. A most obvious answer you are likely to get is because it is an alcoholic drink – a beer satisfies a desire to consume an alcoholic drink. However, given that there are many other alcoholic drinks available in the marketplace, this is likely only part of the picture.

Competitive analysis often involves questions about other functional, emotional and social dimensions of value offered by products and services, and insight on what consumers consider as alternative options. Questions like:

- How do others view Budweiser consumers?
- How do you feel when you consume Budweiser?
- If you didn't buy Budweiser today what else might you have done?
- What is good about these alternatives?

The answers may include insight beyond the selection of Budweiser to quench a thirst, or due to a preference for the taste. For example, it could offer insight on peer status and acceptance of Budweiser as a brand, and of the people who consume it. It could help identify whether drinking Budweiser makes adolescents feel accepted or cool or popular. Considering alternatives, consumers might identify other alcohol brands they may have selected, or even another activity that they may have chosen – playing sport or going for a meal with friends instead of drinking alcohol. By undertaking such competitive analysis, Budweiser can develop a comprehensive understanding of their rivals and their customers.

The Budweiser case here helps identify the utility of competitive analysis. From this process Budweiser executives can learn who and what they are up against – other alcohol brands, the influence of peer groups, social norms and the attraction of other activities besides drinking alcohol. As discussed, competitor analysis can be undertaken using research, but can also be informed by the use of frameworks. Michael Porter (1979), a Harvard university professor and renowned expert on competition in business, offers a useful framework for thinking about competitive analysis through his five forces framework (see Figure 14.1).

As can be seen from Porter's framework, there exists internal and external competition for firms emanating from five different sources. With respect to each of the five forces, we discussed the importance of the first force – competitive rivalry within an industry – earlier in this chapter. We have also extensively examined the second force – the power that the consumer or participant has – throughout much of this book. However, Porter identifies that the amount of power consumers have can vary according to market conditions. For example, consumers have less power under a monopoly, or when economic conditions are challenging. The third force – the power of suppliers of raw material, components, labour and services – is also important but again depends on market conditions. If you make alcohol but there is only one supplier of hops then you have no alternative but to buy from them at the price they set. The fourth force concerns the availability of alternatives, whether that is goods, services, behaviours or even lifestyles. The fifth force concerns the threat of new entrants and considers how easy it is for competitors to enter the marketplace and offer value propositions to consumers.

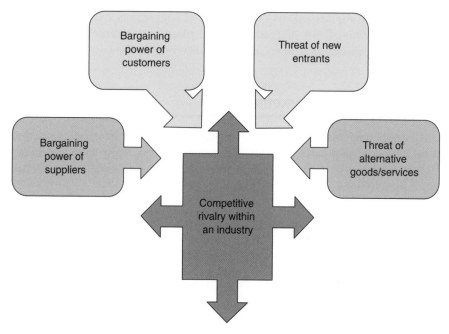

Figure 14.1 Porter's five forces framework for competitive analysis

Source: adapted from Porter, 1979

A useful way then for companies to assess the competition is to undertake SWOT analysis to identify internal and external competitive forces. Returning to the Budweiser example, undertaking a competitive analysis could help them think about their strategic response. For instance, they may want to compete directly against other beer brands such as Coors or Miller, but they may also want to 'sell' drinking alcohol with friends as an attractive lifestyle pursuit – cooler and more fun than other activities. Identifying the importance of consumers' image in front of peers may also lead them to position their brand as youthful and fun – perhaps through things like music or sports sponsor-ship. This exercise in competitive analysis helps us identify that there is a distinction between the core product offering (an alcoholic drink), and the needs of the consumer that are satisfied (lifestyle activity, image in front of peers, a vehicle for socialisation) that act as an *augmented product*, namely non-physical aspects attached to the core product that add value to the consumer. This is an important point: consumers don't just buy products and services to serve functional needs, but as we discussed in Chapter 6, they also perceive and extract other forms of value from consumption, be that emotional (makes you feel good), or social (acceptance from peers). Thus, market-ers need to consider that they are not merely offering a product or service, but a value proposition to the consumer – that stands the test of time and forms a long-term engagement with consumers. Indeed, undertaking competitive analysis involves consideration of the whole marketing mix strategy of competitors and your own organisation from the traditional 4Ps of product, price, place and promotion, to stakeholder marketing, value propositions, advocacy and policy engagement, and so on.

Competition in social marketing

As with commercial marketing, there can be external and internal competition in social marketing. Competitive analysis in social marketing leads to the identification of countervailing forces and the systematic development of strategies to reduce the impact of these external and internal competitive forces.

Internal competition

Internal competition includes such things as people's feelings and attitudes about something; the pleasure involved in the thrill of risk taking; the difficulty of giving up an ingrained habit; or addiction. These essentially act as barriers to change. As Hastings and Domegan (2014: 198) describe, social marketing offerings are often inherently unappealing: 'a bad diet is fun and indulgent, a good one Spartan and dissatisfying; a sedentary life is restful and relaxing, exercise hard work and tiring'. Furthermore, many objectives for social marketing require long-term committed engagement, which brings long-term probabilistic and often intangible benefits. The advantages of using energy efficiently might mean less carbon emissions in your country and a more sustainable future – but these are often concerns in the medium- to long-term future. The convenience of leaving the air conditioning on, or leaving the television on standby, offers short-term definite benefits. Reducing your alcohol intake or abstaining altogether might lead to a healthier and longer life, but the thirst quenching satisfaction of a cold beer on a warm summer day and having fun socialising in the pub with friends offer more attractive and immediate value to consumers.

The key for social marketers is to create an offering that engages and delivers value to participants not just in the far off distant future but also here and now. This is challenging – one of the biggest challenges social marketing faces. In the earlier years of social marketing interventions, much of the focus, perhaps unwisely, was on communicating the negative consequences of not changing behaviours or instilling fear in participants – you will get fat if you eat unhealthily, you will develop cancer and die if you smoke, you will get liver disease if you drink too much (see Hastings et al., 2004). If people acted as rational beings then these often very relevant warnings should be enough to invoke change. However, human beings are emotional creatures and very complex. Just trying to scare people into submission does not work.

Rather, perhaps the focus for social marketers should be on communicating the positive aspects of the offering. Indeed, there are often more immediate benefits from engaging in health, sustainable behaviours and so on. In public health this may mean moving away from the illness paradigm towards the wellbeing paradigm and presenting a more fulfilled and rewarding life. For instance, being fit and healthy can mean you can play with your children more, or have fun by playing five a side football with friends. Drinking less might mean that you don't make a fool of yourself in front of friends, but can remain in command of your senses and be more respected by peers. Eating a healthy diet might give you more energy in the morning, or offer emotional benefits from looking and feeling good. It is these types of incentives and motivational exchanges that social marketers are increasingly focusing on. These approaches have overlaps with ideas from *positive psychology*, which uses psychology theory, research and intervention techniques to understand the positive, adaptive, creative and emotionally fulfilling aspects of human behaviour (Seligman, 1998). Thus there is increasing focus in social marketing on creating attractive and emotionally (as well as functionally) positive exchanges for engaging in behaviour change and social change processes.

External competition

External competition comes from the influence of those people, environments, systems, social norms or organisations that directly or indirectly promote counter-behaviours, or influence people to maintain unhealthy or socially undesirable behaviours. Competitive forces, such as the production and marketing of products and services detrimental to health and society, lobbying or political interference, negative social norms and stress inducing environments make it harder to motivate people to adopt desired behaviours. One of the key sources of external competition to social marketing comes from corporate forces' marketing of potentially harmful products or services such as alcohol, energy dense high fat food, and tobacco. It is these corporate forces that the World Health Organization (WHO, 1998) named the 'Hazard Merchants'.

We must remember that the core objective and responsibility for corporations that sell such products is to deliver shareholder value – which equals selling more and generating profits. Corporations that sell products like cigarettes, alcohol and fast food have been very successful at doing so. British American Tobacco has a market capitalisation of £65.6 billion – the sixth largest in the London Stock Exchange – and McDonalds reported a net quarterly profit of US$1.52 billion in October 2013. The behaviours (smoking, drinking alcohol, eating unhealthy foods) that the Hazard Merchants encourage often push in the opposite direction of what social marketing seeks to achieve. Therefore, such products, the marketing of them, the corporations that produce them, and the institutions, systems and forces in which they reside, act as competition to social marketing. The way in which these corporations do this is through the power of strategic marketing. Take the example of how the tobacco industry used the full extent of the marketing mix to sell their offering.

Although the tobacco industry used more recognisable tactics to sell their products such as branding and advertising, they also used other more strategic approaches such as engaging doctors to be ambassadors for their brands, and funding academic research that questioned the health effects of smoking or argued that there was no influence of tobacco marketing on behaviour. They also deployed extensive advocacy and lobbying of policy makers to ensure the policy, regulatory and legal environment was more favourable to the industry. Importantly, for the tobacco industry their broad strategic marketing efforts worked – extensive research evidence has established associations between exposure to tobacco marketing and smoking (Lovato et al., 2003). Similar research has identified links between exposure to fast food marketing and consumption (Hastings et al., 2003), and alcohol marketing and consumption (Anderson et al., 2009).

Given that we know commercial marketing can act as competition to social marketing, what do we, as social marketers, do in response? This is where much of the work in the critical social marketing paradigm comes in. Following Lazer and Kelley's (1973) lead, social marketing researchers have examined the influence of commercial marketing on behaviours like smoking (MacFadyen et al., 2001), alcohol consumption (Hughes et al., 1997; MacKintosh et al., 1997; Gordon et al., 2010a), and consumption of energy dense high fat food (McDermott et al., 2005), producing key research evidence. Importantly, this research evidence has then been utilised to inform responses such as the development of social marketing interventions tackling youth smoking, and policy and regulatory change such as banning tobacco advertising (see Gordon, 2011a). What is crucial about such research is that it is high quality and rigorous, that analysis and results are transparent and objective, and that the balance of evidence from a series of studies is consistent before evidence-based responses are formed.

As discussed in Chapter 2 social marketing has predominantly tended to focus on individual level behaviour change, rather than the wider environment that influences behaviour – including the impact of commercial marketing. As a result, critical social marketing work is not as widespread. However, in the past fifteen years the critical social marketing paradigm has grown (Hastings and Saren, 2003). Scholars have begun to identify the utility of taking a critical approach to social marketing research, informed by ideas from critical theory, discussed in Chapter 8, and critical marketing (Gordon, 2011a). Critical theory is a social theory informed by several streams of thought including Marxist theory and deconstruction theory aimed at critiquing and changing society (Horkheimer, 1982). Critical marketing is the social and reflexive critique of marketing theory and practice (Gordon, 2011a).

Although much work in critical social marketing has focused on big tobacco, food and alcohol corporations, there are other areas that may warrant attention. For example, the car industry might provide competition to road safety efforts by promoting the speed and excitement of the vehicles they sell; and the airline industry may work against environmental sustainability efforts by encouraging travel and increased carbon emissions. The power and influence of commercial forces are considerable, and doing research on these issues can help generate insight on their effects on citizens and society. These types of critical social marketing research can act as a form of competitive analysis, as it offers insight into the nature and effect of commercial forces that may act in opposition to desired social outcomes. For example, the truth® youth anti-tobacco programme used insight and competitive analysis from years of research on tobacco marketing, to guide the development and implementation of an effective social marketing programme (Farrelly et al., 2005). Critical social marketing research can also help inform strategic decision making in relation to regulation and policy. For example, research on tobacco advertising was influential in the UK government's decision to ban most forms of tobacco promotion in 2002 (Gordon, 2011a). See Chapters 3 and 11 for practical guidance about how competition analysis can be used to develop social marketing strategy and assist with the selection and development of social policy.

Critical social marketing research

Gordon (2011a: 89) outlines a definition for this critical social marketing research as:

> critical research from a marketing perspective on the impact commercial marketing has upon society, to build the evidence base, inform upstream efforts such as advocacy, policy and regulation, and inform the development of downstream social marketing interventions.

As this definition outlines, this work not only involves research but also acting upon it. In a sense, social marketers become activists, engaging in activities like advocacy, policy change and influencing structural conditions as well as trying to facilitate behaviour change among individuals. Critical social marketing research can help contribute to evidence-based policy decisions, by offering insights into the effects of commercial forces on social outcomes. Such insights can then help inform strategic decision making, such as the need to regulate or ban tobacco or alcohol advertising, or to introduce plain packaging for cigarettes. Thus the relevance of this to strategic social marketing becomes clear. The framework presented in Table 14.1, citing an example of using critical social marketing research to influence the UK alcohol environment, outlines a process for doing critical social marketing research and using the insights this generates to inform strategic social marketing approaches including behaviour change programmes and influencing policy and regulation.

As Table 14.1 shows, the streams of activities that critical social marketing can inform are varied, and can form important components of doing strategic social marketing. While using research evidence to advocate and lobby for policy change is one of the most obvious activities we need to be careful how we go about this. Policy makers and opinion formers are participant groups just like anyone else in social marketing, and they have their needs and wants, as well as barriers and incentives to change. Therefore, we must use our marketing nous to influence these stakeholders on their terms – something that is not always done (see French, 2011; Gordon,

2013a). To tackle the competition social marketers need to match their competitors' game; we need ubiquity, to offer convenience, and offer immediate emotional as well as functional value. We also need to use engaging and attractive branding and where relevant warn participants of the activities of commercial marketing (see the example of the truth® counter-marketing programme from Chapter 2). We also need to wield power and influence in the stakeholder and policy environment. It is also important to use social marketing knowledge to influence politicians and policy makers from both the outside via lobbying and from the inside via giving professional marketing support to the policy and strategy development process.

Beyond commercial marketing to institutions, systems and forces

If we are to think strategically, external competition emerges not only from commercial marketing, but also from the institutions, systems and forces that underpin them. Indeed, critical social marketing scholars have called for an increased focus on tackling ideological competitive forces such as corporatism and neo-liberalism, which implicitly support and advocate for unfettered commercial marketing (Hastings, 2012). An aspect of both critical marketing and strategic social marketing is the development of a more cogent, evidence-based and ethically justifiable critique of the current dominant economic discourse, supported by institutions and systems that are singularly focused on lean productivity and efficiencies, generating profits, delivering shareholder value, and strengthening the economic and political power of small numbers of elites and individuals within societies. We argue in this book that a socially progressive strategic social marketing perspective that is focused on value creation, mutualism, social welfare, social justice and social equality is required.

Broader critiques of capitalism have emerged from a variety of sources, not just from those working in social marketing. Indeed, much of the work in *critical marketing* challenges established norms not only in marketing but also in economic and social institutions (see Saren et al., 2007; Tadajewski and Brownlie, 2008). This highlights the relevance of critical marketing to social marketing as understanding broader political, social and economic forces is important to inform strategic social marketing approaches. Beyond marketing, critics of commercialism and capitalism have emerged from disciplines including critical public health, sociology, philosophy, history and political science. Prominent critics of neo-liberalism and free market capitalism include Joel Bakan, author of the 2004 book *The Corporation: The Pathological Pursuit of Power*; Noam Chomsky, a leading political philosopher; Jürgen Habermas, a critical theorist; and Naomi Klein, a social activist and author of *No Logo* (2000). All of these thinkers and others have offered insightful critiques of commercial sector marketing. Crucially, citizens have reacted to the effects of corporate forces. The recent Occupy movement, the 2011 London riots, the Arab Spring – all of these

Table 14.1 Step-by-step schema of critical social marketing research

STEP 1 - Research:	STEP 2 - Dissemination:	STEP 3 - Upstream Social Marketing:	STEP 4 - Social Marketing Interventions:
Using a marketer's perspective to perform research which conducts a critical analysis of the impact of commercial marketing on society.	Production of peer reviewed conference papers and journal articles presenting the findings from research that contribute to the evidence base.	Advocacy, lobbying, informing policy and regulation.	Engagement with relevant stakeholder organisations to inform social marketing programmes.
Including marketing strategy, executions, techniques and principles applied.	Other activities that involve engaging with academic audiences such as workshops, inclusion of study findings in teaching materials, etc.	Achieved through presentation of findings to stakeholder organisations and policy makers such as industry representatives, government departments and supra-national institutions, and industry representative bodies.	Liaison with organisations such as public health bodies to make use of research findings (e.g. youth attitudes towards alcohol, effective channels of communication) to influence the design and delivery of targeted behaviour change interventions, for example to combat under-age drinking. Should involve reflexivity of social marketing systems and approaches chosen to help adapt and refine interventions and drive theory development.
In the case of alcohol marketing this might involve documentary analysis of internal alcohol marketing strategy documents, an audit of alcohol marketing activity, stakeholder interviews, formative consumer research, survey research to assess the impact of alcohol promotion on individual behaviours and the impact upon others (associated harms).		Or may consist of internal stakeholder marketing by policy makers and decision makers to others to influence strategy and policy. For alcohol, relevant stakeholders in the UK may include the Portman Group, Department of Health, European Commission, media and PR activity (newspaper articles, blogs), stakeholder reports (e.g. BMA reports, BMJ opinion pieces), industry stakeholder groups (advertisers, marketing executives, industry representative bodies).	
		Should also include critical reflexivity of commercial marketing systems and approaches.	

Source: Gordon, 2011a

events can be linked to increasing dissatisfaction about inequalities that in part emanate from dominant capitalist systems. Indeed, Michael Porter (one of the world's leading business strategists) and his colleague Mark Kramer have commented;

> the legitimacy of business has fallen to levels not seen in recent history. (Porter and Kramer, 2011: 64)

While these broader concerns may initially seem removed from the focus of social marketing they are actually very important. For strategic social marketing to effect social change that facilitates improved health, wellbeing, sustainability, social equality and social justice, it is important that we understand the broader forces that influence societies. For example, conservative governments may be less supportive of large-scale intervention on health and social issues, preferring a focus on individual responsibility (French, 2011). Institutions and systems in capitalist societies that are geared towards individualism, generating profits, delivering shareholder value and creating corporate goliaths that often transcend national regulatory, legal and economic boundaries, create very real challenges to social marketing.

Hastings (2012) argues that to challenge dominant commercial, political, social and economic forces requires strategic action at many levels. Social programmes and social movements that focus on engaging stakeholder networks, and encouraging mobilisation and participation from all relevant parties, rather than deferring to expert driven top down approaches, is one such suggestion. Movements like Occupy and the Arab Spring also have the power to effect change if they are harnessed effectively. There may also be a need to reclaim marketing and business studies. This refocusing starts in education, teaching students about the real social role of business, including the role of marketing, and embedding the concepts of social value for all and real social responsibility at the core of these disciplines.

Andreasen (2012) has argued that marketing should be reordered with not-for-profit marketing as the dominant form of marketing. Perhaps taking this thinking further, marketing should really be reordered around a consideration of *marketing and society*, with all marketing engaging with its social functions, impacts and responsibilities, and geared towards wellbeing, quality of life, sustainability and equity as first principals, and with making money relegated to a lower order principle. These ideas are not new, indeed Wilkie and Moore (1999) discuss how business has engaged with social issues and social responsibilities in the past. Creating a new generation of socially responsible, reflective and collective thinking business professionals could help drive this agenda. Yet heretofore, the business community has not come up with realistic alternatives – for example, Porter and Kramer's (2011a) concept of creating shared value that we discussed in Chapter 6 has been heavily criticised for still being focused on firms making money and for not really addressing systemic problems in which firms are part of the problem not part of the solution (Crane et al., 2014). Indeed, trusting commercial forces to provide the solutions may seem a stretch considering their previous actions and their primary focus on delivering shareholder value. (See the case study below on how the tobacco and alcohol industries have responded to academic research on links between marketing and consumption behaviour for a discussion on how corporate forces can respond when shareholder value may be threatened).

So, how do we respond? As Hastings (2012) points out, consumers also have a role to play here as we each should think carefully about how we act: what and how should we buy, do we need to keep consuming more, is it acceptable to hold prejudices, or to act only with self-interest, how should we react to unreasonable and intrusive or distorting promotion? Regulation, policy, service delivery, design of systems, products and services, and the environment also have an important part to play. However, policy makers need to show leadership and enlightened thinking – for example despite the discourse about robust new financial regulations following the global financial crisis of 2008, little action took place. It is up to political leaders to help deliver more equitable and sustainable societies by tackling these issues head on. Some scholars go further and argue that rethinking our political, economic and social systems, particularly in Western capitalist societies, may be necessary (Habermas, 1973; Klein, 2000; Chomsky, 2003; Bakan, 2004; Rancière, 2011; Eagleton, 2012; Chomsky, 2013). However, these solutions assume that the answers lie within our current structures and systems. As history shows with events such as the collapse of the Roman Empire, the French Revolution, and the Russian Revolution, it may be that disruptive events could be the driver of deconstruction of our current systems to be replaced by new structures. These challenges are considerable, but the alternative – inaction – holds potentially even greater consequences.

CASE STUDY

Corporate forces respond to the social marketing competition

Strategic and policy context

When corporate forces and their advocates face competition (in the form of research or critique), it is to be expected that they will respond to perceived threats. For example, research conducted on tobacco advertising and tobacco control measures has led to strategies such as harassing researchers who identified associations between advertising and smoking with legislation, public advertising and attempting to cut off research funds (Landman and Glantz, 2009). Hastings (2012: 141) also presents a case of how the tobacco industry

(Continued)

(Continued)

submits freedom of information (FOI) requests to obtain research data or at least divert researchers away from their core research (see also Christie, 2011). The alcohol industry has also employed similar tactics.

Research funded by the National Preventive Research Initiative was the first UK study that assessed the cumulative impact of alcohol marketing on youth drinking. It addressed a complex and important public health problem with a view to having a valuable impact on policy makers and commentators, as well as the research community. The considerable health and social costs of alcohol consumption in the UK are well documented, generating a focus on factors that influence drinking such as social influences and also marketing.

Methodology

The study featured three integrated phases of research. Phase one involved scoping the alcohol marketing environment through an audit of contemporary alcohol promotion in the media and online, supplemented by informant interviews with marketers, health experts and regulators. Phase two featured qualitative focus group research with adolescents to explore the role and meaning of alcohol to them, and their interactions and views on alcohol marketing. Phase three involved a two stage cohort survey questionnaire administered to 920 adolescents aged thirteen, with 552 followed up at age fifteen, to measure their awareness of and involvement with alcohol marketing, and their drinking related knowledge, attitudes and behaviours.

Findings

The media audit revealed that alcohol marketing is ubiquitous in the UK. Most brands were found to have a dedicated online presence featuring sophisticated content that appeals to youth including music, sport and video games. The audit found that alcopop brands concentrated advertising in youth magazines, and that supermarket advertising of alcohol was considerable in the printed press. Focus group research revealed a sophisticated level of awareness of and involvement in alcohol marketing among respondents across several channels. Marketing activities often featuring content with youth appeal seemed to be related to participants' well-developed brand attitudes. Cross-sectional regression analysis of the cohort survey data found significant associations between awareness of, and involvement with, alcohol marketing and drinking status and future drinking intentions. Bivariate and multivariate analysis of the longitudinal data at phase two indicated that alcohol marketing was associated with youth drinking behaviour, including initiation of drinking and increased frequency of drinking between phase one and phase two. The results suggested a small but significant association between alcohol marketing and youth drinking. These findings are consistent with the large body of evidence that has now emerged (Anderson et al., 2009). The findings from the study were disseminated widely in the academic research literature (Gordon et al., 2010a; 2010b; 2011), as well as extensively in policy forums such as the European Alcohol and Health Forum, the House of Commons Health Committee report on alcohol, the Scottish government, and to a broad range of stakeholders including Alcohol Focus Scotland, Alcohol Concern and the British Medical Association, as well as public seminars (Gordon, 2011b).

The critical response from commercial forces

Dissemination of the findings from this study was met with critical reports and public relations efforts by the advertising and alcohol industry stakeholders (Gordon, 2011c). For example a report commissioned by a commercial consultancy agency named BACON appeared in 2013 on behalf of the UK Advertising Association. The report contained 'independent expert views' (Advertising Association, 2013:1) by Professor Adrian Furnham, a Professor of Psychology at University, College London, and Paul Ormerod, an economist and a partner of Volterra Partners, on the research studies.

See the report here: www.adassoc.org.uk/wp-content/uploads/2014/10/Gordon_et_al_expert_views1.pdf

The report questions the methodology and interpretation of the results from each study. This is understandable as scholars often question, critique, disagree and take different views on issues such as methodologies, interpretations, and what the implications are from research. Yet Professor Furnham, states that 'the authors could perhaps be accused of salami slicing – cutting up the same data to publish more than one paper' (Advertising Association, 2013:6). It is unclear what relevance this observation has to the research evidence on associations between alcohol marketing and youth drinking.

Professor Furnham appears to have attended conferences organised by the alcohol industry, see:

www.just-drinks.com/analysis/industry-group-addresses-adolescent-drinking_id85028.aspx. Of further interest is that Professor Furnham has a strong proponent of his work on alcohol in Dr Brian Young, Lecturer in Consumer Psychology at the University of Exeter, see:

www.aim-digest.com/gateway/pages/S&P%20Alcohol%20and%20young%20People/Research%20&%20Studies/articles/furnham.pdf.

Dr Young is a scholar who Hastings (2007) points out published a critique of research suggesting a link between fast food advertising and childhood obesity that was also commissioned by the very same Advertising Association

(Continued)

(Continued)

(Young, 2003). This example perhaps encourages us to reflect upon the moral, social and economic forces that may influence researchers who are employed by independent bodies and organisations who act in the interests of the commercial and private sector.

───────────────── **Discussion question** ─────────────────

Considering the case above, how do you think social marketing researchers – or any researcher working on issues in which there may be conflict between commercial forces and public health or social welfare – should respond to criticisms and attacks from the commercial sector?

Critical debate in social marketing

While most of the focus for critical social marketing has been on the competitive analysis and critique of commercial marketing, and corporate institutions and forces, scholars are increasingly recognising the importance of critical debate (Spotswood et al., 2012).

Despite its continued development as a field, social marketing is still seeking its firm establishment and recognition within academia. As we discussed in Chapter 2 criticism of social marketing is readily evident. One such criticism of social marketing levied by other marketing scholars is that the field is too positivist in nature (Dholakia and Dholakia, 2001). This perhaps reflects the dominant positivist managerialist approach to mainstream marketing (Alvesson, 1994), upon which social marketing is largely based. Sceptics consider that social marketing is dominated by the same pro-marketing ideology, and neo-liberal undertones, as the marketing messages that it is often designed to counter (Hackley, 2009). The view that it is merely a self-serving adaptation of the existing marketing system has also been expressed (Bettany and Woodruffe-Burton, 2009; Tadajewski, 2010). Furthermore, critical marketers have identified that social marketing lacks reflexivity and critical discourse, leading them to reject the identification of social marketing with their paradigm (Tadajewksi and Brownlie, 2008).

This may in part be explained by what Gordon and Gurrieri (2014) describe as the different schools of social marketing thought. They argue that the dominant group of traditionalists in social marketing have focused on individual behaviour change interventions using formulaic concepts and techniques, with little engagement with critical thought. However, as Gordon and Gurrieri (2014) argue, critical debate in social marketing is important, not only to encourage discussion and formulate new ideas to advance the discipline, but also to facilitate more effective social marketing.

However, in contrast to the traditionalists, progressive and critical social marketers have attempted to engage with the critique of existing social marketing concepts and ideas. For example, during the 1990s scholars recognised the limitations of a narrow interpretation of social marketing, and the called for a shift in emphasis towards the influence of multiple forces on behaviour and the incorporation of midstream and upstream activities into the field (Andreasen, 1995; Goldberg, 1995). Progressives have engaged in critical reflexivity to question the narrow focus of social marketing (Andreasen, 2002), arguing that we need to take a strategic approach, the very thrust of this book, and move beyond individual behaviour (Spotswood et al., 2012). These debates have influenced much of the social marketing work that has sought to influence wider stakeholder groups, policy, regulation and law (Gordon, 2013a). Furthermore, as we discussed in this chapter, scholars in this progressive school have long recognised the importance of critical approaches to the discipline (Lazer and Kelley, 1973; Hastings and Saren, 2003; Gordon, 2011a; Lazer, 2013). Critiques of commercial marketing have helped inform social marketing strategies including behaviour change interventions and advocacy for policy change (Gordon, 2011a). Critical social marketers have also critiqued out-dated models and ideas such as the 4Ps marketing mix (Peattie and Peattie, 2003; Gordon, 2012) arguing that they are unsuited to contemporary social marketing contexts. This work has helped encourage ideas and concepts such as new social marketing mix models (Tapp and Spotswood, 2013). Others have identified a lack of theory development as problematic (Andreasen, 2003; Peattie and Peattie, 2003), and have argued for reflection on the unquestioned transference of commercial marketing ideas to social issues. Furthermore, Gurrieri et al. (2013) have argued for a dismantling of managerialist principles and practices and an expansion of the critical social marketing paradigm. Recently, there has been an emerging discourse on moving away from just focusing on behaviour, to engaging with knowledge, attitudes, social norms, cultures and social practices. Such critical debate can help stimulate discussion and the development of new ideas and concepts that may help social marketing advance. We believe that engaging with such critical debate is important to facilitate the emergence of a socially progressive model of social marketing.

Social marketing ethics

Critical debate in social marketing has also led to questions about the ethical, social and moral focus of social marketing (Hastings et al., 2004; Spotswood et al., 2012). For example, are fear campaigns in some social marketing programmes unethical by scaring audiences into changing their behaviour, a practice that would be unacceptable in commercial marketing (Hastings et al., 2004)? In recent years, some social marketing programmes like 'Speeding – No one thinks big of you' have begun to move away from using fear appeals, to use of humour and highlighting the social consequences of behaviours (Stead et al., 2009).

Also, there is debate on how we ethically, morally and equitably select social issues, participant groups and intervention strategies in social marketing (Hastings and Domegan, 2014). For instance, is teen drinking a bigger problem than sedentary behaviours among older adults? As Anker (2013) points out, some health and social issues seem to attract more funding and attention than others. His suggestion that interventions should be targeted at issues based on their overall costs to a society is one way we could decide. We also need to consider which participant groups to work with and address the challenges in doing so. Very low income participants, asylum seekers, people with low literacy and numeracy or prisoners might be hard to reach groups but could benefit from being engaged in social marketing programmes. Using a control group design means that people in the intervention group can participate in a social marketing programme but those in the control group cannot. Making these difficult ethical decisions is not easy, and requires a great deal of reflection and strategic thinking. Selection of intervention strategies is also an important consideration – involving consideration of what tactics should be used. As Gurrieri et al. (2013) and others (Hastings and Domegan, 2014) have discussed, selection of the wrong intervention strategies can cause unintended effects such as stigmatisation of people in obesity campaigns, or adverse economic impacts on smokers through high taxation on tobacco.

Social marketing must also consider debates around gender and feminist perspectives (Gurrieri et al., 2013), for example are females properly represented and respected in social marketing academia, research, practice and programmes – and if, as is likely, not then how can this be critiqued and addressed? Similarly, is ethnic diversity in social marketing knowledge and practice being realised – the suggestion according to Gordon (2013b), at least with respect to academic research, is this is not the case and ethnocentricity in journal publications and disciplinary discourse persists. These are areas in which social marketing must indulge in some navel gazing, reflection and critical debate to identify emancipatory ideas, and emerge as a more ethical and representative discipline.

These critical debates have brought these important issues to the attention of social marketers, and helped us think more carefully about what we do. What all of this work does is show that the critical social marketing paradigm is expanding beyond competitive analysis, and the critique of commercial marketing and commercial forces, to a critique of social marketing itself. While this might seem counter intuitive, it is actually very important. By engaging with and encouraging critical debate in social marketing we can advance knowledge, introduce new ideas and strategies, and potentially facilitate more effective strategic social marketing.

Critical reflexivity

The final area for focus in this chapter is on the topic of critical reflexivity in social marketing (see Gordon and Gurrieri, 2014). Reflexivity is often recognised as a central feature and important part of thinking critically (Fournier and Grey, 2000). Engagement in reflexive practice can help encourage a deep and meaningful consideration of the role of all actors in social processes and actions – including those evident in social marketing. Critical reflexivity builds upon our earlier discussion of the critique of commercial forces, and critical discourse in social marketing in this chapter, as well as our discussion of researcher reflexivity in Chapter 9. Essentially, it acts as a mechanism for thinking critically. Here we propose that it is important to encourage critically reflexive practice among all actors involved in social marketing processes.

Moving beyond researcher reflexivity

While our earlier discussions have focused primarily on critical thinking for social marketing researchers, or practitioners, we must also recognise that programmes do not occur in isolation. Rather, extensive networks of stakeholders are usually involved in some way in social marketing and social change programmes including researchers, practitioners, participants, funding bodies, policy makers, NGOs, lobby groups, media, and commercial industries and organisations. We argue that it is also important that we understand, think critically about and encourage critical reflexivity among the stakeholders and networks involved in social marketing programmes. Having already discussed social marketing researcher and practitioner reflexivity earlier in the book, here we examine *participant* and *other stakeholder* reflexivity.

Participant reflexivity

Within the reflexivity literature, there is increasing recognition of the importance to consider critical thinking and reflexive practice not only for researchers, but also for participants (Reason, 1988; Smith, 1994).

Smith (1994) argues for a consideration of research participants (or by extension participants in social marketing programmes) as reflexive co-researchers and co-analysts. This involves encouraging participants to fully understand and critically deconstruct their values, biases, opinions and attitudes to facilitate greater reflexive practice in research. Using such approaches can provide an important mechanism for discouraging the tendency for researchers to speak for participants and potentially misrepresent their views or marginalise their voices (Gurrieri et al., 2013). Expanding beyond issues of representation, participants should be encouraged to consider and critically reflect upon how their own personal values, biases and experiences may influence their attitudes and behaviours. The alignment of participant reflexivity with social marketing is clear, as scholars have discussed the importance of seeing the world from the perspective of participants, clients and stakeholders and adopting an experiential view (Hastings and Domegan, 2014).

Takhar and Chitakunye (2012) propose three key focus areas for achieving participant reflexivity:

1. Co-research
2. Participant empowerment through trust building
3. Acknowledgment of the ethical and moral dilemmas that may arise.

The idea of participants acting as co-researchers and co-analysts is not a new one, and indeed we discussed this in Chapter 10 when exploring qualitative research methods such as ethnography that espouse the co-production and co-creation of interpretations. Furthermore, in Chapters 6 and 7 we discussed social value creation and the relevance of co-engagement, empowerment and action focused on network activities rather than individual actions. Scholars in social marketing have recognised the importance of collaborative research and espoused co-creation in the selection of social issues, co-participation, co-research and co-representation of meanings (Lefebvre, 2011; Hastings and Domegan, 2014). Importantly, this thinking is starting to transmit to social marketing programmes. For example, the 'Healthy Heroes, Magic Meals' project in Scotland involved community residents as an integral part of the social change process not just as participants but also as decision makers, architects and implementers (Stead et al., 2013).

Empowerment of participants is also of relevance to social marketing. As discussed in Chapters 6 and 7, participant and community empowerment is an increasingly prominent feature of social marketing and social change programmes. This process can be facilitated through strong and meaningful engagement, forming relationships and building trust (Hastings, 2003). Practical strategies for doing this include providing participants with the backstory of who other actors are, establishing credence and competency, speaking to people on their own terms using their own language (Hammersley and Atkinson, 2007), and having an open minded and non-judgemental approach (Prus, 1996).

We have already discussed in Chapters 2 and 9 the relevance of considering ethical and moral issues in social marketing, and engaging with participant reflexivity is part of this overall process. Social marketers have long recognised the range of ethical and moral dilemmas that can emerge (Andreasen, 2001), and extending this critical reflection to participants seems appropriate. This may involve facilitating participants to consider their own ethical and moral dilemmas when engaging in social marketing programmes – for example if a person wishes to reduce their alcohol consumption they may need to consider how this will affect their social life or how friends will perceive them, or if they participate in research to inform drug interventions they may reveal illegal or taboo behaviours to researchers.

Other stakeholder reflexivity

Taking these ideas further, it would seem appropriate to propose that beyond research-ers, practitioners and participants, other stakeholders involved in social marketing programmes should be engaged in reflexive practice. However, heretofore the discus-sion about reflexivity for other stakeholders has only recently emerged (Gordon and Gurrieri, 2014). Social marketers have identified the importance of acknowledging and understanding actor networks in social systems, and of understanding the views and values of stakeholders and working with them to develop strategies that are mutually acceptable (Hastings and Domegan, 2014). For effective social marketing actor net-works to form and to deliver social change, arguably requires all actors in the networks to engage with critical reflexivity. This may involve acknowledgement of institu-tional policies and practices, the function of gatekeepers, and consideration of how knowledge is created and disseminated. Each actor in these networks is likely to have their own agendas and goals. If each actor critically reflects upon the different perspec-tives in the network then this can possibly create greater understanding, facilitate effec-tive working partnerships and create more effective outcomes (Gordon and Gurrieri, 2014). Engaging with this form of stakeholder reflexivity may help avoid issues such as in the 'Road Crew' intervention in rural Wisconsin, which involved the provision of limousines to take groups of men on pub crawls with the goal of reducing rates of drink related road traffic accidents (Rothschild et al., 2006). As Spotswood et al. (2012) and later Eagle et al. (2013) identify, the intervention was criticised by public health stakeholders for being unethical and for sanctioning the wider social issue of excessive alcohol consumption. If those involved in 'Road Crew' had considered all the actors that may have a stake in these issues, and those actors then engaged in stakeholder reflexivity, then such concerns may have been dealt with prior to delivering the pro-gramme. These reflexive considerations can also help us decide if what we are doing is ethical, by thinking through and trying to anticipate potential unintended conse-quences and mitigating these.

Therefore, we propose that engaging with critical reflexivity in social marketing is of vital importance. This can provide a vehicle for doing better research, engaging and empowering participants, and creating more effective partnerships among stakeholders. Engaging with researcher, participant and stakeholder reflexivity, and adopting col-laborative approaches to research and practice are central to our proposals for strategic, ethical and inclusive social marketing. Reflexivity can help facilitate being strategic and taking informed and holistic decisions. Reflexive practice in strategic social marketing involves thinking about, reflecting upon, deconstructing and understanding how knowledge, truths and ideas are formulated and held by the various actors that are often present in the social marketing context. This can help permit greater understand-ing and engagement between actors to form negotiated outcomes. However, the debate on reflexivity in social marketing has only recently emerged (Gordon and Gurrieri, 2014). Thus, we encourage social marketing to strongly engage with these ideas moving forward. This may mean the incorporation of reflexivity into social marketing bench-marks and planning tools, practitioners actively engaging in reflexivity while working in the field, for scholars to integrate reflexivity in research, and for participants in social change programmes to be encouraged to engage with reflexive practice.

Conclusion

In this chapter we have considered the central role of critical thinking in social market-ing. We have proposed that ideas in this space can be organised under the *critical social marketing* concept. We have identified how competitive analysis and addressing the competition are good social marketing practice by helping us understand the bar-riers and oppositional forces to social change. We then outlined how critical social marketing research on the effect of commercial forces on society can offer useful insights and help inform social marketing activities including in the policy arena. The role and importance of critical debate in social marketing were explored, and we identified that such debate can help stimulate new ideas and improve theory and practice. Finally, we concluded with a call for engagement with critical reflexivity for researchers, participants and stakeholders involved in social marketing, aligning with calls for systems thinking in the field (see Chapter 7). We hope to have demonstrated that critical thinking is something that everyone involved in social marketing should engage with, leading to further development of the *critical social marketing* paradigm.

Reflective questions

- What do you think the competition is to men aged fifty to sixty-five pre-senting for bowel screening?
- How could critical social marketing research be used to understand the effects of gambling marketing on young adults? How would you use your research findings to inform social marketing initiatives in response?
- Consider a social issue such as reducing carbon emissions. Identify who you think would be the relevant researchers, practitioners, participants and stakeholders in this space? How might engagement with critical reflexivity across all these actors help achieve support for the introduction of legislation to reduce carbon emissions?

Further reading

Alvesson, M. (1994) 'Critical theory and consumer marketing', *Scandinavian Journal of Management*, 10 (3): 291–313.

Bakan, J. (2004) *The Corporation: The Pathological Pursuit of Power*. London: Constable.

Bettany, S. and Woodruffe-Burton, H. (2009) 'Working the limits of method: the possibilities of critical reflexive practice in marketing and consumer research', *Journal of Marketing Management*, 25 (7/8): 661–679.

Chomsky, N. (2003) *Hegemony or Survival? America's Quest for Global Dominance*. New York: Metropolitan Books.

Dubiel, H. (1985) *Theory and Politics: Studies in the Development of Critical Theory*, trans. Benjamin Gregg. Cambridge, MA: MIT Press.

Gordon, R. (2011) 'Critical social marketing: definition, application and domain', *Journal of Social Marketing*, 1 (2): 82–99.

Gunster, S. (2004) *Capitalizing on Culture: Critical Theory for Cultural Studies*. Toronto: University of Toronto Press.

Gurrieri, L., Previte, J. and Brace-Govan, J. (2013) 'Women's bodies as sites of control: inadvertent stigma and exclusion in social marketing', *Journal of Macromarketing*, 33 (2): 128–143.

Habermas, J. (1973) *Legitimationsprobleme im Spätkapitalismus*. Frankfurt: Suhrkamp.

Waitzkin, H. (1989) 'A critical theory of medical discourse: ideology, social control, and the processing of social context in medical encounters', *Journal of Health and Social Behaviour*, 30 (2): 220–39.

References

Advertising Association (2013) *Expert Views on Recent Academic Research Papers that Argue that Alcohol Marketing Is a Key Influence on Underage Drinking*. Report produced by BACON Research for the Advertising Association. London: The Advertising Association.

Alvesson, M. (1994) 'Critical theory and consumer marketing', *Scandinavian Journal of Management*, 10 (3): 291–313.

Anderson, P., De Bruijn, A., Angus, K., Gordon, R. and Hastings, G. (2009) 'Impact of alcohol advertising and media exposure on adolescent alcohol use: a systematic review of longitudinal studies', *Alcohol and Alcoholism*, 44 (3): 229–243.

Andreasen, A.R. (1995) *Marketing Social Change*. San Francisco, CA: Jossey-Bass.

Andreasen, A.R. (2001) *Ethics in Social Marketing*. Washington, DC: Georgetown University Press.

Andreasen, A.R. (2002) 'Marketing social marketing in the social change marketplace', *Journal of Public Policy and Marketing*, 21 (1): 3–13.

Andreasen, A.R. (2003) 'The life trajectory of social marketing: some implications', *Marketing Theory*, 3 (3): 293–303.

Andreasen, A.R. (2012) 'Rethinking the relationship between social/nonprofit marketing and commercial marketing', *Journal of Public Policy and Marketing*, 31 (1): 36–41.

Anker, T. (2013) 'Cool diseases! Inequality of health attention in a social marketing perspective', World Social Marketing Conference, 21–23 April, Toronto, Canada.

Bakan, J. (2004) *The Corporation: The Pathological Pursuit of Power*. London: Constable.

Bettany, S. and Woodruffe-Burton, H. (2009) 'Working the limits of method: the possibilities of critical reflexive practice in marketing and consumer research', *Journal of Marketing Management*, 25 (7/8): 661–679.

Christie, B. (2011) 'Tobacco company makes freedom of information request for university's research', *British Medical Journal*, 343: d5655.

Chomsky, N. (2003) *Hegemony or Survival? America's Quest for Global Dominance*. New York: Metropolitan Books.

Chomsky, N. (2013) *Power Systems: Conversations on Global Democratic Uprisings and the New Challenges to the US Empire*. New York: Metropolitan Books.

Crane, A., Palazzo, G., Spence, L.J. and Matten, D. (2014) 'Contesting the value of "creating shared value"', *California Management Review*, 56 (2): 130–153.

Dholakia, R.R. and Dholakia, N. (2001) 'Social marketing and development', in P. Bloom and G. Gundlach (eds), *Handbook of Marketing and Society*. Thousand Oaks, CA: SAGE, pp. 486–505.

Eagle, L., Dahl, S., Hill, S., Bird, S., Spotswood, F. and Tapp, A. (2013) *Social Marketing*. London: Pearson.

Eagleton, T. (2012) *Why Marx Was Right*. New Haven, CT: Yale University Press.

Farrelly, M.C., Davis, K.C., Haviland, M.L., Messeri, P. and Healton, C.G. (2005) 'Evidence of a dose–response relationship between "truth" antismoking ads and youth smoking prevalence', *American Journal of Public Health*, 95 (3): 425–431.

Fleisher, C. and Bensoussan, B. (2003) *Strategic and Competitive Analysis: Methods and Techniques for Analyzing Business Competition*. London: Prentice Hall.

Fournier, V. and Grey, C. (2000) 'At the critical moment: conditions and prospects for critical management studies', *Human Relations*, 53 (1): 7–32.

French, J. (2011) 'Why nudging is not enough', *Journal of Social Marketing*, 1 (2): 154–162.

Goldberg, M.E. (1995) 'Social marketing: are we fiddling while Rome burns?', *Journal of Consumer Psychology*, 4 (4): 347–370.

Gordon, R. (2011a) 'Critical social marketing: definition, application and domain', *Journal of Social Marketing*, 1 (2): 82–99.

Gordon, R. (2011b) 'Critical social marketing: assessing the cumulative impact of alcohol marketing on youth drinking', PhD thesis. Stirling: University of Stirling. Available at: https://dspace.stir.ac.uk/bitstream/1893/3135/1/Ross%20Gordon%20PhD%20FINAL%20SUBMITTED.pdf (last accessed 12 August 2014).

Gordon, R. (2011c) 'Alcohol marketing and youth drinking: a rejoinder to the alcohol industry', *Alcohol and Alcoholism*, 46 (4): 369–370.

Gordon, R. (2012) 'Re-thinking and re-tooling the social marketing mix', *Australasian Marketing Journal*, 20 (2): 122–126.

Gordon, R. (2013a) 'Unlocking the potential of upstream social marketing', *European Journal of Marketing*, 47 (9): 1525–1547.

Gordon, R. (2013b) 'New ideas – fresh thinking: towards a broadening of the social marketing concept?', *Journal of Social Marketing*, 3 (3): 200–205.

Gordon, R. and Gurrieri, L. (2014) 'Towards a reflexive turn: social marketing assemblages', *Journal of Social Marketing*, 4 (3): 261–278.

Gordon, R., Harris, F., MacKintosh, A.M. and Moodie, C. (2011) 'Assessing the cumulative impact of alcohol marketing on young people's drinking: cross sectional data findings', *Addiction Research and Theory*, 19 (1): 66–75.

Gordon, R., Hastings, G., Moodie, C. and Eadie, D. (2010b) 'Critical social marketing – The impact of alcohol marketing on youth drinking: qualitative findings', *International Journal of Nonprofit and Voluntary Sector Marketing*, 15 (3): 265–275.

Gordon, R., MacKintosh, A.M. and Moodie, C. (2010a) 'The impact of alcohol marketing on youth drinking behaviour: a two-stage cohort study', *Alcohol and Alcoholism*, 45 (5): 470–480.

Gurrieri, L., Previte, J. and Brace-Govan, J. (2013) 'Women's bodies as sites of control: inadvertent stigma and exclusion in social marketing', *Journal of Macromarketing*, 33 (2): 128–143.

Habermas, J. (1973) *Legitimationsprobleme im Spätkapitalismus*. Frankfurt: Suhrkamp.

Hackley, C. (2009) 'Parallel universes and disciplinary space: the bifurcation of managerialism and social science in marketing studies', *Journal of Marketing Management*, 25 (7/8): 643–659.

Hammersley, M. and Atkinson, P. (2007) *Ethnography: Principles in Practice*. New York: Routledge.

Hastings, G. (2003) 'Relational paradigms in social marketing', *Journal of Macromarketing*, 23 (1): 6–15.

Hastings, G. (2007) *Social Marketing: Why Should the Devil Have All the Best Tunes?* London: Butterworth-Heinemann.

Hastings, G. (2012) *The Marketing Matrix: How the Corporation Gets Its Power and How We Can Reclaim It*. London: Routledge.

Hastings, G. and Domegan, C. (2014) *Social Marketing: From Tunes to Symphonies* (2nd edn). London: Routledge.

Hastings, G. and Saren, M. (2003) 'The critical contribution of social marketing: theory and application', *Marketing Theory*, 3 (3): 305–322.

Hastings, G., Stead, M., McDermott, L., Forsyth, A., MacKintosh, A.M., Rayner, M., Godfrey, G., Carahar, M. and Angus, K. (2003) 'Review of research on the effects of food promotion to children – final report and appendices'. Prepared for the Food Standards Agency. London: Food Standards Agency. Available at: http://tna.europarchive.org/20110116113217/http:/www.food.gov.uk/multimedia/pdfs/foodpromotiontochildren1.pdf (last accessed 10 December 2013)

Hastings, G., Stead, M. and Webb, J. (2004) 'Fear appeals in social marketing: strategic and ethical reasons for concern', *Psychology and Marketing*, 21 (11): 961–986.

Horkheimer, M. (1982) *Critical Theory*. New York: Seabury Press.

Hughes, K., MacKintosh, A.M., Hastings, G., Wheeler, C., Watson, J. and Inglis, J. (1997) 'Young people, alcohol, and designer drinks: quantitative and qualitative study', *British Medical Journal*, 314 (7078): 414–418.

Klein, N. (2000) *No Logo: Taking Aim at the Brand Bullies*. London: Flamingo.

Landman, A. and Glantz, S.A. (2009) 'Tobacco industry efforts to undermine policy relevant research', *American Journal of Public Health*, 99 (1): 45–58.

Lazer, W. (2013) 'William Lazer: reflections on my career', *Journal of Historical Research in Marketing*, 5 (2): 231–243.

Lazer, W. and Kelley, E.J. (1973) *Social Marketing: Perspectives and Viewpoints*. Homewood: Richard D. Irwin.

Lefebvre, R.C. (2012) 'Transformative social marketing', *Journal of Social Marketing*, 2 (2): 118–129.

Lovato, C., Linn, G., Stead, L.F. and Best, A. (2003) 'Impact of tobacco advertising and promotion on increasing adolescent smoking behaviours', *Cochrane Database of Systematic Reviews*, 4: CD003439.

MacFadyen, L., Hastings, G.B. and MacKintosh, A.M. (2001) 'Cross sectional study of young people's awareness of and involvement with tobacco marketing', *British Medical Journal*, 322 (7285): 513–517.

MacKintosh, A.M., Hastings, G.B., Hughes, K., Wheeler, C., Watson, J. and Inglis, J. (1997) 'Adolescent drinking: the role of designer drinks', *Health Education*, 97 (6): 213–224.

McDermott, L., Stead, M. and Hastings, G. (2005) 'What is and what is not social marketing: the challenge of reviewing the evidence', *Journal of Marketing Management*, 21 (5–6): 545–553.

Peattie, S. and Peattie, K. (2003) 'Ready to fly solo: reducing social marketing's reliance of commercial marketing theory', *Marketing Theory*, 3 (3): 365–385.

Porter, M. (1979) 'How competitive forces shape strategy', *Harvard Business Review*, 57 (2): 137–145.

Porter, M.E. and Kramer, M.R. (2011) 'The big ideas: creating shared value – rethinking capitalism', *Harvard Business Review*, 89 (1/2): 62–77.

Prus, R. (1996) *Symbolic Interaction and Ethnographic Research*. New York: State University Press.

Rancière, J. (2011) *Mute Speech: Literature, Critical Theory, and Politics*. New York: Columbia University Press.

Reason, P. (ed.) (1988) *Human Inquiry in Action*. London: SAGE.

Rothschild, M.L., Mastin, B. and Miller, T.W. (2006) 'Reducing alcohol-impaired driving crashes through the use of social marketing', *Accident Analysis and Prevention*, 38 (6): 1218–30.

Saren, M., MacLaran, P., Goulding, C., Elliott, R., Shankar, A. and Catterall, M. (eds) (2007) *Critical Marketing: Defining the Field*. London: Elsevier.

Seligman, M.E.P. (1998) *Learned Optimism*. New York: Pocket Books.

Smith, J.A. (1994) 'Towards reflexive practice: engaging participants as co-researchers or co-analysts in psychological inquiry', *Journal of Community and Applied Social Psychology*, 4 (4): 253–260.

Spotswood, F., French, J., Tapp, A. and Stead, M. (2012) 'Some reasonable but uncomfortable questions about social marketing', *Journal of Social Marketing*, 2 (3): 163–175.

Stead, M., Arnott, L. and Dempsey, E. (2013) 'Healthy heroes, magic meals, and a visiting alien: community-led assets based social marketing', *Social Marketing Quarterly*, 19 (1): 26–39.

Stead, M., Gordon, R., Holme, I., Moodie, C., Hastings, G. and Angus, K. (2009) *Changing Attitudes, Knowledge and Behaviour: A Review of Successful Initiatives*. York: Joseph Rowntree Foundation.

Tadajewski, M. (2010) 'Towards a history of critical marketing studies', *Journal of Marketing Management*, 26 (9/10): 773–824.

Tadajewski, M. and Brownlie, D. (eds) (2008) *Critical Marketing: Issues in Contemporary Marketing*. London: John Wiley.

Takhar, A. and Chitakunye, P. (2012) 'Rich descriptions: evoking informant self-reflexivity in marketing and consumer research', *Journal of Marketing Management*, 28 (7–8): 912–935.

Tapp, A. and Spotswood, F. (2013) 'From the 4Ps to COM-SM: reconfiguring the social marketing mix', *Journal of Social Marketing*, 3 (3): 206–222.

Wilkie, W.L. and Moore, E.S. (1999) 'Marketing's contributions to society', *Journal of Marketing*, 63 (Millennium special issue): 198–218.

WHO (World Health Organization) (1998) *The Pen Is as Mighty as the Surgeon's Scalpel: Improving Health Communication Impact*. Geneva: WHO Regional Office for Europe.

Young, B. (2003) *Advertising and Food Choice in Children: A Review of the Literature*. London: The Advertising Association.

AFTERWORD

We believe that the social marketing principles explored in this book, and the strategic, holistic, creative and reflexive approach we have set out, can assist in the processes of co-creation and delivery of more effective and efficient social policy. The founding premise of this book is that social marketing principles, concepts and techniques when applied to solving social problems add value to policy development as well as its implementation. Moreover this added value is multiplied when marketing principles are applied to policy selection, and strategy development, as well as to operational planning and delivery.

We have defined strategic social marketing as:

> 'The systemic, critical and reflexive application of social marketing principals to enhance social policy selection, objective setting, planning and operational delivery'

We have also tried to illustrate in this book the need to break away from the limitations of simplistic conceptions of social marketing and the formulaic application of outmoded and incomplete theories and models that confine the contribution that marketing can make to solve the world's problems. We have sought to make the case that within the field of social marketing there is a need for:

1. A more systemic, reflexive, creative and critical approach to the application of social marketing that more accurately reflects the reality of dealing with complex issues in dynamic environments and less simplistic analysis and the application of limited formulaic responses.
2. A greater emphasis on the contribution to social marketing at the policy and strategy development end of the social programme selection and delivery spectrum.
3. More focus on social value creation as a means to achieving greater social good. Social value creation should be seen as a central principle of social marketing within the context of the reality of multiple complex webs of exchange and relationships that underpin the creation or destruction of social good.
4. The need for a broader, multidisciplinary focus on objectives that go beyond a predominant focus on individual or group behaviour to include influencing attitudes, beliefs, social norms environments, systems, processes, services, experiences, products, and policy.

5. The need for greater power sharing, co-creation and engagement in the selection development delivery and evaluation of social programmes as a process for the development of more citizen, stakeholder and societal value.

Social marketing is we believe an extremely important set of principles, concepts and techniques that can if applied in a reflexive way add considerable value to all levels of social policy development and delivery. We know that politicians, policy makers and senior civil servants around the world are faced with a raft of complex social challenges, most of which require that systems, processes, environments organisations, markets, groups and individuals be influenced, supported and often changed. Social marketing can help define, develop and deliver such change.

We also argue that a socially progressive model of social marketing with a focus on value creation with and for citizens, and addressing real issues at the individual, community and structural level, is warranted. This citizen centric approach to policy development and delivery supported by evidence, insight and data is one that is growing around the world as citizens demand more influence and more responsive governments and social services.

Social marketing's systematic strategic analysis, planning and evaluation focused approach also make it a natural fit with modern policy development and strategic planning for social good that increasingly emphasises the application of evidence-based policy making, efficiency and evaluation.

We believe however as we have argued in this book that it will not be sufficient to just wait for politicians and policy makers to beat a path to the door of those who believe in the added value of social marketing. The embedding and sustaining of social marketing as a core element of all social programmes will only be achieved if social marketers apply some of their marketing thinking to this challenge. Those who advocate the application of marketing principles as a key strategic element of social programmes have as a first key task the job of marketing the added value of that social marketing to politicians, policy makers, organisations, students and citizens. We hope this book makes a small contribution to taking this work forward.

INDEX